M.E. GIMENEZ
825 33rd ST.
BOULDER, CO 80303

STRUCTURAL SOCIOLOGY

STRUCTURAL
SOCIOLOGY

EDITED BY
INO ROSSI

NEW YORK   COLUMBIA UNIVERSITY PRESS   1982

Ino Rossi is Professor of Sociology and Anthropology
at St. John's University

Library of Congress Cataloging in Publication Data
Main entry under title:

Structural sociology.

Includes bibliographies and index.
1. Sociology—Addresses, essays, lectures.
2. Structuralism—Addresses, essays, lectures.
I. Rossi, Ino.
HM73.S85   301   81-12246
ISBN 0-231-04846-7   AACR2

Columbia University Press
New York   Guildford, Surrey

Copyright © 1982 by Columbia University Press
All Rights Reserved
Printed in the United States of America

Clothbound editions of Columbia University Press books are
Smyth-sewn and printed on permanent and durable acid-free paper.

TO IRENE AND PAUL

CONTENTS

FOREWORD

Professor Rossi has put together an important selection of works on one of the newest and most exciting schools of thought that is currently sweeping over the Western world. That school of thought is called structuralism, or sometimes French structuralism in order to differentiate it from structural functionalism, an older school of thought associated with British social anthropology and American sociology. French structuralism is in some ways a uniquely French orientation. Although it arose most recently out of the anthropological studies of Lévi-Strauss, especially his work in the Brazilian jungles, it has the flavor and style of the French salon and the French coffee house. It is a brilliant kind of armchair aesthetics and also a mythopoetic mode of cultural investigation.

One of the most remarkable features of French structuralism is its ambitiousness. It seeks nothing less than to embrace all of the human studies, including not only the entire range of the social sciences but also the humanities. Because it regards all language as representative of a fundamental mythic structure which can be unearthed through the special techniques developed by French structuralism, there is no subject and no discipline that does not become grist for its intellectual mill. In recent years the greatest breakthroughs and influence of French structuralism have been in the field of literature. In that area it has contributed not only to an entirely new mode of literary criticism but also to the development of a new kind of novel. Another area of importance for French structuralism is psychology and the psychology of linguistics. Influenced most significantly by the work of Piaget, and referring back to the great linguistic work of de Saussure, new perceptions on language, the acquisition of speech, the modes of learning, and the kinds of socialization are being discovered.

The impact of French structuralism on anthropology and sociology has thus far been less pervasive, but it is nevertheless quite
important. In England, because the work of Lévi-Strauss has been
taken up by such important anthropologists as E. R. Leach and
Mary Douglas, there is great interest and new development. In
America, the work of Lévi-Strauss has not so much been recognized by anthropologists as it has been by important literary critics
such as Susan Sontag. It is my suspicion that the mythopoetic style
of French structuralism is less conducive to the modes of operation
of American anthropologists than it is to their European coun-
terparts. Nevertheless, the works of Lévi-Strauss are read widely
on the college campuses. Moreover, the rise of French structuralism in anthropology should cause students of that subject in
America to reinvestigate the works of certain early American anthropologists—especially Frank Hamilton Cushing, whose work
on primitive classification influenced Durkheim and Mauss and
who has been hailed in France by both Levy-Bruhl and Lévi-
Strauss, though long neglected in America.

As some of the essays included in this collection indicate, there
has been some interest in French structuralism by American sociologists. The degree to which French structuralism is compatible
with Parsonian structural-functionalism is controversial, and the
reader will get some idea of the issues entailed in the essays presented in this volume. Essentially the issue turns on the question
of whether what Rossi calls "transformational structuralism" i.e.,
the French approach, can be coordinated with "empirical structuralism," i.e., the American approach. The latter is associated
with Talcott Parsons, Robert Merton, Peter Blau, Lewis Coser,
George Homans, and James Coleman, to name but the leading
figures; the former with C. Lévi-Strauss, Jean Piaget, Maurice Godelier, and Louis Althusser. Rossi, elsewhere, has provided a fine
introduction to this problem and his introduction to the present
collection systematically sets forth the issues and claims of the
various positions.

French structuralism provides a new attitude toward history and
biography. Among the present-day attitudes are those of *abolition*
(as in Mircea Eliade's "archaic man"); *acceptance* (as in K. Bock's
The Acceptance of Histories); *reconstruction* (as in Parsons' *Evolution
of Societies*). To these French structuralism adds a transformational

metaphysical dramatism. Each of the prevailing attitudes mentioned above becomes a mythic or mythopoetical form, subject to structuralist investigation and reformulation. Historiographies become absurdist, biographical monodramas—as the latter were conceived by Evreinov and Beckett—subject to systematic decomposition and discrete characterological re-presentation as individual entities. Thus, to read French structuralism is to attend a performance not unlike that early monodramatic opera by Jacques Offenbach, *The Tales of Hoffman*. In the rarely performed epilogue to that opera, Nicklaus, Hoffman's ever-faithful friend, tells us that the three tales of tragic love that we have just witnessed are but one tale—the story of Hoffman's true love, who has been spirited away from him by his arch-enemy (and, we may add, alterego), Lindorf, even as the tales were told. The characterizations of Hoffman's loves—as a mechanical doll, an alluring courtesan, a gifted singer—are, Nicklaus tells us, but the three faces of a single, complex personality. But, Hoffman, arising from his drunken stupor objects: It is not so. The curtain falls. What are we to believe? That is the exciting challenge that French structuralism offers.

Stanford M. Lyman

Kyoto, Japan
October 1981

PREFACE

Is "French Structuralism" an intellectual "mode" already "passé" in France and slowly fading away in the Anglo-Saxon countries before having established any solid roots? Such seems to be the ill-fated destiny of this movement, if we are to listen to certain "surface" observers of the intellectual scene; but there is plenty of evidence to warrant the opposite prediction—that "French structuralism" (a term under which I include poststructural semiotics) is going to leave deep traces throughout the social sciences and humanities. For one thing, some of the thinkers who have rejected this relatively recent movement have been forced to deeply rethink or clarify positions previously taken for granted. Many young scholars have been caught in a crossfire of prestructuralist and structuralist influences which have forced them to reexamine positions accepted in their early educational training. The editor of this volume has himself traveled through a path of contrasting intellectual orientations. Trained in European philosophy, he has been later exposed to an empiricist-statistical sociology prevailing in America and, finally, to humanistic and critical sociological and anthropological thought. It has been during the later phase that the figure of Lévi-Strauss has begun to emerge among my intellectual interests, first as curiosity, and, later, as a challenging venture. A laborious and cyclical process of interpretation has led me from an existentialist-Marxist reading of Lévi-Strauss to a positivistic, and finally to a "properly structuralist" one.

I have dealt with the interface between Lévi-Strauss' structuralism and competing anthropological orientations in a previous collection (*The Unconscious in Culture*, New York: Dutton, 1974) and a forthcoming one (*The Logic of Culture*, South Hadley, Me.:

J. F. Bergin, Forthcoming). In the last few years I have been witnessing a certain impasse within anthropology between structuralists on the one hand, and cultural ecologists—or even cognitive and symbolic anthropologists—on the other hand; at times, one senses an "outright rejection" or purposeful ignoring of structuralist paradigms. At the same time, various professional meetings and correspondences have made me aware that a good number of young sociologists hold an "open and inquisitive attitude" toward structuralist ideas. Such a realization has prompted me to organize or to participate in various sociological meetings on French structuralism. The present volume is partially a result of these professional activities, since the latter have motivated me to compare and partially integrate anthropological and sociological paradigms. After a few years of such an interdisciplinary endeavor, I have come to the realization that a full appreciation of the enormous potential of French structuralism for sociology is not possible without interdisciplinary thrusts into anthropology (Lévi-Strauss), psychology (Piaget), linguistics (Chomsky), semiotics (Barthes, Kristeva, Eco) and philosophy (Foucault, Derrida, Althusser). It might be true that the Lévi-Straussian structuralism, as a fashionable and facile vogue, is "passé" even in France; but it is also true that there already exists a large body of structuralist and poststructurally influenced literature which documents a pervasive influence of structuralist and poststructuralist problematics in European sociology (see C. Lemert, ed., *French Sociology*, New York: Columbia University Press, 1981). Things are, of course, otherwise within the empiricist dominated atmosphere of American sociology; yet, French structuralism is seen by Robert K. Merton as one instance of that healthy "theoretical pluralism" which "gives rise to a variety of new questions requiring investigation" (Peter Blau and R. K. Merton, eds., *Continuities in Structural Inquiry*, Beverly Hills: Sage Publications, 1981, p. v). It is a matter of fact, however, that the just mentioned volume deals with French structuralism only peripherally and mostly from prestructuralist perspectives. As one might expect, "new questions" when placed in "old barrels" can only produce "old answers."

In the present volume I have undertaken the task of systematically dealing with some of the "new questions" which have been emerging within the sociological "consciousness" under the impact of various forms and phases of French structuralism. As explained in the Introduction, the majority of the essays, all of which have been especially prepared for this volume, deal with aspects of the interface between traditional orientations and recent French structuralism from perspectives which are sympathetic to the latter orientation, without, however, arguing for prejudged positions. In my opinion only such an orientation permits a serious reconsideration of classical sociological paradigms and the incorporation of some aspects of the structuralist perspective within the mainstream of sociological thinking. It is up to the readers of this volume to assess by themselves the revolutionary potential of French structuralism, and, more importantly, to continue the investigation of the many other "new questions" raised by structuralism. It is my firm belief that such an investigation will bring to light the presence within our sociological tradition of much deeper continuities with such pioneers as Durkheim, Mauss, Marx, than have been so far thought of or even suspected. In my forthcoming volume *From the Sociology of Symbols to the Sociology of Signs: Towards a Dialectical Sociology* (New York: Columbia University Press) I will myself undertake the task of documenting some of these continuities and providing a theoretical framework to detect new ones. I hope that such an undertaking will produce an enriched understanding of already established linkages among different sociological traditions and the emerging of new cross-fertilizations not only among diverse sociological schools but also across different disciplines.

New York, October 1981

STRUCTURAL SOCIOLOGY

RELATIONAL STRUCTURALISM AND THE SOCIOLOGICAL TRADITION

RELATIONAL STRUCTURALISM AS AN ALTERNATIVE TO THE STRUCTURAL AND INTERPRETATIVE PARADIGMS OF EMPIRICIST ORIENTATION

INO ROSSI

I have collected essays written by sociologists of different theoretical orientations on the sociological relevance of modern French structuralism—an intellectual movement which still remains little understood and, even worse, misunderstood in the English sociological literature. By the term "modern French structuralism"[1] I refer, first of all, to the semiotic, or linguistically based, structuralism in its systematic and post-systematic phases: The pioneer and systematic phase was inspired by the Geneva linguist Ferdinand de Saussure and later applied in anthropology by Claude Lévi-Strauss, in psychoanalysis by Jacques Lacan, in literary criticism by Roland Barthes—to mention a few pioneer thinkers; the "systematic" phase of semiotics has dealt with the syntactic structure of semiotic systems rather than with the social processes producing the syntactic structure or with the social usage of language. This latter focus of analysis has characterized the works of postsystematic semioticians, prominent among whom are the literary critics Julia Kristeva and the more recent works of Roland Barthes. Michel Foucault, a philosopher often labeled as a "structuralist," also has focused on discursive formation as a strategy indispensable to understanding particular texts (Lemert 1979). Sociological implications of postsystematic semiotics are discussed in this volume by Lemert and Nielsen (selection 12), whereas Eisenstadt (selection 7), Ekeh (6), Katz (5), Parsons (3), and Stinchcombe (4) utilize various elements of Lévi-Strauss' structuralism. The overrepresentation of the systematic phase of structuralism in this volume has a historical and theoretical justification. The systematic phase of structuralism is better known among sociologists; in addition, the postsystematic phase of semiotics can be largely understood as a development or a complement of the systematic phase rather than as a rejection of it. Here I side with Benoist (1978) rather than with Coward and Ellis (1977).

The analytical scope of this volume is not limited to semiotic structuralism since this later movement shares basic assumptions and concepts with the genetic structuralism of Jean Piaget and the transformational grammar of Noam Chomsky—although neither of these two authors derive their approach from the linguistics of Saussure. Condon and Wieting's essay (selection 8) in this volume offers sociological applications of Piagetian ideas, and Lidz (9) utilizes Chomskian ideas to fill gaps in the works of Durkheim and Parsons.

The analytical scope of this volume goes still further, because Lévi-Strauss' ideas have heavily influenced the structural marxism of Maurice Godelier and have certain affinities with the structural marxism of Louis Althusser; Godelier himself offers in this volume (selection 10) a new theory of ideology emanating from his own structural position and Giménez (11) shows the analytical power of the perspectives of Althusser and Godelier in sociological analysis.

As one can see from the list of thinkers I have so far mentioned, relational structuralism is a recent movement which cuts across such disciplines as linguistics, anthropology, psychoanalysis, literary criticism, psychology, and philosophy.[2] As a matter of fact, the interdisciplinary breath of the new approach does not stop at these disciplines, as one can find certain roots and/or convergencies on the structuralist perspective also in the mathematics of the Bourbaki school, the philosophy of Bachelard, and modern biology.[3]

The term "convergence" should not be construed to indicate that the abovementioned thinkers share a homogeneous orientation, or even a neatly definable one. On the contrary, the literature has at times often stressed the profound differences, let us say, among the first and second phase of semiotics or between de Saussure and Chomsky's linguistics or between Althusser and

Godelier; for instance, Althusser has strongly attacked "structuralism" (1976) and Godelier has repeatedly stressed his own differences from Althusser's position (1978:765; 1979:109). I am not concerned here with a discussion of the similarities or differences among these thinkers, but rather with pointing out some assumptions they all share insofar as the latter suffice to characterize their approach as a novel and distinctive one.[4]

What all these thinkers have in common and why their views are very important to sociology is clearly stated by Peter K. Manning, who refers to Lévi-Strauss' ideas as "the ideas of the most important thinker in social sciences in the world." He also states that "the essential thrust" of structuralism "is to challenge the empiricism of sociology and indeed of most social sciences" (1978:142). Obviously, Manning's statement amounts to saying that structuralism represents a direct challenge to most of contemporary American sociology—certainly to its most predominant thrusts. To understand why relational structuralism is against empiricist sociology we must briefly state why structuralism rejects empiricism as such—that is, as a mode of explanation which is common to human, social, and natural sciences.

Briefly, and somewhat simplistically, the gist of empiricism consists in explaining a phenomenon in terms of its content or concrete determinations as they are attainable or observable either in external or internal experience. Examples of empiricists relying on external experiential data are found among sociologists of positivist, behavioral, and operationalist orientation. Empiricists relying on internal experiential data are typically found among phenomenologically oriented sociologists. Semiotic structuralism, structural Marxism, genetic structuralism, and transformational structuralism share a fundamental principle in common: they refuse to consider "experience" as a kind of "recording" or registering of what is immediately "given" or accessible to our sensory apparatus. Structuralists maintain we cannot understand experiential data without building formal models—that is, without isolating from the content of experience a formal set of constitutive elements and relationships among the elements. The meaning of a phenomenon is determined not in terms of its concrete determinations or the subjective intention of the social actors but in terms of the relational constants among the basic constitutive elements. Through this operation we can reconstruct the deep logic, or organizing principles, or conpositional laws of empirical phenomena. Typically, structuralists attempt to identify the rules of the internal composition of a phenomenon and the rules which govern the possible transformations of one phenomenon into related sets of phenomena.

These brief remarks show why the notion of "deep structure" or deep logic of a phenomenon and the notion of "transformation" are the key terms of relational structuralism.[5] The reader will find these two terms used throughout the essays of this volume, whether they are inspired by the formal structuralism of Lévi-Strauss (Eisenstadt, Ekeh, Parsons, Katz, and Stinchcombe), Piaget (Condon and Wieting), Chomsky (Lidz) or based on Eco's structural approach (Lemert and Nielsen) and on structural marxism (Giménez and Godelier).

At this point a basic question must be raised about the nature of that deep logic of phenomena which goes under the names of "structure" and "transformation." Is it a mere product of a mental operation—and so structuralists are "mentalists"—or does it refer to extramental characteristics of data? Does the term "structure" by definition connote a universal logical structure, and hence does it imply a static perspective which prevents structuralists from studying change and history? Is the notion of deep logic of things (and hence their intrinsic rationality) reconcilable with the Marxist notion of dialectic, given that the latter is based on the notion of contradiction?

These questions indicate some of the most common objections raised against relational structuralism. A brief discussion of the mathematical nature of the concepts of "structure" and "transformation" will show the falsity of the first two objections and the validity of the third one. Lévi-Strauss, Piaget, and Chomsky have all been somewhat influenced by mathematical thought; Lévi-Strauss, for instance, has applied the mathematical theory of groups of permutations to the study and classification of the Murngin's marriage systems (1969:169–96). Chomsky has had a training in mathematics and Piaget has extensively used and written about mathematics and formal logic. Piaget defines a mathematical group as "a system consisting of a set of elements" (e.g. the integers, positive and negative) "together with an operation or rule of combination" (e.g. addition) having four specified properties. (For a complete exposition see Piaget 1970:18 where one can find a detailed description of this concept and its properties together with a bibliography; see also Piaget 1949 and Barbut 1966.) Here it suffices to say that a set of operations is not a "group" without the presence of invariant relations—the latter constituting the structure of the group. Similarly, "transformation is an intelligible change which preserves certain basic invariants" (Piaget 1970:20). The Bourbaki school has identified three parent (or most general) structures from which particular structures can be derived through the operations of combination and differentiation.

One can then see that "structure" does not refer to a mentalistic entity but to mathematical properties of the phenomena studied— properties, we should add, which are constitutive of the phenomena. Piaget rightly states that for "relational structuralism" the systems of transformations are the primary reality to which the elements are subordinated; the totality is understood to be constructed out of these transformations (Piaget 1973:22).[6] According to Piaget mathematical structures do not derive their properties directly from things but from our way of acting on them (Piaget 1970:19). Since mathematical structures derive from our operations upon the environment, they are not objective or mental, but interactional. However, our interaction with the environment is an objective and documentable activity, and the mathematical properties describing such interaction are therefore also objective. In this sense mathematical structures are not mere mental projections imposed on the data by the anthropologist or psychologists who carry out the structural analysis. When Piaget defines the development of intellectual operations in terms of algebraic structures (Piaget 1973:23), he inevitably implies that mathematical structures are extramental or objective properties as much as the mathematical laws of engineering or mechanics and the grammatical rules of language (see Rossi, in press).

One can thus argue that to mathematize and axiomatize does not mean to "reduce" things to logical or abstract entities. Lévi-Strauss has well stated that structuralism is quite different from formalism: "'form' is defined by opposition to material other than itself. But 'structure' has no distinct content; it is content itself, apprehended in a logical organization conceived as property of the real" (Lévi-Strauss 1976:115). When Lévi-Strauss interprets a given set of data, he pays close attention to the ecological and cultural context, so that he can rightly differentiate his own structuralism from Propp's formalism: "In formalism there is separation and opposition between structure and content since form alone is intelligible and content is only a residual deprived of any significant value. For structuralism, this opposition does not exist. There is nothing abstract on one side and something concrete on the other. Form and content are of the same nature, susceptible to the same analysis. Content draws its reality from its structure and what is called form is the 'structural formation' of the local structure forming the content" (131).

The objection that relational structuralism can deal only with universal and immutable structures can also be easily disposed of, if we keep in mind the mathematical properties of "structure;" the latter are beyond times and apply to any specific content and to any particular period of history. Hence the attempt to axiomatize history does not entail the denial of history or the impossibility of studying the dynamic aspect of society. The essays of Katz, Eisenstadt, and Ekeh, clearly show the usefulness of structural concepts to study civilizational processes, social movement, and cultural change.

However, the notion of "structural rationality" seems irreconcilable with the Marxist notion of dialectic, since the latter is based on contradictions. Jean Benoist, at least, argues that structuralism substitutes for dialectics the notion of the logic of the heterogeneous. The latter refers to unconscious processes which impinge on and try to change the structure. Benoist incorporates elements of the Lacanian theory of unconscious process into structuralism to guarantee an "open" and "dynamic" quality to structure. The argument is made that the syntactic order (the structure) is changed, but not destroyed, by the semantic productivity of the unconscious and the heterogeneous; the reason is that the entry of the subject (unconscious) into the structure is controlled by the structure itself. For Benoist the essential characteristic of relational structuralism consists precisely in the attempt to map out the logic of heterogeneous processes (Benoist 1978).

At this point we should also briefly mention other important analytical innovations introduced by relational structuralism.

Structural analysis replaces causal explanation and unilineal explanation. Whereas the causal and unilineal explanation is based on essentialistic assumptions, such as the existence of a prime mover or an acting subject, the concept "structure" merely connotes a relational network, reminiscent of the Leibnizian order and Kantian schematism, without the postulation of a moving cause or transcendental (and individual) subject. For this reason Benoist sees in the relational and mathematical perspective of structuralism the promises or potentialities for a universal axiomatization and a general discourse which can unify all scientific discourses.

Relational structuralism has introduced another radical innovation. We have mentioned above that structural axiomatization is based on the notion that structure emerges from the operation of the subject on things; this means that the scientific object of analysis is constructed by the activity of the subject. The notion of the interaction and inseparability of subject and object implies the total rejection of a cardinal tenet of empiricism:—the separation of the subject from the object as a precondition for any objective explanation. For empiricists to be "objective" means to read sociological data as they are "given out there"—outside of the scientist's mind.[7]

The sociological implications of the structural position on this issue are quite important and totally contrary to the conclusion, often drawn by empiricist social scientists, that structuralism is a form of mentalism. Peter K. Manning, a sociologist quoted at the beginning of this essay, seems to be one of the few American sociologists who has captured the specific character of scientific explanation as proposed by Lévi-Strauss. Manning states that Lévi-Strauss "rejects the assertion that the social sciences are hypothesis testing, and argues instead for a reflexive science in which the subject of human sciences, man, is aware of the prejudices involved in the way he defines himself to himself" (Manning 1978:143). Manning's statement goes right to the center of what I consider the crux of the present impasse in sociological theory— and this is true in a much more fundamental sense than Manning can or does explain. My argument is that relational structuralism offers the only viable alternative to the ever-lasting confrontation between the two predominant sociological versions of the objective vs. subjective empiricist explanation—the "natural science" and the "interpretative" paradigms, to use Wagner's typology (1963). Such a confrontation is partially reflected or paralleled in the clash between structural and individualistic explanation. Without claiming to be exhaustive, examples of structural explanation as traditionally understood are frequent among the followers of the "natural science"—hence empiricist—approach—among them Comte, Durkheim, functionalists, exchange structuralists, conflict structuralists (see Wallace 1969: part I). Examples of "interpretative sociology" emphasizing individualistic principles of explanation are found in Weber, some symbolic interactionists, and some phenomenological sociologists. We should add that Georges C. Homans, although not an interpretative sociologist, utilizes psychological principles of explanation; therefore, he fosters a form of individualistic explanation. The dialogue between the two styles of sociology has not been very productive; at times it has turned into a total confrontation and a radical rejection of each other's position. Consider, for instance, Homan's strong attack against functionalism, because of the Functionalists' emphasis on structural principles of explanation (1964; 1975:64), or Jack D. Douglas' rejection of naturalistic and objective sociology. Douglas argues in favor of a "theoretical stance" where the sociologist "stands back from the everyday world, to reflect upon, to re-view the experience taken for granted in the 'natural stance'" (1970:15). Such a theoretical stance demands that sociological phenomena be studied on their own ground (19) and that scientific activity be grounded on the purposes and practical usefulness for which it is carried out. In fact, scientific activity "can never be fully independent of the properties of our minds or of our practical situations" (27).

Alvin W. Gouldner has proposed a similar stance against naturalist sociology. He advocates a "reflexive sociology" whose "historical mission is . . . to transcend sociology as it now exists" by "deepening our understanding of our own sociological selves and of our position in the world" (1970:489). In Gouldner's words, "awareness of the self is seen as an indispensable avenue to the awareness of the social world. For there is no knowledge of the world that is not a knowledge of our own experience with it and our relation to it" (493). As one can see, reflexive sociology rejects the positivistic dichotomy between object and subject, which is accepted by structural and interpretative sociology of traditional orientations, and attempts to realize a total and unprejudged encounter with one's subjectivity as well as social reality. Manning's reference to a "reflexive science" seems to be akin to this kind of thinking.

Even a cursory attention to current sociological debates will show that the overcoming of the subject-object dichotomy produced by positivist thought is one of the most imperative preconditions for the advancement of sociological theory. In his 1975 presidential address to the American Sociological Association, Coser (1975) scolded the inadequacy of two conspicuous examples of what I call the "objective" and "subjective" approaches in sociology—path analysis and ethnomethodology. He finds that the excessive emphasis on measurement has prevented the production of substantive and creative ideas on the part of the practitioners of path analysis. Ethnomethodologists are scolded for the triviality of their inquiry and their radical denial that an objective explanation of society is possible; their sociology would "amount to an orgy of subjectivism" (Coser 1975:698). Worse, the representatives of the two positions talk past each other and at times assume the behavior of sects (697). I do not intend to discuss the merits, which are rather questionable, of Coser's objections, but I emphasize one point: he cannot produce fruitful suggestions for a true dialogue among the two positions as he offers a typically empiricist and pragmatic formula for rescuing them from their sterility: he reminds both sides of the basic importance of studying latent structures of power and domination (695, 698). No one would deny the importance of such a topic of analysis—certainly not the structural Marxists, as Giménez's and Godelier's essays amply document. The problem is that Coser's suggestion is about a specific "topic" of analysis without providing analytical and methological tools which permit one to overcome the empiricist shortcomings of the traditional objective and subjective sociological approaches.

Scott G. McNall in the preface to a recent symposium on Contemporary Sociological Theory has pointed out the need "to bridge the objective–subjective gap in social theory" and has suggested that the Marxist "concept of praxis" specifically bridges that gap (1978:4). However, having indicated a preference for a combination of a critical theory and structural marxism (6), McNall does not spell out how such a combination is possible and of what it consists.[8]

The "objective–subjective gap" is found also within Marxist thought; on the one hand, humanist Marxists stress the predominance of praxis and conscious subjectivity; on the other hand, structural Marxists give a priority to objective contradictions and objective dialectics. Althusser criticizes humanist Marxists for not seeing that it is ideology, as a social practice, which permits individuals to act, and not the other way around; from this notion he infers the priority of structure over individual subjectivity. Coward and Ellis, however, contend that Althusser takes the "subject" for granted and by the term "subject" Althusser refers to an homogenous and coherent subject which supports ideological representations (1977:75).

The subject–object dichotomy, so pervasive in traditional sociological paradigms, permits one to see clearly the importance of relational structuralism. The notions of deep structure and transformational rules permits one to account both for empirical surface structures (which are the focus of traditional structuralism) and the productivity of the subject. Far from denying the personal input of individual subjectivities (performance), relational structuralists refuse to explain it in terms of conscious processes—an explanation which would lead to the subjectivism Coser is castigating; rather, the individual's productivity is explained in terms of "competence" (or the underlying code or deep structure of logical matrix) that must be postulated to account for the subject's ability to interpret a large variety of situations. This important point together with the related notions of deep structure and transformational rules are well explained in Lidz's essay, and so I shall dispense with a lengthy discussion. I shall simply suggest that the notion of deep structure and infinite productivity through transformational rules permits one to avoid both the subjectivism and naïve objectivism of traditional sociology. Subjectivism is avoided because the production of the subject is controlled by his own "competence," which he shares with other members of his own culture. Naïve objectivism is avoided because apparently inconsistent explanations or discrepancies are accounted for and reconciled in terms of basic constitutive rules of human symbolic activity. (For an example see Lévi-Strauss 1963:ch. 8).

Elsewhere, I have discussed in detail the reasons why the notions of deep structure and transformational rules permit one to overcome the dilemma between empiricism and formalism, in which the analytic realism of Talcott Parsons and other traditional sociological paradigms are caught up. Empiricist paradigms lack a satisfactory link between the general level of scientific laws and the particular level of empirical observations (Rossi 1981)—a link which is provided for precisely by transformational rules.

We have so far referred to the sociological importance of the relational structuralism of Lévi-Strauss and Chomsky. The importance of the semiotically inspired Freudianism of Lacan is clearly documented by its capacity to overcome the objective–subjective dichotomy present within Marxist thought. Lacan has shown the crucial role played by language in the construction of the subject out of symbolic representations. With Lacan, Marxist thought has further moved away from mechanical materialism and has been able to elaborate a true dialectic of language, history, and ideology (Coward and Ellis 1977). Both the structural level (the syntactic order) and the subjective level (the unconscious) become indispensable principles of explanation; in fact, as Benoist suggests, the semantic productivity of the unconscious introduces a dynamic element—an openess—into the syntactic order.

At this point, interpretative sociologists can object that Lacanian inspired semioticians are talking about an interaction between the unconscious as a semiotic structure (and hence a "decentered" subjectivity) and structure as a relational network which controls the productivity of the "subject." These notions seem to clearly indicate the predominance of structure and the denial of conscious subjectivity. Apparently such a conclusion seems inescapable once the premise of relational structuralism is accepted—the need to eliminate conscious subjectivity which, in the words of Lévi-Strauss, has for too long dominated the philosophical scene and impeded any serious work (1971:615). Let us, however, recognize that relational structuralism is not necessarily based on the notion of immutable structures; rather, it postulates the existence of matrices which generate an indefinite number of continuously evolving structures—at least for Lévi-Strauss (1971:561). We can see here a clear echo of the notion of algebraic matrix; however, this level of analysis constitutes the point of arrival, the scientific perspective which can ultimately provide a satisfactory explanation of apparently heterogenous cultural systems. Benoist incorporates the notion of decentered subject into the relational perspective implied by the priority of the syntactic order. I would go so far as to suggest that the notion of individual subjectivity can be also incorporated as a starting point of analysis—a starting point which would soon appear inadequate by itself and orient the social scientist toward structural considerations. After all, any subject is a partial actualization of a given structural context and can be seen as an operative principle in the development of new structures through conscious and unconscious processes. A close consideration of the latter processes stimulates the sociologist to move from the level of traditional or empiricist structuralism to that of relational structuralism—hence to the level of relational constants and decentered subject. Yet, the productivity of semantic processes and their ever-present attempts to break into the syntactic order must be always preserved to account for the dynamics of social systems. The semantic process is a potential negation of the syntactic order. Hence it is the negative pole of an ever-present tension. As the "negative" cannot by definition exist without the "positive," so the semantic and syntactic orders mutually constitute each other as analytical principles; such a notion of complementary and relational dialectic seems consistent with the transformational approach and the notion of "reversibility" as a basic property of the mathematical notion of "group."[9]

The notion of complementary dialectic can bridge not only the dichotomy between interpretative and "natural science" sociologies but also the dichotomy between humanist and structural Marxism or between subjective and objective—or natural—(Lévi-Strauss 1971:616) dialectic.

Clearly, various theoretical positions are possible vis à vis relational structuralism. Coward and Ellis (1977) see a discontinuity between the early semiotics of Saussure and Lévi-Strauss and the more recent semiotics of Kristeva and Barthes. Benoist (1978) seems to suggest, however, a relationship of development and complementarity between the two phases of semiotics. I somewhat sympathize with Benoist's view; in addition I suggest that we can establish a dialectic link—not a relationship of continuity—between the relational perspective of the two phases of semiotics (with their emphases on "structure" and "decentered subject"), and the interpretative sociologists and humanist Marxists (with their emphasis on individual subjectivity). None of these three positions rejects the perspective of relational structuralism; the first two claim to be consistent with such a perspective and the third intends to complement it in a dialectical sense.

The same cannot be said of various reactions toward relational structuralism which have appeared in English-language sociological literature. Some authors have proposed strong criticisms of key structural concepts, but those criticisms often betray empiricist misinterpretations of relational structuralism (see Blau 1977, Merton 1975, Homans 1975).[10] Other authors have totally rejected the structural approach on the basis of a complete misinterpretation of its assumptions and thrust (e.g. Badcock 1975). One can find more sympathetic and positive reactions on the part of some sociologists; however, they offer what are essentially marginal reactions. Some authors emphasize elements of continuity between relational structuralism and past intellectual traditions without, however, placing a sharp focus on the specificity of the structural orientation (Bottomore and Nisbet 1978); other authors focus only on particular structural concepts rather than utilizing or corrobating the perspective of relational structuralism as such (Gonos 1977, Katz 1976, Lidz 1976).[11]

The sociological applications found in this volume fall into two categories: some contributors make use of specific structural concepts without endorsing the perspective of rational structuralism as such; other contributors accept the relational perspective and argue that it has a greater analytic power than traditional sociological paradigms. Eisenstadt, Ekeh, Katz, Parsons, Stinchombe—all of whom make selective usage of Lévi-Strauss' concepts—belong to the first category. Their essays have been included in this volume for specific reasons. Parsons suggests analogies and linkages among different intellectual traditions which cut across various disciplines and sociological orientations; for this reason his essay represents much more than a marginal usage of relational structuralism limited to a corroboration of the functional paradigm. The same is true of Eisenstadt's essay, whose theoretical section offers an overview of various structural thinkers; the substantive part of the essay deals with modernization and cultural change in a very innovative way; hence it is a sharp rebuttal to those who argue that relational structuralism is incapable of dealing with cultural change and, more generally, with processes of social dynamics. For the same reason I have included Ekeh's essay on the theory of civilizational developments and Katz's essay on the analysis of social movements. Stinchcombe's essay is interesting because it contrasts structural functionalism with relational structuralism and offers a clear methodological formulation on how to apply structural analysis à la Lévi-Strauss. Stinchcombe also shows that semiotic structuralism can effectively deal with important dimensions of the symbolic and cultural system—systems which have been largely neglected in sociology since the pioneering work of Durkheim and Mauss (1963).

Important dimensions of the symbolic and moral order are also discussed in the Lidz's and Condon and Wieting's articles. Their authors are among those who accept the perspective of relational structuralism and use it to fill gaps of traditional sociological paradigms; this is true of the contributions of Condon and Wieting, Lidz, Lemert and Nielsen, Giménez, and Godelier who apply the perspective of respectively Piaget, Chomsky, recent semiotics, and structural Marxism (Giménez and Godelier). Lidz, Condon, and Wieting have the merit of proposing a theory on the formation of moral judgement and the mechanism of its functioning—a theory which is totally missing from the theories of socialization and institutionalization processes of traditional sociological paradigms Lidz shows that the Chomskian approach is important to fill gaps contained in the way Durkehim, Parsons, and the ethnomethodologists deal with the issue. Lemert and Nielsen also propose suggestions on how to fill gaps present in ethnomethodology— and they do it with the help of Foucault and recent semiotics Lemert and Nielsen squarely face the issues of precise measurement and theory construction which are central in contemporary sociological problematics, and, especially, in path analysis and eth-nomethodology. They show that only in relational structuralism can one find the tools for reading social relations within discursive practices and interpret them in relationship to social structure.

All in all, these essays prove an important point: aspects or forms of relational structuralism can be used to correct shortcom-ings or fill gaps in the three most basic sociological paradigms—to use Wagner's typology (1963): the "natural science" paradigm (here represented by functionalism and path analysis), the inter-pretative paradigm (here represented by ethnomethodology), and the critical paradigm.[12] The latter point is evident in Godelier's brilliant critique of empiricist functionalism and empiricist Marx-ism. In criticizing Lévi-Strauss, Godelier proposes a theory of the relationship between infrastructure and superstructure which is at notable variance with Althusser's structural Marxism; even Go-delier reinstates the importance of analyzing the symbolic and cultural systems, which are largely neglected in the dominant trends of contemporary sociology.

As wide and innovative as these essays might be in terms of analytical scope and substantive applications, they will certainly prove a modest beginning, which is hardly surprising considering that the sociologists' awareness of relational structuralism is at its very beginning, and that such awareness is taking form mostly among young sociologists. One hopes that the large variety of suggestions and pioneering applications proposed by the contrib-utors to this volume will further stimulate the interest of sociol-ogists and make them realize that relational structuralism can add totally new dimensions of epistemological and methodological so-phistication. This volume shows also that relational structuralism can notably extend the range of phenomena sociologists can study and the questions they can raise about culture and social structure. All this can take place without rejecting what is valid in past sociological traditions and, importantly, by placing them in line with recent developments of natural sciences.[13] This latter con-sideration is particularly important since natural sciences have al-ways been a source of and model for sociological methodology. What is contemplated here is a case of sociological continuity in a deeper and more fundamental sense than empiricist sociologists have been so far exposed to or trained for. It implies a rereading of the historical relationship between natural sciences and scientific method in sociology—a rereading made possible only by divesting sociological thinking of its deeply rooted empiricist biases.

ACKNOWLEDGEMENTS

I thank Roslyn W. Bologh, T. Condon, Martha Giménez, Charles Lemert, Charles Lidz, William W. Mayrl, and Stephen Wieting for their comments on an early draft of this introduction. Our somewhat differing and only partially complementary perspectives prevent us from seeing eye to eye on some of the positions herein expressed.

NOTES

1. I refer to this movement with the term "relational structuralism."
2. The recency of relational structuralism is immediately apparent: all the thinkers I have mentioned are still alive with the exception of de Saussure (1857–1914), Roland Barthes, and Jean Piaget; the latter two died in 1980, Barthes prematurely from a traffic accident.
3. For a cross-disciplinary view of the structural movement see Piaget (1970).
4. This question will be amply dealt with in my forthcoming work.
5. For an extended discussion of these notions and related methodological principles see Rossi (1974), especially pp. 60–106 and 238–55.
6. This term is appropriate to indicate certain basic notions common to or consistent with semiotic structuralism, structural marxism, Piaget, and Chomsky.
7. For a recent phenomenological critique of this position see Bologh, (1979:1–6).
8. Pierre Bourdieu (1977) has offered an interesting contribution on this point.
9. This view will be elaborated at length in Rossi (forthcoming).
10. For a discussion of these misunderstandings see Rossi (1981).
11. I do not intend to offer a complete review of the sociological literature but only to mention a few names familiar to American sociologists.
12. A systematic discussion of the relationship between relational structuralism and these three paradigms will be carried out in Rossi (forthcoming).
13. See Lévi-Strauss (1971: Finale); Stent (1972, 1975); Rossi (1978, 1981).

REFERENCES

Althusser, Louis. 1976. *Essays in Self-Criticism*. Grahame Lock, tr. Atlantic Highlands N.J.: Humanities Press.

Badcock, C. R. 1975. *Lévi-Strauss' Structuralism and Sociological Theory.* New York: Holmes and Meier.

Barbut, Marc. 1966. "On the meaning of the word 'structure' in mathematics." *Les Temps Modernes* No. 246; reprinted in English translation, *Lane* (1970):367–88.

Benoist, Jean-Marie. 1978. *The Structural Revolution.* J. M. Benoist, tr. New York: St. Martin's Press.

Blau, Peter, ed. 1975. *Approaches to the Study of Social Structure.* New York: Free Press.

—— 1977. "A macrosociological theory of social structure." *American Journal of Sociology* 83(1):26–54.

Bologh, Roslyn W. 1979. *Dialectical Phenomenology: Marx's Method.* Boston: Routledge & Kegan Paul.

Bottomore, Tom and Robert Nisbet. 1978. "Structuralism." In T. Bottomore and L. Nisbet, eds. *A History of Sociological Analysis,* pp. 557–98. New York: Basic Books.

Bourdieu, Pierre. 1977. *Outline of a Theory of Practice.* Richard Nice, tr. Cambridge: Cambridge University Press.

Coser, L. A. 1975. "Two methods in search of a substance." *American Sociological Review* (December) 4:691–700.

Coward, Rosalind and John Ellis. 1977. *Language and Materialism: Developments in Semiology and the Theory of the Subject.* Boston: Routledge & Kegan Paul.

Douglas, Jack D., ed. 1970. *Understanding Everyday Life,* esp. pp. 3–44. Chicago: Aldine.

Durkheim E. and M. Mauss. 1963. *Primitive Classification.* R. Needham, tr. London: Cohen and West (original 1903).

Godelier, Maurice. 1978. "Infrastructures, societies, and history." *Current Anthropology* 19(4):763–71.

—— 1979. "On infrastructures, societies, and history: reply." *Current Anthropology* 20(1):108–11.

Gonos, George. 1977. "'Situation' versus 'frame': The 'interactionist' and 'structuralist' approaches of everyday life." *American Sociological Review* 42(6):854–67.

Gouldner, A. W. 1970. *The Coming Crisis of Western Sociology.* New York: Basic Books.

Homans, George C. 1964. "Bringing men back in." *American Sociological Review* 29(5):809–18.

—— 1975. "What do we mean by social 'structure'"? In Peter M. Blau, ed. *Approaches to the Study of Social Structure,* pp. 53–65. New York: Free Press.

Katz, Fred E. 1976. *Structuralism in Sociology: An Approach to Knowledge.* Albany: State of New York Press.

Lane, Michael, ed. 1970. *Introduction to Structuralism*. New York: Basic Books.

Lemert, Charles C. 1979. *Sociology and the Twilight of Man: Homocentrism and Discourse in Sociological Theory*. Carbondale: Southern Illinois University Press.

Lévi-Strauss, Claude. 1963. *Structural Anthropology*. Claire Jacobson and Brooke Grundfest Schoepf, tr. New York: Basic Books. (French original 1958).

—— 1969. *The Elementary Structure of Kinship*. J. H. Bell J. R. Von Sturmer, trs. Rodney Needham, ed. Boston: Beacon Press. (French original 1949).

—— 1971. *L'Homme Nu*. Paris: Plon.

—— 1976. *Structural Anthropology*. Monique Layton, tr. New York: Basic Books.

Lidz, Charles W. and Victor Meyer Lidz. 1976. "Piaget's psychology of intelligence and the theory of action." In Loubser et al., eds. *Explorations in General Theory in Social Science: Essays in honor of Talcott Parsons*, pp. 195–239. New York: Free Press.

McNall, Scott G. 1978. "On contemporary social theory." *The American Sociologist* 13(1):2–6.

Manning, Peter K. 1978. "Structuralism—Survey review." *Contemporary Sociology* 7(2):139–43.

Merton, R. K. 1975. "Structural analysis in sociology." In *Blau* (1975):21–52.

Piaget, Jean. 1949. *Traité de Logique*. Paris: P.U.F.

—— 1970. *Structuralism*. C. Maschler, tr. New York: Basic Books.

—— 1973. *Main Trends in Interdisciplinary Research*. New York: Harper Torch Books.

Rossi, Ino. 1978. "Toward the unification of scientific explanation: evidence from biological, psychic, linguistic, cultural universals." In Marvin D. Loflin and James Silverberg, eds. *Discourse and Inference in Cognitive Anthropology*, A volume in the "World Anthropology" series. The Hague: Mouton.

—— 1981. "Transformational structuralism as an alternative to the empiricist and formalist approaches in sociology: On Lévi-Strauss' definition of social structure." In Peter M. Blau and Robert K. Merton, eds., *Continuities in Structural Inquiry*. Beverly Hills: Sage Publications, pp. 51–80.

—— in press. "On the scientific evidence for the existence of deep structures and their objective and mathematical nature: a training session for Rodney Needham, Ronald Cohen, Peter Caws, Paul Chaney." In Ino Rossi, ed. *The Logic of Culture: Advances in Structural Theory and Method* Mount Holyoke: J. F. Bergin. London: Tavistock.

—— forthcoming. *From the Sociology of Symbols to the Sociology of Signs: Toward a Dialectical Sociology.* New York: Columbia University Press.

Rossi, Ino, ed. 1974. *The Unconscious in Culture: The Structuralism of Claude Lévi-Strauss in Perspective.* New York: Dutton.

Stent, Gunther G. 1972. "Cellular communication." In *Communication, a Scientific American Book,* pp. 17–28. San Francisco: W. H. Freeman and Co.

—— 1975. "Limits to the scientific understanding of man." *Science* 187 (4181):1052–57.

Wagner, Helmut R. 1963. "Types of sociological theory." *American Sociological Review* (October) 28:735–42. Reprinted in R. Serge Denisoff, Arel Callahan, and Mark H. Levine, eds. *Theories and Paradigms in Contemporary Sociology,* pp. 41–52. Itasca, Ill.: F. E. Peacock, 1974.

Wallace, Walter, ed. 1969. *Sociological Theory.* Chicago: Aldine.

CHAPTER TWO

THE STRUCTURAL SOURCES OF FRENCH STRUCTURALISM

PRISCILLA P. CLARK and TERRY NICHOLS CLARK

In considering the intellectual and cultural milieu out of which French structuralism emerged, it is important to distinguish three fundamental elements: the structure of the university system, the (dis)organization of the Latin Quarter, and the immediate intellectual background of the Durkheimians. We deal with each in turn.[1]

THE STRUCTURE OF THE FRENCH SYSTEM
OF HIGHER EDUCATION

Institutions of higher education were enmeshed in the national educational system in a manner that demands analysis. The outlines of the system were formed during the late Middle Ages in conjunction with the Church, but most specific institutions were created, or re-created, by the Revolutionary governments and Napoleon. Changes did occur in the period from Napoleon through the 1960s, but many basic characteristics remained constant for that century and a half. Perhaps the most important of these was the predominance of the lycée, the lynchpin that held the system together. Some twentieth-century observers have suggested that to obtain an ideal education a student should attend a French lycée, a British university and an American graduate school. Clearly, the achievements of the lycée have been numerous and impressive. But documenting its excellence is not the present task; the concern here is more with the extent to which its achievements were made at the expense of the rest of the system.

From the early nineteenth century, the lycée was the raison d'être of the faculties of letters and sciences, which served largely as examination committees for lycée teachers. This conception of professional training in the narrow sense was essentially similar in faculties of law, medicine, theology, and pharmacy, and the specialized Grandes Ecoles. The one Grande Ecole which served as a source of scholars was the Ecole Normale Supérieure, although, as its name indicates, it was created to train schoolteachers. The three years of financial support provided for *normaliens* was repaid by the student's contractual agreement to serve the state for at least ten years. Although others attended lectures at the faculties of Letters and Sciences, the national system of examinations (in the Faculties of Letters and Sciences) was structured around this elite core of Ecole Normale students. The examinations, established by the Ministry of Education, in turn constrained the types of professors appointed to faculty chairs and the types of courses they would offer.

Initially the *licence* and *agrégation* degrees were offered in just two subjects, letters and sciences. Although a few more subjects were added during the nineteenth century, differentiation was curtailed as there was no demand for more specialized secondary schoolteachers. Correspondingly, there was no systemic need for university professors or lectures in more specialized subjects. The social sciences, therefore, could enter the system only by infiltrating philosophy or history, or a marginal field like pedagogy. Traditions of social philosophy, social scientific history, and educational psychology and sociology correspondingly emerged within the faculties of letters.

But this was not an easy process. Ambitious lycée teachers could prepare the two theses for the Doctorat d'Etat required of faculty professors. As the thesis had to be completed under a faculty professor, however, and as he often encouraged candidates to work on subjects of interest to him, differentiation at the thesis stage was difficult. With the Doctorat, a man could be named professor in a provincial university. But as the City of Light attracted most eminent professors, and they would normally advise the ministry about examinations and promotions in their particular field, students would tend to complete theses under Parisian professors. Clusters of doctoral candidates, provincial university professors, and, later, research institute staff members consequently emerged around the few holders of chairs at the Sorbonne who served as patrons. Each follower would vie for the patron's favors by contributing to his journal, extending his ideas in publications, and sending him good students.

Institutionalization of innovations thus took place largely when old clusters were displaced by new ones; this generally occurred when the leader of an insurgent cluster was named to a Parisian chair. To achieve such a coup, nascent social scientists had to argue their merits to professors in the faculty, who would vote on candidates when a chair became vacant; or they had to create public pressures on the ministry, which could create a new chair and name its first incumbent.

Extensive preparation was generally necessary because of the system's resistance to piecemeal change. Recognition of a new discipline implied not simply budgetary commitment for one new chair but, generally, provision for a national system of examinations in the subject, and a staff to prepare students for the new examination in many if not all the universities. Hence the necessity for institutionalizing not one man, but an entire cluster.

Structural differentiation and expansion of the system in accordance with the growth of knowledge was thus clearly retarded by such grounding in the secondary schools. Although it was traditional that university professors be appointed and promoted for their original research, there was little provision for training research workers as opposed to teachers. Or, more exactly, the knowledge disseminated in conjunction with the *licence–agrégation* sequence was of the sort essential for a secondary schoolteacher, or as a foundation for research in the traditional fields (those institutionalized at the secondary level). The aggregate of this learning—and the ability, reinforced by oral examinations, to present it with appropriate style—was referred to with no little provincialism as *la culture générale*. Traditionalists would correspondingly invoke the specter of the decline of French civilization whenever creation of a new university chair was discussed. But in a sense they were correct: since the French system (unlike the American, for example) was not sufficiently differentiated internally to provide separate preparation for secondary schoolteachers and advanced research, to emphasize one implied neglecting the other. Committed to training the young, the system could not legitimately introduce subjects irrelevant to this basic concern.

The usual solution was to construct appendages for research: thus were added the Ecole Pratique des Hautes Etudes and the Centre National de la Recherche Scientifique. Outstanding scholars were named to these institutions without the constraints of training schoolteachers, and a few social scientists joined the mathematicians, historians, and other scholars here. But although one could prepare a Doctorat d'Etat, or more abbreviated theses such a Diplôme d'Etudes Supérieures, Doctorat de l'Université, or in later years, a Doctorat du Troisième Cycle at these more research-oriented institutions, this training complemented, but in no way replaced, the traditional secondary school-oriented sequence from *licence* to *agrégation*. Before the 1950s, when career alternatives to the lycée began to become significant, very few students worked with scholars in these institutions. In principle the research sequence could have replaced the teaching sequence; but it never did. The reasons are many and complex—the traditional prestige of general culture; the importance of the lycée as a career base; the continued requirement of the teaching sequence for the most prestigious students, the *normaliens*; and so forth—but the result was the same: the *licence-agrégation* sequence remained most central to the system, but for structural and cultural reasons was subject to only minimal change. In most cases, the "vicious circle of anti-innovation" operated effectively: only less qualified persons would leave traditional careers to specialize in an innovation; critics would point to their work as inferior; and without serious candidates, creating a new chair would remain out of the question.

For these many reasons, ministry officials were most cautious about committing themselves to any new central chair. Then, because an itemized ministerial budget had to be approved by parliament, parliamentary support was generally essential for establishing new disciplines.[2]

Influence could be brought to bear on the ministry and parliament in several ways, but one possible source was opinion in the Latin Quarter. Supported by the generalizing intellectuals of the Latin Quarter, a particular set of ideas, a group of scholars, or a particular individual could attract a popular following. Resulting competition with the official structures might force them to change. Once a field was institutionalized inside the university, the Latin Quarter climate also helped attract or repel talented students, and thus exercised considerable indirect influence on developing lines of thought.

THE LATIN QUARTER

The attractions of Paris, great for all Frenchmen, are perhaps greatest for students; since 1900, with less than 10 percent of the total population residing in Paris, over one-third of all students in France have been enrolled in Parisian institutions. Most students in Paris thus migrate from the provinces, and many of those enrolled in the provinces manage to spend a few months or a year in Paris at some point in their student career. In any case, whether the student is physically present or not, Paris supplies the dominant reference point.

In migrating to Paris, students shake off the integrative bonds linking them to the rest of society: parents, siblings, relatives, family priest, school teachers, and childhood friends. Moving to Paris is thus no mere change of address; it is a *rite de passage* glorified for shiftless youths and bored provincial housewives from the novels of Balzac and Stendhal to the lonely-hearts articles of the penny press. The provincial student knows that when he returns home he will be expected to act as a Parisian, and consequently must learn his part. But acculturation to new and often radically different norms can only be achieved through great psychic strain on the individual. The crucial period, when anomie is most profound, occurs during the year or two after old norms have been cast off, while the new ones have not quite been internalized. (To a lesser degree this is true as well of students coming to the provincial university centers from the surrounding rural or small-town areas.)

For the student no less than the tourist, the City of Light offers wondrous enticements, but companionship seldom is cited as one of them. On the contrary, documentation of every nature suggests that new students find life in Paris extremely lonely. It has been one of the largest student centers in the world since the late middle ages and had by the 1880s acquired most of the characteristics considered here. The bustling metropolis nearly swallows up the separate faculties and institutes that constitute the University of Paris. The university, moreover, can muster precious little defense

against engulfment, for its possesses almost no integrative structures outside the administrative hierarchy of the Ministry of
Education.

For the vast majority of students, Paris was a cold, fragmented
multiversity long before the term was invented. Here and there
closely integrated structures can be found—most Grandes Ecoles,
and various laboratories and research institutes, for example—but
these are generally not accessible to the newcomer. The small
classes and personal contacts with professors, made possible in
other countries by departmental or collegiate structures, have increasingly become all but unknown. The crowding of more recent
years, in addition to the availability of published course notes and
Radio Sorbonne broadcasts, has enabled many to elude contact
with the university entirely, save the annual ceremonies of reg-
istration and examinations.

Nor do extra-academic structures afford free-floating psyches
much in the way of anchoring points: dormitories, *Studentenheims*,
clubs, and fraternities are practically unknown; special restaurants
for students became widespread only after World War II; the
extracurricular activities that assume such importance in Anglo-
Saxon countries are few in number and attract only a handful of
enthusiasts; organized sports are meager. Since the loci so important for the development of distinctive student activities in
other countries are almost nonexistent, it is no suprise that there
is virtually no student culture to which a lonely student might
attach himself.

More than any other, the cultural style which does dominate
in the Latin Quarter is that of the individual creative artist, the
freelance writer, the critical intellectual. The Left Bank has long
been the favorite location for adult artists and intellectuals, plus
such ancillary *commerçants* as publishers, art dealers, and bookstore
proprietors, around whom have congregated streetcorner philosophers, unemployed journalists, and would-be men of letters who
with the students constitute much of the shifting, gesticulating,
rootless crowd of cafe habitués and *flâneurs*. This ecological prox-
imity to adult intellectuals, along with a national culture that ac-
cords great prestige to individual creativity, seriously diminishes
the significance of other adult models. The military officer, the
civil servant, the entrepreneurial industrialist, or the liberal profes-

sional—who serve as important models for students in many other countries—are ridiculed more often than emulated by students in France.[3]

Because of the central role in launching tastes and styles, philosophical systems, and political doctrines that have devolved historically upon the creative artist, French student life is perhaps best considered in conjunction with the men who have so often served as its stylistic models. Consequently, in the following sections, we shall discuss some of the men of letters and intellectuals who in some way illuminate the distinctive *Zeitgeist* of different periods.

Clearcut lines of causality in these matters cannot readily be established: writers may propagate ideals, and students may adopt some of them, but seldom without modification. Further, the relationships of writers to students vary considerably: Romain Rolland was a distant voice that intoned ideals, Péguy a comrade of street fights, Martin du Gard largely a post mortem scribe. But one can understand the mood of student life in the early twentieth century far better by considering certain men of letters and intellectuals fastened on by the young than by focusing on the students alone in their cultural semi-nudity.

The fundamental question is how students resolved the problem of anomie. In general, the anomie characteristic of French student life prompted solutions which students (and others) nurtured in more temperate surroundings would consider extremist.[4] Extremism was compounded by the increasing importance accorded youth near the end of the nineteenth century by literature as well as by society at large. Adolescents were not unknown quantities in earlier years—*Le Lys dans la Vallée, L'Education sentimentale,* and *Dominique* are three random examples that depict the strains of adolescence, although in the context of the hero's adult life— but the end of the nineteenth century saw a spate of literature devoted to youth and its crises.

A brief historical survey of shifts in mood and outlook in the Latin Quarter is useful. We have had recourse to the best indicators, quantitative or qualitative, that currently exist. We have, when possible, made use of information about organizational memberships; we have also sought indicators of other sorts, often relying upon statements by contemporary or later observers concerning the success of a particular writer. We have then examined the similarities between the works of writers considered influential and attempted to isolate reasons for this influence. We have considered, in addition, the changing reputations of certain other popular figures, such as professors.

Better than ever before, the flood of statements, diatribes, and rebuttals during the Dreyfus Affair illuminated the values upon which the Third Republic stood. The Dreyfusards appealed to those values, most coherently expressed in the writings of the *philosophes*, which had begun to emerge during the Enlightenment and had been partially institutionalized in the successive efforts, largely of bourgeois Frenchmen, to remake their society into a republic. The basic elements of this configuration of beliefs, which may be summarized as *secular rationalism*, included rationalism, a civic lay morality, internationalism, and social solidarity.

This eminently bourgeois rationalism penetrated most of the university as a result of reforms in the 1880s and 1890s. These reforms were aimed at applying to all areas of learning the scholarly and methodical procedures from across the Rhine sanctified as *echte Wissenschaft*. In their many writings, Renan and Taine established the ideological bases for the new scientific university, and by the end of the century these ideals had risen to quasi-official dogma. Even here, however, we may note that the two most illustrious exponents of "scientism" were not themselves scientists but fundamentally *littérateurs*; in demonstrating the varied benefits of careful, exact analysis of historical or literary materials, they elevated the approach of the natural sciences to a philosophy and lauded the benefits of science as a philosophical ideal with an audacity and conviction that most lowly practitioners of the natural sciences would have been too timid to suggest. It was with support from this climate that Durkheim rose to the Sorbonne and attracted his most important followers. The period ended with mounting nationalism which culminated in the Great War, as it is still called in France.

For the majority of students as for many intellectuals, the 1920s were years of intensive searching and little discovery. Commitment to this search was perhaps the only consistent commitment.

A time series on an anomie scale would be certain to reveal an increase during the 1920s. Secular rationalism, still important inside the university, found little support outside; the spontaneous nationalism of the immediate pre-war years had spent itself in combat; the Wilsonian ideals were pleasant, but too remote for most. Montherland, Rolland, and Gide were read and debated yet did not provide a firm set of values. That they were so widely read in these years suggests the extent of moral hesitation among their younger readers.

In more than one respect the 1920s now appear as years of transition. The elite characteristics of the entire educational system—the small number of students, their solidly bourgeois origins, the sure careers awaiting those who passed their exams (and for that matter most who did not), the polished style of life—were gradually eroding.

The 1930s presented new alternatives, and the student culture once again became far more polarized. The economic dislocations struck considerable numbers with great severity, even though the depression was less pronounced than in Germany or the U.S., undermining further the security of a bourgeoisie already shaken by postwar inflation. Many students viewed the university as little more than a vehicle for disseminating the superannuated ideals of the bourgeoisie; they found the government precarious and the economy ailing, and sought more positive models abroad (Nizan 1932). Some saw the solution in the fascist models of Italy, Germany, and Spain and supported the neofascist leagues which built on the tradition of the Action Française. Others who in former years might have elected socialism now found the most dynamic movement the one linked with the young and promising Soviet Union. The rise of the Parti Communiste Français and the migration to Paris of a few Russian intellectuals, such as Alexandre Kojève, also stimulated a few French intellectuals to read Marx seriously for the first time. Numerous solutions between fascism and communism were sought in little groupings that published a number of generally ephemeral journals in the 1930s. Although highly politicized, these journals—*Esprit, Réaction, Combat, L'Ordre nouveau, Plans, L'Homme nouveau*—printed poetry and short stories along with their more ideological articles (Touchard 1960).

In many ways the Latin Quarter mood of ideological *engagement* that developed in the 1930s continued through the 1950s. Like the journals, the men of letters who served as student heroes were more politicized than in the decade before: Malraux, Paul Nizan, Jean-Paul Sartre, Simone de Beauvoir, and several younger men around the Action Française (Lüthy 1955). Then, after about 1960, social scientific models came to dominate the Latin Quarter (Bourdieu and Passeron 1967). If orthodox Marxism lost much of its appeal, the widespread and often indiscriminate use of such terms as "neo-Marxism," "post-industrial society," and "structuralism" indicated that the search for ideological solutions continued, now based on more or less social scientific approaches.

If any constant emerges from the 1920s to the present, it would seem to be the decline of the man of letters as a primary source of charismatic Latin Quarter leadership (and as a means of mitigating student anomie). His mantle has been passed on to others: certain university professors, freelance political commentators, and, to an increasing degree, student leaders. It therefore becomes less and less profitable to assay changes in student orientation by examining the views of popular men of letters. This decline would seem not to rest on the formal structure of the university system, which had not altered substantially before the uprising of May 1968. Paris attracted roughly the same proportion of students as at the turn of the century, so the change would not seem to reside in the students' location or in their relationship to the city of Paris. At first glance the increase in the number of students is indeed impressive (from 29,377 in 1900 to 73,600 in 1930 to 192,178 in 1959 to 499, 442 in 1967–1968: Boudon 1969), and demographic pressures doubtless exercised influence in and of themselves.

But probably the most important single factor behind the decline of literature as a reference point for student culture lies in the lower social backgrounds of students and their insecurity concerning post-university occupations. Since formal instruction accounted only minimally for the taste for literature, literary consciousness depended first on the outlook and orientation acquired from one's family and second on a student culture that glorified artistic, especially literary, pursuits.[5] A core of student dilettantes sufficiently confident of their ultimate careers to indulge their literary predilections was important for setting and maintaining this style.

Whereas even today the French system of higher education is not one of mass education in the American sense—the proportion of students of working class and peasant origins is small compared to the U.S.—considerable democratization nevertheless has impressively augmented the number and proportion of students from *les couches moyennes*, a trend which will most likely be accentuated still further in the future.[6] In the process, the university is likely to adapt itself more closely to the changing technological and industrial needs of an expanding economy. At the same time, if the future elites of France pass through institutions where literature is decreasingly central to the student culture and if this is not compensated by the family milieu, most probably the general prestige of literature and the literary man will recede further still.[7] With no major structural changes to modify the tendencies toward student anomie, other sources of values will tend to be sought as alternatives to the man of letters.

THE SOURCES OF STRUCTURALISM AMONG THE DURKHEIMIANS

How did these shifts of mood affect the emergence and successful reception of structuralism? To answer this, we must look at the followers of Durkheim after the death of the master in 1917.

No one could claim Durkheim's charisma, but efforts could be made to channel it into more solid structures. As Durkheim's nephew and longtime collaborator, Mauss was an important symbol of the cluster. But he remained marginal to the university: not a *normalien*, not a Docteur, not the author of a single weighty volume, he was at the EPHE until a chair (in Sociology!) was created for him at the Collège de France in 1931. His distinctly nonprophetic temperament, his egalitarian camaraderie, and his gourmandise inclined him to convene meetings in carefully selected restaurants. Such meetings could provide undeniable integration for the cluster, but more formal organizations were necessary to perpetuate its collective consciousness. Mauss played a leading role in maintaining these institutions.

A first and natural choice was continuation of the *Année sociologique*. All prewar issues were out of print, and Alcan was not prepared to continue the earlier arrangements. However, the cluster now had friends in important positions. The Confédération des Sociétés Scientifiques made available support from Parliament. The Académie des Sciences Morales et Politiques (of which Lévy-Bruhl and Meillet were members) made a special research award to Mauss and Hubert. Private donations came from affluent friends. These funds permitted the launching of the New Series of the *Année* in 1925. Only two volumes appeared in the New Series, however, in 1925 and 1926, and these only with considerable effort on the part of Mauss.

With the disappearance of the *Année*, the main integrating institution became the Institut Français de Sociologie. Mauss served as its first president (1924–1927) and was succeeded at four-year intervals first by Lévy-Bruhl, and then by Simiand, Granet, Fauçonnet, and Halbwachs. The Institut's *Bulletin*, the official cluster publication from 1926 to 1934, included papers presented at the Institut's monthly sessions and subsequent discussions. This format was better adapted than the *Année* to the cluster's new egalitarianism.

With leading members aging, and younger ones lost in the war, new talent was essential for the cluster's survival. Restaurant meetings and sessions at the Institut Français de Sociologie were too exclusive for attracting young collaborators. Two new structures were thus created, financed through connections of the cluster, in which for the first time ethnology became institutionally differentiated from sociology.

Students in philosophy would still be exposed primarily to Lucien Lévy-Bruhl, who offered courses for the certificat in *moral et sociologie*. An additional certificat in *sociologie générale* was created at the Paris Faculty of Letters in 1921, but it attracted fewer students. Bouglé's ideological pose may have appealed to students about 1900, but as he grew older, he attracted more followers through his institutional activities. In 1927 he became *directeur adjoint* of the Ecole Normale Supérieure, and in 1935 *directeur*, continuing until his death in 1940. He sought to play a role similar to Lucien Herr's in an earlier period. He created a Centre de Documentation Sociale, where, like Herr, he built up an excellent library. His views, and those of persons with whom he sympathized, were presented in seminars at the Centre. Such *normaliens* as Raymond Aron, Georges Friedmann, Jean Stoetzel, and René Marjolin, as well as certain non-*normaliens*, were to benefit from Bouglé's support in Paris as well as in obtaining traveling fellowships.

A second subcluster was less oriented toward political ideology and contemporary society than the circle around Bouglé; its concerns were more ethnological than sociological. Like the *normaliens* around Bouglé, most ethnology students began with a *licence* in philosophy, and after 1927 they could also prepare a *certificat* in ethnology. Mauss offered the main course for the new certificat; in this way, although still at the EPHE, he had a respectable number of students channeled to him for the first time. His course was offered at the Institut d'Ethnologie, created in 1925 by Mauss, Lévy-Bruhl, and Paul Rivet, with a budget coming largely from the Ministry of Colonies. These funds provided fellowships so that career alternatives to the lycée became available to young *agrégés*. In this way, serious field work was undertaken for the first time by trained French ethnologists. Young scholars associated with the Institut included Marcel Griaule, Mme. Dieterlen, André Leroi-Gourhan, Michel Leiris, Denise Paulme, Jacques Soustelle, and Claude Lévi-Strauss.

The generation of the 1930s followed several quite different lines. One began with Marxism. A few scattered individuals had read Marx in earlier years, but there was no serious French tradition of Marxian scholarship as in Germany or Italy. One precipitating event was the arrival in Paris of certain Russian and then German émigrés in the 1930s: Maurice Merleau-Ponty, Henri Lefevbre, and a handful of others developed a philosophical approach to Marx after attending Alexandre Kojève's lectures on Hegel at the EPHE. The Frankfurt Institute for Social Research of T. W. Adorno, Max Horkheimer, Herbert Marcuse, Erich Fromm, et al. was in Paris for part of the 1930s, but did not have a significant impact.

Raymond Aron and Georges Friedmann studied Marx seriously in these years and developed certain themes in Marx by building on advances of others abroad: Aron went to Germany and brought back Max Weber to the French public, as well as a more sophisticated interpretation of Wilhelm Dilthey, Heinrich Rickert, Georg Simmel, and Karl Mannheim than was previously available inside France. Friedmann went to the Soviet Union and returned with a heightened concern for technology and industrialism. Aron and Friedmann both began academic careers which were interrupted by World War II: Aron became associated with the Gaullists in London, while Friedmann participated in the metropolitan Resistance movement. After the war, Marxism and associated ideological concerns (defining proper political involvement: inside or outside the Communist party, which petitions to sign, and so forth) were among the most widely debated issues in the Latin Quarter. Maurice Merleau-Ponty and Jean-Paul Sartre had many common experiences with Aron and Friedmann (Ecole Normale, philosophy, study of Marx, the Resistance), and the debates waged among them in *Les temps modernes* and various polemical volumes dominated much of the Latin Quarter and French sociology until the mid-1950s (Aron 1955; Lüthy 1955, Bourdieu and Passeron 1967). Assuming a new Sorbonne chair in sociology in 1955, Aron developed his non-Marxian approach to industrial society in greater detail in several lecture courses.

A second line of development led Jean Stoetzel to the United States in the late 1930s. His contact with Halbwachs was partly responsible for both a theoretical concern with collective social psychology and a methodological interest in quantification. But whereas Halbwachs never combined the two, Stoetzel did through attitude theory and public opinion measurement as they had emerged in the United States. At his Institut Français d'Opinion Publique and later the Centre d'études Sociologiques, he developed an important following of persons interested in survey research. Some observers suggest that this tendency dominated in the mid-1950s after disillusionment with Marxian-inspired ideology, although there were occasional efforts to combine the two.

A third line that spread out in many directions was that of Georges Gurvitch. Born in 1894, he was about a decade older than other members of the 1930s generation, although he formulated many of his ideas with them. After studying law in Russia, he emigrated to Prague (1921–1924) and then to France, becoming a French citizen in 1928. His works in the late 1920s grappled with German phenomenology, but in the 1930s he worked through the legacy of the Durkheimians; his earlier legal studies merged with the Durkheimian tradition of the sociology of law in a Doctorat d'Etat. After spending most of the war in New York, Gurvitch brought back a mild sympathy for empirical work, returning to Strasbourg (1945) and then the Sorbonne (1948) where, in keeping with the times, he focused on Marxian-inspired themes. He became one of the leading interpreters of the young Marx, and continued work on social class relationships and the sociology of knowledge; in both of these latter areas he combined Durkheimian themes with phenomenology as well as Theodor Geiger, Mannheim, and Georg Lukács. His work on social time drew on Halbwachs as well as Bergson. But despite influences from the French, like his counterpart Sorokin in America, he never became integrated into French sociology.

The fourth line of development contrasted sharply with the others; this was the ethnological tradition of students of Mauss. Unlike the *normalien* philosophers Aron, Friedmann, and Stoetzel, Lévi-Strauss and many French ethnologists seem to have had a less traditional academic background. Associated less often with Bouglé than with Mauss and Rivet at the Institut d'Ethnologie and the Musée de l'Homme, they avoided the ideological hothouse of the Latin Quarter during long periods of field work.[8] Their integration into an international professional community was also greater than that of the more politicized sociologists. When they listened to Mauss, it was at the EPHE and the Collège de France (and on his famous walks home through the Latin Quarter), rather than at the Sorbonne or the Ecole Normale. Their ancillary work often took them into highly specialized courses in linguistics, history, and area studies at the EPHE, Collège de France, or the Ecole des Langues Vivantes Orientales. Here they came into contact with professionally eminent if less politically involved figures, like the linguist Antoine Meillet, the Indologist Sylvain Lévi, or the Sinologist Marcel Granet—all of whom had collaborated on the *Année Sociologique*. Initial temperamental differences, field work, and study in less central institutions seem to have generated a certain detachment from the dominant Latin Quarter mood. Then, too, Mauss remained a supple and creative thinker until the end of the 1930s, while Bouglé had become rigid and ideological even before 1914 (Lévi-Strauss 1945, 1965).[9] Mauss was by no means the oratorical professor that other Durkheimians could be; indeed, in later years he sought to differentiate himself from them as well as from the philosophical legacy of his uncle.[10] He never had a large following. However, his followers remained personally devoted and spent their lives developing ideas which he passed on. Through a certain detachment from their national traditions, they were able to build on the strongest at home and integrate the best from abroad, rather than rejecting their training and starting almost from scratch without the support of a professional critical mass.

STRUCTURAL CHANGES SINCE 1945

More than continuous traditions maintained by a professional community, the social sciences in France, since entering the university, have been characterized by discontinuous successions of clusters. As the clusters overlapped in some areas while ignoring others, their disagreements led potential followers to be skeptical of professional standards and insecure about their careers. In this respect the immediate postwar period saw few structural changes from earlier years. But in the late 1950s and 1960s continuing economic prosperity, political stability, and other factors led to considerable growth in financial support. The CNRS and the Sixth Section of the EPHE increased the number of posts for research and teaching, and with other sources provided research funds in quantities considerably greater than ever before. More chairs were added to existing universities and new universities were created.

Initially these new resources were channeled to support traditional cluster patterns, but as the number of researchers, laboratories, and activities increased, the clusters grew so unwieldy that the system became fragmented. Increased resources, *ceteris paribus*, lead to decentralization of authority; this tendency seems to have been accentuated by the increasing number of sources (especially for applied research) as well as a greater tendency to award contracts directly to younger persons.

With sufficient increase in size and certain structural changes, the system might have evolved toward a German or American pattern, including relatively autonomous centers for research and training united through various professional activities. Many ardently desired such a pattern, which was seriously considered at the Caen colloquia and in the early stages of "reform" proposals after May 1968. But despite discussions over many years, such a pattern seems to have been scarcely adopted in the humanities or social sciences, and only slightly more in the natural sciences. Persons in most basic disciplines, and in many professional schools, have offered the same essential criticisms of the system and the same proposals for change. With the exceptions of history and geography, the social sciences have not been fully incorporated in the secondary school curriculum, and have remained excluded from the *licence-agrégation* sequence. Sociologists, anthropologists, and psychologists thus would generally prepare the philosophy *agrégation* even though *licences* were created for these three fields after 1945. Economics in the Faculties of Law and political science in the Institutes of Political Studies have continued training largely for nonacademic careers. None has developed strong disciplinary communities.

While the *agrégations* also were an obstacle to research training in the natural sciences, they were apparently more successful than other fields in establishing contacts abroad—through research and teaching exchanges, international congresses, journals, and so forth. These contacts seem to have derived both from more universalistic standards in the natural sciences and their less intimate association with French national culture. Citizens of a country that once dominated the civilized world in intellectual, economic, and military matters find egalitarian international relationships difficult to accept. Imposed cognizance of military inferiority in two world wars, and additional colonial losses, led to considerable emphasis on cultural superiority—and correspondingly generous subsidies. The impact which international relationships might have had in stimulating French intellectual life was thus diminished.

Still, many problems for France are similar to those of other middle-sized countries, such as Germany or England: small enough that self-sufficiency invites stultification, their national traditions are still so rich as to hinder international cooperation. Internationalist tendencies in France also suffer from the brilliance of

Paris—not only the artistic, architectural, and gastronomical attractions—but also the presence of leading writers and scholars from all disciplines. Any one university abroad pales by comparison. The whole of Paris is more of a multiversity than any single American center, and such Latin Quarter institutions as the café, the bookshop, and the little magazine link the specialized fields with French general culture. National cultural factors aside, it is much easier to leave a small European university, or even a minor European capital, than it is to leave Paris, especially if one is French.

One means of attaining excellence is to build on the best work abroad; but to do so necessitates international contacts. Such contacts in the social sciences have been most frequent in those areas least associated with French national culture, such as mathematical models and research methods, and in those substantive fields—such as ethnology or parts of history—which are particularly strong in France. Outstanding individuals from less advanced fields also tend to have a wide range of international ties. Thus it is the less advanced substantive fields and the less qualified individuals—precisely those who most need the challenge and support of extensive professional ties—that often rely on immersion in French civilization and Parisian intellectual life as a substitute for a professional community.

This situation is aggravated of course by the structural incompatibility of the entire system with distinct disciplinary communities. Even in the natural sciences, the national professional community is seldom large enough, especially near the top, to foster the universalistic standards that are less difficult for a larger system. Given the cultural barriers to integration with American professional communities, many French natural scientists, and at least some social scientists, have sought greater association with fellow professionals in other European countries. Extensive relationships with intellectually underdeveloped countries have continued as in earlier years, but these have seldom provided serious professional criticism.

An alternative to international contacts is ties with adjoining disciplines, especially those of greater stature. A third possibility is closer integration into the general intellectual community—by reading and writing in unspecialized journals, participating in Latin

Quarter intellectual life, and so forth. Finally, one can turn to governmental, political, or industrial groups, and participate in many clubs, colloquia, and applied research projects they have supported. These last three choices, however, imply contacts channeling activities away from basic disciplinary research—the principal foundation for international standing. The choice among local and cosmopolitan reference groups therefore is crucial in establishing standards to guide development of a field. These four choices, each of which was followed to some degree through the 1960s, were affected by a broad range of factors, but, as in earlier years, some of the most important were shifts in temper of the Latin Quarter, funding policies, and the position of the individual in the national system.

Financial support for social science seems to have come increasingly from governmental and industrial sources demanding applied work. But pressures toward applied research often were delicately counterbalanced by Latin Quarter ideology.[11] Individuals could seek to avoid role-conflict through role-segmentation, but with increased pressures from student demands, many delicate balances gave way. Considerable role-differentiation has persisted within the system, but individuals seem to have narrowed their range of roles.

The many potential reference groups have appealed differently according to an individual's location in the system, a first obvious distinction being between graduates of the Grandes Ecoles and those of other institutions. (Touraine 1968; Bourdieu 1970; Bourdieu et al. 1970). Graduates of the Ecole Polytechnique, often in economics and statistical institutes, have established linkages with governmental and industrial groups; but despite rigorous training in mathematics, a weak background in economic or other social science theory narrowed the impact of much of their work. Including more social science instruction in the Polytechnique curriculum, or that of other Grandes Ecoles, could effect dramatic changes in this regard.

The Ecole Normale graduates have remained for many the major source of hope. In history there have constantly been internationally eminent *normaliens*. Most others in the social sciences have prepared the *agrégation* in philosophy, and thus have been largely social scientific "autodidacts." This lack of systematic social science training, coupled with the strain toward system building expected of the patron, provided a major source of intellectual discontinuity. Abolition of the *agrégation* requirement for *normaliens*, declining importance of the lycée as a career base, new training possibilities at the EPHE Sixth Section and elsewhere, and the broad choice of apprenticeships in small research institutes seemed, in the late 1960s, to be leading some *normaliens* toward more cumulative development.

The possibilities for innovation created by a certain marginality also should not be ignored. The ambition for large-scale contributions inculcated at the Ecole Normale, combined with the creativity of Latin Quarter intellectuals, but still grounded in the rigor of an international professional community, could potentially lead to path-breaking work. Many have no doubt sensed this opportunity, but to achieve the optimal combination of reference groups is no easy task. General intellectual capacity is clearly essential, but by no means sufficient; more than one capable mind has been crippled by the French system. On the other hand, just a single brilliant example can exercise enormous influence. While individual genius can emerge anywhere, the operation of the American system does not provide the same strains toward brilliance as found at the top of the French system.

To date, the Ecole Normale has in principle provided training for this sort of leadership. But without strong professional norms inside the national system, leading patrons have sometimes deviated considerably from international standards. In such instances, the level of private discontent has often been so high but that of public criticism so low that patrons and observers, especially younger observers, have seen their own standards erode. Essential for assuring the informed evaluation and criticism of supposedly original contributions, and for allocating proper rewards, are a minimal number of reasonably advanced and institutionally autonomous individuals. In their research such persons also can provide a sort of middle-level consolidation of ideas. Precisely such middle-level persons, however, have often been absent from the French system (and, on the other hand, produced in large numbers by the American system). The recent growth of posts with the CNRS, EPHE, and other organizations would seem to correspond to this middle-level category. But in fact many researchers in them have become integrated into existing clusters, or if isolated, would tend not to criticize others publicly. There seem to have been recent changes in this respect, although responsible criticism deriving neither from other clusters nor from spontaneous outsiders has not become an important tradition. The absence of such middle-level persons and the lack of clear criteria for professional evaluation have derived largely from the importance of clusters.

Both the structural supports for the Cartesianism-spontaneity dichotomy and organization of the university system into clusters depend, as has been pointed out, on certain traditional elements of French society. Demands for change, however, and actual changes in the political system and, even more, the economy, have been so great that the university and associated structures have experienced considerable pressure. If scientific achievement depended simply on the number and quality of researchers, the prospects of French social science would be excellent. One can only hope that structural arrangements can be adapted to make effective use of these talents.

STRUCTURALISM AND FRENCH INTELLECTUAL ORGANIZATION

The course of structuralism, or more accurately structural thinking in its many guises, in the 1960s illustrates the interaction of the formal and informal intellectual institutions of French life. Perhaps the primary characteristic of structuralism, certainly the one which made it a byword in the most diverse intellectual quarters, is that it represents an attitude toward, a perspective on, cultural phenomena, rather than a distinct analytical approach or theory. It is a "movement of the mind" (Scholes 1974:1–7) which finds its terrain in many areas—in the social sciences and well beyond.

The distinctiveness of structuralism in France is clearest in terms of its intellectual antecedents and antagonists, in the university as well as in the Latin Quarter. It is customary to trace the primary impulse of structural thought to the linguistic analyses of Ferdinand de Saussure, who broke with the German tradition of philological analysis of specific languages to focus on the structures or elements of language itself. Because de Saussure's *Cours de linguistique générale* did not become widely known until mid-century (although published in 1915), the impact of de Saussure coincided to a large degree with that of Lévi-Strauss.

As de Saussure looked beyond historically oriented philology to a theory of language and what he termed structural linguistics, so Lévi-Strauss went beyond culture specific ethnography to what he called structural anthropology. Richly varied ethnographic field material becomes in Lévi-Straussian focus so many variations of invariant basic models of thought. Lévi-Strauss' analyses of social relations, myths, and customs, mark his effort to establish the identity—the structures—from which apparently very different phenomena are derived. The many structuralisms which have in one way or another built on the work of de Saussure and Lévi-Strauss likewise seek to identify the phenomenon, or the structure, which determines and defines the variegated profusion of epiphenomena.

Given the organization of the French university and the implantation of certain clusters, it is not surprising that structuralism should have had its greatest success in disciplines, or parts of disciplines, which were not solidly entrenched in the university. Certainly the most prominent advocates of structural analysis have been outside the university, or in institutions marginal to it, and they have not formed clusters. Marcel Mauss, whom Lévi-Strauss considers the founder of structural anthropology, taught at the EPHE and later at the Collège de France. Lévi-Strauss himself has taught at the Collège de France since 1959, as has Michel Foucault since the late 1960s. The seminar of Louis Althusser was at the Ecole Normale. Jean Piaget, while he offered a course in Paris for a number of years, teaches at the University of Geneva. Roland Barthes, now at the Collège de France, was early identified with a structural approach to literary criticism (although he now speaks of his "structuralist phase"), and was a study director at the EPHE as was Lucien Goldmann and as is Gérard Genette currently.

The ahistoricity of structural thinking distinguishes it from most Marxian positions while the insistence on the objective existence of ultimately rational models of thought behind apparently irrational behavior makes clear structuralism's differences with the hermeneutics of Ricoeur, the phenomenology of Merleau-Ponty, and the existentialism of Sartre, which stress the dependence of the perception upon the perceiving subject, hence dependence upon the particular. Thus even though a writer like Sartre may draw on structuralist vocabulary for his literary-historical works, the Sartrean position is fundamentally antithetical to what Sartre (and others) view as the reductionist formalism and the holistic perspective and stasis of structural thinking. It was perhaps to be expected that structuralism would come under attack, especially as one after another of its variants became institutionalized, for alleged political conservatism, an accusation summed up most succinctly by a graffito which appeared during the events of 1968: "Structures don't take to the streets."

Nevertheless, in cafés if not on the streets, in journals, reviews and a profusion of books, structuralism was a key word, if an untidy concept, in French intellectual life in the 1960s. Then as now much of its course was necessarily determined by the organization of French intellectual life. The same stricture will no doubt hold true for whatever structuralism in France becomes in the future.

NOTES

1. Permission is acknowledged to reprint excerpts from Terry Nichols Clark, *Prophets and Patrons—The French University and the Emergence of the Social Sciences* (Cambridge: Harvard University Press, 1973), © 1973 by the President and Fellows of Harvard College. Interested readers should consult this work as well as Clark and Clark (1969) for further information and documentation.

2. See the reports on ministerial budgets in the *Revue Internationale de l'Enseignement* from 1881 to 1914 and the associated discussions of parliamentary attitudes.

3. While this is more true for the Faculty of Letters than other Parisian institutions, the cultural and demographic importance of the Faculty of Letters has increased throughout most of the twentieth century.

4. Clearly we are arguing that literature provided important elements of an ideology for students, utilizing what Geertz labels a "strain theory," specifically the "morale," "solidarity," and occasionally the "advocacy" explanations (Geertz 1964).

5. The emphasis on artistic sophistication in French student culture consistently has been related to the social background of the students, independent of formal training, in the research of the Centre de Sociologie Européen, (Bourdieu et al., 1966; Bourdieu and Passeron, 1964).

6. The percentage of the population between 20 and 24 years of age attending

institutions of higher education in France has increased from 6.9 in 1955 to 17.4 in 1965; in the U.S. the analogous figures are 24.9 and 40.8 (if one ignores differences in the meaning of "higher education"). O.E.C.D., 1969.

Of those attending institutions of higher education in France in 1960, some 3 percent had fathers who were industrial workers and 6 percent farm owners and workers, while a national sample of 33,982 graduates of American colleges and universities in 1961 included 31 percent with fathers in working class occupations and 8 percent farmers and farm workers (*Informations statistiques* 1961;268; Davis 1964:6).

Even though the percentage of French students from working class and farm backgrounds has increased since 1960, the most impressive change concerns those from *les couches moyennes* (artisans, shopkeepers, etc.). The ratio of students from this level to those from higher levels increased by a multiple of four between 1950 and 1965 (Boudon 1969; *Informations statistiques*, 1968:886).

7. Preliminary analysis of occupational prestige scores for a sample of Frenchmen tends to indicate that occupations associated with literary activities are lower than most traditional discussions of the subject would indicate.

8. Although often referred to as the circle around Marcel Mauss, the organizational leader of the subcluster was Paul Rivet. Despite his intellectual leadership, Mauss performed few activities of a traditional grand patron.

9. Louis Dumont criticizes Bouglé, but asks the reader to look twice if he seems to deviate from Mauss, for "en tout cas que ce serait affaire de capacité insuffisante et non d'intention" (Dumont 1966:7ff).

10. In doing so, he mentioned Durkheim's name so seldom that students, on reading Durkheim, were occasionally surprised to learn how many of Mauss's ideas could be found there. Personal communication, M. Claude Lévi-Strauss.

11. At least one observer perceived that "le sociologue français d'aujourd'hui s'efforce de garder le contact à la fois avec le Commissariat au Plan et avec *les Temps Modernes*" (Touraine 1967:130).

REFERENCES

Aron, Raymond. 1955. *L'Opium des Intellectuels*. Paris: Calmann-Lévy.

Boudon, Raymond. 1969. "La Crise universitaire française: Essai de diagnostic sociologique." *Annales: Economies, Sociétés, Civilisations* (May-June), 24(3):739.

Bourdieu, Pierre. 1970. "Reproduction culturelle et reproduction sociale." Centre de Sociologie Européenne. Manuscript.

Bourdieu, Pierre, Yvette Delsaut, and Monique de Saint Martin. 1970. "Les Fonctions du système d'enseignement." Centre de Sociologie Européenne. Manuscript.

Bourdieu, Pierre, Alain Darbel, and Dominique Schnapper. 1966. *L'Amour de l'art*. Paris: Editions de Minuit.

Bourdieu, Pierre and Jean-Claude Passeron. 1964. *Les Héritiers*. Paris: Editions de Minuit.

——— 1967. "Sociology and philosophy in France since 1945: Death and resurrection of a philosophy without a subject." *Social Research* (Spring), 34:162–212.

Clark, Priscilla P. and Terry N. Clark. 1969. "Writers, literature, and student movements in France." *Sociology of Education* (Fall), 43:293–314.

Clark, Terry Nichols. 1973. *Prophets and Patrons: The French University and the Emergence of the Social Sciences*. Cambridge: Harvard University Press.

Davis, James A. 1964. *Great Aspirations*. Chicago: Aldine.

Dumont, Louis. 1966. *Homo hierarchicus*. Paris: Gallimard.

Geertz, Clifford. 1964. "Ideology as a cultural system." In David Apter, ed., *Ideology and Discontent*. New York: Free Press.

Informations Statistiques. 1961. No. 12, October-November.

——— 1968. No. 108, December.

Lévi-Strauss, Claude. 1945. "French sociology." In Georges Gurvitch and Wilbert Moore, eds. *Twentieth Century Sociology* pp. 503–57. New York: Philosophical Library.

——— 1965. *Tristes Tropiques*. New York: Atheneum.

Lüthy, Herbert. 1955. "The French Intellectuals." *Encounter* (August):5–15.

Nizan, Paul. 1932. *Les Chiens de garde*. Paris: Rieder.

O.E.C.D. 1969. "Development of higher Education in O.E.C.D. member Countries: Quantitative trends." Paris: O.E.C.D., mimeo.

Piaget, Jean. 1968. *Le Structuralisme*. Paris: Presses Universitaires de France.

Scholes, Robert. 1974. *Structuralism in Literature*. New Haven: Yale University Press.

Touchard, Jean. 1960. "L'esprit des années 1930." In *Tendances de la vie française depuis 1789*, pp. 89–121. Paris: Hachette.

Touraine, Alain. 1967. "Unité et diversité de la sociologie." *Transactions of the Sixth World Congress of Sociology*. Louvain: International Sociological Association.

——— 1968. *Le Mouvement de mai ou le communisme utopique*. Paris: Seuil.

PART ONE

PERSPECTIVES INSPIRED BY LÉVI-STRAUSS, 1

THE STUDY OF SOCIAL STRUCTURE

CHAPTER THREE

ACTION, SYMBOLS, AND CYBERNETIC CONTROL

TALCOTT PARSONS

As a social scientist, I have been made vividly aware, over a rather long career, of what may well deserve to be called an intellectual revolution touching the whole range of the sciences dealing with living systems and, indeed, going beyond that. By the phrase "living systems," however, I mean those which comprise two principal universes of analysis and discourse, namely that of organic life on the one hand and of what many of us have come to call human action on the other.

In the early stages of my own career, going back to the 1920s, the proponents of such ideas as self-regulation, boundary maintenance, the operation of codes and programs, or teleonomy, were quite definitely on the defensive. For example, in biological theory, "mechanistic explanations" were exceedingly popular, exemplified most notably perhaps in the work of Jacques Loeb (1906). In the disciplines dealing with human action a kind of "interest-materialism" was by and large in the ascendency. One version of this lay in Marx's historical materialism, but it was much more widespread than that.

A convenient reference point is to be found in the pair of concepts *Realfaktoren* and *Idealfaktoren* as this dichotomy was formulated and very widely suscribed to by philosophically minded people in the Germany of my student days in the mid-1920s (Parsons 1937: part I and II). In the background of course lay the philosophical traditions of German Idealism and, in European thought more generally, somewhat less prevalent in Germany, the ideas of Positivism and Scientific Materialism. Marx's famous feat of "standing Hegel on his head" was to provide a substitute for the Hegeliam stress on ideal factors by introducing a theory of history grounded in the so-called real factors. More generally, however, tough-minded social scientists were under very heavy pressure to be sure not to underestimate the importance of such entities as economic interests and political power, which may be said to have been at the core of Marxian theory.

The movement of social thought in which I first came to be strongly interested essentially broke through this either-or dilemma. I think by far the most significant figures of my early concern were those of Max Weber, who lived in this German intellectual *milieu* and with somewhat different emphasis, Emile Durkheim in France (Parsons 1937). They had to contend, not only with the ghost of Karl Marx, but with much else that could better be called positivism, behaviorism, and the like, and as a callow young American graduate student, I was under pressure to come to terms on these problems. My first major statement, the book entitled, *The Structure of Social Action* (Parsons 1937), was very largely preoccupied with this order of issue. By that time it should however be noted that a certain amount of support was available outside the sociological tradition, notably in Freud's psychology (Freud 1958), in that of Piaget (1965), the Gestalt psychologists (Kohler 1929), and the philosophy of science of A. N. Whitehead (1925), by sharp contrast with his collaborator, Bertrand Russell, and finally certain trends in biological thinking, notably the popular book of Walter B. Cannon, *The Wisdom of the Body* (1932).

In the period since the 1920s, the movement away from the tendency to identify real social science with the *Realfaktoren* has steadily gained force through a number of intellectual movements. These movements have covered the whole range from macrosociology and the theory of culture to microbiology and the new theories of biochemical genetics. There is, however, a very striking unity of pattern in the movement over this enormously wide range.

In what follows, I should like to deal with certain developments in genetic and evolutionary biology, with linguistics, with certain aspects of cybernetic theory, and then with matters closer to my own field. There will be occasion toward the end to raise a few questions about the relation of my own work to that of Lévi-Strauss, in whom Professor Rossi is particularly interested.

As I noted above, a particularly striking set of comparisons or analogies between social theory and the physiological level of biological sciences was brought to a head and came to my attention very early through the work of W. B. Cannon (1932), which in turn rested on the earlier physiological work of Claude Bernard (1957). This particularly had to do with the self-regulatory properties of the highly differentiated individual organism, including of course, the human. Cannon introduced the term *homeostasis* for the general idea of the capacity of such organisms to maintain relatively constant internal states in the face of substantially greater fluctuations in the state of the environment in which they lived (Cannon, 1932). One of Cannon's principal illustrations was the maintenance of a constant body temperature by certain classes of the higher organisms, notably mammals and birds, but he dealt with many other examples. His point of view, following that of Bernard, was strongly influenced by the idea of a distinction between an internal environment of the organism, notably, for the higher organisms, mainly the bloodstream, and the external environment. The distinction between internal and external environments clearly also implies that the organism as system maintains boundaries *vis-à-vis* its external environment (Parsons 1975a).[1]

At the level of the species rather than the individual organism, another development came into my own awareness some years later. This came to my attention through the contributions of a biologist, Alfred Emerson (1956), at an interdisciplinary conference on system ideas, which was held in Chicago over several years in the early 1950s. The most important idea which Emerson advances is phrased in terms of what he himself called the analogy between symbol and gene. This clearly is a shorthand formula and could be elaborated to the effect that there is an important parallel between the genetic component of the determination of the structure and functioning of species at the organic level, and the role of culture in the structure and functioning of systems of human action. This parallel is developed at some length in the paper in the volume in honor of Merton referred to above (Parsons 1975a, Merton 1957). Let me say essentially, that in biological theory, with increasing emphasis, as a function of progress in its branch of the science of genetics, stress had come to be put on the independence of genetic heritage of species from individual organisms as members of species of what many biologists have called the level of the "phenotype," that is the living individual member of the species, which had developed from a fertilized ovum by a process of growth involving interaction with an environment at every step.

It was later that ideas like that of code and program came to enter prominently into genetics and other branches of biology. The full development came with the discovery of, or unravelling of the chemical structure of DNA and the subsequent understanding of the genetic code (Stent 1972; Stern 1972).

A very notable feature of the new genetics, of which a convenient short account is given by Stent, is the extent to which linguistic terminology is employed (Stent 1972). Thus, it is said that the information contained in the structure of the DNA molecule is "transcribed onto RNA." RNA then, to omit various complications, is the agent of the "translation" of this information, in connection with the functioning of enzymes, into the constitution of functionally important protein molecules within the cell. Indeed, the usage goes farther than this. In one of the later developments an entity appeared in the microgenetic theory called the "codon." As Stent explicates this concept, it is a series of adjacent genes (on the DNA molecule), the relations of which to each other are directly analogous to the relations of the parts of a sentence in linguistic usage. Thus in figure 7 of Stent's article (1972:222), the codon is represented by three adjacent genes labelled Z, Y and a. These explicitly are designated as the subject, the verb and the predicate respectively of a "sentence." Furthermore, in the usage of microgeneticists, the enzymes are often referred to as the alphabet of the information system, or one could even in quotes say, "language" which operates in the genetic process.

This usage on the part of microbiologists is surely meant to be more than metaphor. Genetic information is indeed transmitted by signification. Furthermore, it articulates with the very notable development in the field of linguistics, which had been going on more or less simultaneously with that in microbiology. In my own awareness of these developments, on a background to which Charles Morris (1964) contributed significantly, the most prominent names are Roman Jakobson (Jakobson and Halle 1956) and Noam Chomsky (1968). The movement symbolized by these names has introduced a new era into linguistic science. The version of it most frequently refered to contemporaneously, of course, has been that of Chomsky. Chomsky in particular makes much of a distinction between what he calls the "deep structures" of a language and the "surface structures." The deep structures do not as such articulate any sentences which could convey coherent meaning. The surface structures constitute the level at which this occurs. The connecting link between them is a set of rules of transformation, to use Chomsky's own phrase, by which elementary symbolic components of linguistic expression are manipulated and combined with each other and with others to constitute meaningful sentences. One of the extremely important tenets of this school is the conception that language opens the possibility of an indefinitely wide range of meaningful statements or sentences, many of which will never have been formulated before in the history of speakers of the language.

Before attempting to pull some of these themes together in relation to the theory of action, something should be said about the advent of the idea of cybernetics. This was a movement in general science, the most important leader of which was the late Norbert Wiener (1961), who was a professor of mathematics at MIT. As in so many other cases, Wiener coined the term by adaptation of a Greek expression which refers to "the helmsman." The relation of this idea to the Bernard-Cannon (Bernard 1957) (Cannon 1932) ideas in physiology is extremely close and it is significant that many of the most important of the earliest applications of, and investigations in, cybernetics, occurred in the realm of physiological processes. It also, however, appeared to have an extremely important bearing on the more general cognitive structure of theory underlying engineering processes. The governor of the steam engine was thus one of Wiener's favorite illustrations (Wiener 1961). The essential theme in engineering is meeting the conditions whereby a humanly contrived mechanical system can indeed come to be, within limits, self-regulating.

The idea has, of course, been transformed in a very important way to the electronic field in applications to such inventions as radar and, with particularly far-reaching consequences, to the development of the modern computer. It is notable again, that far from unconnected with Wiener's work, the theoretical father of the computer is widely believed to be another mathematician, John Von Neumann.

To adhere to very simple-minded levels, we may quote the central formula of cybernetic theory, that cybernetics concerns the conditions under which it is possible for systems which are high in information but low in energy to exert effective control over systems where energy and information stand in the reverse relationship, that is, which are high in energy but low in information. In my own teaching for some years, I have used the example of the thermostat, controlling the temperature levels of a small enclosed space heated in cold weather by something like an oil-burning furnace. The electricity consumed by operation of the thermostat constitutes a negligible fraction from the energy involved in the oil used for heating, for example, in severe New England winter conditions. Nevertheless, the control of the turning on and off of the burner unit rests in the thermostat, not in the energy aspect of the burner itself or its fuel. This very simple device is indeed a prototype of the idea of cybernetic control. Quite clearly the information which is relevant is information as to the temperature status of the space in which the thermostatic instrument is placed.

In the biological field, comparable developments were not confined to the microbiological level. Broadly the same period saw extremely important developments in what Ernst Mayr has called "the other half of biology," namely that concerned with evolutionary theory. There has been, particularly in the work of Mayr himself (1970), enormous clarification of the nature of the evolutionary process, linking on a level of sophistication well beyond Darwin's own work, the genetic and the natural selection aspects of the problem. I shall have somewhat more to say about these problems before the end of this article, but in particular would like to call attention to the importance for the present theoretical context of Mayr's concept of teleonomy (Mayr 1974:78–104).

At a certain kind of first sight, these three great developments, namely in microbiology, linguistics, and cybernetic theory, seem to have little to do with the disciplines dealing with action at the human level. In my own experience the most important early hint of a relationship was given in the idea promulgated by Alfred

Emerson (1956) by stating the analogy, or at least partial equi-valance, of what he refered to as gene and symbol. I would now like, however, to bring the discussion back to the older theme with which I opened it, namely the relation between what many German intellectuals, in the early part of the century, were calling *Realfaktoren* and *Idealfaktoren*. The most dramatic shift of atmos-phere may perhaps be characterized by saying that cybernetic theory had undermined the presumptive superiority of laying ex-planatory emphasis overwhelmingly on the side of *Realfaktoren* because these are precisely the categories of human action which are high in the equivalent of energy. The possibility however clearly needed to be explored that another set of factors which were high, in the cybernetic sense, in information, but low in energy might have crucial determinative consequences. On much reflection on these matters, it seemed to me increasingly that both Weber and Durkheim had hit on action parallels to the phenomena which had emerged as so important in these other intellectual contexts. Thus Weber's treatment (1963) of the role of religious ideas in the larger processes of differentiated social development fitted that, as did, in a less sharply formulated way, Durkheim's ideas (1915) about the importance of the belief component in what in his later work he came to call collective representations.

If there is a set of components in the theory of human action comparable to DNA and the genetic code and to programs of different levels, to the deep structures of a language in Chomsky's sense (Chomsky 1968), and to the high information, low energy systems of cybernetic theory, clearly they must lie in the area ordinarily called that of the *Idealfaktoren* in the German expression I have refered to. In the formal terms of the theory of action, such factors or components come to a head in the cultural system. A major clue is given in Emerson's formula relating the gene and the symbol (1956), for the structure of culture as this concept has developed has come increasingly to focus on symbols and their relations in patterns of meaning (Parsons and Platt 1973).[2] From the point of view of the theory of action a particularly important sub-category is that of values or value-commitments, because this has served as such an important bridge between the cultural system and those lower in the cybernetic hierarchy of action, notably the social system and the personality of the individual.

Before the advent of the theories from disciplines other than the analysis of human action, there was indeed a long struggle to validate the importance of this set of components precisely in the determination of empirical outcomes. The position they took on these matters was one of the main bases on which I was originally attracted to the work of the authors dealt with in my book *The Structure of Social Action*, namely Pareto, Durkheim, and Weber, especially in contrast on the one hand to the tradition of Marx, on the other hand that of utilitarianism and positivism more generally. By the time some of these other intellectual movements crystallized, however, it can, I think, correctly be said that a fundamental outline of theoretical concepts and their relations which fitted these desiderata had been worked out. This is, in a certain sense, the structural core of what has come to be called "structural-functional" theory in the social and action fields (Parsons and Smelser 1956; Parsons 1961, 1967, 1969; Parsons and Platt 1973).

Though the point of view I have stated is still contested from time to time, I think it can be regarded as rather firmly established. The confirmation of it by the relations between these aspects of the theory of action and the work in biology, linguistics, and cybernetics which has been reviewed, greatly strengthens the case for the essential correctness of this line of thinking (Watson 1970).

I shall now discuss a few of the highlights of the common conceptual structures which are found in these fields and in the theory of action. A particularly important key to the relationship lies in the theoretical developments which have taken place in linguistics. The reason for this is that, on one side, there would be now serious argument that linguistics deals with symbolic phenomena and on the other side, there is no serious question about the prominence of the role of symbolic phenomena in the general field of culture. Indeed, it has long been anthropological tradition that language should be treated as a part of culture, though anthropologists have not been very precise as to how it should be located in relation to other parts of the cultural system (Leach 1970).

Perhaps we can discuss this matter in terms of the relation between three primary categories. In both linguistics and genetics the first of these has been called *code*. A second central concept, used particularly by geneticists and other biologists, is that of *program*. Finally, a third category is a very substantial general significance which may be called a *mediating agency*. I have in mind in the biological context two categories in particular, namely the hormones, which figure prominently in the Cannon type of physiology (Cannon 1932), and the enzymes, which figure very prominently in microbiological thinking (Luria 1973). In linguistics, the speaker is assumed as the active agent of sentence construction, hence, I think a somewhat comparable concept in linguistic theory is that of the transformative rules by which deep structures are linked to surface structures. It is very striking in Chomsky's theory that the linkage requires crossing from one level to another (Chomsky 1968), the deep structures are components of the semantic aspect of a language whereas the surface structures are much more prominently characterized by the role of phonetic sounds and their combinations (Jakobson and Halle, 1956).[3]

In the field of the theory of human action we can, I think, ground the high information factors in something very comparable to the genetic code and the deep structures of language. I think the best name we can give to these symbolic entities is something along the line of Max Weber's concept of complexes which state the premises of answers to what Weber called "problems of meaning" in the context of his sociology of religion (1963). Concepts of meaning, however, do not automatically transform themselves into concrete human action. The tendency to believe that they do seems to me to constitute the basic fallacy of idealistic thought. They require intermediate structures and processes, of which perhaps the most important for our purposes are what sociologists sometimes call institutions, and also the concomitant type of process by which symbolic components come to be part of the going structure of action systems, a process which may be called institutionalization.

There is another central concept developed over the last few years in the theory of action which bears an important relationship to the comparison we are making. This is the concept of "generalized symbolic media of interchange" (Parsons 1969, 1975b; Parsons and Platt 1973). At one level the principal model for the conception of a generalized symbolic medium has been money as that concept crystalized in the work of the classical economists.

At a somewhat different level a prototype has been language itself, the relevance of which to our analysis needs no further comment. The basic tenet of use of the concept in the theory of action has been the assumption that neither money nor language should be treated as a unique phenomenon but that both should be treated as members of a much larger family of mediating agencies. Since in the title of this category we have used the word symbolic, it is quite clear that from the point of view of the determination of human action such media belong in the high information, low energy category. It also seems clear that at the macrophysiological level the hormones are very closely analogous to action media. A good example is insulin in its physiological functions of controlling the level of sugar in the blood of higher organisms. At the microbiological level a somewhat similar set of functions seem to be performed by the enzymes as agents of what the microbiologists call the synthesis of proteins. It is a notable fact that these substances exist in the living systems of reference only in small quantities and that they are neither factor inputs into the primary physiological results, nor are they categories of output. Enzymes, that is to say, are not to be confused with the proteins that constitute the main concrete structure of cells.

A code I would define as a framework of symbolic categories or patterned arrangements, for example, within a complex chemical molecule, such as DNA, which can serve as the framework for embodying and conveying information. As such, however, a code, like Chomsky's deep structures (Chomsky 1968), does not "say anything"; it is not part of the operative structure of the system, many of the properties of which it regulates and governs. The genes, this is to say at both the macro and microbiological levels, are not anatomical parts of the phenotypical organism, nor are they physiological processes. They constitute a quite different order of factors.

We would consider the genetic code, the deep structure of a language, and the structural paradigm of an action system to be, for the purposes of the present discussion, essentially equivalent entities. It is indeed to me extremely striking that the fundamental structure of the genetic code, as delineated by Gunther Stent (1972:220), is formally identical to the structure of an action system as that has been worked out in the theory of action. I think it probable that comparable things can also be said about the corresponding linguistic structures.

Essentially, such structures are built on principles of binary differentiation. The genetic code is built on the framework of the four constitutive bases on DNA, which it will be remembered always occur in two pairs. I think it can fairly be said that the pattern variable scheme is in some sense a formal equivalent of the base structure of DNA. The genetic code then, in order to code for particular amino acids, of which there appear to be twenty, must select on three different dimensions, which are portrayed in Stent's diagram (Stent 1972; Olby 1972) as the outside vertical axis, the outside horizontal axis, and, on the right of the diagram, repeated within each of the four horizontal rows. This carries the complication of a binary diagram to the 64 cell level. In action system diagrams, we have habitually carried it out only to the 16 cell level, but the logic of carrying it two steps further does not pose any difficulties.

There seems furthermore to be an important relation between this structure of the genetic code and the Mendelian principle of segregation according to which the genes for heritable traits occur in dominant and recessive pairs, called alleles, which are continually reshuffled in the process of genetic inheritance, certainly when it is bisexual. We suggest that this binary pattern is of a fundamental significance for living systems and is to be contrasted with the pattern of continuous variation of linear variables as these have been formalized in terms of the differential calculus.

Another very striking fact, as noted, is the extent to which the microbiologists use linguistic terminology in describing the events of the biochemical relations between DNA and the synthesis of proteins. In the first place they speak of DNA as the bearer of *information*, quite explicitly using that term. They then speak of the *transcription* of the DNA information onto RNA, and finally, of the *translation* of this information in the process of the synthesis of proteins by messenger RNA. Finally, perhaps most striking of all, is the description provided of the *Codon* (Stent 1972), which consists mainly of three adjacent genes which are explicitly labeled as subject, verb, and object, or predicate, that is, as constituting a sentence in the linguistic sense. It would scarcely be possible to come closer to the idea that the mechanisms of genetic inheritance are special cases of information processing mechanisms which can be systematically linked to the symbolic levels of human action.

One further point may be mentioned: Ernst Mayr in particular has made a distinction between a code and a program (Mayr 1974). In going back over the microgenetic material, so far as a layman can understand it, it has seemed to me that the concept program probably best fitted that of the codon because this is the sector of the information in DNA which is utilized for the synthesis of particular amino acids and eventually classes of proteins.

The upshot of this analysis is that the presumption seems to be strong indeed that the basic code and program structure is basically the same for language, for the transmission of genetic heritage, and for human action. If this is a tenable position, it surely is one that has extremely wide implications. The similarity quite clearly rests on the fact that they are all ways of carrying and implementing, or transmitting, information.

I would like in this connection to call the reader's attention to still a further very striking parallel between the organic levels of the functioning of living systems and that of action. The first point of reference for the comparison to follow now came from the concept of natural selection as that has been inherited from Darwin and in revised form, formulated among others by Mayr (1970). On careful reconsideration of the writings of some of the microbiologists, notably Stent (1972), Watson (1970), and Luria (1973), it struck me that the process of the synthesis of proteins, as they describe it at the level of the interaction between DNA, RNA, and the enzymes in the cell, carries with it the same basic logical structure that natural selection, at the macro-organic level does, according to an evolutionary biologist such as Mayr (1970). The central fact is that by no means all of the organic compounds which are present in the ordinary cell come to be synthesized as parts of protein molecules, which can perform certain kinds of physiological function within the cell. The process of protein synthesis involves a rather drastic *selection* among the materials present and available and their *combination* in highly specific ways. In a similar way, at the macro-organic level, by no means every trait which is carried in the genetic heritage of a species, survives in the phenotypic populations of individual organisms which characterize a species. Many variations are eliminated in the process of natural selection, that is, are not selected, and those which are selected are combined in highly specific ways.

The process in systems of human action which is analogous, on the one hand to natural selection, on the other to the synthesis of proteins, is what some sociologists have come to call the process of institutionalization. Notably at the cultural levels of symbolic organization, innovations continually occur. However, only part of these become part of the going structure and determinative of it, of going action systems at the social system level, and of their future developments (for purposes of the present argument, I shall ignore that of personality). Cultural innovations have to be institutionalized for this to occur, and institutionalization, from this point of view, is a process of selection on the one hand, of combination on the other (Parsons 1971:97–139). It seems to me that here, as in the nature and role of codes and programs, the parallel is very close indeed, a closeness which has not been widely appreciated.

Finally, I may note that the editor of this volume, Professor Rossi, has been particularly interested in the work of Claude Lévi-Strauss, which has, in its later phases, borne the name of "structuralism" (Lévi-Strauss 1963). The question has a number of times been raised of defining the relations between the theoretical scheme used by Lévi-Strauss, and that used by myself and various associates under the heading, the theory of action. An important contribution to clarifying this problem has been made in an article by Adrian C. Hayes (1974). Hayes in particular calls attention to the fact that Lévi-Strauss confines his empirical analyses entirely to what Hayes calls primitive societies, and does not attempt a comparable analysis of societies of the modern type. It seems to me that this is a very striking feature of the Lévi-Strauss work and suggests a solution of the problem of relation, which Hayes poses.

By and large, primitive societies stand on a level of greater simplicity of structure, notably with respect to structural differentiation, than is the case for more advanced societies, which are more advanced on an evolutionary scale. It seems to me to be a reasonable hypothesis that since Lévi-Strauss deals only with primitive societies, the conceptual scheme he uses is less differentiated than that of the theory of action which was to a very large extent developed for the analysis of modern societies. This circumstance may account for a feature of Lévi-Strauss' analysis which has very much concerned me since I have become acquainted with his more recent work. This consists in what seems to me to be a very strong emphasis on the cognitive aspect which might even be considered to constitute a cognitive bias. Lévi-Strauss himself frequently refers to the paradigm he uses as expressing "the structure of the human mind," but it seems to me that he means human mind in a cognitive, almost directly Cartesian, sense. At the level of primitive society, however, it would be less inappropriate to suppress the distinction between the cognitive and noncognitive components of action, or the rational and nonrational, to put it in Max Weber's terms, and I have the impression that this is the tendency of Lévi-Strauss' position. By contrast, for the theory of action, the problem of the relations between rational and nonrational components has constituted a very central point of reference for the whole theoretical enterprise. It would seem to me, therefore, that Lévi-Strauss' structuralism could be interpreted as a less differentiated version of the same fundamental conceptual scheme which has been presented in a more highly differentiated and elaborated form in the theory of action.

In closing let me mention merely that it seems to me to be a very striking feature of the development of a number of disciplines in the twentieth century, that they have, to the extent to which this has been the case as reviewed in the article, converged on the use of what increasingly have seemed to me to be common conceptual elements. This convergence particularly concerns the understanding of the structure and processes involved at low energy levels, to use the cybernetic theory expression. These are structures and processes having to do with the organization and transmission of information which fit in with the emphasis on the important role of symbols and symbolic levels of the organization of meanings. Even though the connections between the theoretical schemes used in the science of language, in various branches of biology, and in the social sciences, which I have grouped together under the concept of the theory of action, are not very widely known and appreciated, it seemed appropriate to review them together and point out the close resemblances which they bear to each other.

NOTES

1. The homeostatic idea clearly has an extremely important bearing on the status of the very central and controversial concept of function. I would hold that this is common to the theory dealing with all levels of living systems. For a discussion of this, see my contribution to the Festschrift for Robert Merton (1975a). My paper deals with the present status of "structural-functional" theory. It is notable that Merton (1957, ch. 1) as well as myself among so-called "functional" social scientists, have taken a very positive attitude to Cannon's point of view.

2. Of course both terms which Emerson used, gene and symbol, constitute part of a relatively cryptic shorthand. "The gene" does not individually determine specific hereditary patterns of a species or an organism at the organic level, but it is a unit in a complex system of symbols which constitutes a culture. Although a language is only part of a cultural system, it of course comprises a very large number of particular symbols which can have exceedingly complex grammatical and semantic relations to each other. Just as we use values as units of one particularly important subsystem of a cultural system, but discuss the complex relations of particular symbols when we try to analyze the system, so the study of language must consider very complex concatenations of interrelated symbolic components in considering the functioning of a language. On the relations of culture to the rest of human action, especially illustrated by cognitive structures and processes, cf. Parsons and Platt (1973).

3. There is some question about the use of the term code in linguistics. It was used by Jakobson and Halle (1956) who spoke of *code* and *message* as the two primary components of a language. Chomsky, however, has not followed this usage, preferring the terms *deep* structures and *surface* structures in the above meaning. How directly comparable the term code as used in microgenetics and by Jakobson and Halle is not altogether clear, but the main point of the present discussion seems to hold, namely that the genetic code and the deep structures constitute cybernetically controlling factors in the sense of cybernetic theory that they are entities high in information which act to control those which are relatively lower in information but higher in "energy." Just how the corresponding components of the theory of action stand will be discussed further.

REFERENCES

Bernard, C. 1957. *An Introduction to the Study of Experimental Medicine.* H. C. Greene, trans. New York: Dover (orig. 1865 in French).

Cannon, W. B. 1932. *The Wisdom of the Body.* New York: Norton.

Chomsky, Noam. 1968. *Language and Mind.* New York: Harcourt, Brace and World.

Durkheim, E. 1915. *The Elementary Forms of the Religious Life.* J. W. Swain, trans. New York: Macmillan (org. 1912 in French).

Emerson, A. E. 1956. "Homeostasis and the comparison of systems." In Roy R. Grinker Sr., ed. *Towards A Unified Theory of Human Behavior: An Introduction to General Systems Theory.* New York: Basic Books.

Freud, S. 1958. *The Interpretation of Dreams.* vols. 4 and 5 of *The Standard Edition of the Complete Psychological Works of Sigmund Freud.* London: The Hogarth Press and the Institute of Psychoanalysis (orig. 1900 in German).

Hayes, A. C. 1974. "A comparative study of the theoretical orientations of Parsons and Lévi-Strauss," In *Indian Journal of Social Research,* August-December.

Jakobson, R. and M. Halle. 1956. *Fundamentals of Language.* The Hague: Mouton.

Kohler, W. 1929. *Gelstalt Psychology.* New York: Liverwright.

Leach, E. R. 1970. *Claude Lévi-Strauss.* New York: Viking Press.

Lévi-Strauss, C. 1963. *Structural Anthropology.* C. Jacobson and B. G. Schoepf, trans. Garden City, New York: Doubleday Anchor Books.

Loeb, Jacques. 1906. *The Dynamics of Living Matter.* New York: Columbia University Press, McMillan Co.

Luria, S. E. 1973. *Life: The Unfinished Experiment.* New York: Scribner.

Mayr, E. 1970. *Populations, Species and Evolution.* Cambridge: Harvard University Press.

—— 1974. "Teleological and teleonomic: A new analysis." In Marx Wartousky, ed. *Method and Metaphysics: Methodological and Historical Essays in the Natural and Social Sciences,* pp. 78–104. Proceedings of the Boston Colloquium for the Philosophy of Science 1969–1972, vol. 6. Holland: Brill.

Merton, R. K. 1957. "Manifest and latent functions." In *Social Theory and Social Structure* (rev. ed.). New York: The Free Press.

Morris, C. 1964. *Signification and Significance.* Cambridge: MIT Press.

Olby, R. 1972. "Francis Crick, DNA, and the central dogma." In Gerald Holton, ed. *The Twentieth Century Sciences: Studies in the Biography of Ideas.* New York: Norton.

Parsons, T. 1937. *The Structure of Social Action.* New York: McGraw-Hill. reprint, New York: The Free Press.

—— 1961. "An outline of the social system," and "Editorial Foreword: The General Interpretation of Action." In Talcott Parsons, Edward Shils, K. D. Naegele and J. R. Pitts, eds. *Theories of Society.* New York: The Free Press.

—— 1967. *Sociological Theory and Modern Society,* New York: The Free Press.

—— 1969. *Politics and Social Structure.* New York: The Free Press.

—— 1971. "Comparative studies and evolutionary change." In Ivan Vallier, ed. *Comparative Methods in Sociology*. Berkeley: University of California Press.

—— 1975a. "The present state of structural-functional theory." In Lewis Coser, ed. *The Idea of Social Structure: Papers in Honor of Robert K. Merton*. New York: Harcourt Brace Jovanovich.

—— 1975b. "Social structure and the symbolic media of interchange." In Peter M. Blau, ed. *Approaches to the Study of Social Structure*. New York: The Free Press.

Parsons, T. and G. M. Platt. 1973. *The American University*. Cambridge: Harvard University.

Parsons, T. and N. J. Smelser. 1956. *Economy and Society*. New York: The Free Press.

Piaget, J. 1965. *The Moral Judgement of the Child*. New York: The Free Press.

Stent, G. S. 1972. "DNA." In Gerald Holton, ed. *The Twentieth Century Sciences: Studies in the Biography of Ideas*. New York: Norton.

Stern, G. 1972. "The continuity of genetics." In Gerald Holton, ed. *The Twentieth Century Sciences: Studies in the Biography of Ideas*. New York: Norton.

Watson, J. D. 1970. *Molecular Biology of the Gene*, 2nd ed. New York: W. A. Benjamin.

Weber, M. 1963. *The Sociology of Religion*. Trans. by Ephraim Fischoff. Boston: Beacon Press. (orig. 1922 in German).

Whitehead, A. N. 1925. *Science and the Modern World*. New York: McMillan.

Wiener, N. 1961. *Cybernetics, or Control and Communication in the Animal and the Machine*. 2d ed. Cambridge: The MIT Press.

CHAPTER FOUR

THE DEEP STRUCTURE OF MORAL CATEGORIES

EIGHTEENTH-CENTURY FRENCH STRATIFICATION, AND THE REVOLUTION

ARTHUR L. STINCHCOMBE

I shall apply structural analysis to the system of moral categories into which any society's population is classified, to the categories of the stratification of the old regime in eighteenth-century France, and discuss how the deep structures of the stratification culture of the old society shaped the nature of the Revolution, which abolished that stratification structure.

THE SOCIAL FUNCTIONS OF MORAL CATEGORIES

In every society there are some categories into which people can be classified that pervade their whole lives: child-adult; male-female; citizen-alien; black-white; crazy-sane are examples of such categories in the United States. Further, there are other categories that pervade particular situations or social systems: in a house there is the owner or renter (and his or her family) and the guests. These categories dominate the situation of the particular house, in the sense that few of a guest's are not affected by his being a guest.

Furthermore, these categories have extension into the larger institutional order. If a guest oversteps his rights, the police and the courts will distinguish the tenant from the guest. If an insane person comes to criminal court he or she will be treated differently from a sane person. Blacks appear in the administrative records of fair employment enforcement with a different significance than do whites. Children are required to go to school—adults not.

These categories used to classify people for social purposes have moral obligations attached to them. A guest has responsibilities, ranging from the most subtle obligation to pick up cues about when to go home to the legal responsibility not to break and enter. Children have privileges and obligations distinct from adults; citizens privileges and obligations distinct from noncitizens (e.g. noncitizens are not expected to be "loyal"); a white or a black come by accident to a neighborhood bar with the opposite color clientele can feel his lack of moral privilege with the hair on the back of his neck.

On the one hand these categories seem to be features of institutions. For example, the category "child" is a part of the institution of the school, and its moral significance constituted by the obligations it lays on the child in the teacher-child relation, the principal-child relation, the child-bringing-home-grades-from-the-teacher-to-his-parents relation, and so on. Child is also a category in the institution of the family, as a person subject to adult authority; in the political system as a nonvoter; in the system of civil law as a person who cannot sign contracts. We do find a certain amount of variation between these institutions in exactly who is a child: In schools there is a variable age of final graduation to an adult role (from about 16 to about 30); for voting there is a single age of 18; for the family adult rights and duties are granted so gradually and so variably among families and among children that legal majority has little to do with it. In any event, the age of legal majority varies for different areas of life.

But somehow this misses the essence of the social status of being a child. After all, being a child in the civil courts (i.e. not being able to be held liable for contracts) is very closely related to being a child in the family (being subject to the head of the household's decisions about money) and in the labor market (not being employable) and the school (being prepared for the labor market). The status of a child is pervasive among institutional areas, and "hangs together" in a meaningful sense. That is, it is dominated in each institutional area by the notion that this is a person who needs to be taken care of, who cannot make his or her own decisions. Though the details (e.g., the age of majority) vary among institutions, the child-adult contrast has roughly the same significance in all of them. It is a "structural" distinction, in the sense that it gives structure to a wide variety of superficially different situations.

Likewise the status of "owner or tenant" and "guest" is structural in the same sense. A guest in a restaurant is a client whose rights and obligations differ substantially from those of the man who came to dinner, but beneath the superficial differences we find that both the housewife and the waiter can keep the guest out of the kitchen, and can send him home at closing time. Thus there is a deeper continuity in meaning in the tenant-guest distinction between superficially different situations.

Now consider the problem of quickly constructing a moral order for conversations at a dinner party. Who is in charge? The owner or tenant, the "host." Who can be shooed out? Children. How should people be arranged at the table? Alternate men and women, but do not seat women next to their husbands. The moral order is thus quickly blocked in—its main features are known—just by making use of the structural or pervasive distinctions of the culture. Although the montage of a particular dinner party may have aesthetically unique qualities, its basis is constructed from standard materials. These categories are, so to speak, the ideological raw materials from which a moral order may be constructed to suit the occasion. Since, by and large, one can depend on children to be willing to be shooed, husbands to give up their wives for the sake of dinner conversation, hosts to take charge, there is a certain amount of reliability, of known qualities, in the raw materials.

Much more complex and continuing systems can be built with the same sort of raw materials. Schools shoo children on a complex and well worked out schedule, combining the shooability of children with many other moral characteristics of the structural position of a child (such as listening when he or she is told to listen) to build the complex moral order of "education."

The problem of structural analysis of a moral order is therefore one of finding the basic or pervasive categories of the normative system, out of which (with suitable modifications) the basic moral order for different situations is constructed.

UNIVERSAL MORAL CATEGORIES?

People categorize other people into morally significant categories primarily in order to carry out action toward, or with, them.

Commonalities of human action therefore tend to produce commonalities of moral categorization. For example, in most male social groups in all societies, women are of more sexual interest than are other men, and women in child-bearing ages are of more reproductive interest than are girls or older women. In all societies this sexual and reproductive interest results in men classifying women differently from men. The reproductive interest results, in all societies, in the classification of women according to who their children "belong to," by marital status, by who is responsible for supporting the children, for claiming children's labor services, for arranging their social placement, marriage, etc. This classification by marital status often also results in the establishment of moral (if not always practical) sexual monopoly over the woman, so that she becomes (morally) of no sexual interest to men aside from her husband.

That is, in all societies there is a moral category of female, and a moral category of wife.

Likewise for age—all societies distinguish children and adults. All must take some cognizance of those adults who cannot assume adult responsibilities because of mental or physical disabilities. All must recognize that a dead person can no longer fulfill his social obligations in the same way as one who is alive, and consequently (for example) that a *widow* is in a somewhat different situation than a wife, and a farm or herd whose owner has just died has to be run in some different way (by an "heir").

And finally we come to the most pervasive category of all, the category that distinguishes those people who can be trusted to form reliable parts for the moral constructions we make to run our lives, and those who are outside the pale. Moral reliability usually depends on social enforcement, ultimately economic sanctions or violent punishment. People whose social and economic fate, or their life and liberty, are not subject to the moral order are not reliable parts of it. The boundaries around a "society" are boundaries that mark off people who are moral entities in the normative system, in the sense that their behavior is subject to that system and can, to that degree, be relied upon.

For example, there is a reasonably close correspondence between "residing" in the United States and being a "citizen" of the United States. About 1 percent of the population in the territorial

United States at any one time is likely to consist of aliens. But in hundreds of ways, aliens living in the United States are part of American society—and when they are not, as some diplomats are not, the legal status of diplomat is defined by American law and American treaty obligations. Aliens (except perhaps diplomats) must drive on the right, pay their bills, send their children to school, leave when the host starts yawning after a dinner party, and keep their hands off other men's wives in public. Thus the category "resident alien" is a status in American society. But there is no morally significant sense in which "Japanese citizen living in Japan" is a category of the moral system of the United States. Such people are merely "foreigners."

Every society, indeed every corporate moral system whatever, has a categorical distinction between members and nonmembers, that is, between morally responsible constituent elements for social action governed by the norms of the group, and people who are not governed by those norms. These categories may be shadings of grey rather than black and white distinctions, and there may be "resident aliens" or "apprentices" or "probationary members." And there are always ways of showing oneself to be sufficiently unreliable, and hence read out of the society as criminal, insane, incompetent, or disloyal, so that membership is never completely inheritable.

But having said all this, we must recognize that we have said very little. Although there is a category "wife" in all societies, the moral accompaniments of the category are not very similar at all. For example, in eighteenth-century France and in Karimoja in Northern Uganda (Dipson-Hudson 1966) a wife is only represented in the legal system by her husband or father-in-law; in the United States she can make contracts and sue in her own name. In the United States and Karimoja she can get divorced, while in old regime France she could not, but in Karimoja she leaves the children to her husband's family, while in the United States she almost invariably takes them with her on divorce. In Karimoja the wife works in agriculture, the husband does not—in eighteenth-century France the reverse. The amusement of playing with fire by encouraging conversations between a wife and other men, so characteristic of the upper middle classes in the United States, would be foreign to the conversational role of a wife in eighteenth-century France or Karimoja. A wife among the Karimojong has no legitimate claim to sexual monopoly over her husband; in eighteenth-century France she had a strong claim unless her husband was politically upper class, in which case she shared him with mistresses. In the United States she has a strong claim to sexual monopoly *especially* if the husband is in the political upper class, and people lose political offices for scandals that would have contributed to political prestige in eighteenth-century Paris.

Thus except for one common feature of these moral situations of wives—that they are all centrally determined by what men want women to do as wives—the category wife is a different one in the three societies. In each case there will be a moderate degree of predictability, so that by and large one can depend on wives' behaving as they are supposed to. In each case one builds the moral order of families *and* conversations *and* casual sexual encounters with the moral raw material that includes the concept wife.

In the same way "foreigner" means to the modern United States "the subject or citizen of another state, or a refugee." Foreigner to a Karimojong means "enemy" (with some exceptions), a person to be either attacked or avoided. In eighteenth-century France, the category of foreigner was in rapid evolution, as a medieval jumble of crosscutting feudal ties were being reorganized into nation-states; roughly speaking, it had the modern meaning of someone to be dealt with through his political leaders. The Karimojong do not have diplomacy, so foreigners cannot have the moral meaning of "people dealt with by diplomacy." There is a similarity again at a deeper level, like the similarity in the meaning of "wife" as "someone at the disposal, in certain respects, of her husband." Foreigners in all three moral systems come under a "principle of lesser eligibility" for all sorts of privileges and rights created by the moral order. Only if diplomacy gives a foreigner a right to travel in the United States, or to sell his or her goods there, does he have that right—all American adults except prisoners or mental patients have those rights.

We are clearly in a dilemma here if we treat such concepts as "wife" and "foreigner" as universal components of normative systems, and to ignore the immense variety. If we do, we shall not take into account that foreigners entering Karimojong territory get killed, while foreigners entering the United States only get humiliated by an Immigration Officer. The difference between getting killed and getting humiliated is sufficiently important to take account of, at least if one is a foreigner rather than a social theorist. Nevertheless, there is a good deal in common between an Immigration Officer and his enforcement of lesser eligibility and an indignant Karimojong meeting a foreigner at his waterhole.

THE METHOD OF STRUCTURAL ANALYSIS

The problem we have just outlined is basic to the cultural sciences. It is the question of whether it makes sense at all to use common categories across cultures for cultural or "mental" phenomena. Clearly it makes sense to talk of sexual intercourse or eating as phenomena that take place everywhere. But is "wife" a phenomenon everywhere? If so, what about "mistress"? Is "feast" a cross-cultural category? If so, what about "communion"? Unfortunately these empirical questions have become tangled up with epistemological questions, about whether we can ever know what is in someone else's mind, and if we can, whether we can measure it. Though this is a very interesting question, it is only in the case of the solipsist resolution of it that it has any implications for scientific practice. If we resolve the epistemological question by saying that there are better and worse guesses about what people have on their minds, and that we know generally speaking how to make our guesses gradually more accurate, we can address the question of what to do with the guess that "foreigner" means something similar, yet crucially different, to a Karimojong and to an Immigration and Naturalization Hearing Examiner. That is, we suppose that we have solved the epistemological problem enough to guess that intending to kill someone is different from intending to change the conditions of a visa, and that in both cases the principle of lesser eligibility is applied to foreigners. Now we want to know what to do with this guess. We leave the question of the ultimate philosophical value of that guess to philosophers.

There are two main methods that have been proposed to deal with this question: the "ideal type" method and the "structuralist" method. In both cases "method" is perhaps too strong a word: "intellectual strategy" or "orientation" might be better.

The "ideal type" strategy starts with a common problem of human action, for example, of a decision-maker controlling an administrative apparatus which he wants to have execute his decision, or a religious leader justifying God's ways to Man by explaining how evil and injustice come about. The notion is that there will be a limited number of basic types of cultural patterns that *can* do the job: charismatic, traditional, or bureaucratic authority; transcendental gods, exorable gods, or a purposeless universe. The reason that only a limited number of basic strategies will be found is that the nature of the problems of human action everywhere have basic similarities. Getting willful men to obey, or explaining to a man with boils all over himself why he should love God, are everywhere basically similar. And since the problems are similar, only a few types of cultural frames will provide the materials for constructing a moral order that can solve them. Thus the ideal type approach depends on what might be called "strong functionalism." Although the kinds of gods may vary, the nature of the problem of explaining evil and injustice is everywhere sufficiently the same that only a few basic forms of solution will be found.

The "structuralist" strategy tries to avoid the strong functionalist postulate by analyzing each cultural concept in terms of the particular cultural system as a whole. For example, the concept "wife" among the Karimojong would be described by the conjunction of all the contrasts between adult women and children, all the contrasts between unmarried and married adult women, all the contrasts between married women and widows. Thus "wife" among the Karimojong means a person without the right to own cattle but with the right to use a garden and a milk cow, without the right to participate in religion and politics, without the right to take lovers, but with the right to have a baby's father support it, with the right to live with the husband she married rather than one of her husband's heirs (as a widow must), and so on.

The bundle of distinctions, of rights and duties, liberties and immunities, that make up the moral concept "wife" among the Karimojong may be unique. There is no "strong functional" hypothesis here that only a few sorts of cultural patterns can fill the role of bearing legitimate children. Where then does the universality come in? It comes with the attempt to specify a cross-cultural set of contrasts which *will be a sufficient language* for, say, describing all roles as wives. The question is now, if we take all the components used in the description of a Karimojong wife's status, can we use that set to describe any other human family system we choose?

What then would this language look like? First we have a set of exclusions: in all known societies some family members are excluded from some ownership roles but not others, from some religious ritual roles but not others, from some political decisions but not others. Thus in every society family roles can be divided from each other by ownership, by ritual capacities, by citizenship rights.

Now we know that this small set of distinctions is not a complete language for describing the role of a wife, for even among the Karimojong it does not yet distinguish a wife from a widow. And yet it makes perfect sense to us to use the same language to say that in the United States wives typically own family property jointly with husbands, but the children and grandparents typically own none of the nuclear family's property; that wives and children participate in religious ceremonies but usually in subordinate roles, that wives but not children have legal political citizenship.

The reason for calling this approach "structural" is that it presumes that the concrete concepts of a moral order such as the concept "wife," will vary from one "moral language" to another. But the basic pattern of contrasts out of which these concepts are constructed, say contrasts between excluded and included roles in property, religion, and politics, will tend to be universal.

An example of the contrasting strategies would be in the analysis of rules of succession. Radcliffe-Brown's famous essay argues that the predominance of *either* matrilineal *or* patrilineal succession in most societies of the world was caused by the fact that only a few cultural solutions existed to the problem of continuity of corporate action, when the corporation consisted of relatives and when it managed a valuable estate (1952). Thus Radcliffe-Brown constructs a couple of ideal types, cultural patterns having a good deal in common in spite of superficial differences, starting from a very common problem of ensuring the continuity of a family corporation managing a family farm or herd or whatnot.

To manufacture a structuralist approach to the same problem, we set out a series of contrasts likely to be taken into account in the moral evaluation of a succession problem. People may be classified by:

1. Is the person dependent for support on the estate or not?
2. Is the person closely or distantly related to the deceased?
3. Is the relation created by marriage or by blood?
4. If by blood, was the deceased married to the mother or not?
5. Did the deceased have a substantial moral debt to the person for service or not?
6. Is the person competent to take over the authority of the deceased or not? (Both actual and ritual competence are relevant.)
7. Is there enough of an estate so that anybody really cares?
8. Is the potential heir a person who can be trusted to act honorably in cases where his self-interest conflicts with his obligations to others having an interest in the estate?
9. Was the relation of the deceased to the property in question that of "owner" or not? (etc.)

A complete classification of all the people involved with the deceased in all his roles by all the criteria above would be very complex. No doubt very few systems of succession use all of the distinctions, and when they do they do not use them in all cases. But already the above list of considerations looks as if it would describe the main brunt of conversations about succession problems in authors as diverse as Jane Austen, Fyodor Dostoyevsky, and Tsao Hsueh-chin (*The Dream of the Red Chamber*).

THE STRUCTURAL METHOD: A ROUGH OUTLINE

When we turn to the analysis of a particular normative order, using either of these methods, we run a grave risk of oversimplification. It is clear, for example, that the categories king, clergyman, nobleman, and commoner were fundamental moral categories for eighteenth-century France. The king could never be treated as merely another nobleman, and although he was a very powerful official of the Church he could not be mistaken for a cardinal. King was a pervasive status, relating a man to all institutional areas in a distinctive way. So was "nobleman" pervasive, carrying legal privileges, economic advantages, and career opportunities in both the royal bureaucracy and the Church. And of course the status "clergyman" likewise pervaded family life, political life, legal privileges, etc.

But after some detail about the classification into four estates, and some internal legal differentiation of them, we shall have to discuss in some detail the enormous variation in status and privileges within them. When writing about American society we are much less likely to forget that one resident alien is a distinguished Visiting Professor of Anthropology, while another picks grapes in the Salinas Valley, than we are to forget that some noblemen were prime ministers and others petty landowners.

But even in the face of personal variations, this pervasive classification of people in many parts of the normative system determine the dominant status of people—that is, classification decisively shapes the opportunities, rights, and obligations to which a given person is exposed. This in turn means that from a psychological point of view, classification shapes people's dominant conception of their identities, of the continuities in their own lives: continuities in the way they are treated by others, in the purposes which it is appropriate for them to pursue, in what they amount to in terms of the values and functions of the society as a whole.

Such pervasive classification also shapes the stratification systems and the role systems of the component institutions of the society. The line between minors and adults in the society as a whole decisively shapes families (adults always run them), schools (teachers and parents run them in all respects in elementary and secondary schools, in colleges only in areas connected to academic life), factories (minors are excluded), automobile and real estate markets (minors cannot get credit, so must have adult agreement), and so on.

MAJOR MORAL CATEGORIES AND PREJUDICE

Women, foreigners, children are all categories about which people have stereotypes. That is, at the same time that the category "young woman" may be defined normatively as "not capable of consequential actions and so not to be taken seriously; sexually attractive and fecund and so to be protected," the same category also functions in a belief system, in such beliefs as "women are more emotional than men; women can rarely achieve the highest peaks of aesthetic or intellectual performance." Likewise children are commonly believed to be less intelligent or worse informed than adults, and usually required or encouraged to go to school.

The actual institutional actions which cause women, children, foreigners, or Black people to have different normative rights and duties are called "discrimination" and the beliefs associated with those categories are called "stereotypes" or "prejudice." The relation between prejudice and discrimination has been subject to acrimonious debate because it touches on the political questions of who is to blame and what is to be done. If prejudice causes discrimination, then a person who does not believe the stereotype is innocent, and what is needed is education. If the prejudiced beliefs are merely surface manifestations of pervasive categories in the whole normative order, "institutional racism" or "institutional sexism," then it is not so easy for a person with liberal beliefs to hold himself innocent, and what is required is the use of power to stop discrimination rather than education to stop prejudice.

A person's first reaction to this causal question is likely to depend on his attitude toward the discrimination. For example, in the United States children up to about 16 are required to be in school and to be out of the labor market. This discrimination is much greater and more uniform than labor market discrimination against blacks or women. This has not always been the case, of course. Before 1865 most blacks were legally prohibited from selling their labor, and children were allowed and even encouraged to sell theirs. This discrimination against children is associated with a stereotyped belief that children are more ignorant than adults. Like other stereotypes, a few moments examination of the evidence available in one's own experience is generally enough to show it to be false. All of us can certainly match, to the child's advantage, a youngster under 16 we know against some adult we know.

In this case hardly anyone would urge that it was their unexamined stereotype that makes them support discrimination against children in the labor market. A proposal to apply the criterion of ignorance "fairly," so that people of whatever age who failed a test were required to go to school, and those who passed it were free to get jobs, would strike them as preposterous. The idea that by educating people out of their stereotypes one could get them to support a "fairer" system in which brilliant 10 year olds could hold jobs and dull 50 year olds had to learn algebra would not appeal to anyone.

Historically the logic of the inquiry in sociology usually has proceeded from stereotype to emotions. Sociologists have reasoned that if people do not decide how to treat others by reason of the explanations they give, then it must be emotions, irrationality. When one *favors* the discrimination the emotion postulated is often called love, love of children, love of country; when one opposes it it is often called hate, or a word ending in "-ism" (racism, sexism). It is clear from our daily experience that indeed a few people are passionate haters of blacks or women or foreigners, or passionate patriots, or always so squishy when children are around. It thus is fairly easy to imagine that pervasive normative categories are the result of a widespread *mild* infection of public opinion with the affect that we see in strong form among the virtuosi of emotions, among fanatic patriots or bigots.

But this will not do either. The virtuosi of emotional anticommunism hate American radicals worse than Southeast Asian ones. But the nation they "love" kills Southeast Asian Communists, and makes speeches against American ones. That is, their discrimination does not fall where their hatred does. The emotional tone of a congressional debate on family property law, bearing on women, or the setting up of Civil Service qualifications which exclude many blacks, or of the negotiation in a firm of the retirement age, is not that of a lynch mob. People change their emotions nearly as fast as their stereotypes, loving the noble mysterious Russian peasant soul or hating the Asiatic barbarian posing as a European according to what emotion the State Department suggests this year. Survey studies show that most people, most of the time, hardly notice what emotion they have to abstract categories like "young woman," "child," "foreigner," or even "black." And when they do notice the emotion, it is quite often a generous one.

The problem is that reason and emotion are both individual causes, but the thing to be explained is a social construction. It is, to be sure, mental, as all moral systems are mental, from the grammar and phonology of a language to the highest flights of philosophical jurisprudence. But when we observe that the rule passed and past be pronounced the same way in English must in some sense be in people's minds, we are not inclined to look either for a process by which the individual reasoned it out, nor for an emotion toward the "t" sound. The characteristics of the normative role of "young woman" are much like the rules of phonology:socially established mental structures that people use to construct, on the one hand, the sounds of particular sentences, or on the other, the particular moral structures of a concrete family or a concrete office staff. To look for reason or emotion in the individual as a cause of such a moral category is therefore looking in the wrong place. Instead we have to look for principles of evolution and growth of (more or less) integrated structures of symbols, moral categories, and their manifestations in particular concrete institutions. The key symptom we use to determine when "prejudice" is likely to be connected with "discrimination" is when the prejudice is about a category which is a pervasive element of the institutional order in many areas of social life. For that will indicate that instead of being a random belief, it is a belief serving the function of making cognitive sense of the moral order. People may have a wild stereotype of, say, Turks, and never discriminate, but have moderate and changeable stereotypes of women, and discriminate in all areas of their social life. It is the structural function of the category woman in the normative order as a whole which accounts for the disproportionate effects of mild emotions and stereotypes.

We must think of the problem of the relations between prejudice (stereotypes or hatred) and moral categories in a much more complex way. In the first place, by the fact of being fundamental categories of social thought, moral categories form a catch basin for generalizing tendencies of beliefs, emotions, and moral injunctions. To some degree stereotypes of men and women, emotions of sexual solidarity and generalized interest in the opposite sex, and moral injunctions about the care of children or the responsibilities of child support are all organized around the distinction of men versus women because the distinction is there. Such a socially instituted category channels the generalizing impulse toward itself, as the most readily available reservoir for general ideas and feelings.

Second, a socially instituted category makes use of human mental capacities, whatever they are, to construct an ideology in its defense. Faculty with an interest in maintaining their authority, or plantation owners running a place whose basic moral category is racial, attach now beliefs, now emotions, now moral injunctions to the categories student or black. But the insistence with which faculty urge on parents that students are ignorant and should be educated, or plantation owners urge on hill farmers that blacks should not be uppity, comes from their dependence on a manifestation *in a particular moral order* (the plantation or university) of a pervasive social category. Of course, reproduction of the same dependence on a moral category in multiple areas of life, as in the pervasive interest of South African whites in the color bar, can make many groups ready to receive, amplify, and return each other's ideology; a feedback leading to an extraordinary ideological screech so difficult for moderate English and American racists to live with.

Third, the close relation of pervasive categories to identity, to the confidence that both you and others know who you are, renders all change of basic moral categories a soul-wrenching experience. When such a displacement is forced on a person by someone on the disadvantageous side of the boundary, a sudden growth of prejudice is more a protest of wounded vanity than a continuous repressive policy.

And finally, most of the time people are treated as women, or children, or blacks, or too old, because the possibility of treating them otherwise has never occurred to the discriminating person. Giving another person an individual identity, an individual place in the moral order, is an effort. The deep wound in a sensitive woman, child, black, or old person is often caused more by thousands of instances of cruel indifference, or minor thoughtless insult, than by the massive apparatus of systematic oppression.

That is, the relation of prejudice and discrimination to moral categories is one of overdetermination. Once the categories exist, different sorts of causes cumulate to produce both prejudice and discrimination organized around the same categories.

THE LEGAL PHILOSOPHY OF THE SYSTEM OF PRIVILEGE IN THE OLD REGIME

The legal organization of the old regime is nowadays generally viewed as a system of monopolistic corporate privileges, organized to favor the rich and oppress the poor. This view had its origin in the efforts of reformers like Turgot and publicists who wrote during the eighteenth century. It became the official view because it was the official ideology of the Revolution. The whole system looks queer and irrational to modern eyes, because it was based on different ideas about what law was for, what its relation to government should be, what the role of "private" interests should be. The system as a whole was more similar to modern university administration than to modern law or modern corporations (a modern business-school eye has equal difficulty understanding the administration of a university).

There are four basic principles that make the old regime's legal philosophy different from the modern one:

The first is the idea that every important administrative official was basically a judge. An old regime official decided cases according to two principles simultaneously: the public purpose for which he was appointed, and the general body of legal doctrine to which citizens, "corporations," and the government itself were subject. His practical decisions about how his job should be done had the force of law, were subject to legal appeal, and constituted the jurisdiction of his court. The extensive conflict between royal officers, especially the *intendents* who were chief administrative officers of provinces, and other courts (seigneurial or baillage courts, *parlements*) reflects the fact that a royal officer's legal jurisdiction, as a judge, tended to expand into all areas for which he had practical responsibility. The legal device by which this was done in general was the King's right to withdraw any case from any court and to decide it himself; i.e. in a different "court." Thus every important shift in administrative organization simultaneously reorganized the legal system, and undermined the rights of some court or administrative body. We shall call this the principle of legalistic administration.

The second principle was that every socially important function in the society was a public function, a responsibility of the state.

Supplying food to Paris, for example, was not merely a business that some people happened to be in; it was of the nature of a public office, and the wholesalers and navigators who did the work were responsible to the King and his officers for it. This meant in turn that they had to have judges and courts and special legal standing, so that they could be legally obliged to fulfill their offices, and legally defended in the profits and wages of that office. The extensive legal provisions about how work was to be done, and who could do it, represented an extension of the idea described above—the idea that a public administrative officer was basically a judge and an origin of law, in his area of competence, to "private" social functions. A guild was therefore something like a court of law in an area of the economy, and simultaneously something like an administrative arm of the government. This identification of private and public functions was especially prevalent in the administration of the basic economic resource of the Old Regime, agricultural land, and much of what is called "feudalism" has to do with the conception of land ownership as a public office, as a part of the government, and of a public office as a court of law and an origin of law. We shall call this the principle of mixture of civil law and public law.

The third principle, perhaps by the end of the Old Regime more of a contradiction in the system than a principle, was the legal unity of the individual. That is, the general presumption was that all of a man's life was devoted to a single public or social function, and that this single dominant status determined which courts and laws he was subject to. His taxes, for example, should be administered by the same law court (cum administrative apparatus) that determined his qualifications as, say, a goldsmith; the body of law, the court, and the administrative section of the state apparatus to which he was subject had to correspond to his overall status. Thus, theoretically, every social function and all the people who performed it had a distinct legal status, responded in their own courts, had their taxes determined by their own courts, and so on. We will call this the principle of an "estate" legal system.

The final principle was that the people in a given legal niche, a given legally created status, had a legitimate right to representation in the law court (cum administrative apparatus) that governed them. This right of representation was not egalitarian, and did not extend to government as a whole but only to their own guild or estate. But, for example, the officers of a guild who served as a court or administration for the legal jurisdiction of the guild (the *jurés*) were almost invariably masters in the guild, and often were either elected by some class within the guild or (when the office was a venal office bought from the king) selected by the guild to buy the appointment. We shall call this the principle of corporate administration.

The principle of legalistic administration is analogous to two principles in university administration: that all important administrators should have scholarly qualifications so that they can be judges of the academic merits of decisions, and that many administrative decisions are reviewable by bodies of faculty. The principle of mixture of civil law and public law has only a distant analogy in a modern university, though the incorporation of student residences as teaching organizations in the more ancient "college" organizations of Oxford and Cambridge is more closely analogous. That is, a residence was conceived of as a university institution devoted to public university purposes, rather than the private purposes of students. The principle of an "estate" legal system is analogous to the university principle that a man's competence corresponds to his discipline, and that he should be judged (in the first instance) by his peers (i.e., his superiors) in that discipline. He is to be judged by the *jurés* of his own guild. The principle of corporate administration is analogous to the role of departments as the lowest unit of the administrative hierarchy and simultaneously a body of colleagues who are responsible for the detailed regulation of their disciplinary jurisdiction.

The overall result of a legal system organized according to these principles is that everyone (or more practically, everyone important) has legal privileges which depend on his social function and are manifested by his being subject to a special court. But also his privileges depend on his status *within* the corporation which administers that court. From the point of view of political dynamics it also means that every (important) social interest group has a legal and administrative arm, embedded in the legal organization of society as a whole, which can be defended by appeal to the king's laws and regulations that legally "create" that guild or estate. The politics of interest groups become, above all, matters of corporate litigation, in which the central issue is very often which court has jurisdiction over a given matter, or a given person.

THE LEGAL BOUNDARIES

The social functions of most interest to the government, and hence those which had the most solidly institutionalized positions of legal privilege, were the cosmopolitan functions—those which tied localities into the national and international system. These functions in turn were divided into two main sets: those of "the court" (the king and *les grands* or "the great"), and those of the cities and localities; the court controlled *all* the cosmopolitans, and some of those cosmopolitans controlled local areas directly. There were always great distinctions of wealth, prestige, organized deference, and power between people directly involved in royal policy and in contact with the king, and the rest of the nobility and privileged classes. The special legal status of the king himself extended, for many purposes, to his ministers and his household. All the top members of the royal administration were noblemen (except for a couple of foreign financiers), but by no means were all noblemen among *les grands*.

Below *les grands* were five basic types of cosmopolitan functions that usually either resulted in the conferment of nobility or were recruited from among nobles: taxation and internal administration (the Intendents and various royal officials of municipalities and provinces); large-scale wholesale trade and the associated administration of taxes on commerce; law courts and judges above the local level and in the more important localities; the higher clergy (those with more than parish responsibility); and the military.

Each of these social functions, except the military, requires the person in charge to so manage the local system that he gets something from it which circulates in the society as a whole or, in the case of higher courts, defends the rights of those who circulate from local interference. The king's interest in these functions was straightforward: his fluid resources all came from these supra-local streams of money and goods. The majority of the tax money by the end of the Old Regime came from taxes on commerce, managed by the General Farms, a "private" corporation that supervised the public officials who actually collected the taxes. The corporation advanced the money to be collected to the royal treasury. In rural areas, although the majority of the *taille* was used for local purposes, part of it, and most of the *capitation* and *dixième* or *vingtième* taxes went to the royal treasury. Part of the revenues of the Church, which came both from the tithe and from the returns of church lands, were given as a "free gift" to the king, and of course they supported the Church itself, which was more like a government department than a private congregation. In earlier times the services of men in the army had been directly extracted from the local system by noblemen and brought to the front by them, a so-called "feudal" army. The direct interest of the royal administration in cosmopolitan social functions was then a taxation interest. It spent resources that it could only get from local systems by cosmopolitan intervention in them.

In an old fashioned feudal system, of, say, around the year 1200, all these cosmopolitan functions were concentrated for a given area (in legal theory) in one person—the head of the local noble family. It is he who collected taxes, made and judged laws, recruited military resources from the local area and led them to battle, and saw to the support of the church. The core governmental institution was, in the pure case, an assembly of noblemen, of all the people who could support supralocal functions (especially warfare and the Church) because they were the *origin* of all supralocal resources. The growing complexity of cosmopolitan relations in the areas of France with the most extensive commerce, the most bureaucratization of the royal administration, the most developed system of legal professionalism, and the most penetration of "modern" monastic and episcopal religious organization undermined this monopoly of cosmopolitan functions by the local lord.

In the less cosmopolitan economies of Brittany, the *Massif Central*, the Alps, and the Pyrenees, the identification of the basic economic function of landlord and the basic cosmopolitan governmental functions was more nearly preserved. The government was run more by assemblies of landed nobles, taxation was both less productive and less complex, and there was less occasion to create new bureaucratic nobility. The legal organization of taxation, in the Old Regime the crucial aspect of the legal organization of government, required the consent of these assemblies. This was the main significance of the distinction between *pays d'états*, where the estates consented to taxation, and the *pays d'election*, where special local officials (*élus*) were appointed for judging taxation assessments and functioned under the supervision of royal officials (receivers, and ultimately the *Intendent*). The ratio of what was ideologically "new" nobility (the *noblesse du robe* of the law courts, noble merchants—almost entirely in large-scale wholesaling—and ennobled government officials) was therefore much higher on the plains, in the Seine, Loire, and Aquitaine basins (the jurisdiction of the Paris *Parlement*). In addition, of course, the landed nobility of highly commercialized agriculture developed many more commercial interests and moved more easily into commercial enterprises. And there were many more rich local bourgeois in such areas to buy noble estates. So the lord of a local area was himself often involved in commerce.

The legal boundary of noble privilege therefore was changing, with the increasing commercialization of the plains of France, and the increasing dependence of the royal government on commerce for taxes. The ideological ground for this change was royal favor. The king, in theory, created new nobles. The change was most rapid in the areas most subject to the royal bureaucracy and most commercialized. But the change had built-in lags, both because nobility was generally inheritable, and because once created it could not easily be destroyed, for it had formidable legal and political resources.

The system of legal privilege for the third estate was both more complex and more obscure. It is partly obscure because of Marxist misinterpretation of its nature. First, it is not true that large-scale businessmen were excluded from the nobility. This would have been very difficult in any case, since most of commerce dealt with agricultural goods. It is not within reason that a large-scale noble supplier of the main article of commerce should take no interest in its marketing, especially when large profits are to be made in marketing, and especially when wholesale commerce is intimately regulated by a government run by nobles. Not only is it not within reason—it was not true. Nobles engaged in commerce. Second it was not true that those businessmen who were not nobles had no legal privileges which they were interested in defending, and that they were therefore thrown willy-nilly, rich and poor alike, into alliance against the government. Third, it is not true that the philosophy of reorganization of the government (of taxation and monopoly of social functions, that is) was radically different between the nobles and the third estate in 1787–89. What they disagreed on was mainly which estate should run things. Finally it is not true that the third estate uniformly favored the "capitalistic" freedom of commerce that was one of the main legal results of the Revolution, a result carried through, in large part, by the assembly of the third estate. In order to understand the skein of causes that ultimately led the third estate to carry through a revolution they had had no real intention to carry through, we need to address the problem of the legal organization of cities and guilds.

THE EIGHTEENTH-CENTURY CITY AS A PRODUCTIVE SYSTEM

What makes it so hard for a modern student to see what was going on in a medieval or early modern city is that he has to imagine away the bureaucratic control of production. *Nobody was there* to tell a baker, or a goldsmith, or a mason, or a shoemaker, what to do and how to do it. The "company" that made wine did not have a national distribution system that relied on Gallo Burgundy always being, for better or worse, the same stuff. Instead production was organized in family firms with a few apprentices, and whatever was not sold directly by the artisan to consumers was bought by wholesalers to ship elsewhere. The key sources of non-local income to the city were people who could tap the flow of tax and rent money in the society—government officials, bishops and abbots, landowners—and people engaged in wholesale commerce. The people who functioned to relate a city to the economy of France were *not* manufacturing corporations.

The notion that a design or quality control engineer or marketing executive would decide what a man should produce was as foreign to the eighteenth-century city as the notion that a university president should specify what advances in linguistics the anthropology department should produce would be today. The bureaucratic superior was a legally trained official or a rich bourgeois who had bought an office, hardly anyone to consult on the quality of leather to make shoes.

As in modern cities, the great majority of work done (two-thirds or more) was for the local population. Only a small part was working in industries that "exported" products or services from the city to the rest of the country or abroad. In the eighteenth century the "export" goods were rarely manufactured goods. An artisan shoemaker in one city was no more efficient than an artisan shoemaker in another city, or in a village in the countryside, so there was no reason to concentrate artisan production in a single city in a "factory." Instead the "exports" were higher government services, higher religious services, and wholesale trade. Within a given city, then, the *menu peuple* were mainly *artisans and retail traders working for the local market of the city*, with no particular national significance. Manufacturing and retail trade were not the big businesses of the society; government, religion, and wholesale trade were.

Thus within the city there was a sharp division between an elite of government officers, higher clergymen, wholesale traders, and large landowners of the region, on the one hand, and the retail, manufacturing and service workers that served the city population, on the other. The powerful guilds that ran "municipal" governments were largely drawn from wholesale traders. They of course had some conflicts with the local royal representatives, the higher clergy, and local landowners, about who should really run the city, who should pay for local public services, and how much money should be sent to Paris. But this is quite a different conflict from the conflict of the *menu peuple* with the elite for representation of their interests (low food prices, higher prices for their products and services, control of competition in a given line of business, especially competition from shoddy work, reduction of their tax load, and so on).

LEGAL BOUNDARIES IN CITIES

The legal boundaries that were central in cities were organized in the guild system. But there were very different kinds of guilds. They can be classified into three broad types: (1) guilds with representation in the municipal government, (2) guilds with royal charters but without significant representation in city government, and (3) guilds without autonomous legal powers. Broadly speaking, the guilds with representation were the merchant guilds en-

gaged in wholesale trade and finance. The guilds with royal charters but no significant representation had a legally established
monopoly over the provision of certain local goods and services
(bakers, masons, shoemakers, and the like), with the legal right
to challenge any other group who competed in the industry, and
the right to admit apprentices, journeymen, and masters to the
guild. Their economic regulations and taxation powers were reviewed by local royal officials and by the courts, and administered
by sworn officials (*jurés*) of the guilds (who usually had to have
approval both of the guild masters and of the royal or municipal
officials).

But this system of craft guilds in its turn gave legal significance
and monopoly value to the *internal* status of a man within his
guild, as a master rather than a journeyman or apprentice. A
general tendency of even the less privileged guilds to give rise to
an oligarchy of masters with legal monopolies tended to set up
a class conflict *within* the guild between masters and journeymen,
and an interest group conflict over prices with the consuming
public. Finally there were craft associations without royal charters,
with precarious legal standing, and few monopolistic privileges,
often trying to gain royal charters and monopolies.

Thus the early modern city in France was organized in a series
of nested conflicts, each revolving around a legal boundary between corporately organized status groups. The first level was the
conflict between the privileged wholesale bourgeoisie and rich
rentiers, controlling "municipal" government through representation of merchant guilds, with the royal bureaucracy, the clergy,
and sometimes local landed rentier nobility, over taxation and
other governmental powers. The second was between the citywide
legally privileged cosmopolitan oligarchy of wholesalers, often together with the royal government, and the privileged elites of
local service guild, masters in the artisan trades, over the latter's
claim to representation and to monopoly powers. The third was
the conflict between the local guild elites and the journeymen and
apprentices who were excluded from opening their own shops by
the legal monopoly power of the guild. And finally all local monopolies had price conflicts with the general population, and conflicts over status honor, taxation privileges, and legal rights.

This nested set of conflicts, as Max Weber argued extensively,

(1968:1301–68) have always tended to produce a revolutionary "democratic" tendency in cities. But the more democratic the government that these conflicts produced (where cities have some legal autonomy), the more opposition it gets from national governmental institutions that depend on controlling tax flows through local privileged groups, so the more such a democratic government tends to be undermined by a drift of power back toward the merchant and rentier oligarchy that controls the flow of exports and imports to the city, the group that is rich and nationally powerful.

In times of religious excitement, bad harvests, famine, and food riots, or in military conflicts of the city with other cities or with rural or royal authorities, a rapid movement toward democratic constitution of the city tends to take place. But in times of peace, plenty, and ecclesiastical control, those democratic constitutions decay into systems of monopolistic privilege and oligarchical control. This drift is reinforced by a strong royal government interested in tax returns, though strong royal government also tends to bring about a substitution of royal power for local oligarchic control.

To put it another way, a social movement of city oligarchs to increase their powers relative to the royal government is faced with a dilemma. Such movement tends to ignite in a chain reaction the claims of craft guilds against the oligarchy, and then of the *menu people* against corporate privilege in general. This chain reaction happens especially when it is combined with a shortage of food (focusing resentment against wholesale merchants) or with popular religious enthusiasm (e.g., the Jansenist conflict). It is this ignition of nested conflicts that made the city of Paris such a revolutionary place, and forced the moderate constitutional demands of privileged cosmopolitans in the Estates General into a democratically revolutionary course.

LAW, GRACE, AND VENALITY IN THE SYSTEM OF PRIVILEGE

The system of legal privileges for classes of people described previously is a great oversimplification. From a legal point of view, the added complexity of the system depended on the role of the king's "grace," his capacity to make exceptions to the laws he had established or to any general administrative arrangement of the government. Concretely one of the most important manifestations of this "grace" was the system of venal offices. For the crucial aspect of a venal office is that it is a privilege extended by the king to a particular person, not on the ground of some general principle of administration or general legal principle, but rather because that person was willing to pay for the privilege. Thus it created types of legal inequalities which were not rationalized by an overall public purpose (except the purpose of getting more money for public purposes), nor built into the system of law as whole, nor administered with control from the central authority subjecting them to overall shifts in public purposes. In the telling phrase, in the old regime "even the inequality was unequal."

The jurisdiction of a venal office became much like a right of private property, defended by the interest of its holder rather than by the public purpose it served. That jurisdiction in its turn had to be created by carving up the legal obligations created by the state into pieces that could be sold as private property. But this tended to set the interests of bureaucratic state administrators and the higher law courts (interested in legal uniformity) against those of venal officers. Further this competition of jurisdictions made the exact state of the law uncertain—whether or not a claim of a bureaucratic administrator of jurisdiction would hold up, or whether it would turn out to be in the jurisdiction of a venal officer, were matters to be decided each time a new special regulation was made creating a venal office.

Finally, the solidity of the value of a venal office depended on the reliability of enforcement of those legal obligations of citizens which brought in the fees. Insofar as that enforcement depended on the bureaucratic apparatus of the state, it tended to be uncertain. An *Intendent* might well think he had better things to do with his small budget than to insure the fees of a venal officer by providing police when and where that officer said they were needed.

The most valuable venal offices tended to be of one of two kinds. First, offices which carried nobility with them, with the corresponding legal and social privileges, were valuable as means of social ascent, regardless, to some degree, of their value in money returns. Second, some venal offices were valuable because they settled "constitutional" questions, especially in city and guild government. That is, the question of who should rule a guild or a city could be resolved by buying the offices that had jurisdiction over the guild or city. the corporate group, especially the wealthier members of it, could help insure their monopoly position in the economy by buying the offices through which the state regulated corporate matters.

Thus by the time of the meeting of the Estates General in 1789, questions of the distribution of privilege were intimately tied up with constitutional questions, especially questions of the powers of the king. And the queer phenomenon of the *parlements* (made up of nobles), and the noble estate itself in the Estates General, attacking many aspects of the system of privilege becomes much more understandable. One of the most common demands in the noble *cahiers* was, for example, that nobility should be granted only on the basis of merit. Aside from challenging the simple notion that people who inherit their status should be unequivocal supporters of ascription, this is representative of a great many demands by the nobility "to make inequality more equal," to ground privilege in generally understood laws and regulations rather than on arbitrary grace from the uncontrolled will of the king. A nobleman who got his status through buying an office that carried nobility with it was a nobleman only because he was rich, not because he was deserving.

In addition, of course, the king could only charge for the offices that established corporate self government of a guild or a city if he rendered the constitutional status of that group's corporate liberties precarious. He could not charge them for their constitutional status unless he was willing (and claimed the right) to take it from them if they did not pay.

And finally, the multiplication of jurisdictions, and the lack of bureaucratic and legislative control over those jurisdictions since the jurisdiction was private property, interfered with bureaucratic officials when they were discharging their duties. When we remember that the bureaucracy was a noble bureaucracy, in the sense that the people in positions of high responsibility for seeing to it that governmental and public objectives were achieved were virtually all noblemen, it is not surprising that there were powerful currents within the nobility for restricting and regularizing the system of privilege.

The legal reflection of this whole problem of irregular privilege was one part of a crucial legal privilege of the king, the right to withdraw any legal case from any jurisdiction in which it fell, and to allocate it to a court more to the king's liking, especially one more under his own thumb. Even though a rather similar right was granted to noblemen (the right of *committimus*, which allowed all noblemen to bring their cases to the appropriate *parlement*), it divorced the control over the allocation of status so thoroughly from a regularly organized legal system that many noblemen objected to it. This is manifested in the high percentage of noble *cahiers* just before the Revolution which asked that courts of exceptional jurisdiction (courts to which the king committed certain matters which he did not want to have decided by the regular *parlements*, especially a good many tax matters) should be abolished. We shall not treat the constitutional conflicts involved. Our interest here is in what it implied for the system of legal distinctions whose rough outline is given above. Aside from the organized system of distinctions among estates, there was in the old regime a massive organization of purely personal privileges of a normative kind, reflected in treatment at law and in public policy, granted to individuals on the basis of a systematic administration of the king's grace, i.e., on the basis of "exceptions to the law." The principle that there should be, beside the normative system, an extensive system of *justice d'exception* rendered the scheme of normative boundaries much less regular and systematic than is implied by a schematic characterization of the old regime as a *Standestaat*, an estate society.

THE LANGUAGE OF MORAL CATEGORIES IN OLD REGIME STRATIFICATION

Much of the language of the old regime has a feudal ring: king, noblemen, commoner, estates general, and the like. The point of the discussion above is that the feudal language was now a language for discussing quite a different stratification order, especially in the plains of northern France and of the Aquitaine basin, and most especially in the cities of those regions. That is, the system of distinctions between, say, nobleman and commoner, was used in the old regime and sounds like the distinctions of feudal society. But a great deal of legal activity, especially by the royal bureaucracy, had changed the moral obligations and the social role attached to the categories. One of *les grands* at the king's court or an *Intendent* in charge of the royal bureaucracy in a province was not an ordinary nobleman—certainly not the same sort of nobleman as a landowner in Brittany or a wholesale merchant in Orleans was.

Thus in many ways the language of feudalism had enough distinctions in it to be able, with the aid of some centuries of ingenuity, to describe a moral order of a highly commercialized bureaucratic empire, governing an estate society in which there were multiple social functions in each estate. No strong functionalism connected the feudal language to a feudal mode of production. Instead the feudal language formed a structure of distinctions that could be utilized to block in a moral order of quite a different kind. In Brittany or in the Alps the language still described an older moral order.

That is, the system of basic moral categories was a "deep structure," in which moral paragraphs could be written to explain the obligations and rights of relatively traditional feudal lords, modern wholesale grain and wine merchants in cities, and ennobled royal officers.

This deep structure of common moral categories was a culture of stratification that unified a stratification system consisting of very disparate parts.

Probably eighteenth-century Frenchmen, as well as modern scholars, believed that they lived in a single stratification system. This is shown by the fact that the Parisan-based Revolution abolished the system throughout the country, substituting a new moral language: citizenship for status, liberties for privileges, representation in government for guild membership, landownership for seigneurial rights, and so on. One major consequence of the Revolution then was to treat disparate stratification systems, in cities, on the Northern and Aquitaine plains, and in the peripheral *pays d'état*, as if they were the same, and to abolish the culture of stratification that had made them appear to be the same.

But this shows the power of the deep structure of the culture of stratification categories to assimilate and shape the views of people differently situated, people with different grievances in the old regime and different hopes for the new, so that they believe themselves governed by a common value system and a common moral order when they are not. The deep structure of moral categories shapes the prejudices of revolutionaries about what features of society are the source of their difficulties as well as the prejudices of racists.

REFERENCES

Dyson-Hudson, Neville. 1966. *Karimojong Politics.* Oxford: Clarendon Press.
Radcliffe-Brown. A. R. 1952. *Structure and Function in Primitive Society.* Glencoe, Illinois: The Free Press.
Weber, Max. 1968. *Economy and Society.* New York: Bedminster Press.

PART TWO

PERSPECTIVES INSPIRED BY LÉVI-STRAUSS, 2

THE STUDY OF SOCIAL DYNAMICS

CHAPTER FIVE

STRUCTURAL AUTONOMY AND THE DYNAMICS OF SOCIAL SYSTEMS

FRED E. KATZ

Structural theories in such diverse fields as genetics, chemistry, Chomskyan linguistics, and Lévi-Straussian anthropology regard an observed event as "an instance of the possible" (Piaget 1970:38). What one actually encounters in events is a very inadequate version of basic scientific reality. That basic reality is made up of rules—laws, natural principles—that regulate what is possible: What can exist and what cannot exist. Not, what does exist at any particular moment or has existed in the past. Nature deals with options. Options make up the substructure beneath the surface. This surface, the reality we encounter in behavior, is made up of options.

Concern with options differs from the reigning orthodoxy of Western sociology. That orthodoxy has been emphasizing the analysis of what actually exists or events that have actually occurred. It has roots in Functionalists' acceptance of social behavior patterns that currently exist (and, then, assessing how these existing patterns are interrelated). In addition, the orthodoxy has roots in the coupling of pragmatism and empiricism in Western, chiefly American, sociology of the present century. Here one has "hard-nosed" focus on empirical research methods to yield untarnished facts. A major shortcoming, however, is that one's "facts" tend to exclude the range of possibilities within which those facts exist.

The structuralist's credo, it seems to me, is that scientists must clarify the existing range of options—and the principles governing the choice of some options over others. To the sociologists this can be taken to mean: What sort of behavioral *autonomy* do people have when they interact with one another? Or, stated more generally: How does behavioral autonomy operate within social systems?

I have for some time been working on models that focus on the nature of autonomy within social systems. These models indicate how autonomy is organized, and how this organization of autonomy contributes to social systems. As I use it, such *socially structured autonomy* exists within definite limits and in definite locations within social systems. It differs from autonomy in the psychological sense, such as personal freedom or self-enhancement.

The rationale for focusing on socially structured autonomy is based on two grounds: (1) Human social systems are very distinctive types of *cybernetic systems*. (2) There is need to develop more adequate theory of what behavior is possible, and what behavior is not possible, in any variant of social system.

Human social systems are cybernetic systems, but they are cybernetic systems of a very special kind. The traditional conception of a cybernetic system is based on an analogy to the sort of processing of information that takes place in the human body. That is, the total system is influenced by, and reactive to, information. But there is a central "governing" entity, the brain, that regulates the management of information. It is the central agency for decision-making, for coding and storing information, for reacting to information feedback.

In human social systems there may also be an overall governing agency, the government for example, analogous to the brain of a person. But additionally *all the constituent parts of human social systems are capable of acting as complete cybernetic systems*, including decision-making, coding and storing of information, and reacting to feedback. For instance, the persons within a group, the departments within a large bureaucratic organization, and the complex organizations and institutions within a large society each contain the full gamut of decision-making capabilities. Each component part of a social system is capable of manipulating information. Each can gather, store, and sort information. Each can make decisions based on selective use of information. In short, each component part of a social system has the potentials for manipulating information autonomously. A crucial sociological question then emerges: How do social systems actually cope with this potential for cybernetic autonomy that exists among its component parts?

The second rationale for focusing on autonomy is that a major objective of structural theory is to develop systemic and conceptual formulations about what is possible. As already mentioned, Piaget has pointed out that "structure is conceived as a set of possible states" (Piaget 1970:38). Structural theory is not mere description of what actually exists. It seeks to explain that what exists is an instance of what *can* exist. In formal logical terms, what-does-exist is a subset of the universal set that consists of what-can-exist. The real objective of structural theory is to explain what *can* exist—and what *cannot* exist. In the natural sciences a well developed structural scheme exists in the form of the periodic table in chemistry. That table includes a stipulation of the capacity-to-combine (*Valence*) of each component. On this basis one can develop models that show the capacity of combination of various molecular and submolecular units: What can combine and what cannot combine? The criteria are theoretical—not empirical—as to whether it has actually happened.

The crux of the matter is not what exists? but what can exist? Not, which options have been exercised, now or in the past? But, which behavior options exist at all? And, how are options organized systemically?

In order to work toward such a sociology of options, I have developed models that show how *autonomy*—as the operational version of optional social behavior—is incorporated in social structures. I shall briefly describe some of these models in the following pages.

Before proceeding, however, it is necessary to emphasize that it is not enough to know which options—what sorts of autonomy—exist. One must also know how the options are organized. How the autonomy is itself structured within the context of ongoing social relationships. Here the emphasis is on the morphology of social systems. Morphologically, one tries to discover where, within a matrix of social relationships, spheres of autonomous activity are located. Do these spheres of autonomy have definite boundaries; and, if so, where do the different spheres interpenetrate one another? What "adjoins" these spheres of autonomy?

The thrust of the approach is threefold:

1) Autonomy is definitely locatable; it exists in specific sectors within social systems.[1]

2) Such morphologically "located" autonomy plays distinctive parts in the operation of social systems.

3) The operation of structural autonomy lends itself to developing theorems that have general validity in social systems.

This essay is essentially a progress report that applies the perspective of "structured autonomy" to complex bureaucratic organizations, social roles, and social movements. For each of these the focus will be on different problems. For complex organizations, the focus is on *morphology*: how autonomy is built into the fabric of social systems and how it influences *separation, link,* and *interpenetrations* among different structures; and on *exchange* processes: how autonomy is exchanged among different component parts of such organizations, and how this can serve distinct adaptive functions for the organizations. For social roles, the focus is on how autonomy within a role ensures a necessary degree of separation of that role from other roles. For social movements, the focus is on the fact that whenever a part of a system has autonomy, the rest of the system is faced with uncertainty as to how the autonomy will be used. Here the focus is on how the rest of the system copes with such uncertainty.

I suggest theorems only in relation to autonomy in social movements. (For additional theorems, see Katz 1976:34–51). I support the theorems about structured autonomy with historical and recent political evidence, but do not prove them in a full-fledged, rigorous sense. No explicit systematic tests are devised; the theorems are offered as a beginning for working with the construct of structured autonomy in social systems. Further work can doubtless lead to revisions and improvements.

STRUCTURED AUTONOMY WITHIN COMPLEX ORGANIZATIONS: THE CASE OF INFORMAL WORKER CULTURE IN FACTORIES

The well-known informal behavior patterns of factory workers are an example of relatively autonomous worker behavior—behavior that is not controlled by management. Workers carry on minute-by-minute activities, such as induction hurdles for new members, banter and joking, discussions and arguments. These activities are not at all trivial. Some of them, such as workers' informal control over production quotas, have direct bearing on work. But many of the activities have little bearing on work. Stated more analytically: workers have very narrowly defined technical tasks; here their behavior is closely controlled. But all else—what the worker actually thinks and talks about most of the day while on the job—is not controlled by the work prescriptions. Here he has autonomy by default. This autonomy arises because the technical work tasks make a narrow claim on the life-space of the individual worker. It is enacted outside of the worker's tasks but still within his day-to-day life within the factory. From the vantage point of his work tasks, it is *external* autonomy, although carried out within the factory. The worker can, and often does, use the resultant autonomy to re-create within the factory a truncated version of his working-class culture that exists in more fully developed forms outside the factory. I do not need to describe this in detail. Donald Roy and many others have done this long ago. Suffice it to say that working-class habits and outlooks are openly enacted as newcomers are "razzed," as informal status rankings crystallize, as daily talk of the young males centers on sexual exploits, the talk of young women on attracting and evaluating young men, the talk of older men on health and economic troubles in the home. It must be emphasized that these problems are not being resolved in the work context. They are merely, in Simmelian sense, enacted in "play" form. This means that some aspects of the problems are enacted again and again, but others—such as actually solving problems, there and then—are left out.

From a structural point of view, the following features are important: The working-class culture[2] is at variance with the ethos of bureaucracy, namely with bureaucracy's emphasis on orderly, rational procedures, paperwork, impersonality, etc. It is permitted to exist in specific locations within the factory, but it is not permitted to circulate freely within the factory. It is localized in the work realm of the manual worker. This means that the outside world penetrates into the organization. But within the organization the impact of the outside culture is strictly controlled because its circulation is restricted.

The opposite happens in the higher echelon of factories. Managerial persons have far more autonomy in their work than do laborers. An essential part of their tasks is the fact that they have discretion in making and executing policy. Here is internal autonomy—i.e., autonomy within their work. But their tasks are defined very broadly, making a broad claim upon the life-space of the manager. Hence, as the "organization man" syndrome shows, their organizational role tends to spill over into their life in the community and in the family, influencing how the manager participates in the community and in his family. He will help run his community's fund-raising drives for charitable causes *because* he is the Third Vice-President of the Fourth National Bank. He is using his internal, task-based, autonomy outside of the bank, within the community. He does so in the expectation that his fund-raising activity will augur well for the Fourth National Bank and, in turn, for the Third Vice-President's chances of becoming the Second Vice-President. In short, some of the drama of competition among executives of the Fourth National Bank is enacted in the community, outside of the immediate confines of the bank. This is fostered by the fact that each executive has a measure of autonomy in deciding how, and on which battlefield, he will fight his status battles.

Structurally, then, the organization penetrates into its environment. It does so by exporting the "culture" of the administrator and his involvement in his work. Conversely, some components of the workingman's outside culture penetrate into the organization. Within the organization these two cultures tend to be segregated; they do not blend and neutralize one another.

I have also applied this model to schools and hospitals. The model lends itself to analyzing relations between organizations and their environment and also to relations between different units within single organizations. In all of them the processes of interpenetration—by the environment into an organization and by an organization into its environment—serve very decided adaptive functions. A crucial underlying factor is that the *processes of penetration are facilitated by ways in which autonomy is selectively built into social structures*. Stated differently, structured autonomy can foster interpenetration among different social systems.

This, then, is one sort of structural model. It does not utilize a particular theory of the mind, as the more orthodox structuralist models do. Instead, it adopts a morphological perspective to structure. In this perspective structures are shown to be linked in very special ways. They are separate from one another and, at the same time, they have definite ways of interpenetrating one another.

In contrast to such a morphological perspective one can apply a perspective of *exchange processes* to these same data.

Let me again turn to the factory situation. Here the exchange process works somewhat as follows—although this is not usually acknowledged in official work agreements: Briefly stated, workers have a low degree of autonomy in their tasks and in their participation in the factory's official concerns. In exchange, they have high autonomy to participate in a truncated version of their "outside' life while in the factory. Roughly speaking, the converse is the case for the managerial staff.[3]

To be more explicit: Factories need working-class people. To get them—to have them participate in the factory and give some measure of allegiance to an alien, bureaucratic world—factories permit a limited amount of intrusion of the working-class culture. The factory's adaptation toward workers consists of permitting workers a certain *sector* of autonomy, namely autonomy to engage in activities that are essentially alien to bureaucratic patterns, with its emphasis on record-keeping and paperwork. In exchange for receiving this autonomy, workers give up the opportunity for participating—and exercising autonomy—in the factory's decision-making processes and reward system. Workers are disfranchised from ownership of the organization and from real participation in making policy decisions about the organization. They remain outsiders while working inside the organization. In the "outsider" role they have autonomy. But this autonomy exists only in those sectors that have little bearing on policy-making of the organization. (For the sake of illustrating the model, I have deliberately relied on a rather traditional picture of worker-management relationships. Actually, the nature of the tradeoff between workers and management varies where workers participate in some administrative decision-making.)

In the role of factory manager there are also distinctive sectors of autonomy that are exchanged for ways of participating in the social system of the factory. To be sure the managers' sectors of autonomy are very different from those of the working-class, blue-collar worker. The well-known organization man syndrome exemplifies this well. Typically, the manager has autonomy to formulate and interpret policy of the organization, but the price for a high degree of autonomy in his job is a low degree of autonomy outside of it. More specifically, as William Whyte described it, this is not merely a matter of carrying papers home in the evening. It is a matter of having one's job dominate one's family and community life. The traditional organization man has little autonomy to engage in activities other than those relatable to his organization role. He has exchanged them, consciously or not, for a measure of autonomy in his role.

This description contains the ingredients of a distinctly structural perspective to exchange processes. In this perspective things are not merely exchanged for other things. They are also placed in a structural context. Their "worth" depends on where they fit in that context. In short, morphology enters the picture. Let me now make this perspective more explicit.

Social systems adapt to their environment by exchanging *blocks* of behavioral options, where each block contains a *sphere* of behavioral autonomy. There is trading in such blocks. And, at any moment, a social system can be regarded as an *arrangement of blocks of behavioral options*. A particular arrangement is likely to be the result of past trading in such blocks.

The closest analogy to this model is a game of cards. Each card represents a range of options as to things the player can do while playing the game. There is trading in cards. When a new card is acquired, it is placed in the player's "arrangement" within his total set of cards. The worth of a particular block is not determined by its own inherent character. It is determined by its "fit" into an arrangement of blocks. Each block contributes to the arrangement, the totality, of the set. This totality is more than the sum of the parts. It is a configuration, a Gestalt. In a system of direct, specialized exchange (I have an extra spear and you need a spear; you have an extra loincloth, and I need a loincloth) the exchanged items fit into one specific location. On the other hand, in a system of generalized exchange (I don't need your loincloth, but I do need your money, which I can exchange for a variety of things) the exchanged items can be fitted into diverse locations. They fit a variety of human social behavior arrangements.

The playing card analogy can be taken even farther. Most cards have a limited number of locations into which they can possibly fit. But some cards—the joker, for instance—may fit into all arrangements. They have virtually unlimited capacity for attachment. The joker is analogous to money (and power, as Parsons notes) in a system of generalized exchange. Blocks consisting of money or power have the capacity to become attached to very diverse social arrangements, and influencing them. Of course the capacity of money or power for being attached to varied arrangements does not depend on any inherent properties of money or power. It depends on institutionalized guarantees that underwrite those uses of money. In short, then, there are types of blocks that are highly "attachable"—blocks that can fit into very different sorts of arrangements of social behavior. And there are blocks that are relatively limited in their "attachability"—blocks that can be attached only to a limited series of arrangements.

Two additional types of things can be known about blocks of behavior options: One, figuratively, is the "size and shape" of each block; that is, what behavior options—what spheres of autonomy—are contained in a block? The second is the placement of a block in relation to other blocks; that is, the arrangement of blocks. Both can be illustrated from the example of factory workers' autonomy described earlier. Workers' options for spending much of their time discussing "outside" interest—sports, sex, health—while at work exist alongside the fact that they are disfranchised from decision-making in the factory. That is, their autonomy to discuss outside interests seriously and at length exists within a definite arrangement of blocks of options. It is an arrangement that specifically excludes options about decision-making in regard to policies for the factory. Conversely, those who do have options within the policy-making sector, the organization men, tend to lack options for involving themselves in "external" matters while they are at work, except if these can be shown to relate to work. Here, too, life in the organization consists of an arrangement of definite blocks of options.

In sum, "arrangements' of blocks of options constitute organization of behavior. The mutual fit between the different blocks of behavior options are crucial aspects of social structures.

So far I have discussed the operation of structured autonomy in complex organizations. These are relatively large structures. Let me now turn to much smaller structures, namely, social roles.

STRUCTURED AUTONOMY IN SOCIAL ROLES: A NOTE REGARDING SEPARATION, LINKAGE, AND VIABILITY OF SOCIAL STRUCTURES

How can very diverse social roles coexist while, at the same time, each role remains viable? There is need for theory about the conditions that make for viability of social roles (and, for that matter, about the conditions that make for viability of every sort of social structure). As a step in this direction it is useful to develop a structural perspective to the functioning of autonomy in social roles. Specifically, one should be able to answer a question such as: Are there minimal amounts of autonomy that are necessary for the viability of each kind of role? In order to answer this sort of question it is necessary to develop models showing how autonomy is structured in roles. Such models need not emphasize ways in which the person who enacts roles achieves reconciliation between the different roles. (This was the typical focus of role-conflict studies in the 1950s). Instead, the models need to emphasize ways of balancing the autonomy requirements of different roles so that each role can be performed: i.e., each role remains viable. Co-existing roles exercise constraints upon one another. Yet beyond some level of constraint a role presumably loses its viability. How can one pinpoint the balance between a role's having a degree of autonomy and, at the same time, being subject to external constraint?

The larger picture is as follows: Present-day sociology contains the doctrine—based on the evolutionary theories of the previous century—that modern societies are increasingly made up of highly specialized component parts. Unlike primitive societies, modern societies are said to contain fairly *separate* economic, religious, governmental and educational components. These typically involve specialized social arrangements, including separate locations and separate social collectivities. Under the mantle of specialized macrostructures individuals enact specialized roles—be it as businessman or businesswoman, parishioner, civil servant, or teacher.

In actual fact, however, the separation of structures is much less clear-cut than our reigning orthodoxy presupposes. Let us take the macrolevel, for example. Businesses not only have to relate themselves externally to governments—paying taxes, obtaining licenses, and so forth, but also their external operations are permeated by governmental activities—credit policies, regulatory practices regarding trade, labor policies regarding minimum salaries and other employee rights, and so forth. Similarly, one can point to interpenetrations between religion and family, and between schools and the economy and governments.

On the microlevel, when we examine social roles of individuals, we similarly see interpenetrations. The businessman's participation cannot be *completely* separated from his participation in his family, for example. If he spends most of his time at work, he has very little time to devote to family matters. This, in turn, is apt to influence his standing in his family, regardless of his standing in the business community.

The theoretical side of all this is that sociological descriptions of functional specialization are not describing structural separation or, for that matter, how structures are connected with one another. Such scholars as Marion Levy and Talcott Parsons have been well aware of this. They have emphasized all along that functional systems tend to be analytic and, therefore, abstract; that concrete systems are very different from analytic systems; and that it is very difficult, if not impossible, to study functional systems concretely. If we want to put some flesh on these scholarly bones we must face up to the fact that concrete structures or processes cannot be clearly separated from one another. Analytically, we can often speak elegantly about being able to delineate specialized functions clearly and unambiguously. But when we look at concrete social structures—at families, at complex bureaucratic organizations, at groups, at specific roles being enacted—it just does not work this way. "Separate" structures are routinely interpenetrated by other structures. The task facing us is to clarify how interpenetration and separateness actually operate, how both coexist, and how one can retain some faith in talking about "structure" in the face of simultaneous separation and interpenetration of structures.

The separation of a social structure is obviously a relative matter, since no structure is utterly and completely separate. Yet some separation doubtless exists. The question is: How much separation? For an operational way of discovering the amount of separation among the structures within a system, one can measure the amount of autonomy in each structure. Autonomy is here taken to be an operational definition of separateness. I have developed two kinds of models of autonomy in social roles (Katz 1976:52–98 contains a fuller description). They are methodological devices for describing degrees of *actual* separation among roles. Obviously it is important to eventually develop models of *optimal* degrees of separation. This can greatly enhance our ability to design social systems that have predictable characteristics.

One model rates the amount of *participation* against the level of autonomy between roles. This model lends itself very nicely to graphic presentation. The model assumes a zero-sum situation; i.e., the amount of participation in two roles (but not the amount of autonomy) has a fixed upper limit. The profile for autonomy for each role, in relation to the other role, can take many forms. It is not a matter of maximizing autonomy for each role. Some roles can be performed very effectively at low levels of autonomy. Other roles require very high levels of autonomy. Thus, for example, the social critic needs a great deal of autonomy from the existing authorities if he is to perform his role. On the other hand, the low-ranking bureaucratic clerk may perform his role most effectively at a low level of autonomy from administrative control.

The model can also be applied to dynamic situations. For example, the innocent prisoner who faces prosecution in a totalitarian police state loses autonomy in his role as a free person as he continues to participate in the prisoner role, regardless of his actual behavior. If he remains silent, this is interpreted as hostility and guilt; if he admits "guilt" he is, of course, believed to be guilty; if he denies guilt, he is believed to be lying and, therefore, doubly guilty. In short, he loses autonomy in his role as free person by every form of participation in the prisoner role. He can only remain a free person by leaving the system.

This model, then, is a quantitative indicator of the degree of separation between two roles (or between a dichotomized aggregate of roles). As such it is a step in the direction of clarifying the conditions that make for viability of different, but coexisting, roles.

The second model concentrates on the *location* of role-based autonomy. Where, in which sort of behavior, does the autonomy lie? Here I use the distinction between internal and external autonomy already mentioned in comparing factory workers with factory managers. The worker, *while in his job*, has a low degree of autonomy in his tasks (low "internal" autonomy). But, at the same time, he has a high degree of autonomy in behavior not related to his tasks (high "external" autonomy). The manager, on the other hand, has a high degree of autonomy in his work tasks but a low degree of autonomy, while on the job, to engage in non-work-related behavior. The distinction between internal and external role autonomy lends itself to an explanation of a variety of social situations. Thus, for example, the hospitalized psychotic patient can enact many fantasies—he can pitch to Joe DiMaggio and then adjust his crown as King of Transylvania—while renouncing participation in life outside the hospital. In short, in his role as inmate he has considerable autonomy to live a life of fantasy in exchange for giving up autonomy in normal outside life, including the autonomy to regulate most of his own, day-to-day activities.

This model, too, is a methodological device for looking at the viability of social roles. It focuses on types of arrangements of behavior autonomy and on how each type of "arrangement" is a distinct form of adaptive strategy.

So far I have discussed autonomy without reference to one of its most obvious consequences: Autonomy of any part of a system creates uncertainty for the remaining parts of that system. Let me now turn to this corollary of autonomy, the existence of uncertainty whenever any part of a system has autonomy.

AUTONOMY AS PRODUCER OF INDETERMINACY

When one sector of a system has autonomy then the other sectors of that system necessarily experience uncertainty in relation to that sector. Thus, if the doctor has autonomy to make medical judgments about his patient, it follows that the patient does not know precisely what the doctor will order him to do. For the patient there exists an element of uncertainty in the doctor's behavior. The same applies to larger social processes. If the Internal Revenue Service has the autonomy to decide which tax transgressions will be investigated and which will not, then the citizen, and even other government departments, cannot know precisely which transgressions will be investigated. For them the Internal Revenue Service's autonomy constitutes uncertain behavior.

How do social systems adapt to such uncertainty? To begin

with, I must reiterate that the sort of autonomy I have been describing is not random and free-floating. It exists in definitely specified sectors of the system. It has definite boundaries. In short, it is structured. Yet from within its legitimated boundaries there emanates activity that cannot be predicted with precision by the remainder of the system. The latter only knows the legitimated outer limits of the uncertain activities. But the remainder of the system is an accomplice to that uncertainty. After all, the structured autonomy of the parts of the system is ordinarily acknowledged and accepted by the rest of the system—at least when the system is in a stable, equilibral state: Patients do accept doctors' autonomy to make decisions about their illness; citizens do accept the Internal Revenue Service's autonomy to make unannounced checks of their tax returns. I am calling such institutionally accepted uncertainty *structured indeterminacy*. It is indeterminacy that has boundaries. In a sense these boundaries insulate the system, protecting it from disintegration.[4]

However, indeterminacy creates distinct problems for social systems. And these problems demand responses.

I shall briefly describe some systemic responses to structured indeterminacy, and I shall offer some generalizations in the form of theorems. The generalizations are based on historical events, but are necessarily provisional, since they are not subjected to full-fledged and comprehensive testing.

The historical events are the social movements of Father Coughlin and Senator Joseph McCarthy, the Watergate Affair, and anti-Semitism in Nazi Germany. The focus, here, is on the nature of autonomy and the nature of the responses to indeterminacy in these events. Briefly summarized, the events are as follows.[5]

Father Coughlin and Senator McCarthy led movements that achieved dramatic and seemingly ever-expanding autonomy, with corresponding increase of indeterminacy for their respective environments. Senator McCarthy led an anti-Communist movement. He began by claiming to have discovered a number of Communists in the U.S. government. The movement grew with great rapidity, leading to widespread searches for Communists in many sectors of public and private life. Indeterminacy, in the case of the McCarthy movement, meant that no one seemed immune from the charge of being a Communist or Communist sympathizer, and the consequent likelihood of public disgrace, loss of job, and possible imprisonment.

Father Coughlin's movement started in the 1920s as a form of populism against economic injustices in Coughlin's native Midwest. Over time its scope expanded dramatically. By the late 1930s Father Coughlin had his own national radio program and a weekly newspaper that was widely read. The focus of the Coughlin crusade had, by then, expanded beyond the local level and beyond economic injustices. It had moved toward broad national and international issues. Its pronouncements included outspoken anti-Semitism and strong support for the wave of Fascism in Europe (Mussolini was once cited as "Man of the Week" in the Coughlin newspaper). Indeterminacy took the form of increasingly virulent attacks on the national government and many citizens and agencies who supported it.

Father Coughlin's downfall was accomplished by his religious superiors. Senator McCarthy's demise was brought about by censure in the U.S. Senate. In each case the respective *significant* environment acted when certain limits appeared to have been transcended. (The concept *significant environment* bears some analogy to G. H. Mead's "significant other"—the person who is crucial to the individual's self-esteem. As used here, in a more sociological sense, the significant environment is the part of the environment that is crucial to the viability of a particular social entity. A social entity can be a position, a social movement, a group, or a social organization.)

The Watergate Affair also manifested autonomy that transcended institutionalized limits of existing norms. During the presidential election campaign of 1972 a team of followers of President Nixon did things, such as burglarizing the campaign headquarters of their opponents, that transcended existing rules of the game for political elections. Since the Executive Branch of the U.S. Government was implicated in the crime, including the Attorney General, it seemed unlikely that a significant environment existed to enforce the traditional norms. But a significant environment did materialize because of a coalition of the U.S. Senate and the mass media. It produced drastic action, including the President's resignation and terms of imprisonment for some high officials.

Anti-Semitism in Nazi Germany built upon long-standing anti-

Semitism in Germany.[6] But it included enormously expanded autonomy in the scope and practical implementation of anti-Semitism. This resulted in the murder of 6 million Jews in Germany and areas controlled by Germany during the Second World War. Although this went far beyond then existing norms of "acceptable" autonomy in persecuting Jews, there was no concerted action against the Nazi movement that carried out this action. By the 1940s no significant environment to counter the Nazi party existed within Germany, because opposition parties no longer existed; an independent mass media no longer existed; an independent judiciary no longer existed (the judiciary has been thoroughly subverted, and indeed much of the campaign against Jews was conducted through the "legal" means of passing and enforcing ever-more restrictive laws against Jews). And, finally, much of the German citizenry was actively coopted into the Nazi party and was actively carrying out its policies.

In the Coughlin, McCarthy, and Watergate situations a significant environment acted to curb the part of the social system that had exceeded the normatively permitted range of autonomy. But where no significant environment existed (or where none could emerge), as in Nazi Germany, no counteraction took place. I am not saying that an environment is significant because it succeeded in destroying the autonomy-transcending part. To avoid such a tautology it must be made clear that the existence of the significant environment is indicated independently of its actions against the autonomy-transcending part of the system. For example, in the case of the environment to Nazism, I have indicated the subversion of the judiciary, the cooptation of much of the citizenry, the lack of opposition parties. All these are indicators of a weak environment to Nazism. They existed independently of any specific failure to curb anti-Semitism.

THE RESPONSE TO UNCERTAINTY

The adaptations to uncertainty can now be summarized in more conceptual terms: Social systems contain an institutionalized level of uncertainty. That uncertainty is part of the orderly character of social systems. It derives from the fact that when one part of a system—a person, a group, a social process—has autonomy the other parts cannot predict precisely what its behavior will be. There *is* uncertainty.

If uncertainty is so prevalent, how can one continue to approach the study of social processes as though they were systemic? Two reasons suggest themselves for preserving a systemic perspective:

(1) The kind of uncertainty identified here exists within certain limits; it is not expanding. It is locatable; it is not free-floating. It is a component of stable systems; it is not an entropic condition.

All this follows from the conception that ranges (or blocks) of behavior options can be regarded as the core ingredients of social structure. Observers of social activity, whether members of the system or researchers, frequently cannot predict which specific behavior options will be enacted. But in a stable social system the limits—the range within which the options fall—are likely to be known quite precisely. This is what is meant by the statement that there is structured indeterminacy, that uncertainty exists within known boundaries. Such structured indeterminacy is part of the "arrangement" under which social processes take place. It is a component part of social systems.

(2) Social systems have definite adaptive mechanisms toward structured indeterminacy.

The *adaptive mechanisms* can be formulated in terms of the following theorems:

Theorem I:
If the system contains a viable significant environment to the component parts, (i.e., the environment has the capacity to influence the existence of the component parts), the following principles prevail:
  A. When the uncertain activity occurs within the area of legitimated indeterminacy, the environment accepts this behavior.

The environment does not challenge the appropriateness of this kind of uncertain activity. The environment does not react against it. This may be called the *principle of limited reactivity by the environment.* It amounts to a social mandate for a degree of indeterminacy. This was exemplified by the early period of the McCarthy and Coughlin movements. A drastic change occurs, however, when the legitimated boundaries have been transcended (and the environment remains intact).

B. When the uncertain activity goes beyond the boundaries of the legitimated indeterminacy, the environment adopts a totalistic response against it and against the social arrangements in which it is embedded.

The environment renounces the legitimacy of the indeterminacy altogether once it is ascertained that the uncertain activity goes beyond its socially accepted boundaries. Typically this involves a full-scale attack on the social arrangements that include the uncertain activity. It may range from terminating a particular dyadic relationship to crushing a social movement. This may be called the *principle of totalistic attack by the environment*. The environment does not merely limit the indeterminacy, by having the offending unit return to the bounded level of indeterminacy. It acts to eliminate the offending unit altogether as a functioning entity. This was exemplified by the last stages of the McCarthy and Coughlin movements and in the aftermath of the Watergate Affair.

Theorem II:

If there is no viable significant environment to the component parts there can be no reaction against transgressions of the boundaries of legitimated indeterminacy.[7]

This was exemplified by lack of environmental response to extreme anti-Semitism in Nazi Germany.

The danger of tautological thinking must be reiterated. One does not rely on reaction by the environment to indicate whether existing norms have been transgressed. There are independent ways of ascertaining whether legitimated norms have been transgressed. For instance, one can ask people whether they think the boundaries have been transgressed; one can use nonobtrusive indicators, such as analysis of existing writings by intellectuals; one can survey the folk culture of popular jokes and anti-Establishment stories.

CONCLUSION

A. THE CHARACTER OF SOCIALLY STRUCTURED AUTONOMY

This article has sought to go beyond the truism that some forms of autonomous behavior are useful and indeed necessary or, to put it in more scholarly language, that autonomy serves functions in social systems). My premises were:

(1) There exists autonomy that is locatable within social structures. Such autonomy exists within boundaries. It is delimited. It exists in a distinct place within the system. It is part of the morphology of social systems. It is structured.

(2) The structured autonomy can be quantified. Models can be developed as to the amount and the kind of autonomy located in different social systems. (For a start, see Katz 1976:53–98. I have not dwelled extensively on these models in the present paper.)

(3) Autonomy can be traded. This occurs in two senses.

 a) There is trading (or exchange) of autonomy in *activities* that exist within relatively stable boundaries. For example, the research-minded physician may take little part in the day-to-day administrative matters of his hospital. This enables him to spend much of his time doing research. This physician's lack of participation in administrative matters is very likely to mean that he has little autonomy to influence administrative matters. Conversely, he is apt to have autonomy in doing research because of his attention to research matters. This pattern, where autonomy exists and where autonomy does not exist, constitutes an important dimension of the structure of the physician's work situation.

 b) There is trading of spheres (or *blocks*) of autonomy. At some point the just-mentioned physician may give up his autonomy to do research in return for a higher salary, with the resulting autonomy to solve his economic problems; or he may give it up in return for an administrative position, with the resulting autonomy to make administrative policy decisions in his hospital. Here, then, the structure of the system is undergoing change. We have a rearrangement of the parts of the system, including the rearrangement of spheres of structured autonomy.

(4) Autonomy of the parts of social systems necessarily contributes uncertainty for the remainder of social systems. This is a ubiquitous fact of life, and one to which social systems appear to have developed definite adaptive strategies.

(5) The operation of autonomy in social systems is subject to lawful principles; these principles can be discovered. Two such principles have been suggested (in the form of theorems). As

offered here, the theorems are provisional. They need to be subjected to systematic proof.

B. A NOTE ON STRUCTURAL THEORY IN SOCIOLOGY

By focusing on the place of autonomy amid orderly social processes I have departed from some important sociological traditions. At the same time I have linked up with certain aspects of these traditions.

The Parsonian structure-functional scheme emphasizes *controlled* social behavior as perhaps the central factor in social structure. Such control takes the form of norms that are internalized by people who carry out roles and are enforced additionally by external enforcement agents. In a larger sense, control is regarded as the central features in the operation of institutions, whereby whole syndromes of interrelated norms are socially implemented.

This is an overly controlled conception of society (a slight rephrasing of Dennis Wrong's statement that the structure-functionalists have an "overly socialized" view of people). But this statement is only true when one caricatures the structure-functional approach somewhat. In actuality Parsons and his followers are well aware that social norms do not specify *items* of behavior, but *ranges* of behavior. The norm is typically a statement of outer limits within which behavior is expected to fall. This implies that "normative" behavior contains some autonomy as to precisely which items of behavior, from within the approved range, will be enacted.

But the Parsonians have not paid explicit attention to autonomy itself being a core ingredient of social structures. In contrast to this, I suggest that autonomy is indeed a central ingredient of social systems. It needs to be included in theoretical models of social order, on a par with "control," as a basic building block of social structure.

Conflict theorists, in contrast to structure-functionalists, have explicitly paid attention to autonomy. They have concentrated on showing ways in which existing social constraints deny people—individuals, groups, classes, strata—their necessary or fair amount of autonomy. But autonomy is typically viewed as something one must struggle to obtain. The focus is on struggle.

By concentrating on the struggle for autonomy, on the deprivation-of-autonomy syndrome, the conflictists are omitting from view a central theme of this essay: that autonomy is distributed throughout social systems, though structured in different forms in different sectors of these systems. I am advocating a less warlike posture to studying autonomy than that of the conflictists. Such an approach can yield a more dispassionate and more adequate understanding of the place of autonomy in social systems.

I have outlined a form of structural sociology that deviates to some extent from Lévi-Straussian structuralism. Yet any discussion of structuralism in the field of sociology must acknowledge indebtedness to Lévi-Strauss. First, the structural sociology outlined here shares Lévi-Strauss' (and other structuralists') concern with *options*. One must clarify which options exist and why some options come to be actualized, in behavior, while others are not. Sociological reality does not consist only of what does exist; it consists of what can exist.

The present approach diverges from Lévi-Strauss in rejecting the idea that ultimately the mind generates social structure; that the underlying principles of social structure must be sought in how the human mind works. The claim here, in contrast, is that social structures have a distinctive morphology of their own, one that is not reducible to the workings of the mind of individuals. Social structures are not merely the summation of the behavior of the individual. A macrosociology, as Amitai Etzioni and others have pointed out, is not reducible to the behavior of individual persons, let alone the minds of these individuals. It operates on sociological principles of its own, principles that can be discovered.

Concentrating on the distinctive morphology of structures— whether social structures or others—also owes much to the work of d'Arcy Thompson (1952). His work on physical properties of organic structures remains a beacon of light to the scientific community. My own development also owes much to medical histologists and pathologists, who served as my first victims for sociological study. I have preempted some facts of their scientific perspective, notably the concern with *links, separations,* and *interpenetrations* of structures.

The present approach bears some similarity to Lévi-Strauss'

concern with "deep" structures, but it also departs from it. Here the view is that some patterns of behavior are activated and others are not, yet remain within a repertoire of potentially activated behavior. Unactivated behavior is currently dormant. Lévi-Strauss' emphasis is on *deep, hidden* patterns of behavior, particularly in the psychological sense of being part of the subconscious of individuals. These patterns are difficult to discover—except by a trained structuralist—but they are always active. The present approach does not claim that "deep" structures do not exist. It merely concentrates on a different aspect of structures.

In the final analysis, Lévi-Strauss remains the preeminent theorist about the workings of social structure. Sociologists such as Stinchcombe (1975:57–64) and Eisenstadt (selection 7) have shown that his work has direct relevance to sociologists' work on institutional processes. The approach outlined here departs rather drastically from some features of Lévi-Strauss' structuralism. But it remains indebted to him for its main guiding principles: that structures are not self-evident and observable from behavior and that structure is concerned with options. As these insights are adopted by sociologists, sociological theory will be greatly enhanced.

NOTES

1. This structural approach to autonomy differs from looking upon autonomy as something that part of a system carves out for itself while facing a hostile environment. I do not deny that the latter approach can be fruitful, as Gouldner has shown. But I claim that one can also fruitfully consider autonomy to be a structural component part of social systems. Here the process whereby autonomy is carved out, usually against an environment that opposes the granting of autonomy, is of secondary importance. What is important in the present approach is how autonomy actually operates alongside the other components of social systems.

2. To be sure, "working-class culture" is not one unitary phenomenon. It is complex and contains many variants. I am deliberately simplifying matters somewhat.

3. I have left out the consideration of money. I do not claim, of course, that monetary considerations play no part in these exchanges. I do not elaborate on the ways in which the monetary and social participation processes augment each other. But obviously they do. The present model needs to be seen as an additional dimension to the purely monetary version of exchanges between factories and their employees.

4. I am indebted to Professor Victor Lidz for drawing my attention to such insulating mechanisms. However, Professor Lidz is not responsible for the way I am using this concept here.

5. A fuller report on these data and their analysis will be found in a forthcoming book, *Autonomy and Social Movements*.

6. Perhaps the best survey of German anti-Semitism before and during the Hitler period is found in Dawidowicz (1975). She demonstrates that anti-Semitism was deep and widespread before Hitler came to power.

7. It may be asked: Why place such reliance on the "environment"? The answer is that the environment of any one component part of a social system is the rest of that system. We are here dealing with the actions of social systems.

REFERENCES

Dawidowicz, Lucy S. 1975. *The War Against the Jews 1933–1945*. New York: Bantam Books.

Katz, Fred E. 1968. *Autonomy and Organization*. New York: Random House.

—— 1976. *Structuralism in Sociology: An Approach to Knowledge*. Albany: State University of New York Press.

—— 1979. "Organizational theory and cultural intrusions into organizations." A Note. *American Sociological Review* (August) 44.

Piaget, Jean. 1970. *Structuralism*. New York: Basic Books.

Stinchcombe, Arthur L. 1975. "A structural analysis of sociology." *The American Sociologist* (May) 10:57–64.

Thompson, d'Arcy. 1952. *On Growth and Form*. 2d ed. Cambridge: Harvard University Press.

CHAPTER SIX

STRUCTURALISM, THE PRINCIPLE OF ELEMENTARISM, AND THE THEORY OF CIVILIZATION

PETER P. EKEH

THE METHODOLOGY AND THE THEORETIC OBJECTIVES OF STRUCTURALISM: A SOCIOLOGICAL PERSPECTIVE

It will be useful to begin this essay by differentiating between the *methodological* concerns of structuralism and its *theoretic* objectives. This is so because a virile scientific perspective advances on both of these fronts of knowledge and suffers from imbalanced growth when one of them is developed while the other is retarded. The need to differentiate between the two is all the more important in the case of structuralism because focus on the methodology of structuralism threatens to overwhelm attention to its theoretic objectives.

The methodology of a scientific perspective gains strength through analysis; its theoretic potential is realized in its ability to explain. Analysis is achieved when a whole phenomenon is so broken up that it falls into logical parts, with established linkages between the parts. Explanation is of a higher order: here, the meaning of a phenomenon is understood when its mode of operation is subsumed under superior laws—laws preferably developed and borrowed from different orders of phenomena. Thus analysis is inductive, while explanation is deductive. When an anthropologist takes up a myth and arranges it into its several parts in order to make sense of the whole of the myth, he is engaged in analysis—informed by the methodology of structuralism. But when his exercise is aimed at deriving laws from the operation of the myth with the ultimate aim of applying such laws to the understanding of the nature of a phenomenon of a different order—of the nature of modern complex civilization, for instance—he is being influenced by the theoretic mission of structuralism. Analysis is applied to a phenomenon as an entity sufficient unto itself. An explanation joins two or more orders, linked together by laws derived from one order in an attempt to explain the other. Thus when a myth is being investigated with the aim of yielding laws that will help one to understand more complex phenomena, such as civilization, one has only begun one's mission when a law offers itself from the analysis of such a myth.

The methodology of a scientific perspective may and usually does cut across various disciplines. Its theoretic objectives are more specialized and vary from discipline to discipline. But whenever a new scientific perspective, such as structuralism, is introduced into new disciplines, they gain both from its methodology and from the new theoretic objectives it helps to bring to the new fields of inquiry. The importation of the methodology of structuralism from linguistics into anthropology has led anthropologists to a better understanding of traditional materials such as kinship behaviors. And by increasing its theoretical concerns, the new scientific perspective leads to the expansion of the discipline to include new materials previously considered marginal or even irrelevant to the discipline. Thus mythology, previously considered in epiphenomenal terms, has acquired new status in anthropology because of the new theoretical insights yielded by structuralism.

I discuss here the relevance of the foregoing considerations for the possibility of strengthening structuralism in sociology. While I believe that the methodology of structuralism, as it has been developed in linguistics and anthropology, will be beneficial to some aspects of sociological analysis, structuralism will turn out to be one of the many passing fads in sociology unless attention is paid to the unique theoretical contributions it can make to this discipline dedicated to the understanding of modern complex man and society. The longevity of structuralism in sociological theory and research will be assured (a) if it can strengthen the ability of sociologists to deepen their traditional theoretic objectives and (b) if it can legitimately expand the scope of the discipline by including new material, particularly at the level of the unconscious, without rejecting the old concerns of the discipline.

It is helpful to introduce structuralism, at least in its formal dimensions, into sociology from anthropology rather than from linguistics. This is so because sociology is closer to anthropology and in fact shares some theoretic concerns with it. But this closeness itself imposes the need for caution: for any wholesale importation of Lévi-Strauss' structuralism will limit the contributions of structuralism as a scientific perspective to sociology.

Two different types of concerns may be discerned in Lévi-Strauss' structuralism. The first is contained in *The Elementary Structures of Kinship*. Although in this book he contributes a great deal to the intrinsic understanding of elementary kinship behaviors as such, he engages in generalizations in a manner which suggests that he treats such behaviors as a baseline for gaining deeper understanding of more complex institutions and behaviors. It is in fact a book of discovery—of the meaning of elementary kinship behavior, of course, but also a discovery of how such elementary structures could help one to explain more complex structures.[1] In other words, structuralism in the early stages of Lévi-Strauss' work was partially concerned with the way elementary structures would help the theorist to understand complex structures. But as Lévi-Strauss' commitments to structuralism have become more explicit and more elaborate he has shed this theoretic mission of structuralism and has come to stress its methodology—with a great deal of emphasis on the intrinsic nature of myths themselves, rather than on how much myths can help the investigator to understand more complex phenomena. Now, this latter characteristic of Lévi-Strauss' work, limited to the understand of archaic and primitive structures, is removed from the age-long commitments of the sociologist to the understanding and explanation of complex modern man and society. Lévi-Strauss (1958:338) himself concedes this much: "I am not a sociologist, and my interest in our own society is only a secondary one. Those societies which I seek first to understand are the so-called primitive societies with which anthropologists are concerned."

But the first concern attributed to Lévi-Strauss closer to the sociologist's—and flows directly from Emile Durkheim and Marcel Mauss' brush with structuralism. If the sociologist is to exploit the resources of structuralism in the furtherance of his time honored objective of explaining the complexity of modern man and modern institutions, one must recover the perspective of Durkheim and Mauss in their *indirect* approach to unraveling the principles of the operation of modern society through the structural laws yielded by the study of primitive and archaic institutions. Thus, in concluding their study on primitive classifications, they felt justified to assert that

Primitive classifications are therefore not singular or exceptional, having no analogy with those employed by more civilized peoples: on the contrary, they seem to be connected with no break in continuity, to the first scientific classifications. In fact, however different they may be in certain respects from the latter, they nevertheless have all their essential characteristics. (Durkheim and Mauss 1903:81)

In their separate works after *Primitive Classification*, Durkheim and Mauss singlemindedly applied themselves to the sociological exploitation of ethnographic data from primitive and archaic societies in order to understand more fully modern man and modern institutions. Nowhere is this indirect approach of structuralism plainer than in the first six pages of *The Elementary Forms of the Religious Life*. On the very first two pages of this book, Durkheim asserts the distinction of his profession vis-à-vis structuralism:

We shall set ourselves to describe the organization of this system [of the most primitive and simple religion which is actually known] with all the exactness and fidelity that an ethnographer or an historian could give it. But our task will not be limited to that: Sociology raises other problems than history or ethnography. It does not seek to know the passed forms of civilization with the sole end of knowing them and reconstructing them. But rather . . . it has as its object the explanation of some actual reality which is near to us, and which consequently is capable of affecting our ideas and our acts: this reality is man, and more precisely, the man of today, for there is nothing which we are more interested in knowing. Then we are not going to study a very archaic religion simply for the pleasure of telling its peculiarities and its singularities. If we have taken it as the subject of our research, it is because it has seemed to us better adapted than any other to lead to an understanding of the religious nature of man, that is to say, to show us an essential and permanent aspect of humanity. (Durkheim 1915:1–2)

It is the search of these permanencies and commonalities in humanity that forms the bedrock of the theoretic objectives of sociological structuralism. And it is the quest for these invariant structural laws of humanity that led Marcel Mauss to study primitive exchange so that "we may draw conclusions of a moral nature about some of the problems confronting us in our present economic crisis" because, he believed, "the same morality and economy [in primitive and archaic societies] are at work, albeit less noticeably, in our societies, and we believe that in them we have discovered one of the bases of social life" (1925:2).

Both Durkheim and Marcel Mauss have thus pioneered those aspects of structuralism that deal with the *explanation* of complex institutions by way of understanding elementary structures. But the methodology for realizing such theoretic objectives of structuralism is highly limited in their work. Durkheim was dimly aware that his theoretical commitments called for an examination of unconscious materials. Thus he writes:

One must know how to go underneath the symbol to the reality which it represents and which gives it its meaning. The most barbarous and the most fantastic rites and the strangest myths translate some human need, some aspect of life, either individual or social. The reasons with which the faithful justify them may be, and generally are, erroneous; but the true reasons do not cease to exist, and it is the duty of science to discover them. (Durkheim 1915:2–3)

Despite this insight, Durkheim's structuralism is circumscribed by his rigorous functionalism—in confining the operation of the unconscious materials of human experience to the needs of the immediate social group. Thus his structuralism could not go far enough to underline the essence of common humanity.

In fact, both Durkheim and Mauss directed attention more to conscious data than to unconscious human processes. Lévi-Strauss has correctly pointed out the limitations of these pioneer sociologists in this respect:

Durkheim and Mauss, for instance, have always taken care to substitute, as a starting point for the survey of native categories of thought, the conscious representations prevailing among the natives themselves for those stemming from the anthropologists' own culture. This was undoubtedly an important step, which, nevertheless, fell short of its goals because these authors were not sufficiently aware that native conscious representations, important as they are, may be just as remote from the unconscious reality as any other. (Lévi-Strauss 1958:28)

That is, Durkheim and Mauss stayed too close to conscious reality to discover the "inmost" structural laws that would have enabled them to master the essential principles of modern life. The methodology of authentic structuralism calls for an examination of unconscious layers of the human mind—not just of the individual unconscious but of the collective unconscious; not just the unconscious products of individual ontogenetic development, but of the unconscious materials derived from the phylogenetic development of collective groupings.

Sociological structuralism would seem to be well founded if it combines the strength of Durkheim and Marcel Mauss on the one hand and of Lévi-Strauss on the other. Durkheim's and Mauss' pioneer efforts—stressing the significance of the materials of elementary societies for the explanation of complex ones—have charted a course for sociological structuralism. Nevertheless, there is a need to deepen this theoretic objective of structuralism by exploiting the methodology of Lévi-Straussian structuralism by way of analyzing the unconscious data of elementary societies in our effort to understand the complexity of modern social life. And it is in this area of unconscious representations that one must seek Lévi-Strauss' contributions to the sociological imagination.

It seems necessary, in fact, to forewarn the sociologist that the sociological tradition inherent in structuralism encourages collectivistic rather than individualistic modes of sociological imagination. This is especially the case when the emphasis switches from *conscious* representations, as in Durkheim and Mauss, to *unconscious* representations. Lévi-Strauss puts this point emphatically:

I therefore claim to show, not how men think in myths, but how the myths operate in men's minds without their being aware of the fact. . . . it would perhaps be better to go still further and, disregarding the thinking subject completely, proceed as if the thinking process were taking place in the myths, in their reflection upon themselves and their interrelation. For what I am concerned to clarify is . . . the system of axioms and postulates defining the best possible code, capable of conferring a common significance on unconscious formulations which are the works of minds, societies, and civilizations chosen among the most remote from each other. (Lévi-Strauss 1964:12)

Lévi-Strauss may appear to have exaggerated matters a little, but the fact is that structuralism as a theoretical perspective has very little room for the individual, endowed with self-consciousness. Its proper subject matter consists of supra-individual entities.

THE PRINCIPLE OF ELEMENTARISM

I shall now proceed to highlight the distinctive sociological attributes of structuralism by embodying its concerns in what I have elsewhere labeled the principle of elementarism (Ekeh: 1976). This sociological principle may be stated as follows: Structuralism is based on the assumption that there are universal and invariant laws of humanity that are operative at all levels of human life—at the most primitive and at the most advanced. The search for these laws constitutes the theoretical mission of structuralism. However, they are difficult to grasp and to discern at the most advanced stages of social life, in complex civilizations. This is so because these laws are masked by surplus and nonessential acquisitions, so to say. In order to capture these invariant laws, one goes to "reduced models" at the most elementary stages of social development—to a point in its development where the essence of the phenomenon has not been confounded by nonessential accretions. The laws yielded by such elementary institutions and societies provide the basis for the understanding of the essence of institutions and societies in their complex forms. This principle of elementarism has an operative corollary—namely, that at the elementary stages of development, every feature of a phenomenon should be carefully examined for relevance in the context of the totality of the phenomenon. Such a procedure would be costly at the higher reaches of development because many of its complex features are only acquired in luxury and are inconsequental for the essential operation of the phenomenon.

This principle underlies such classics in the social sciences as Emile Durkheim's *The Elementary Forms of the Religious Life*, Marcel Mauss' *The Gift* and, to a limited extent, Claude Lévi-Strauss' *The Elementary Structures of Kinship*. These examples are all French. Although structuralism is not exclusively limited to French social scientists, nor in fact is it to be entirely identified with the brand of French sociology following Durkheim's works, the principle of elementarism has received its fullest expression in the works of Durkheim and his followers. To give one contrary example: even though Sigmund Freud's work can be legitimately characterized as structuralist in that he too was in search of the universal laws of the human mind, his structuralism is not informed by the principle of elementarism. Rather, Freud derived his laws and principles by studying the psyches of the most complex human beings of his day and he later on sought to generalize the principles thus yielded to archaic and primitive institutions and men (e.g. Freud 1913). The early points of objection raised by Malinowski (1927, 1929) to Freud's interpretations indicate the danger of ignoring this principle of elementarism, when a theorist generalizes from the complex to the elementary.

The principle of elementarism manifests itself also at the ontogenetic level. The mind and behavior of the child may be assumed to be more elementary than those of the adult. Sometimes, a social scientist may undertake to cut through the complexity of adult behaviors and his masked mental life by going through child psychology. Certainly Piaget's studies of childhood behaviors were at least partially carried out with this aim in mind.[2]

Formal concern with this principle of elementarism is not new in sociology and is already well emphasized in *The Elementary Forms of the Religious Life*. Durkheim was interested in flushing out "fundamental representations or conceptions" of religion:

These are the permanent elements which constitute that which is permanent and human in religion. . . . How is it possible to pick them out?

Surely it is not by observing the complex religions which appear in the course of history. Everyone of these is made up of such a variety of elements that it is very difficult to distinguish what is secondary from what is principal, the essential from the accessory. . . .

Things are quite different in the lower societies. . . . That which is assessory or secondary, the development of luxury, has not yet come to hide the principal elements. All is reduced to that which is indispensable, to that without which there could be no religion. But that which is indispensable is also that which is essential, that is to say, that which we must know before all else.

Primitive civilizations offer privileged cases, then, because they are simple cases. (Durkheim 1915:5–6)

This statement at once represents the kernel of the principle of elementarism as well as Durkheim's contribution to structuralism.

"Reduced models" in the form of the most elementary societies and institutions should remain central to sociological structuralism.

DURKHEIM: EVOLUTIONIST OR ELEMENTARIST?

The linking of Durkheim to the principle of elementarism raises a significant point of interpretation in sociological theory. The orthodox interpretation of Durkheim's sociology is that the worth of his work is vitiated by a nineteenth-century evolutionism which he unfortunately inherited from the intellectual milieu in which he worked. It is usually further assumed that this evolutionary aspect of Durkheim's work is something to be purged from his sociology. Unquestionably, there is something that looks like evolutionism in Durkheim's sociology. Stretching back to Merton's (1934) review of *The Division of Labor in Society*, several scholars have chastised Durkheim for his unilinear evolutionism. Even the most sympathetic interpreter of Durkheim's writings in recent times, Robert Nisbet, sees a pervasive evolutionism in his sociology—as early as in *The Division of Labor* and as late as in *The Elementary Forms* (Nisbet 1965, 1975).

I believe that any impression that Durkheim was a straight-faced evolutionist is at best an exaggeration. This issue will benefit from a clear-cut distinction between *evolutionism* and *elementarism*. Evolutionism is an *analytical* principle employed in the characterization of the growth of a phenomenon through various stages. Intermediate stages are of the utmost importance for the accurate analysis of the growth of the phenomenon whose evolution is being traced. The pattern of such evolution would be indeterminate if one were only given its point of origin and its end-stage. Elementarism is different. It is an *explanatory* principle that makes the fundamental assumption that the discovery of the elementary forms of a phenomenon is worthwhile because they help to capture the essence of the phenomenon as well as to explain its complexity by ferreting out those features of the phenomenon that persist from its elementary forms to its complexity. Elementarism requires only two points in order to determine the character of the phenomenon: its nature at the beginning and at the end-stage. Strictly speaking, the intermediate stages are unnecessary for the principle of elementarism. Or to put the matter differently, an elementarist explanation would be indeterminate were the intermediate stages to be given without either a knowledge of its beginnings or its state of complexity. An elementarist is interested in the intermediate stages only if they would lead him to determine the nature of the elementary forms of the phenomenon. And he is interested in the most elementary state of the phenomenon for one principal reason: in order to explain the nature of the phenomenon, especially in its complexity. To repeat a point of distinction here: evolutionism emphasizes stages of development; elementarism is not uniquely interested in the stages of development but rather in the characterization of the elementary forms of the phenomenon with a view to understanding it in its complexity. Evolutionism stresses the changes that occur in the structure of the phenomenon as a result of its stage-related differentiations. Elementarism, on the other hand, stresses those aspects of a phenomenon that remain permanent despite the changes in the structure of the phenomenon.

It is in the context of this distinction between evolutionism and elementarism that Durkheim's work must be placed for maximum understanding. Perhaps the passage that has the most overt appearance of evolutionism in Durkheim's writings, and so labeled by Nisbet (1975:167, 244), is the following:

Every time we undertake to explain something human, taken at a given moment in history—be it a religious belief, a moral precept, a legal principle, an esthetic style or an economic system—it is necessary to commence by *going back to its most primitive and simple form*, to try to account for the characteristics by which it was marked at that time, and then to show how it developed and became complicated little by little, and *how it became that which it is at the moment in question*. (Durkheim 1915:3; emphasis added)

Why is Durkheim interested in the "most primitive and simple form" of the religious life, "the characteristics by which it was marked" at that elementary state? It is not to construct, in the tradition of the great nineteenth-century evolutionists, such as Spencer, the panorama and stages of the religious life. It is rather to trace the elementary forms of it—so that we may more easily understand its complex forms. Thus defined, the interests of Durkheim in this area lie in the structuralist quest for the universals and permanencies of common humanity. For here we are searching for the enduring forms of the religious life, forms that not only exist in its elementary states, but that are also important for understanding and explaining the complexity of the religious life, even in its sublimated forms.

On the face of it, this distinction between evolutionism and elementarism may appear thin, but it is of the utmost significance in considering the modern relevance of structuralism. Evolutionism, with its compelling emphasis on stages and stage-related differentiations, may be outdated in social science; elementarism as an explanatory principle is not. Information concerning the characteristics of the elementary forms of a human phenomenon is still one important source for understanding the complexity of modern life. In this, sociology still has a great deal to gain from Durkheim.

THE ELEMENTARY FORMS OF CIVILIZATION

One of the softest spots in Durkheim's sociology lies in his undifferentiated conception of the dynamic processes in elementary societies. To him all were the same. That is why he could talk of "primitive civilizations" as broadly meaning non-Western societies or what he also called "lower societies." But one must take exception to so bizarre a phrase as "primitive civilizations." It seems to me preferable to talk of "elementary civilizations," in which the bare bones of civilization are clearly discernible. But such elementary civilizations must be considered apart from what have usually been styled primitive societies. Elementary civilizations are not to be found in all human organizations; rather, they constitute the essence of the great civilizations, at a reduced level. It seems to me that Durkheim erred in equating "human" with "civilized." At what point may we say that we have arrived at the threshold of civilization?

I think we can answer this question in terms of the Lévi-Straussian distinction between *nature* and *culture*. Human development consists in the shifting balance between nature and culture. At the primitive stage of human development nature asserts its potency most strongly whereas culture is weakly represented. But at the stage of elementary civilizations, a crucial transition takes place in this dialectic. The nature of which I seek to characterize here. The assertion of culture and the relative taming of nature in elementary civilizations may be difficult to ascertain because it occurs at the level of the *unconscious*. It is this attribute of elementary civilizations that provides a more stable characterization of elementary civilizations than their ecological settings, mostly in city-states.

Given the commitments of Anglo-Saxon sociology, it seems necessary to amplify the significance of two points raised here. These concern the distinction between nature and culture and the legitimacy of *unconscious* collective data, such as myths and legends, in sociology. Both points are relevant in any attempt to introduce structuralism into sociology, and yet sociologists are unused to them. First, about the distinction between nature and culture: Sociology is distantly associated with the analogous distinction between nature and nurture in the area of socialization theory. This distinction deals with individual ontogenetic development—with the way the individual is molded in his development by an interaction of biological with environmental factors. But the study of human development covers a wider area and must include a consideration of phylogenetic societal development, issuing in the institutions of society. The investigation of collective phylogenetic development of society requires the distinction between nature and culture. But such distinction must be seen in dialectic terms, not in terms of a historically dated transition from nature to culture, from a state of nature to human life. Nature is a theoretical construct that represents the reality of subhuman existence in which biological forces control collective action.[3] Culture is a theoretical construct which represents the human dimensions of social reality, embodying those aspects of social existence which are the products of collective human efforts and actions. The institutions of society are molded within the dialetics between nature and culture. As Lévi-Strauss recognizes, "it is beginning to emerge that this distinction between nature and culture, while of no acceptable historical significance, does contain a logic, fully justifying its use by modern sociology as a methodological tool. Man is both a biological being and a social individual" (1949:3).

Sociologists are also apt to be uneasy about the inclusion of another main preoccupation of structuralism, namely, collective *unconscious* data, in sociological theory and research. While they may be distantly sympathetic with the psychoanalyst or psychologist investigating unconscious mental activities in the individual, sociologists are less likely to see the need for expanding the scope of their discipline into this region. But the unconscious data I refer to are different from the individual unconscious. Rather, they are contained in unconscious collective data, which are the attributes of supra-individual collectivities. Thus, legends and myths are the creation of cultures and societies, unlike dreams which are the products of individual mental activities. There is every reason to hope that structuralism will expand the scope of sociology by bringing to it not only the distinction between nature and culture but also unconscious collective data as legitimate material for sociological theorizing and analysis. At least my approach to the understanding of elementary civilizations compels the distinction between nature and culture and the decoding of unconscious collective material.

Let me illustrate the relevance of these points through a consideration of incest—a baffling phenomenon because, as Lévi-Strauss has observantly noted, it represents a meeting point between nature and culture. "Wherever there are rules we know for certain that the cultural stage has been reached. Likewise, it is easy to recognize universality as the criterion of nature, for what is constant in man falls necessarily beyond the scope of customs, techniques, and institutions whereby his groups are differentiated and contrasted" (Lévi-Strauss 1949:8). Now, incest is *cultural* in the sense that the rules governing it vary from group to group; and it is *natural* in that there is universal abhorrence of incest in every known society.

But the proper meaning of incest in human development emerges when one considers *conscious* and *unconscious* reactions to incest. At the primitive stage of human development, incest is condemned at the *conscious* level but is approved of, or at least tolerated, at the *unconscious* level. To cite Lévi-Strauss, "there is so little 'exception' to the prohibition of incest that the native *conscience* is very sensitive about it. When a household is sterile, an incestuous relationship, although unknown, is taken for granted, and prescribed expiatory ceremonies are celebrated automatically" (1949:9; emphasis added). This universal conscious revulsion against incest in primitive communities is to be contrasted with its approval, or its toleration, at the unconscious level. The lightness with which incest is treated in primitive mythology is revealed in *The Raw and the Cooked*:

The initial theme of the key myth is the incest committed by the hero with the mother. Yet the idea that he is "guilty" seems to exist mainly in the mind of the father, who desires his son's death and schemes to bring it about. The myth itself, however, does not render a verdict, since the hero begs for and obtains help from his grandmother, thanks to whom he survives all ordeals. In the long run, it is the father who appears guilty, through having tried to avenge himself, and it is he who is killed by his son.

[In the myth in which the wronged husband is punished], as in the key myth, the person who committed incest appeared less guilty than the wronged husband who sought to avenge himself. In each instance it was vengeance, and not incest, that prompted supernatural sanctions. (Lévi-Strauss 1964:55)

This inconsistency in "primitive" societies with regard to incest (*conscious* condemnation and *unconscious* approval) is remarkably different from that at the level of human development that I characterize as elementary civilizations. It is at this stage that for the first time revulsion against incest is registered at both the conscious and the unconscious level.[4] It is at this stage that the eternal human dialectic between nature and culture is tilted toward culture.

THE SOCIAL SURVIVAL HYPOTHESIS AS A PRINCIPLE OF ELEMENTARY CIVILIZATIONS

Elementary civilizations have their own characteristic mythical unconscious representations. One prominent example is the Oedipal myth. Although incest and patricide are common themes in mythology at various levels of human development, the distinguishing features of Oedipal myths as a manifestation of elementary civilizations are the presence of royalty in the myths and the assumption that incest is wrong even when unwittingly committed. Roheim (1930:309) has remarked that "It is significant that the greater part of the mythical material in which we find an open or nearly open statement of the Oedipus situation should be connected with divine rulers." And the emphasis on incest as a crime is a feature of mythology that begins to distinguish elementary civilizations from primitive human organizations. As I emphasized elsewhere (Ekeh 1976), these Oedipal myths are found in elementary civilizations as far separated in time and space as ancient Greek city-state organization and city-state civilization in Benin, Africa.

Now, elementary civilizations are usually small-scale civilizations, in many cases organized around city-states. There is an ever-present threat to their survival. The example of Carthage or the fate of Troy (whether seen in the light of history or mythology) is a clear indication that elementary civilizations can be destroyed. Concern with survival is thus a major preoccupation of elementary civilizations.

This concern with social survival is fully carried over to the unconscious realm of mythical reproduction. In a previous study (see Ekeh 1976), I contended that the two dominant interpretations of the Oedipus myth, by Sigmund Freud and by Erich Fromm, are inadequate. In their place, I offered what I labeled as a social-survival hypothesis to account more adequately for the role of the actors. At the level of elementary civilizations, the dialectic between nature and culture is informed by the concern for social survival. Indeed, Oedipal myths, as prominent unconscious representations of elementary civilizations, can be seen in terms of this collective concern for social survival. The polar opposites in this dialectic are *potency* (representing natural inclinations) and *legitimacy* (indicating the tamed influence of culture).[5] Since the focal actors in the Oedipus myth are "fathers" and "sons," the transformation equation of the Oedipus myth may be rendered as follows:

$$\text{Son}:\text{Father}::\text{POTENCY}:\text{LEGITIMACY}$$

The element of royalty in the Oedipus myth heightens the dialectic tension between potency and legitimacy, largely because royalty symbolizes legitimacy and the killing of a royal father combines at once patricide and regicide and deepens the significance of the attack on legitimacy.

As I have pointed out, this dialectic between potency and legitimacy at the level of elementary civilizations can be related to the wider terms of the dialectic as follows:

POTENCY : LEGITIMACY :: NATURE : CULTURE

The needs of the social survival of elementary civilizations demand that a delicate balance be maintained between the two terms of the dialectic. An exclusive emphasis on potency would lead to a return to the dominance of nature—to a societal regression to primitivism. An exclusive emphasis on legitimacy would put too much accent on tamed culture and threaten the physical survival of elementary civilizations—by way of ineffectual response to attacks from the outside, for instance.

The survival of elementary civilizations depends on the judicious choice of which of these terms of the dialectic is to be asserted in response to given situations. If the challenge facing an elementary civilization were to be of the physical type, say, military threat from within or from without a city-state civilization, it would be more successful to assert the principle of potency. On the other hand, if the challenges concerned matters of values and norms of the elementary civilization it would be more successful to assert the principle of legitimacy. But when responses to all types of challenges are fixated—and are cast entirely in terms of the consistent assertion of either legitimacy or potency but not both—then the survival of elementary civilizations is put boldly to question. It is this contrapuntal interplay between potency and legitimacy that sustains elementary civilizations.

Here indeed one must distinguish between a true and a false Toynbean challenge-and-response. The challenges that threaten the survival of civilization may be one of two types: *externalized* challenge, which is of a physical nature, of military threat, for instance; and *internalized* challenge, which attacks the basic value and normative premises of the civilization. Now successful responses require that elementary civilizations assert the principle of potency in the face of externalized challenge and that they assert the principle of legitimacy when confronted with internalized challenge. But when the responses emitted by elementary civilizations are unvaried—in the uniform assertion of either potency or legitimacy, but not of both—then their survival is threatened.

THE DIALECTICS OF COMPLEX CIVILIZATIONS

Modern complex civilizations are infinitely more complex than the civilizations that I have characterized as "elementary." But this is a difference in degree only, clearly not of kind. For the structural laws of the dialectic between potency and legitimacy, representing the larger human dialectic between nature and culture, are operative in the more complex civilizations as well, albeit in sublimated forms. The discovery of these sublimated forms of this dialectic should shed considerable light on the character of civilizations as a whole.

It seems necessary to emphasize that we are considering civilization as a special phase in the movement of human development, bracketed off by typical outward complex social organization and characterized by specialized thought patterns. In the area of unconscious collective representations, certain mythical patterns typify elementary civilizations and reveal the nature of civilizations, complex civilizations included. Here, one must sympathize with Ricoeur's (1963) complaint that all Lévi-Strauss' examples of mythic thought have been taken from the geographical regions of totemism and never from the areas from which modern complex Western civilization sprang—Semitic, pre-Hellenic, or Indo-European areas. For Lévi-Strauss, humanity is all of a piece at the level of the unconscious. My position is different. I assume that, the eternal human dialectic between nature and culture takes on different forms, depending on the level of human development. Although the dialectical confrontation between nature and culture can be discerned at the level of conscious collective representations in primitive human organizations, nature is more strongly depicted in their unconscious collective representations. It is at the stage of elementary civilizations that one begins to discern the ascendance of culture more clearly, even at the depth of unconscious collective representations, such as myths. Hence the discovery of the laws of civilization may more aptly be gained by decoding such unconscious collective representations at this stage of human development. The Oedipus myth, emphasizing incest, and especially patricide and regicide, is typical of mythic thought at the level of elementary civilizations.

The indirect approach of sociological structuralism is relevant for the study of complex civilizations because at this stage of human development, the deep structural laws that give ultimate meaning to societal dynamics have become *sublimated*. At their depth, complex civilizations represent the sublimated dialectics between nature and culture, transformed, as in elementary civilizations, to a contrapuntal relationship between potency and legitimacy. The vitality of a complex civilization is realized at that point in its history when this contrapuntal relationship exists— when such a civilization is selectively responsive to social problems and societal crises either by choosing strategies that emphasize potency and force (that is, its natural inclinations) or by invoking the resiliency of its normative and value order by asserting the principle of legitimacy.

This position is discernible in the history of various nations which enjoy complex civilizations. The alternations between Pareto's lions and foxes is an attribute of the politics of a viable complex civilization and the lions and foxes represent nature and culture in a sublimated fashion. This view of politics is true for French social history as it is for the outline of American politics. To cite one interpretation of French history: Roger Prioueret attributed to Raymond Aron the following position:

Raymond Aron follows the views of Andre Siegfried, according to which there are two basic political attitudes in France. This country is sometimes Bonapartist and sometimes Orleanist. Bonapartism consists in the acceptance and even desire for personal power, Orleanism in leaving the administration of public affairs to representatives. In the face of crises like the defeat of 1871 or a protracted war like the one in Algiers, France changes in attitude, that is, turns from Bonapartism to Orleanism as in 1871 or from Orleanism to Bonapartism, as on 13 May 1958. (Cited in Lévi-Strauss 1962:70)

In French history, then, Bonapartism represents potency, leaning on natural inclinations, and violates the principle of legitimacy. On the other hand, Orleanism symbolizes legitimacy, representing culture in the human dialectic between nature and culture. Of course, these tendencies have become greatly sublimated in these complex civilizations and require a considerable amount of interpretation before one can see the outline of the dialectics.

I am inclined to see Lipset's (1963) distinction between "status politics" and "class politics" in American political life in the same light. During periods of economic crises, class distinctions—predicated on economic positioning in the social order—is emphasized. The disadvantaged classes became assertive in their demands for social equality. On the other hand, in periods of high national wealth and economic boom, "status politics" prevail, with the privileged groups emphasizing the cultural differences between them and the lower status groups and the value of moral distinctions. The inference may look distant, but is it really outlandish to say that the contrapuntal relationship depicted by Professor Lipset rests on the larger human dialectics between nature and culture—that "class politics" signifies the strength of natural inclinations with its emphasis on natural equality while "status politics" signifies the hierachical distinctions implicit in the realm of culture? The difficulty posed in entertaining these thoughts ultimately flows from the sublimated nature of the dialectics that govern modern civilizations.

Like elementary civilizations, complex civilizations are subject to decay. It is true that they are less subject to violent termination and can thus avoid the fate of Troy or Carthage. But the problem of gradual erosion is a significant one for complex civilizations. And such erosion, leading to decay, can be partially traced to the tendency to false responses to problems raised by the dialectics. The survival problems of complex civilizations do not yield to uniform solution—either exclusively in terms of the persistent assertion of potency by use of natural force or by way of consistent emphasis on the legitimacy of normative values and cultural standards for the solution of societal problems. The continuity and the viability of complex civilizations require that externalized crises be met with solutions relying on potency and that value crises, crises that threaten the cultural order, be met by invigorating the values and norms of the social order. Failure is inevitable where responses to all forms of crises are unyieldingly uniform and unvaried.

STRUCTURALISM AND THE ANALYSIS OF SOCIAL CHANGE

Modern complex societies are distinguished from simple and elementary societies above all else by the fact that in complex societies social change is normal and that any adequate conceptualization of these societies must account for the dynamics of social change. In elementary and simple societies, on the other hand, social change is unusual and one would be doing no violence to social reality in these societies by failing to include a notion of social change in conceptualizing their social dynamics. Accordingly, what anthropologists ask of a theory tends to be different from what social scientists engaged in the study of modern societies demand of a theory. The adequacy of any theoretical perspective admitted into sociology requires that it should contribute to the understanding of the phenomenon of social change. It is because of its inadequacy in this respect that functionalism faced its first serious challenge in sociology, whereas it was generally considered adequate for the subject matter of anthropology: namely, simple societies.

One may thus pose the following questions: Can structuralism, as a theoretical perspective, shed any light on the nature of social change in modern society? The question is especially significant in the case of structuralism because of its emphasis on the discovery of invariant laws of humanity. Is it not a theory of permanent structures rather than of change?

To answer these questions adequately, it seems necessary to understand the meaning of social change. Social change poses an intriguing intellectual problem because it deals at once with continuities and discontinuities in societal processes. The problem that faces any theorist of social change is that he needs to master the ways in which a society with a continuity and history stretching into the past has nevertheless experienced discontinuities by leaping through some stages of development and thus leaving behind some characteristics that formerly marked its past while acquiring others that were absent from it. A theory may be judged adequate with respect to its capacity to deal with social change if it can account for these continuities and discontinuities in societal dynamics.

Structuralism can contribute to the understanding of social change in two separate ways. First, it can help in the discovery of the various forms and meanings of the terms of the eternal human dialectics between nature and culture. As I argued previously, these human dialectics operate differently, particularly at the level of the collective unconscious, in simple and elementary societies and in complex societies. Because of its commitments to the discovery of the invariant laws of humanity, structuralism is especially suited to carry out a program of the investigation of the various forms that the dialectics assume at different levels of human development. More generally, even beyond the postulation of the dialectics between nature and culture, the structuralist program entails the discovery of the various forms that the *constancies of human existence* assume.

Thus, Weinstein and Platt's (1969) study of the impact of modern Western civilization on the human psyche—issuing in what they characterize as the "introspective revolution" in which individuals turn inwards for self-examination, self-analysis, and self-criticism—points to an important area of social change experienced by modern man. Change here refers to the sublimation of overt acts and institutions at the more elementary stages into more subtle representations at the higher stages. These latter require structuralist analysis in order to be more fully understood. Social change in this case does not involve the acquisition of materials that were not in existence previously, but rather to aspects of human existence that remain constant over centuries but which assume different, more refined forms. Thus, the constructs that psychoanalysts call superego and the Oedipus complex are presumed to be a stable aspect of humanity, which have been operative for as long as man has led organized life. Weinstein and Platt deal with the refined forms that the Oedipus complex and the superego assume with the onset of Western civilization. This is an aspect of social change that does not lend itself to the ordinary tools of sociological analysis and that requires the methodological outfit of structuralism.[6]

Secondly, the structuralist analysis of social change engenders a differentiated attitude to the understanding of the subject. There are core areas of society and of institutions in society that cannot be lost without the complete loss of the society as previously constituted. They mark the area of continuity. When a social scientists deals with the national character of a people he is engaged in the intellectual discernment of this continuity in society. If social change were so profound as to change these continuous areas of social life, then we would have to say the society has been lost and reborn. But even social revolutions cannot destroy these core areas of society. On the other hand, there are areas of society that can be shed in the process of social change without affecting the genius of the society; similarly, other attributes can be acquired in the process of social change without altering the essence of the society. In a sense, then, the form a society assumes in complex civilizations is predetermined by its core attributes. It is also affected by the course of change it is exposed to. The final outcome of social change is thus determined by the interaction of its distinguishing essential attributes and the type of changing experiences it goes through in its history.

The potential of sociological structuralism for contributing to the study of social change, may be seen in a second way when it is considered in the light of the two dominant doctrines of social change: preformationism, and epigenesis. The doctrine of preformationism suggests that there are core areas of social life that are impervious to change; the doctrine of epigenesis stresses that the product of societal dynamics is the result of successive stage-related differentiations issuing in new structures and new functions. Now, by organizing a program of discovery that seeks to disentangle the various meanings and forms the core structures assume, structuralism should be able to differentiate between epigenetic influence and preformationist tendencies in societal development. From the point of view of structuralism, modern complex society cannot be adequately conceptualized in epigenetic terms only; it can only be fully understood if epigenesis is considered in the light of preformationist structures.

CONCLUSIONS

Durkheim has justly been hailed as a pioneer in establishing sociology as a discipline and in giving it its professional direction. Of Durkheim's works, two may be cited as his most significant accomplishments. These are *Suicide* and *The Elementary Forms of Religious Life*. Both were committed to the same goal: the understanding of modern man and modern complex institutions, but their strategies were vastly different. *Suicide*, as did *The Division of Labor in Society*, approached the problem of understanding complex society directly. By constrast, *The Elementary Forms* sought to understand modern society only indirectly—by way of laws yielded by the study of "primitive" men and primitive institutions.

In accepting Durkheim, Anglo-Saxon sociology, which now dominates Western sociology almost completely, has been selective. It has accepted the Durkheim of *Suicide* and has apparently rejected the Durkheim of *The Elementary Forms*. In doing so, modern sociology has restricted itself to the exploitation of the virtues of *Suicide*, while denying itself the rich resources for deciphering the underlying meaning of modern complex institutions that the indirect approach of *The Elementary Forms* would have made available to sociology. Moreover, exclusive focus on the direct approach of *Suicide*, with a heavy accent on the here-and-now observation of data, has plunged sociology into what may be called an empiricist illusion—namely, the view that social reality can only be captured by direct observation. In fact, the intellectual wealth of *The Elementary Forms* lies in its pioneering venture in attempting to discover the laws of complex modern man and society *indirectly* from the dynamics of simple and elementary societies.

And this should be the central concern of sociological structuralism. All structuralists assume that there are fundamental laws and principles of humanity. While structural anthropology attempts to discover such laws and principles in order to understand simple and "primitive" societies more fully, sociological structuralism has a higher assignment: it strains to understand modern man and modern complex institutions through the laws and principles yielded by simple societies. This concern constitutes what I have characterized as the principle of elementarism.

We need not be dismayed by the certain objection that we shall be doing violence to Western culture by assuming that it is one with the rest of humanity. Those who are swayed by the appeal of the uniqueness of the so-called Judeo-Christian civilization will have enough to engage them in the elementary institutions and societies of Greek and Roman city-state civilizations. But it must be stressed that structuralism is a program of generalization from the elementary to the complex, not the reverse. Alvin Gouldner (1965) studied Greek city-state society in the light of the principles of modern sociology; we may applaud his efforts but we must acknowledge that his investigations are not informed by the program of structuralism and the principle of elementarism. Gouldner's benchmark is modern complex Western society; in effect he generalized from complex societies to elementary societies by, for instance, applying the principles of social stratification in modern societies to the study of ancient Greek city-state society. In doing so, the sociologists may be yielding to what Bendix (1964:13) has called the "fallacy of retrospective determinism"—the attribution of modern modes of thought and behavior, complicated by nonessential luxury, to elementary societies of the past. The reverse, which is the program of sociological structuralism, is based on the methodologically sound grounding that in their simplicity elementary societies will yield fundamental laws and principles that will enable us to separate what is essential from what is nonessential in the functioning of modern institutions.

But if we do uphold Durkheim as the pioneer of sociological structuralism, we must nevertheless recognize that pioneering efforts have their own limitations. Durkheim's, chief limitation is that he stayed too close to conscious collective representations to enable him to discover what Lévi-Strauss has termed "innermost" laws of humanity. Sociological structuralism must include in its program of discovery unconscious collective representations.

It is here, however, that sociological structuralism may well face resistence from established intellectual patterns in the discipline. Collective representations, or social entities, have hardly had a respectable hearing in sociology. There is the danger that when used in the context of structuralism, collective representations may be received with that indifference which continuous reference to, but lack of action on, this term has engendered in sociology. This would almost certainly be fatal to sociological structuralism. For sociological structuralism that is not predicated on the legitimacy of collective representations is impoverished from the start. In addition, sociology has been timid in the area of the study of unconscious collective representations, such as myths. True, mythology does not appear to be an attribute of modern society, but why should we disregard unconscious collective data if they will help us to understand modern man and society by abstracting them from elementary and simple societies?

That sociology is facing a crisis is by now well recognized by those engaged in the assessment of the field. Typically, there are two ways of facing up to the crisis. The first is the attempt to replace the old theoretical perspectives, considered as ineffectual in matters regarding the explanation and analysis of modern society, with theoretical view points which are considered more elevated. Instead of Parsonian functionalism, we are urged to substitute ethnomethodology or "critical" sociology. However, it is becoming clear that the various new perspectives that seek to do away with the old have not gained the acceptability necessary to endow them with the legitimacy required for success. This is because they have not provided viable alternatives. There is an alternative solution, which promises to be more rewarding: to expand the scope of sociology to include new commitments. This is the area in which sociological structuralism should attempt to establish a footing. Not only does it claim parentage from one of the eminent founders of sociology, but it seeks to expand the frontiers of the discipline to the region of the collective unconscious—an area long ignored by sociologists. It is by no means certain that sociologists are sufficiently prepared for such a venture in a new territory. Perhaps what anthropologists can do, sociologists can do as well—differently of course, but with benefits to our discipline.

NOTES

1. Cf. Lévi-Strauss (1949:xxiv): "Properly speaking, then, this work is an introduction to a general theory of kinship systems. Following this study of elementary structures there is need for another on complex structures." This explanatory relationship between elementary structures and complex structures is particularly stressed in the last two chapters of *The Elementary Structures of Kinship*.

2. In the realm of American sociology, it appears that Bales' small group studies have been governed by the principles of elementarism. There is no doubt that Bales' prolific small group experiments can be exploited so as to derive laws that can help to master the operation of more complex structures. Such for instance, is Bales and Borgatta's (1955) study of the effect of size on the operation of the group (Cf. Ekeh 1974:50, 52, 56). But it is not clear whether Bales' small group categories and rules were derived from formulations pertaining to complex structures, or whether the contrary is the case. Clearly Parsons' four-functions social system paradigm has close ties with Bales' four-phases small group interactions; but it is not clear which of them is derived from the other. It is noteworthy, though, that originally Parsons (1951) had a tripartite division of func-

tions, but that he later on added a fourth function to make his theory a four-systems poradigm (see Ekeh 1974:71). Was this derived from Bales' small group experimental formulations? It may also be noted that Simmel's study of small groups was motivated by the desire to understand more complex structures. As such, his work may be described as not only structuralist (since he too was interested in invariant laws of human association) but as also informed by the principle of elementarism.

3. By theoretical constructs, I mean mental constructions which are not amenable to sensory observations but which are validated by aspects of observable sensory social reality.

4. What Freud (1900:222–25) said about universal expressions of horror evoked by *Oedipus Rex* is really more characteristic of elementary civilizations and complex civilizations than of humanity as a whole. Clearly, incest—especially that involving royalty—is much more tolerated at the primitive level of human development than at the level of elementary civilization or of complex civilization.

5. Cf. Ekeh (1976:86): "The principle of legitimacy is predicated on the preeminence of traditional beliefs concerning what institutions and values are considered right *in* society. The customs, the norms, the ethos in society are given stress by this principle. On the other hand, the principle of potency gives emphasis to what is considered right *for* society at any given time. While the principle of legitimacy flows from the cultural heritage of members of a society and plays up what *ought* to be done, the principle of potency emphasises the problems of society at a specified time and plays up what can be done to meet them. Potency is a violation of legitimacy. The former operates on the note of *possibility*; legitimacy operates on the note of *ought*. A potent action is taken because it *works*; a legitimate action is taken because it is *right*."

6. Similarly, Arnold Toynbee's (e.g., 1946:198) "law of progressive simplification" or "etherialization" in which elaborate forms are changed into more coherent forms requires structuralist analysis for its elucidation. For what is involved here is the operation of a phenomenon that assumes different shapes at different levels of human development, marked by more subtle representations at the higher stages.

REFERENCES

Bales, Robert F. and Edgar F. Borgatta. 1955. "Size of group as a factor in the Interaction Profile." In A. Paul Hare, E. F. Borgatta, and R. F. Bales, eds. *Small Groups: Studies in Social Interaction*, pp. 396–413. New York: Knopf.

Bendix, Reinhard. 1964. *Nation-Building and Citizenship*. New York: Wiley.

Durkheim, Emile. 1893. *The Division of Labor in Society*. New York: Free Press, 1933.

—— 1897. *Suicide*. New York: Free Press, 1951.

—— 1915. *The Elementary Forms of the Religious Life* London: George Allen and Unwin.

Durkheim, Emile and Marcel Hauss. 1903. *Primitive Classification*. London: Cohen & West, 1963.

Ekeh, Peter P. 1974. *Social Exchange Theory: The Two Traditions*. London: Heinemann Educational Books; Cambridge: Harvard University Press.

—— 1976. "Benin and Thebes: Elementary forms of civilization." In Werner Muensterberger and Aaron Esman, eds. *The Psychoanalytic Study of Society*, 7:65–93. New Haven, Conn: Yale University Press.

Freud, Sigmund. 1900. *The Interpretation of Dreams*. London: George Allen and Unwin, 1915.

—— 1913. *Totem and Taboo*. New York: Vintage Books.

Gouldner, Alvin W. 1965. *Enter Plato: Classical Greece and the Origins of Social Theory*. New York: Basic Books.

Lévi-Strauss, Claude. 1949. *The Elementary Structures of Kinship*. Boston: Beacon Press, 1969.

—— 1958. *Structural Anthropology*. New York: Basic Books, 1963.

—— 1962. *The Savage Mind*. London: Widenfeld and Nicolson, 1966.

—— 1964. *The Raw and the Cooked*. London: Jonathan Cape, 1969.

Lipset, S. M. 1963. "The sources of the 'radical right.'" In Daniel Bell, ed. *The Radical Right*. New York: Doubleday.

Malinowski, B. 1927. *Sex and Repression in Savage Society*. London: Routledge and Kegan Paul, 1957.

—— 1929 *The Sexual Life of Savages*. London: Routledge and Kegan Paul, 1953.

Mauss, Marcel. 1925. *The Gift: Forms and Functions of Exchange in Archaic Societies*. London: Cohen and West Ltd. 1954.

Merton, Robert K. 1934. "Durkheim's division of labor in society." *American Journal of Sociology* 40:319–28.

Nisbet, Robert A. 1965. *Emile Durkheim*. Englewood Cliffs, N.J.: Prentice-Hall.

—— 1975. *The Sociology of Emile Durkheim*. London: Heinemann Educational Books.

Parsons, Talcott. 1951. *The Social System*. New York: The Free Press.

Ricoeur, P. 1963. "Structure et hermeneutique." *Esprit* (November), pp. 598–625.

Roheim, Geza. 1930. *Animism, Magic and the Devine King*. London: Kegan Paul, Trench Trubner & Co.

Toynbee, Arnold J. 1946. *A Study of History. Abridgement of Volumes 1–6* by D. C. Sommervell. London: Oxford University Press.

Weinstein, Fred and Gerald M. Platt. 1969. *The Wish to Be Free: Society, Psyche and Value Change*. Berkeley: The University of California Press.

CHAPTER SEVEN

SYMBOLIC STRUCTURES AND SOCIAL DYNAMICS

WITH SPECIAL REFERENCE TO STUDIES OF MODERNIZATION

S. N. EISENSTADT

In this article I analyze the possibilities and limitations of "structuralist" approaches to the analysis of societies. The central problem discussed is how to apply the concept of hidden structure, as rooted in some basic symbolic or cultural orientations, to the analysis of the working of institutions. My analysis is based on comparative macrosocietal materials especially in the fields of political institutions and social stratification and I evaluate the major conclusions in terms of anthropological and social theory.

I. THE PREMISES OF STRUCTURALISM AND ITS CONFRONTATION WITH PROBLEMS OF SOCIAL ORGANIZATION

A discussion of some of the possibilities and limitations of the structuralist approach to the analysis of societies is of interest. In the last 20 years there have been debates and controversies in social sciences which dealt with the place of symbolic dimension in the construction of social life and its relationship to the organizational aspects and workings of social groups and systems.

The structuralist approach, to some degree initially developed as a contrast to the then-prevailing emphasis in anthropological literature on the integrative role of rituals and symbols in the functioning of social systems. It stressed the autonomy, and possibly the predominance of the symbolic sphere in the construction of social and cultural reality.

Structuralism, as developed by Lévi-Strauss (1963, 1966, 1969); Hayes and Hayes (1970); Lane (1970); Scholte (1973), however, goes beyond the mere emphasis on autonomy, importance, or even predominance of the symbolic dimension in the construction of culture and society. (See, for instance, Boon 1972). It combines such emphasis with more specific assumptions about the structure and working of the symbolic sphere and its relations to human behavior and to social organization (MacRae 1968; Hammel 1972).

The crux of the structuralist claim (Lane 1970; Leach 1965; Hayes and Hayes 1970) is, first, that there exists within any society or culture some "hidden structure" which is more real and permeating than the overt social organization or behavioral patterns. Second, the rules according to which this structure is constituted are crystallized in code in the "human" mind. They are not concrete rules of social organization, nor are they derived from organizational or institutional needs or problems. Third, the most important of these rules at (at least according to Lévi-Strauss and his followers) are those of binary oppositions and consequent rules of transformation which govern the ways these oppositions are resolved. Fourth, it is these rules which are the constitutive element of culture and society, and which provide the deeper ordering principles of social and cultural realms. Fifth, these principles constitute the real models of any society—those according to which society is structured. They need not be identical with the conscious models represented in the minds of its participants or symbolized in various concrete situations and representations (like myths) although it is mostly through a structural analysis of these representations that such rules can be analyzed and understood.

The discussions between the structuralists and the more "orthodox" anthropologists, although very heated, were often rather unproductive. Because of the mixture of "principled" philosophical, ontological, metaphysical, and sociological assertions, they tended to talk past one another. (For analysis and illustration of some of these discussions see H. Geertz 1965; P. E. Josselin de Jong 1965a, b; Kobben 1966; Pouwer (1966a, b, c); Scholte 1966; Rotenstreich 1972; Rossi 1973.)

Lévi-Strauss and his followers were often criticized for a failure to provide empirical evidence for their assumptions. These were countered by arguments about "irrelevance" of evidence based on empirical "positivist" assumptions as against the importance of discovering "hidden" models of societies in which the working of the basic rules of human mind is manifest (Maybury-Lewis 1960; Needham 1960; Lévi-Strauss 1966). Each side tended often to dismiss the other as "irrelevant" or as dealing with a different level of reality. And yet the structuralist approach presented a major challenge to anthropologists and sociologists of all camps. First, is it possible to specify the concrete institutional loci and derivatives of the symbolic systems and orientations of the so-called general rule of the human mind (beyond the concrete and immediate organizational exigencies and processes) by means of studies in "conventional" sociological analysis? (See for instance, Parsons 1961; Mayhew 1971; Parsons and Platt 1973). Second, how do these rules impinge on the actual working of social systems? To which aspects of the institutional structure are they related?

Some preliminary answers have developed in recent sociological and anthropological literature in two directions. One, the indication of the ways "deeper" symbolic principles may influence the working of institutions, could indeed be found in several recent studies in anthropology and sociology. They could be found first in the work of the Dutch anthropologists of the Leyden school (J. P. B. Josselin de Jong 1922; P. E. Josselin de Jong 1951, 1960, 1964, 1965a, 1971; Schulte-Nordholdt 1971; Pouwer 1964, 1966c), all of whom attempted to indicate how various symbolic orientations may explain different patterns of kinship and territorial arrangements.

Similarly the work of Louis Dumont (1971) on India attempts (however great the criticism of detail) to derive at least some of the organizational aspects of Indian society from the symbolic structure of Indian civilization; Luc de Heusch (1971) studied the interweaving of symbolic realm and of social organization in African tribes; E. Leach, Lévi-Strauss' major critical follower among the senior group of the British anthropologists, worked on the succession of Solomon (Leach 1968) and on Burma and Ceylon (Leach 1954, 1960, 1961), and stressed the importance of such symbolic orientations in defining the boundaries of the different ethnic, religious, and political collectivities.

Similarly, one may also include some attempts by Marxists like

Maurice Godelier (1973) or Lucien Sebag (1964) to specify the institutional loci of principles of a society's "hidden structure" which are of great interest for our discussion. In this context D. M. Schneider's (1968, 1972; Schneider and Smith 1973) efforts to clearly distinguish the symbolic from the more behavioral and organizational aspects of kinship in general and the American one in particular (while at the same time indicating the ways in which the two are interwoven) have been extremely significant.

A second major direction toward which the search for the institutional anchorages and specifications of the symbolic dimension developed was, as in the case of scholars like C. Geertz, V. Turner, or T. O. Beidelman in anthropology, in the analysis of how symbolizaton of social and cultural orders takes place in special social situations. Among sociologists, important studies are E. Shils' (1961, 1965) analyses of the nature of the charismatic identification in particular, as well as E. Tiryakian's (1970) attempts to combine the "structural"-symbolic with the structural-functional approach. Tiryakian's attempt was based on designating the sphere of the sacred or the symbolic as the crucial element in the construction of the boundaries and identity of a society. This provides the "meaning" (the normative and cognitive focus) through which the "structuralization" of social organization takes place. In addition, he emphasized the concept that social structures are normative phenomena of intersubjective consciousness which frame social space. Finally, he indicated various institutional and subinstitutional loci (whether the more fully ritualized situations or the less formalized but very pervasive "esoteric" situation of social relation) where symbolic orientations may be especially visible.

II. THE INSTITUTIONAL IMPACT OF CULTURAL ORIENTATIONS: SOME COMPARATIVE DATA

A. INSTITUTIONAL CONTINUITIES IN TRADITIONAL AND MODERN SOCIETIES

These indications about the institutional anchorage of symbolic orientations may now be systematized on the basis of more recent comparative sociological analysis. Comparative macrosocietal studies in general, and those of modernization in particular, have provided some highly pertinent insights about these institutional problems. The revisions of the initial model of modernization has, among other factors, given rise to a very strong stress on tradition and continuity that has some important relevance to our concern about both the possible institutional anchorages of symbolic orientations and the implications of such orientations for the working of social systems.

In these studies two major aspects of social order were indicated as potentially important from these points of view. First was the possible importance of some "abstract" or symbolic principles which tend to influence the organizational patterns of societies— very often cutting across changes in regimes, in organizational patterns, or in levels of social modernization or economic development—thus coming seemingly very close to the structuralists rules of the "hidden structure." Second, there developed an emphasis (in a way not dissimilar from Tiryakian's analysis of the importance of understanding the nature of society) on the portrayal of a society's own "real," often "unconscious," self-image in some symbols of collective identity. Such symbols, most fully enacted in symbolic ritual occasions, are also pervasive in more "dispersed" situations.

With respect to the first area, comparative research has identified some aspects in institutional spheres in which some continuity (which may be indicative of some broader cultural orientations) could be discerned. Some of these continuities have indeed been identified in central aspects of two focal institutional complexes of a society: the political sphere and that of social stratification. Striking similarities were found in how central institutional-regulative problems in these two areas were dealt with in the "same societies" (in their traditional and "modern" phases) and in different traditional and modern societies.

In the political sphere the most important were the nature of the loci of centers of political decision and innovation, the types of center-periphery relations prevalent within a society, the relative emphasis by the rulers or elites on different types of components of centers or activities of centers, the types of policies developed by the ruler and the types of public goods developed in a society, and some aspects of political struggle and organization.

Within the field of stratification the most important of such institutional aspects found to be relatively continuous are the type of attributes emphasized as constituting the basis of societal evaluation and hierarchy, the degree of status autonomy of different groups (as manifested in their access to such attributes irrespective of centers of the society), and the degree of broader status association as opposed to status segregation of relatively close occupational and professional groups.

B. THE COALESCENCE OF INSTITUTIONAL FEATURES INTO PATTERNS OF SOCIAL AND POLITICAL SYSTEMS

These characteristics tend to coalesce into some broader institutional complexes, or patterns of sociopolitical orders. One may cite those which have been designed as "absolutist," "estate," and "nation-states" models in Western Europe; the autocratic-Imperial and revolutionary-class models of Russia or China; and various patrimonial and neopatrimonial models. Others, such as those which crystallized in, say, the Japanese or Turkish complexes may also be noted. Each of these complexes or broader patterns shows evidence of specific continuous structural characteristics.

Thus, for example, the modern sociopolitical order of Western Europe has been characterized by a high degree of congruence between the cultural and political identities of the population as well as a high level of symbolic and affective commitments to the political and cultural centers. There has been a marked emphasis on politically defined collective goals for all members of the national community, while access of broad strata to symbols and centers has been relatively autonomous.

Many of these characteristics of the European nation-states are similar to those which existed in their premodern sociopolitical traditions—those of the Imperial, city-state, and feudal systems. The strong activism characteristic of these nation-states derives from the traditions of city-states, while the conception of the political order as being actively related to the cosmic or cultural order has its origin in many Imperial traditions or in the traditions of Great Religions. The strong emphasis on the autonomous access of different groups to the major attributes of social and cultural orders prevalent in these regimes find their sources, at least in part, in the pluralist-feudal structure. Continuation and expansion of these premodern structures and orientations have been greatly facilitated by the commercial and industrial revolutions as well as by the development of absolutism on the one hand, and of Protestantism on the other.

In the Imperial Eastern societies such as Russia, Japan, or China, the pluralistic elements have been much weaker than those found in the feudal or city-states of the traditional Western European order (for greater detail, see Eisenstadt 1973b). Their political traditions have rarely entailed a dichotomy between State and Society. Rather, they have tended to stress the congruent, but often passive, relations between the cosmic order and the sociopolitical order. The interrelation between the political and the social orders is not stated in terms of an antithesis between these entities, but envisaged as the coalescence of different functions within the same group or organization with a common focus in the cosmic order. In Russia, for example, this constellation of attitudes has encouraged neither the conception of relatively autonomous access to the political and cultural centers for the major strata nor the autonomy of the social and cultural orders in relation to the political one.

In traditional as well as modern patrimonial regimes (Eisenstadt 1973c) the broader social or cultural order is perceived mostly as something to be mastered or accommodated, not as something commanding a high level of commitment. Within these societies, acceptance of the givenness of the cultural and social order tends to be strong, while the possibility of active autonomous participation is barely perceived by any social groups that could shape the contours of that order— even to the extent that such shaping is possible in traditional systems. Tension between a "higher" transcendental order and the social order seldom appears; and when it does, it constitutes an important element in the "religious" sphere, but not in the political or social ones.

Such societies place little emphasis on the autonomous access of the major groups or strata to the predominant attributes of these orders. Such access is usually seen as mediated by ascriptive individual groups or ritual experts who represent the "given" order and are mostly appointed by the center or subcenters. The connections between broader universalistic percepts—be they religious or ideological—and the actual social order tends to be weak.

Ritualistic participation in the society's broad orientations plays a more prominent role than deep commitment to such concepts. The basic premises of the cultural order are accepted with relative passivity, while the givenness of that order often goes unquestioned.

As a result of these perceptions of the sociopolitical order, the inclination to active participation in the centers of these societies is weak. And the center is depended upon to provide resources and to regulate internal affairs insofar as these are related to the broader society. In such situations the development of autonomous mechanisms of self-regulation is inhibited.

In these societies demands on the center have nevertheless abated with the spread of the basic assumptions of modernity. But such demands have not usually focused on control of the center, but on change in its contents and symbols or on the possible creation of new types of social and cultural orders by the center.

III. SYMBOLIC ORIENTATIONS AND PATTERNS OF CODES AS "HIDDEN STRUCTURE" OF SOCIAL ORDER

These patterns point out broad institutional similarities that persist in the "same" society in different periods of its development. The patterns also cut across different levels of social differentiation, as well as changes of regimes, boundaries, collectivities, and symbols of collective identity. All of this attests to similarities in the ways of coping with problems specific to traditional and modern settings—even though the concrete organizational problems themselves vary greatly between such settings. Crucial to our analysis of these different institutional patterns is that these ways of coping with societal problems are related to some type of symbolic orientation.

The available comparative macrosociological analyses and studies indicate that there is a rather close relation between the broad principles of institutional patterns or constellations analyzed and some cultural orientations. Two types of cultural orientations seem to have a great impact on institutional life.

One type of orientation refers to the "cosmic," existential problems of human life: (1) (and above all) the relative evaluation of these problems of the major dimensions of human existence (the ritualistic, the political, and the economic). (2) the conception of the degree of autonomy or interrelations of the cosmic, cultural, social, and political orders and of their mutual relevance and the concomitant problems of theodicy. (3) the relative emphasis on active or passive attitudes toward participation in the social and cultural orders and their formation. (4) the different conceptions of change, attitudes to change, and the possibility of an active rather than passive participation in the formation of such changes in the major social and cultural spheres. (5) the bases of legitimation of cosmic social orders, especially with regard to the degree in which the relations to these orders are mostly adaptive ones, as opposed to an attitude of commitment.

Another set of such orientations is those related to symbolic evaluation of the fundamental dilemmas of social life and the bases of acceptance of social order—i.e. to the relative emphasis on power, solidarity, or instrumental relations and the underlying bases of social order; or the conception of social life as being harmonious or conflict-ridden; or the relative emphasis on equality or hierarchy and on individualism or communalism.

These themes or problems constitute some of the major loci of the symbolic domains in human culture. Of course, they are manifested in the most speculative and intellectually articulated symbolic expression of human creativity in the fields of aesthetics, philosophy, or theology. But they also constitute some of the major symbolic foci of the quest for the construction of a good or just social and cultural order, and of participation in it. In such an order, people's discrete social activities would be brought into some patterns of meaningful experience, encompassing the maintenance of a meaningful personal life in some relation to these orders.

The impingement of such orientations on the working of institutions is effected through the transformation or crystallization of such general broad orientations into what may be called cultural codes. Such codes are very close to what Max Weber (1947, esp. p. iv, 1958; 1964) has called *Wirtschaftsethik* generalized modes of "religious" or "ethical" orientation to a specific institutional sphere and its problems—the evaluation of this sphere, the provision of guidelines for its organization and for behavior within it in terms of the perception of major problems of human existence outlined above. In a somewhat different paraphrase, such *Ethik* or "code" connotes a general mode of orientation to a given sphere of social life, based on, or derived from, the "answer" to the basic symbolic problems mentioned above.

It is through the institutional derivatives of the programmatic specification of these codes that the symbolic and organizational dimensions of the structuring of human activities are most closely interwoven in the process of institutionalization and in all these ways they may seem to provide different principles of the hidden structure of any given social order.

Support for this supposition can be found, first of all, in the fact that some regularity can be discerned in the way any such specific orientation influences certain aspects of the institutional structure. To give a few initial and random illustrations based on the materials presented above, it seems that when (as in Western Europe) the social and cultural orders are perceived as relevant to one another and mutually autonomous, the greater will be the degree of political autonomy of different groups and of the development of independent foci of political struggle, and of the ideological dimension in politics. The more the access to these orders is, as in Russia, fused, or the more they are dissociated from one another (as in many patrimonial societies), the smaller will be the degree of such autonomy. In the first case the center will tend to permeate the periphery without permitting independent impingement by the periphery on the center; while in the second (and third) cases adaptive relations will tend to develop between the center and the periphery.

Similarly, the more the center is conceived of as the single focus of broader cultural order, the more the emphasis tends to be on functional attributes of status and on closed segregated status groups. The greater the "adaptive" attitude to the center, the greater also the degree of status segregation and emphasis on restricted prestige of closed communities. The greater the commitment of broader groups to the social order, the greater the centers' permeation on the periphery.

Emphasis on power usually tends to create, among other things, a greater distinction between center and periphery, a very strong control on social mobility by the center, and dissociation between kinship groups and status units. The autonomy of strata is minimized. An emphasis on solidarity, however, tends to minimize the distinctions between center and periphery, to increase the formation of autonomous strata, and to strengthen the relations between strata and kinship units. (For greater detail, see Eisenstadt 1971b.)

IV. PATTERNS OF CODES AND INSTITUTIONAL ORDER: THE ESTABLISHMENT OF THE GROUND RULES OF SOCIAL INTERACTION AND THE DEVELOPMENT OF SYSTEMIC SENSITIVITIES OF SOCIAL ORGANIZATIONS

Several questions crucial to our analysis are raised here. What is the place of the institutional derivatives of these orientations in the context of institutional social order? What is the relation of these principles to other aspects of social organization, especially to organizational problems, "needs," and exigencies of social groups, collectivities, or systems with which sociological analysis has been so greatly concerned? (Parsons 1961; Mayhew 1971; Parsons and Platt 1973). What are the mechanisms through which these orientations are concretely institutionalized?

The preceding illustrations (as well as the data in the various researches referred to above) indicate that the basic institutional derivatives of the symbolic orientations are the specifications of the following: goals "appropriate" for different categories of people in major types of societal situations; attributes of similarity and of criteria of membership in different collectivities; criteria of regulation of power over resources in different social situations and institutional spheres; interrelations among them all; and legitimation in terms of criteria of distributive justice which are perceived as incumbent in such different situations and in different collectives of social and cultural orders (see Eisenstadt and Curelaru 1976).

Such programmatic derivatives of codes provide the normative and evaluative specification—in terms of some of the tensions inherent in major problems of human existence analyzed above—of a range of goals or of desiderata available or permitted to the members of a certain group or social-cultural category (sex, age, occupation, territorial belongingness) and of the combinations of discrete "goals" into some broader styles of life.

In addition, such programmatic derivatives of codes define the basic attributes of social and cultural similarity which constitute the criteria of membership in different collectivities, including the symbolic and institutional boundaries of these collectives. The establishment of attributes of similarity involves the definition of the contents of the sociocultural orders, of the rules of access to them, and of their legitimation in terms of some broader "charismatic" conceptions of justice, order, or appropriateness.

These attributes provide the starting points for the definition of criteria of membership in various collectivities and orders; for the specification of the rights and limitation of access to such attributes and the consequent rights of participation in the order or community; of the range of conditional and unconditional obligations and rights accruing through membership in such collectivities or orders; and of the consequent terms of conditional and unconditional access to the various resources and positions which are available according to such criteria. Thus membership in collectivities entitles one to benefit from and participate in certain rules of distributive justice, to be subject to certain rules of exchange. And it defines the duties symmetric to these rights, which are interlinked in the process of interaction that makes a clear distinction between members' and nonmembers' rights to participation (Eisenstadt 1971c).

Thus, side by side with the specification of attributes of membership and solidarity, the programmatic derivatives of codes also specify the general principles of distribution of power within the major institutional spheres of a society. Indeed, the major focus of the institutional derivatives of such codes is on membership criteria and boundaries of collectivities with regulation of power over resources and with the major mechanism and criteria of allocation of roles, rewards, and principles of integration in the various institutional spheres. This connection is effected by establishing the major criteria according to which public and semipublic goods—as well as of institutional credit in institutional spheres (Kuhn 1963, ch. 9; Olson 1968; Coleman 1971)—are organized. Or, in greater detail, it sets up the criteria of the differential payment of the costs of the payment of such goods—of the public distribution of semipublic and private goods (i.e. the direct allocation of various resources and rewards to different groups of the population according to criteria which differ greatly from those of pure exchange). These criteria also specify the ways in which different groups, organizations, and institutional spheres enjoy institutional credit—i.e. the degree to which resources provided to any such group or institution are not channeled into immediate exchange, but relinquished unconditionally to a certain group or institutional complex. Thus such group or institution is provided with what may be called "credit autonomy," which supplies the prerequisites of any long-range working of such institution.

A closer look at these various institutional derivatives of the major cultural codes indicate that they are not randomly distributed in social interaction, but are found in some specific institutional locations and that they work through specific institutional mechanisms. The programmatic derivatives of such codes touch especially on those areas of institutional life within which, in principle, there exists a strong possibility of randomness, uncertainty, and potential conflict of the original Hobbesian state of war of all against all.

The major institutional derivatives of the various codes provide some of the mechanisms through which these areas of potential randomness and conflict became structured in ways which can then assure some continuity of frameworks of interaction. They circumscribe those uncertainties inherent in any social interaction which are taken for granted and which have to be overcome in order to assure the continuity of any interaction. And they provide some of the rules according to which the boundaries of any given collectivity or of social interaction are structured *vis-à-vis* their respective internal and external environments.

These programmatic specifications of codes and their derivatives impose some limitations on what may be called free exchange between people interacting in institutional frameworks, thus setting up some of what, in Durkheim's terminology, can be called the precontractual elements of social life, the bases of mechanical solidarity (Durkheim 1933; Davis 1963; Bloch 1974). Or, to use Schneider's (1968, 1972) nomenclature: they combine the construction of "identity" and membership in different collectivities with the range of "codes" incumbent on those participating in such collectivities.

In this way the precondition for the effective participation of members of a society in terms of broader rules of ethics and criteria of justice prevalent in such a society is also established (Piaget 1932; Mead 1934; Parsons 1961, 1973a; Kohlberg 1971).

In the language of game theory, these limitations of free exchange and interaction which are set up by programmatic specification of codes define, first, "the ground rules that structure the basic frameworks within which decision-making in different areas of social life is possible, and, second (albeit in various degrees in different societies or parts thereof) some of the broad criteria of the rules that guide choices among the options which such frameworks allow" (Buchler and Nutini 1969).

Similarly the institutional specification of the codes defines the range of concrete needs of a society. Even if we accept that groups and societies do have general common needs or problems, such as those of allocation or regulation, or the famous Parsonian problems of adaptation, goal orientation, and pattern maintenance (Parsons and Shils 1951), the nature of any concrete definition of such a particular group or society's needs is not simply given by the coalescence of the people and the resources generated and available in any situation into some patterns of division of labor— i.e. in groups, role sets, and institutional spheres. Within each concrete situation, such needs or problems can be defined in different ways and different answers can be given to them (Eisenstadt 1971a). These definitions are crystallized through the specification of the institutional derivatives of the codes. Such crystallization is effected firstly by specifying the range of "permissible" questions and answers about some of the basic problems of social and cultural existence. Second, it is effected by relating these questions and answers to the definition of criteria for boundaries and membership of collectivities, and combining them with the principles of criteria of allocation of power within societies.

All these specify the broader parameters within which the organizational problems of any such group are set—i.e., the boundaries of the environment of the respective groups and the ranges of possible responses to the "pressures" of such environment. Above all they play a central role in the cybernetic mechanisms of any social system—both primary and secondary cybernetics (Maruyama 1964)—and in the crystallization of the specific morphostatic and morphogenic tendencies of any such system (Buckley 1967).

Above all, they influence the ways in which the general functions necessary for the working of social systems will perform within any concrete setting. In this way they also influence, once such systems or congeries of codes are institutionalized, the range of their systemic sensitivities, the salience of different potential conflicts and problems of the continuity of the given systems, and the ways in which different systems cope with the specific range of problems and crises they face, as well as the possible outcome of such crises—especially of modes of "incorporation" or various dimensions of social and political expansion.

These patterns of codes influence the conception of the major political problems: the specific types of conflicts to which they are especially sensitive, the types of conditions under which the potentialities for such conflicts become articulated into more specific "boiling points" which may threaten the stability of any regime, the ways in which the regimes cope with these problems of conflict, and especially the ways of incorporating various types of political demands—those of growing participation in the political order. In particular, such codes influence the intensity of these types of conflicts and the perception of their acuteness—the range of "flexibility" or of rigidity in response to them and the relative importance of regressive (as against expansive) policies in coping with them (a fuller exposition of such differential systemic sensitivities of one type of politics is given in Eisenstadt 1973c). Different patterns of codes do also shape the mode of change that develops in different societies; thus it has been shown that revolutionary changes develop only in those civilizations within which there is prevalent a strong perception of tension between the transcendental and the mundane order, and a this-worldly, or combined this- and other-worldly mode of resolution of such tension (Eisenstadt 1978).

V. THE OPENNESS OF SYSTEMS OF CODES IN RELATION TO CONCRETE INSTITUTIONALIZATION

The preceding analysis bears out in fuller detail the assertion made earlier that these basic institutional derivatives of codes which constitute the ground rules of social interaction and "hidden structure" are not concretized through some sort of direct "emanation" of the institutional rules derived from symbolic premises of the codes and models of social structure, or from some general laws of the human mind. The process of their concrete crystallization or institutionalization involves elements of openness, choice and uncertainty.

This can be demonstrated even more forcefully by the fact that there exists no simple one-to-one relation between such cultural models or patterns of codes and any specific regime or macrosocietal order. The ways in which basic problems and dilemmas are defined and resolved in an articulated cultural model, or in the broad pattern of codes, do not necessarily correspond only to one specific pattern of institutionalization.

Within any tradition or social order, the possible relations among its different components are not exhausted by their actual coalescence in the existing institutionalized system. Within each such order there exist several ranges of freedom with respect to the concrete possibilities of institutionalization of the various derivatives of codes.

Concretely, such openness of different cultural models and systems of codes is evident in the fact that the same cultural model or pattern of codes can be institutionalized in different—if not endless—types of political regimes or economic systems. Thus, for instance, codes that specify the general types of relations between, let us say, the political and social or cultural order can leave undefined the concrete settings or boundaries of such organizations and units. For example, while an emphasis on the importance of the fusion of the political and cultural communities is basic to all of Islam, the way it can be institutionalized has varied greatly from one situation to another—from the tribal setting of Arabia, to the centralized empires of the Middle East, to the more shifting centers of North Africa (Gellner 1973; Mardin 1973; Yalman 1973). Within each such situation, rather different societal orientations may operate and different cultural themes emphasized.

Even in the more "compact" traditional societies, like China, Japan, and Burma, where there is greater coalescence between the cultural and political orders, these codes have been institutionalized in various ways (Bellah 1972; Wakeman 1972). Thus in China, the tension between the ideals of sociopolitical involvement of the individual and of inner harmony can be played out in the distinction between the lonely scholar and the bureaucrat on the one hand, and between the legalistic official and the Taoist-Buddhist mystic on the other (Wakeman 1972).

The fact that there is great choice in the institutionalization of codes is manifest on several levels. To begin with, there exists some openness in the coalescence between the two major types of codes—those oriented to the existential problems of human life and those oriented to the symbolism of the special dilemmas of social life. Thus any specific institutional concretization of, let us say, a strong emphasis on the political dimension of human life, together with conceptions of a very strong correlation—and tension—between the cosmic and cultural order may be defined in a strongly ritualistic, Third-World manner, as in China, or transcendentally, as in Islam. The concretization may be combined in different historical situations, in different concrete regimes, and with varying emphasis on hierarchy or equality, conflict or harmony; and great or small value may be placed upon the relative importance of power, solidarity, or instrumental attributes of social order.

Second, any such institutionalization of a model or pattern of codes entails the specification of the appropriate "here and now"—the concrete setting, groups, or collectivity—as distinct from other such groups; the *concrete* criteria of membership, with an emphasis on a specific group with its primordial symbols, or its particular dogma.

Such specification is very closely related to the other major type of institutional derivative of symbolic orientations—to the concretization of the symbols of collective identity which are taken up and crystallized in any such situation. The various symbols of collective and personal identity which are constructed in the process of institutionalization of such models and patterns of codes—even if they are taken out of the reservoir of traditional symbols—are rarely simply given. They are continuously being reconstituted and reconstructed. This becomes especially vivid in situations of far-reaching social and cultural change. In such situations, cultural traditions, symbols, artifacts, and organizations become more elaborate, more rationally organized, or at least more formalized and articulated, as different groups and individuals in a society become increasingly aware of these traditions and symbols. That is, "tradition" becomes differentiated in layers. Simple "given" usages or patterns of behavior may become quite distinct from these more articulated and formalized symbols of the cultural order—such as the great ritual centers and offices, theological codices, or special buildings. The layers of tradition tend also to vary in the degree and nature of their prescriptive validity and in their relevance to different spheres of life. These processes are often related to a growing "partialization" and privatization of various older existing traditions or customs. Even if the "old" customs and symbols are not negated or "thrown out" they undergo far-reaching changes (Eisenstadt 1973b; Yalman 1973).

VI. THE SPECIAL CHARACTERISTICS AND MECHANISMS OF THE PROCESS OF INSTITUTIONALIZATION OF THE GROUND RULES OF SOCIAL INTERACTION: THE CONDITIONALITIES, TITLES, AND INSTITUTIONAL ENTREPRENEURS

It is only through all these processes of selection, through the combination of these different elements—each with its own tendencies or rules—that any model of cultural and social order, as well as of patterns of codes, can become concretized and impinge on the working of concrete social groups or collectivities.

Such concretization is effected through processes of institutionalization with very strong elements of struggle, choice, and coalition making. But the processes of institutionalization of the institutional derivatives of codes, of the ground rules of social interaction, contrast rather sharply with relatively free exchange of resources in open institutionalized markets regulated either by rules of supply and demand or rules of operant psychology or with the "direct" provision for the "needs" of social groups. We are only beginning to analyze these problems, and only some very preliminary indications can be discerned.

The most general mechanism of the regulations of the patterns of interaction and of the flow of resources in a society (Coleman 1971), through which these aspects of institutional life are regulated is the specification of unconditionalities—of patterns of interaction in social institutional settings which are not based on the direct conditional but rather on indirect giving and receiving of services, resources, and rewards, and on the setting up of "titles" (Eisenstadt 1971c). The construction of unconditionalities takes place through the institutionalization of various ascriptive limitations on institutional interaction or exchange on access to positions as well as on the use of resources for establishing the rules of such access. Ascriptive restrictions on exchange mean that an actor, even if he possesses the commodities relevant to a given exchange and is willing to enter into the exchange, is excluded because he belongs to some group or category of people.

The most important aspect of such restrictions, from the point of view of the regulation of the flow of resources, is the combination of economic resources and power with prestige—not only with prestige as a symbolic dimension of interpersonal relations but, above all, as the structural principle which regulates the access to participation in some relatively "exclusive" order: membership in a collective, in societal centers, or in the cultural orders (Eisenstadt 1973b). The pursuit of discrete goals—whether for economic gain, power, or interpersonal prestige—is linked to such participation in various societal and cultural orders. This linkage creates the structural, as distinct from the purely interpersonal, aspects of prestige and underlies the central role of prestige as the potential transformer or regulator of other media (Eisenstadt 1973b).

The formation of these institutional patterns is effected in special frameworks and through interaction among the occupants of special types of social positions. Thus the establishment of such unconditionalities and their continuous regulation takes place, in contrast to markets based on barter or on the free interchange of various media and resources, in special hierarchical frameworks. Among such frameworks are ritual and communicative situations (analyzed above) in which reference orientations of different population groups are set up. Various legal and political frameworks are included as well (see also Williamson 1973a,b).

These unconditionalities and organizational frameworks and the consequent restrictions on exchange they entail are constituted by the cross-cutting of two levels of social interaction. The first is interaction (cooperative or conflictual) between those people, holders of different positions or members of different groups, who can be designated as institutional entrepreneurs (Barth 1963;

Eisenstadt 1973a,b,c). Such people articulate models of social order, set up new norms and organizational frameworks, and mobilize the necessary public resources. Second is the interaction between social units (or their representatives). They are mostly oriented to the assuring the flow of some mutual solidarity and of the establishment of continuity of social interaction among those individuals, strata, and groups who are ready to provide such resources—i.e. those who are willing to pay something for these entrepreneurial activities. (See also Cartwright and Schwartz 1973 for one of the few concrete analytical studies of the development of such norms.)

It is through these types of interaction that the ground rules of social interaction are institutionalized and, above all, combinations of membership with principles of power—of "codes and identity"—are institutionalized. They are derived from the "meeting" of the symbolic with the organizational aspects of social life. They differ from "regular" institutional interaction in that they regulate not only the flow, exchange, and conversion of organizational resources (especially economic resources and power), but also that they combine—above all through the different mechanisms of prestige—such resources with the symbolic orientations in general, and with different symbols of identity in particular.

The institutionalization of these ground rules does not "solve" the problems of social order. Rather it transposes it and its ambivalences to the meeting of the symbolic and the organizational aspects of social life. The nature of these ambivalences and their selection to the institutionalization of the ground rules of social interaction can be best seen in the situations in which such institutionalization is symbolized.

VII. THE SYMBOLIZATION OF MODELS OF SOCIAL ORDER AND THEIR INSTITUTIONALIZATION IN RITUAL AND COMMUNICATIVE SITUATIONS

Any such normative specification and legitimation inherent in the institutionalization of the selection of the derivatives of patterns of codes involves the prohibition and sanctioning of some patterns of behavior, as well as the exclusion of other situations and groups. Hence it is only natural that such specification also creates a very strong ambivalence about the concrete "resolution" of human predicaments provided in any such model and about the consequent exclusion of other possibilities. Ambivalence is also created about the need to employ sanctions through which these models and the norms derived from them are maintained.

Hence, each model or system or complexes of codes contains within it several points of tension, which are inherent in the contradictions that develop within any such system itself and in its application to the creation of institutional complexes.

These contradictions tend to cluster around certain themes or poles, according to their perception and formulation on the symbolic level. Among such themes the most important are the varying ways of structuring the differences in human life between nature and culture; the perennial encounter between the quest for solidarity and the exigencies of division of labor and political struggle; the tension between the givens of power and its exercise and the search for more transcendental types of legitimation of the social order; and the degree to which various models of cosmic, human, and social order can provide foci for meaningful human endeavor. Such themes tend to coalesce in different ways in different models.

These ambivalences are most fully and dramatically played out in special social situations (Geertz 1973, ch. 15; Peacock 1968b; Eisenstadt 1965, section V)—in plays, public displays, private encounters, jokes, and various types of myths (Peacock 1968a,b; Munn 1973b). But they tend to be most fully articulated in those ritual occasions which are most closely related to individual and collective *rites de passage*—be they rituals of birth, initiation, wedding, and death; or of first-fruits collective ceremonies, and those occasions in which routine is to some extent broken or disturbed (Eisenstadt 1968). Rites of passage tend to become fully articulated in (a) situations where there is some transition from one institutional sphere to another; contemporaneous activity in several institutional spheres, or in several subsystems of a society; (b) situations where various subsystems must be directly connected with the central values and activities of a society; (c) situations where people are faced with a choice among various roles; (d) situations where the routine of a given role of an individual or group is endangered or disrupted.

In all such situations the individual is placed in potentially ambiguous, undefined, and conflicting conditions in which his identity and status image and the continuity of his perception of other actions are endangered.

These various situations—the more structured individual and collective rites of passage reported in anthropological studies, and the less structured "communicative situations" of modern societies—have a common denominator: people or groups involved in these situations experience some shattering of the existing social and cultural order to which they are bound. Hence they become more sensitive to symbols or messages that attempt to symbolize such order, and are more ready to respond to people who are able to present new symbols to them. Such new symbols could give meaning to their experience in terms of some broader fundamental, cosmic, social, or political order; they may prescribe the proper norms of behavior, relate the individual to collective identification, and reassure him of his status and in place in a given collectivity.

Such situations do not arise only in catastrophic conditions. They constitute part of any orderly social life—of the life of individuals as they pass from one stage in their lifespan to another, or from one sphere of activities to another. They also occur in organizations of groups and societies.

In all these situations the cognitive, evaluative, and affective aspects of such symbolization are focused on the ambivalences inherent in the concretization of the models of social and cultural order, and around the dilemmas of human existence and social life. In such situations these dilemmas, and the various subconscious orientations toward them, serve as focal points of the meeting between the cultural evaluation of different attributes (natural and cultural) of people and of the organizational problems of social division of labor and of participation in it, and of the tensions inherent in any such meeting. Especially important here are the tensions between the ideal models of social and cosmic orders and the possibilities of their actualization in life; between different dimensions of prestige; between dimensions of solidarity and between the givens of social division of labor (Turner 1968; Geertz 1973).

Thus in such situations the models of cosmic, social, and cultural orders, and the choices of action they imply, are often focused around the evaluation of interpersonal relations in basic groups—family, work, etc.—the tensions involved and their resolution are formulated in terms of the evaluation of life and death or sexual prowess, age, or symbols of purity and pollution. Hence such symbolization is also focused around the major primordial symbols of personal and collective identity (Douglas 1966, 1970; Turner 1968; Silverman 1971; Munn 1973b).

In the construction of such answers, the objects closest to these problems—bodily characteristics and functions, some basic aspects of the natural environment, as well as of the major attributes of solidarity, or power—become foci of evaluative symbolism, of purity, and pollution. They become components and symbols of personal and collective identity and guides in performance of many social tasks and activities (Douglass 1966, 1970; Schneider 1968, 1972; Schneider and Smith 1973).

Hence in all such communicative and ritual situations, what may be called the natural givens of any of the respective institutional spheres—sex, age, and procreation in the family, power and force in politics, or the extraction of resources from nature in economics—are usually dramatized, evaluated, and related to the organizational problems of each sphere. In fact, however, there is no "natural" predestined correspondence between any organizational problem and any given fixed set of symbols (Schneider 1968, 1972; Silverman 1971; Meggit 1972). For instance, although in most societies there is a predilection toward combining the placement of new members with symbols of procreation, this need not always be the case. Similarly, although some symbols of blood do indeed enter into the definition of familial identity, in some societies such natural biological data may be crystallized as symbols of polity, or of different types of cultural orders, and not of family or kinship (Ossowski 1948).

All such situations are characterized by a very high element of ritualization. Such ritualization highlights two strongly connected functions of the ground rules of social interaction that are derived from the meeting between the symbolic and the organizational aspects of social life. The strong element of formalization inherent in ritualization restricts the freedom potentially given in any human discourse (Maurice Bloch 1974). In this way it defines and symbolizes the given environment of any group or society and maintains some cybernetic control within it (Rappaport 1971; Munn 1973b).

VIII. CONCLUSION: THE POSSIBILITIES AND LIMITATIONS OF THE APPLICATION OF STRUCTURAL ANALYSIS TO SOCIAL ORGANIZATION

The preceding analysis has illustrated in relatively detailed ways that the "hidden structure" of social order, as presumably represented by the programmatic derivatives of codes, is not just a set of abstract rules of the "human mind" which are somehow reflected in social organization. Hidden structure is effected through complicated institutional processes and mechanisms. This analysis has indicated that, as in other spheres of symbolic patterning of human experience, it is the "schemata" of the respective sphere and not the "objective" contents of the objects of such experience that provides the decisive principles of cognitive and evaluative organization of human behavior, of the hidden structure or contexts or such behavior. (Munn 1973b; Turner 1973; and for a classical exposition, Cassirer 1953). But the schemata operative in the social field are not purely cognitive, "prelogical" or logical ones. They are (Geertz 1973, chs. 1, 13) closely combined with the more existential dimension of human life and social organization.

It may be true of course that on a very high level of abstraction some very common general tendencies of such coding or structuring—like those of "mediation" between polar opposites—are common to all systems of human creativity and activity. But this, in itself, does not tell us about the ways in which these principles influence the construction and operation of different concrete spheres of human activity. Whatever the degree or scope of such universal rules, their concrete crystallization (and hence the possibility of creation of new contents and combinations) is possible only when they unfold in concrete interaction.

The most crucial aspect of such interaction (probably contrary to the exposition of some structuralists) is the openness of both "models and "codes" with respect to the ranges of their concretization in institutional life. Such openness implies that the concretization of such rules and models entails some potentialities of innovation, and that it is effected through some concrete processes of human activity—which have some rules or tendencies of their own. Hence the concretization of such codes and models is mediated by those different problems specific to these different spheres of activity.

Thus, insofar as it is meaningful to talk about hidden structure with respect to social organization, the meaning of the term structure here is much nearer to the way Piaget (1970) tends to use it, as Terry Turner has put it (1973:371): "Structures . . . are not conceived as directly fulfilling functions, or indeed, as 'acting.' They consist rather, in generalized codes or mechanisms for regulating the functional activities of 'subjects.' . . .

"As against this concept Lévi-Strauss' concept of structure, as Piaget notes is static, atemporal, anti-functionalist, and leaves no place for the activity of the subject." (See also Geertz 1973, ch. 13.)

But here we encounter some limitation of Piaget's own analysis in general and its bearing on the problems of social organization in particular. Piaget's definition of structure does not distinguish between different types of structure that are specific to different types of objects and organizations—mathematical or logical operations as contrasted with, for instance, social organization.

Our analysis has provided some indications about these problems. We have discussed the nature of the specific symbolic orientations and of the problems of these models and codes, oriented to the working of systems and the institutional loci on which they impinge.

We have also discussed the relations between such rules and the organizational aspects of social life. It has shown that these orientations and rules are indeed related to such problems—but at the same time they are not identical with the concrete organizational "functional" problems of any specific social group or system.

Thus, the influence of cultural models and systems of codes in the social field does not automatically stem from some natural emanation of these models and codes. It constitutes a crucial—although special—aspect of the process of institutionalization, with very strong elements of power struggle, choice, resolution of conflicts, and coalition-making. But these elements refer to a level, or aspect, of institutionalization which differs from concrete organizational interaction and from the concrete organizational interaction of groups and collectivities. It therefore entails possibly different rules, carriers, and modes of continuity. We do indeed encounter one of the most difficult problems of our analysis—the identification of the different social carriers and mechanisms through which distinct levels of the institutional order are crystallized. The analysis of the different characteristics of these levels of institutionalization and of their interrelation constitutes one of the basic challenges for sociological and anthropological analysis in general, and for the further elucidation of structuralist approaches to social organization in particular. In the preceding pages we have attempted to provide some initial indications in this direction.

REFERENCES

Barth, F. 1963. *The Role of Entrepreneur in Social Change in Northern Norway.* Bergen: Artok.

Bellah, R. N. 1972. "Intellectual and society in Japan." *Daedalus* (Spring 1972):89–117.

Bloch, Maurice. 1974. "Symbols and songs, dance and features of articulation; or, Is religion an extreme form of traditional authority?" *Archives Europeens de Sociologie* 15:55–82.

Boon, J. A. 1972. *From Symbolism to Structuralism.* Oxford, Basil Blackwell.

Buchler, Ira R., and Hugo G. Nutini, eds. 1969. *Introduction to Game Theory in the Behavioral Sciences,* pp. 1–23. Pittsburgh: University of Pittsburgh Press.

Buckley, W. 1967. *Sociology and Modern Systems Theory.* Englewood Cliffs, N.J., Prentice-Hall.

Cartwright, B. C., and R. D. Schwartz. 1973. "The invocation of legal norms: An empirical investigation of Durkheim and Weber." *American Sociological Review* (June) 38:340–54.

Cassirer, E. 1953. *The Philosophy of Symbolic Forms.* New Haven: Yale University Press.

Coleman, J. S. 1971. *Resources for Social Change.* New York: Wiley.

Davis, J. A. 1963. "Structural balance, mechanical solidarity and interpersonal relations." *American Journal of Sociology* 68:446–62.

Douglas, M. 1966. *Purity and Danger.* London: Routledge & Kegan Paul.

———1970 *Natural Symbols.* Harmondsworth, Middlesex: Penguin Books.

Dumont, L. 1971. *Homo Hierarchicus.* Chicago: University of Chicago Press.

Durkheim, E. 1933. *On the Division of Labor in Society.* New York: Macmillan.

Eisenstadt, S. N. 1965. *Essays on Comparative Institutions.* New York: Wiley.

——— 1968. *Charisma and Institution Building: Max Weber and Modern Sociology.* Chicago: University of Chicago Press.

——— 1971a. "General introduction: The scope and problems of political sociology." In Eisenstadt, ed. *Political Sociology.* New York: Basic Books.

——— 1971b. *Social Differentiation and Stratification.* Glenview: Scott, Foresman.

——— 1971c. "Societal goals, systemic needs, social interaction and individual behavior: Some tentative explanations." In Herman Turk and Richard R. Simpson, eds. *Institutions and Social Exchange—The Sociologies of Talcott Parsons and George C. Homans,* pp. 36–56. New York: Bobbs-Merrill.

——— 1973a. "Post-traditional societies and the continuity and reconstruction of tradition." *Daedalus* (Winter), pp. 1–29.

——— 1973b. *Tradition, Change and Modernity.* New York: Wiley.

——— 1973c. "Traditional patrimonialism and modern neopatrimonialism." *Sage Research Papers in the Social Sciences* 1 (90-003). (Studies in Comparative Modernization Series.) Beverly Hills, London: Sage Publications.

——— 1978. *Revolution and the Transformation of Societies.* New York: The Free Press.

Eisenstadt, S. N. and M. Curelaru. 1976. *The Form of Sociology—Paradigms and Crises.* New York: Wiley.

Geertz, C. 1973. *The Interpretation of Cultures.* New York: Basic Books.

Geertz, H. 1965. Comment on Professor P. E. Josselin de Jong [1965a]. *Journal of Asian Studies* 24(2):294–97.

Gellner, C. 1973. "Post-traditional forms in Islam: The turf and trades, and votes and peanuts." *Daedalus* (Winter), pp. 191–207.

Godelier, M. 1973. *Horizons, Trajets Marxistes en Anthropologie.* Paris: E. Anthropos.

Hammel, D. 1972. "The myth of structural analysis." Addison-Wesley Modules in the Social Sciences. New York: Addison-Wesley.

Hayes, E. N. and T. Hayes, eds. 1970. *Claude Lévi-Strauss, The Anthropologist as Hero.* Cambridge: MIT Press.

de Heusch, L. 1971. *Pourquoi s'epouser.* Paris: Gallimard.

Josselin de Jong, J. P. B. 1922. "De Couvade." *Mededeelingen der Koninklijke Akademie Van Wetenschappen* 54(B):53–84.

Josselin de Jong, P. E. 1951. *Minanqkaba and Negri Sembilan. Socio-Political Structure in Indonesia.* Leiden: Eduard Ijdo.

—— 1960. "Cultural anthropology in the Netherlands." *Higher Education and Research in the Netherlands,* 4:13.

—— 1964. "Circulerent connubium en het dubbelunilineals principe." *Bijdragen Tot de Taal-, Land- en Volkenkunde* 120:181–94.

—— 1965a "An interpretation of agricultural rites in Southeast Asia, with a demonstration of use of data from both continental and insular areas." *Journal of Asian Studies* 24(2):283–91.

—— 1965b. Reply to Professor Hildred Geertz [1965]. *Ibid.,* pp. 297–98.

—— 1971. "Presumed behavior: Comments on Cara E. Richards' brief communication." *American Anthropologist* 73:270–73.

Kobben, A. J. F. 1966. "Structuralism versus comparative functionalism: Some comments." *Bijdragen Tot de Taal-, Land- en Volkenkunde* 122:145–50.

Kohlberg, L. 1971. "Stage and sequence: The cognitive developmental approach to socialization." In David A. Goslin, ed. *Handbook of Socialization Theory and Research,* pp. 347–481. Chicago: Rand McNally.

Kuhn, A. 1963. *The Study of Society—A Unified Approach.* Homewood, Illinois: Dorsey.

Lane, M., ed. 1970. *Structuralism.* London: Jonathan Cape.

Leach, E. 1954. *Political Systems of Highland Burma.* London: C. Bell & Sons.

—— 1960. "The frontiers of Burma." *Comparative Studies in Sociology and History* 3(11):49–68.

—— 1961. *Paul Eliya. A Village in Ceylon.* Cambridge: Cambridge University Press.

—— 1965. "Claude Lévi-Strauss—anthropologist and philosopher." *New Left Review* 34:12–28.

—— 1968. *Genesis as Myth and Other Essays,* eds. W. Lepenies and H. Ritter. London: Jonathan Cape.

—— 1972. *Orte des Wilden Denkens.* Frankfurt: Suhrkampf.

Lévi-Strauss, C. 1963. *Structural Anthropology.* New York: Basic Books.

—— 1966. *The Savage Mind.* Chicago: University of Chicago Press.

—— 1969. *The Elementary Structures of Kinship,* ed. Rodney Needham. London: Eyre & Spottiswoodle.

MacRae, D. 1968. Introduction to Raymond Boudon, *The Uses of Structuralism.* London: Heimann.

Mardin, S. 1973. "Center periphery relations: A key to Turkish politics? *Daedalus* (Winter), pp. 169–91.

Maruyama, M. 1963. "The second cybernetics: Deviation amplifying mutual causal processes." *American Scientist* 51:64–79.

Maybury-Lewis, D. 1960. "The analysis of dual organisation: A methodological critique." *Antropologica. Bijdragen Tot de Taal-, Land- en Volkenkunde* 116:17–45.

Mayhew, L. 1971. *Society; Institutions and Action.* Glencoe, Illinois: Scott Forseman.

Mead, G. H. 1934. *Mind, Self, and Society.* Chicago: University of Chicago Press.

Meggit, M. 1972. "Understanding Australian Aboriginal society: Kinship systems or cultural categories." In P. Reining, ed. *Kinship Studies in the Morgan Centennial Year.* Washington, D.C.: Anthropological Society of Washington.

Munn, Nancy D. 1973a. *Waibiri Iconography. Graphic Representation and Cultural Symbols in a Central Australian Society.* Ithaca, N.Y.: Cornell University Press.

—— 1973b "Symbolism in ritual context—aspects of symbolic action." In J. Honigman, ed. *A Handbook of Social and Cultural Anthropology,* pp. 579–613. Chicago: Rand McNally.

Needham, R. 1960. "A Structural Analysis of Aimol Society." *Antropologica. Bijdragen Tot de Taal-, Land- en Volkenkunde* 116:81–109.

Olson, M. Jr. 1968. *The Logic of Collective Action.* New York: Schocken.

Ossowski, S. 1948. *Wiez Spoleczna l Dziedzichwo Krwi* (Social Bond and Block Inheritance). Warsawa: Ksiazka.

Parsons, T. 1951. *The Social System.* Glencoe, Ill.: The Free Press.

—— 1961. "Introduction to culture and the social system." In T. Parsons and E. Shils, eds. *Theories of Society,* part 4, 2:963–992. Glencoe, Ill.: The Free Press.

—— 1973a. "Durkheim on religion revisited: Another look at the elementary forms of the religious life." In Charles Y. Glock and Phillip E. Hammond, eds. *Beyond the Classics,* pp. 156–80. New York: Harper & Row.

Parsons, T. and G. Platt. 1973. *The American University.* Cambridge, Mass.: Harvard University Press.

Parsons, T. and E. Shils, eds. 1951. *Toward a General Theory of Action.* Cambridge: Harvard University Press.

Peacock, J. L. 1968a. "A problem in the study of ideals: Lévi-Strauss' statistical and mechanical models." Paper prepared for Symposium No. 41, Wenner-Gren Foundation for Anthropological Research.

—— 1968b. *Rites of Modernization: Symbols and Social Aspects of Indonesian Proletarian Dramas.* Chicago: University of Chicago Press.

Piaget, J. 1932. *The Moral Judgement of the Child.* London: Routledge & Kegan Paul.

—— 1970, *Structuralism.* New York: Basic Books.

Pouwer, J. 1964. "A social system in the star mountains: Toward a reorientation of the study of social systems." *American Anthropologist* 66:133–61.

—— 1966a. "Referential and inferential Reality. A rejoinder." *Bijdragen Tot de Taal-, Land- en Volkenkunde,* 122:151–57.

—— 1966b. "Structure and flexibility in a new society." *Ibid.* pp. 158–69.

—— 1966c. "The structural and functional approach in cultural anthropology: Theoretical reflections with reference to research in western New Guinea." *Ibid.* pp. 129–44.

Rappaport, R. 1971. "The sacred in human evolution." *Annual Review of Ecology and Systematics* 2:23–24.

Rossi, I. 1973. "The unconscious in the anthropology of Claude Lévi-Strauss." *American Anthropologist* 25:20–49.

Rotenstreich, N. 1972. "On Lévi-Strauss' concept of structure." *The Review of Metaphysics* 25(3):489–526.

Schneider, D. M. 1968. *American Kinship: A Cultural Account.* Englewood Cliffs, New Jersey: Prentice-Hall, Inc.

—— 1972. "What is kinship all about?" In P. Reining, ed. *Kinship Studies in the Morgan Centennial Year,* pp. 32–64. Washington, D.C.: Anthropological Society of Washington.

Schneider, D. M., and R. T. Smith. 1973. *Class Differences and Sex Roles in American Kinship and Family Structure.* Englewood Cliffs, N.J.: Prentice-Hall.

Scholte, B. 1966. "Epistemic paradigms: Some problems in cross-cultural research on social anthropological history and theory." *American Anthropologist* 68:1192–1200.

—— 1973. "The structural anthropology of Claude Lévi-Strauss." J. Honigman, ed. In *A Handbook of Social and Cultural Anthropology,* pp. 637–717. Chicago: Rand McNally.

Schulte-Nordholdt, G. H. 1971. *The Political System of the Atoni of Timor.* The Hague: Martinus Nijhoff.

Sebag, L. 1964. *Marxisme et Structuralisme.* Paris: Payot

Shils, E. 1961. "Center and periphery." In *The Logic of Personal Knowledge: Essays Presented to M. Polanyi,* pp. 117–31. London: Routledge and Kegan Paul.

—— 1965. "Charisma, order, and status." *American Sociological Review* 30(2):199–213.

Silverman, Martin G. 1971. *Disconcerting Issue: Meaning and Struggle in a Resettled Pacific Community*. Chicago, London: The University of Chicago Press.

Tiryakian, E. A. 1970. "Structural sociology." In J. C. McKinney and E. A. Tiryahian, eds. *Theoretical Sociology: Perspectives and Developments*, pp. 112–35. New York: Appleton, Century-Crofts.

Turner, T. 1973. "Piaget's structuralism." *American Anthropologist* 75:351–73.

Turner, V. 1968. "Myth and symbol." *International Encyclopedia of the Social Sciences*, pp. 576–82. New York: Collier Macmillan.

Wakeman, F. J. 1972. "The Price of autonomy: Intellectuals in Ming and Ching politics." *Daedalus* (Spring), p. 351.

Weber, M. 1947. *From Max Weber, Essays in Sociology*. London: Routledge & Kegan Paul.

—— 1958. *The Religion of India: The Sociology of Hinduism and Buddhism*. New York: The Free Press.

—— 1964. *The Religion of China: Confucianism and Taoism*. New York: Macmillan.

Williamson, D. E. 1973a. "Some notes on the economics of Atmosphere." Fels Discussion Paper No. 29. University of Pennsylvania, The Fels Center of Government.

—— 1973b. "Markets and hierarchies: Some elementary considerations." *American Economic Review*, pp. 316–25.

Yalman, N. 1973. "Some observations on Secularism in Islam: The cultural revolution in Turkey." *Daedalus* 1:139–69.

PART THREE

THE STRUCTURE OF MORAL ORDER

PIAGETIAN AND CHOMSKIAN PERSPECTIVES

CHAPTER EIGHT

MORALITY, JUSTICE, AND SOCIAL CHOICE

NATURAL FOUNDATIONS FOR THE CONSTRUCTION OF SOCIAL ORDER

THOMAS F. CONDON and STEPHEN G. WIETING

I. GENERAL INTRODUCTION

The concept "social structure" carries a variety of meanings and applications. Our unifying aim here is to clarify and illustrate a "constructivist" approach to social structure. Here, "construction" implies a reciprocal relationship between "structure" and the processes of "structuring." More specifically, our aims are twofold: (a) to introduce sociologists to the "genetic structuralism" of Jean Piaget (1970a), posing this as an alternative to the more familiar, empirically oriented approach to structure; (b) to indicate how his "genetic structuralism" provides new insights into both the origins of structure and the process by which new social structures may be constructed.

Piaget is generally construed as a developmental psychologist, so his program of research is not apt to be familiar to sociologists. However, by considering what he means by "developmental," we can lay a foundation for demonstrating his relevance. Piaget typically begins one of his numerous inquiries by comparing and contrasting three alternative answers to the question of the "origins of structure" (e.g., 1970a:60–68). These three, exhaustive possibilities are:

(1) *Preformed*, as in archetypes, "innate" dispositions or predispositions of behavior, or the genetic determinism of the new synthesis of sociobiology;

(2) *Contingent Emergence*, as structures seen as given or whose origins are simply unquestioned, as in gestalt psychology or macrosociology;

(3) *Constructed*, where structures arise and consolidate as the product of the irreducible interaction between properties of the actors, *and* properties of their conventional social environment.

Piaget refers to the first alternative as "genesis without structure," to the second as "structure without genesis," and the third as "genetic structuralism." To clarify what he means by these labels, we shall illustrate each of these three alternatives.

A. PREFORMED STRUCTURES: GENESIS WITHOUT STRUCTURE

The publication of *Sociobiology: The New Synthesis* (Wilson 1975) provides an exceptional opportunity to clarify the first alternative; it is also highly relevant to sociology, since it seeks to assimilate sociology into its theoretical perspective—i.e. to "biologicize" sociology. On its own terms, sociobiology is: (a) *materialistic* (mind and behavior "have an entirely materialist basis"; Wilson 1978:65); (b) inclined to view the actor as a "robot" or pawn (Dawkins 1978); (c) *reductionistic* (see Wilson's discussion of disciplines/anti-disciplines, 1978:1–13); (d) *deterministic* (while he acknowledges the principle of indeterminacy [1978], Wilson believes that even in a coin-toss we could, with sufficient information, determine the exact outcome [Wilson and Bossert 1971]); (e) somewhat ambiguous on the core "motives" underlying behavior ("gene selectionists" see man as inherently "selfish" [Dawkins 1978], while group-selection implies altruism as a prime motive [Wilson 1978]); (f) *atomistic* (the core theory is based upon Mendelian populations—i.e. independent elements, such as "genes"—hence is opposed to the "holism" of Durkheim [Wilson 1978:78]). All of these properties reflect a priority of "genesis" over "structure." Hence, before assenting to the proposed "biologicizing" of their discipline, sociologists ought to recognize this disequilibrium.

For instance, Dawkins argues that the flow of causality between genotype and phenotype is, strictly, gene to phenotype (1978:24). But this is rotten genetics since the environment (selection pressure) may favor one phenotype over others, thus indirectly affecting genotype frequencies. Similarly, Dawkins overemphasizes "stability" (1978; ch. 2) at the neglect of "variety."[1] While stability is essential for the very slow course of natural selection to design organisms, variety is essential any time a shift occurs in selection pressure. In point of fact, "genetic variance" is the *fundamental theorem of natural selection* (Wilson and Bossert 1971:79). So, the overemphasis on *stability* arises at the neglect of its complement, *variety*, giving the theory of sociobiology a decided one-sidedness.

In discussing "disciplines" and "antidisciplines," Wilson argues that, just as the laws of biology must be consistent with those of its antidiscipline, chemistry, so, the laws of sociology must be reducible and consistent with those of biology. In context, he sees a simple, singular hierarchy of science: mathematics and physics constituting the base, followed by chemistry, biology and genetics, and then the social sciences/humanities. But such "objectivity" is highly controversial and neglects historical facts. In Karl Popper's terms (e.g., Popper and Eccles 1977) "objective knowledge" is first and foremost a cultural (World 3) product. While natural selection may have occurred for millennia, it took a cultural construction for the theories of Darwin and Wallace, and the experiments of Mendel, to be developed. In this light, culture and social structure are the base sciences upon which are erected all other sciences. Having missed this crucial point, Wilson was taken by surprise when he was accused of racism, sexism, etc.

Finally, in his discussion of "ethics" (Wilson 1978: ch. 1 and 7, 8, 9), we find the following ideas: humans, while "consistent in their codes of honor"—presumably reflecting deep structures in the hypothalamus-limbic[2] structures of the brain, which in turn has been programmed by genes—are notoriously "fickle" in choosing to whom the codes apply. The terms "consistent" and "fickle" obviously connote "strength" and "weakness," respectively, from an objective, scientific viewpoint. Theoretical progress depends upon objects which are stable, consistent, and persevere in their manifestations. At the same time, however, change and the production of new structures requires a degree of fickle unpredictability. Furthermore, the choice of whom the codes of ethics apply to depends crucially upon existing patterns of social structure—e.g., in-group allegiances vs. the outgroups. Hence, the study of ethics implies, in Wilson's own terms, the interaction between innate dispositions *and* social structural arrangements; in fact *all* applications of the natural selection theory implies such an interactive term. We shall return to this theme of the code of ethics and its application shortly.

In sum, sociobiology well illustrates a preformed, genesis-without-structure alternative. All of the properties outlined above, and which characterize the sociobiological enterprise, reflect an undue emphasis on sturdy, material substructures, or "genotypes," at the neglect of complementary properties which are essential for understanding both structure and structuring-as-process. We turn now to a consideration of these complements.

B. CONTINGENT EMERGENCE: STRUCTURE WITHOUT GENESIS

If we think of sociology as a science of the environment, *vis à vis* sociobiology, then it is marked by the following properties (complementary to those of sociobiology): (1) symbol-systems, where actors are producers and not merely robots; (2) attention focuses on emergent qualities, indeterminacy and the contextual-relational nexus of meanings, motives, etc. Whereas genetics views motive as a pre-wired disposition, sociology recognizes that motive comes from a derived grammar/meaning system. In short, *meaning* implicates system and context; any one term gets its meaning in a context of similarities and oppositions with other terms. Hence, a core opposition between genetics and sociology is that between (1) an autonomous, elementary unit, as is required in Mendelian theory; and (2) a holistic, systemic context for units as in language and social structure. Relatedly, where biology is Darwinian selection, sociology is Lamarckian (see Bronowski 1973) selection. Finally, Lamarckian selection means that acquired characteristics can be transmitted to future generations as through socialization. We might expect, then, that sociocultural systems contain more information than do genes; just as brains, with their incredible degree of interconnectedness, may contain more information than do genes (Sagan 1977).

If this characterization of sociology is anywhere near the mark, then we must conclude that sociology requires orientations to theory and procedure which are quite distinct from those of sociobiology. Let us look into the matter through the lens of a particular and pertinent example.

Peter Blau (1974) pays close attention to theories of social structure, some actual states of social structure, and some procedures for linking theory with states. He begins by defining structure as consisting of *elements* (actors, social positions), *and their interrelations* (systemic properties). He then proceeds to identify two generically different conceptions of structure. His preferred conception "describes *observable empirical* conditions and is merely the basis for a theory (genetic or systemic?) yet to be constructed" (p. 615 emphasis added). The rejected conception holds that "social structure is a system of logical relationships among *general principles* [and] which is *not* designed as a conceptual framework to reflect *empirical* conditions" *ibid.*). Instead, this second conception is to be used to "interpret" social structure.

Respectively, these two approaches characterize orthodox sociology and the structuralism of Claude Lévi-Strauss. Orthodox sociology addresses "actual" arrangements, seeks to describe (not interpret) them, and, *then*, to construct a theory to explain the arrangements. This gives the enterprise a clear "structure without genesis" quality. This can be compared with Lévi-Strauss' approach. Here the emphasis is clearly upon: (a) the actual in the context of the possible (logical relations); (b) general principles—the symbolic "rules" (values, norms, etc.), which can be used to "test" for consistency, contradiction, and construction; and, (c) interpretations—taking account of the relations between goals and actual-structures-as-means for achieving these goals.

What is most ironic about Blau's preferred approach, and the orthodox sociology it is modeled after, is that in the end he is forced to abandon it. In the body of his paper, after he has developed his two parameters and the appropriate procedures for applying these, Blau identifies two *actual but contradictory* trends with respect to social integration. On the one hand, "multiform heterogeneity" (pp. 622f.) represents an actual trend toward an increasing and more dynamic form of integration. In his words, "Multiform differentiation is at the roots of . . . social change. It attenuates ingroup relations, which confine people's perspectives, and intensifies intergroup relations, which foster tolerance and flexibility" (p. 631).[3] On the other hand, "status consolidation" (p. 630), where power and influence become increasingly concentrated in the hands of a few, tends to "aggravate inequalities," as well as posing a serious threat to intergroup relations and adaptive social change. It is also "incompatible with democracy." But clearly the "threats" Blau identifies cannot be derived from "actual" patterns in social structure—i.e. from descriptions of observable conditions. To reach such a judgment he has to invoke general principles, values, what *could be* as well as what *is*. In other words, prescriptions."

To summarize, orthodox sociology, while addressing an "object" which is radically different from the substructural "elements" of sociobiology, tends to employ procedures and theoretical models borrowed from biology and other objective sciences. This borrowing is what gives sociology its "structure without genesis" quality, for our "genesis" lies not in the realm of genes, but in superstructures of symbols, ideas, values, etc., viewed as contextual systems. In other words, the "fact" in "social fact" is not an objective, material element which can be isolated and manipulated; it is a contextual meaning depending upon its *relationship* to other meanings.

C. CONSTRUCTION: GENETIC STRUCTURALISM

Genetic structuralism is an interactive synthesis of relevant aspects of the two previous positions. Since we shall detail Piaget's theoretical program in the two succeeding sections, we pause here merely to highlight it.

In his early years, Piaget was a naturalist. Once, on a visit, he noticed a mollusk in a lake. Unlike the familiar mollusks of Lake Geneva, this one's shape was elongated rather than round. To satisfy his curiosity, Piaget took the strangely shaped mollusk back to Lake Geneva. His "hypothesis" was based upon the fact that Lake Geneva, being larger, was a rougher ambience because it was buffeted by winds and currents. Quite interestingly, the little mollusk soon assumed the more familiar round shape. From this little experiment, Piaget began to reason that observable (phenotypic) structures always reflect the joint action of genes and environment. Hence, rather then worrying about estimating the contributions of each, Piaget decided to employ a developmental framework in order to study the interaction of genotype (e.g., children of different ages) *and* environment (problems of time, space, chance, geometry, etc.). In all of these studies, his basic question is: what are the stages through which the mind (brain, environment) constructs realities. Now, let us see how this imagery might be applied to select and synthesize aspects of socio-biology and orthodox sociology.

We have called sociobiology "genesis without structure" for good reason. As Wilson himself indicates (1975:70f), the models of classical population genetics consider only the competition be-tween alleles on a single locus. In short, Mendelian assumptions treat each gene in a random framework as though it were an independent element. While this proves adequate for simple mor-phological traits, it is not adequate for complex (especially be-havioral) traits. If the human genome contains 10,000 or more genes, we can expect them to work in concert.[4] Hence, we have more than $2^{10,000}$ possible combinations with which to contend in estimating "heritability." Add to this complexity the notions of "dominance deviations," "epistatic interactions" (a kind of power hierarchy among genes at different loci), and the problems of covariance of gene/environment, and we can begin to appreciate why sociobiology is imputed to lack structure. The actual progress in population genetics is, quite simply, much too primitive to support Wilson's claims. It is this juxtaposition of evidence/model with Wilson's claims that lead us to characterize sociobiology as mechanistic, atomistic, and reductionistic (table 8.1).

It is also *overly* deterministic. Suppose we have two populations (in-breeders), which, in a given year, differ by one standard de-viation in mean intelligence as measured by IQ. It is a plausible hypothesis that this mean difference is due to gene quality. How-ever, it is equally plausible to assume that this difference in gene quality reflects a social policy of dysgenic breeding in previous years and centuries. This would seem especially likely if the in-ferior population had been slaves for several hundreds of years. Slave masters are very likely to prefer a slave-husbandry policy which produces docile, dull, but powerful workers. But the point of this despicable scenario is that genes *do not determine* morpho-logical or behavioral traits. They may set limits on what is possible, but their affects are, in balance, equally attributable to an envi-ronmental context.

Piaget's theory of development is rooted in biology, but is con-cerned with emergent, not mechanical structure; it is interactive rather than analytically reductive and deterministic. Furthermore, while the theory antedates modern neurophysiology (e.g., Eccles

Table 8.1. A Comparison of the Innatist and the Environmentalist Approaches to Structures

Structure Is	Model Orientation	Associated Researcher	Implied Image of Behavior
I. Preformed.	A. Atomistic—genes—is without structure.	Richard Dawkins, Edward O. Wilson.	Seeks general laws of behavior. Actor is robot, programmed by genes for selfish, deceptive behavior.
II. Continent Emergent.	B. Holistic—structure without genesis.	Kenneth Arrow (associated with A and B) (see Section III. below).	Uses "market mechanism" as means for aggregating individual values into collective decisions. Each actor pursues his self-interest, with majority rule.
	C. Relational—distinctive patterns of structure without genesis.	Peter Blau (associated with B and C)	Actors created by society. Aim is to describe social positions and their network of relations as a basis for theory yet to be constructed.
III. Constructed.	D. Rules—genetic structuralism.[a] Structures arise as interaction of genes and environment.	Jean Piaget, John Rawls	Social Behavior is the observable outcome of the interaction of native properties of mind and the symbolic environment, hence, combines "structure" with the "structuring" process. Actor and social structure are copartners in construction.

[a] Piaget defines "morality" and "justice" in terms of the four stages of respect which the individual acquires for "rules." In the fourth, "formal operational," stage, rules have their origin in the social group, both in terms of their production and the respect given to them.

1977), it anticipates many of the recent developments. First, the brain, which is a product of gene "orchestration," contains billions of neurons, each of which is *connected*—i.e. non-atomistic—to thousands of other neurons. Secondly, the "split-brain" phenomenon appears to have demonstrated that "reductionism" vs. "holism," analytic "atomism" vs. "synthesis," reflect a division of labor between the two brain hemispheres.[5] Finally, there is ample evidence to suggest that the brain is extremely active, and, unlike a robot or computer, that neuronal assemblies will atrophy through disuse; conversely, action tends to build new and richer structure. So, in a biological context, Piaget's theory is both genetic and structural.

Blau, as representative sociologist, described two sociologies. One version is concerned with *actual* social structure, after which to build a theory. But this typification of the sociological enterprise leads to the characterization of "structure without genesis." If social structure is at least partially guided by ideas, values, and norms (i.e., by choice, however unconscious) then symbols are the "genesis" of social structure. Since symbols are learned, social genesis is Lamarckian in its form of evolution. This gives social structure its "fickle" quality, and means that social theory is oriented to "rules," not to universal "laws." But this way of viewing social genesis is precisely what characterizes the nonpreferred approach to structure: concern for general principles, employing the quasi-necessity of logic (e.g., consistency between principles in their applications) rather than empirical necessity. In other words, the enterprise of sociology is no more lawful, deterministic, and materialistic than is biology. Instead, sociology is "rule-full," capable of change and adaptation in a self-regulating fashion, and is based upon symbols. Furthermore, unlike the atomism of genetics, symbols are first and foremost contextual; meaning and significance is constituted within a total system of similarities and oppositions.

So, Piaget's constructionism is an interactive hybrid. Substantively, it views behavior as the emerging product of the interaction and experiences of a material substructure (e.g., the active brain) with a symbolic superstructural *system*. Hence, the procedures focus primarily upon developments and the "quasi-necessity" of logic (including interpretation) as a means of mapping the developmental stages. In the next two sections, we shall further develop this substantive-procedural nexus. For the moment, we turn to a preview of the arguments to follow in order to indicate their organization.

We begin the arguments at the level of the individual (table 8.1; fig. 8.1). Here the main issue is an adequate representation of how the individual gradually constructs reality. Once this image is established, we can consider how Piaget's general theory can be applied to the specific issue of the evolution of moral judgments. Morality is deemed important since it constitutes the individual substructure for social justice and social choice (the ideational genesis of social structuring).

Once we have outlined Piaget's general and special theories, we can entertain questions of sociological import: the choice of mechanisms, and the attendant problems, for deriving social choices from individual inputs. We start (section III.) by explicating Arrow's elegant treatment of the problem. Arrow's work is significant in three interrelated ways. First, he adopts a "utilitarian" approach to social good. Now, this doctrine or principle suffers from the same kinds of defects which bedevil sociobiology. Whereas "good" implies both a material *and* a symbolic component, as does "behavior," it gets treated in a deterministic fashion. The solution to this problem is to separate "procedures" from "significance." Secondly, Arrow focuses on a "market mechanism" as the ideal social-choice procedure.[6] This mechanism has common ideational roots with the theory of "natural selection," but if social structure is Lamarckian, we might anticipate a rapid divergence between "actual" and "ideal." Finally, the conclusion which Arrow reaches—his "impossibility theorem"—indicates that the mechanism cannot consistently lead to social decisions. As table 8.1. indicates, the market mechanism does not take account of relationships—e.g. status consolidation—in the social structure.[7] Because of its emphasis upon "independence" (like classical population genetics) of elements, a market mechanism works best at the incipient stage of structuring. As networks develop, it becomes increasingly impotent, skewed, and irrelevant as a procedure for reaching social consensus.

With this negative result in hand, we finally come to Rawls' theory, which is a positive application of Piagetian construction.

Figure 8.1. A General Schematic of the Social Construction Problem[a]

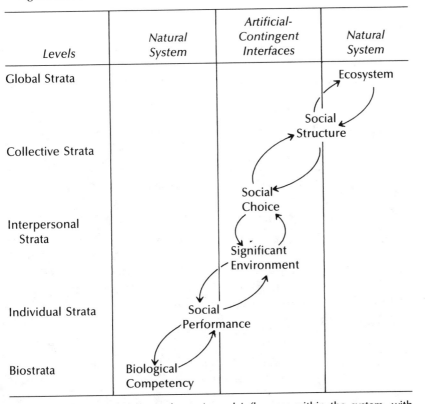

Levels	Natural System	Artificial-Contingent Interfaces	Natural System
Global Strata			Ecosystem
Collective Strata		Social Structure	
Interpersonal Strata		Social Choice / Significant Environment	
Individual Strata	Social Performance		
Biostrata	Biological Competency		

[a] The double arrows represent the reciprocal influences within the system, with biological competency and the global ecosystem as terminals. For a discussion of the "natural" and "artificial" distinction, see Simon (1969).

On the one hand, it recognizes that social structuring is guided by *rules*, not laws or random aggregation. For instance, suppose we experimented with collegiate football by enacting two rules of substitution: unlimited in one section of the country, severely restricted in another (see Coombs 1964: 245–49). We can expect that both recruitment (i.e., "selection") and the organization of teams (highly specialized vs. generalists) would vary considerably between the two sections.

On the other hand, Rawls is attuned to the symbolic, the accidental and conventional, origins of structure. Consequently, he seeks to "veil" the actual fabric of relationships to promote the workings of Piaget's "formal operations" in the choice of fundamental rules of sociation. Once basic and inviolable rules have been chosen the "veil" is lifted to restructure society. Two implications follow from this procedure. First, unlike the "market mechanism," Rawls' theory remains relevant to social choice no matter how much relational structure is produced.[8] Secondly, like Piaget (through his concept of decentering from "egocentrism"), Rawls does not believe that individuals are inherently "selfish." Rather, they are fundamentally symbolic; they create, and are created by, society viewed as a contextual system.

Three thoughts about Piaget's general theory should be kept in mind. It is "interactive," always viewing behavior as a composite of nature and nurture (the reciprocal arrows of fig. 8.1. capture this). Secondly, the focus on development means that the procedures are attuned both to observable structure and to the transformations leading to new structures. Finally, the substantive problem of morality, and of justice, is the choice between competing "rules" for social construction—e.g. between the social elaboration of "multiform heterogeneity" vs. the social dissection of "status consolidation."

II. THE INQUIRY INTO MORALITY: BEHAVIOR AND CONSCIOUSNESS

A. INTRODUCTION TO THE GENERAL THEORY

Before we go on to consider the results of the inquiry into the evolution of moral judgments, it is essential that we do a bit of spade work on Piaget's underlying structural theory. While his program of research has spanned a number of content domains, we shall primarily be concerned here with his model of the underlying structural properties—the inferred organizational characteristics which explain the contents of behavior. These remarks are intended as a summary framework, which, when combined with the substantive results of the study of morality, will carry us beyond the psychological realm to the considerations of a just social order.

1. Examples of the Structuring Process. To illustrate how structures arise, we shall briefly review two research programs which employ computer simulations to represent an information-pro-

Figure 8.2. Three Stages in the Development of "Cell Assemblies" Representing the First Few Months of Life[a]

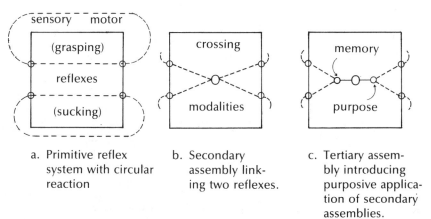

a. Primitive reflex system with circular reaction

b. Secondary assembly linking two reflexes.

c. Tertiary assembly introducing purposive application of secondary assemblies.

[a] Adapted from Cunningham (1972).

cessing view of the individual. The first of these exemplifies the process of intellectual growth during the first two years of life—i.e. how structures are developed, via "circular reactions" between a system and its environment, during the sensorimotor period.[9] The second provides an example of how adults apply these underlying structures to rather limited aspects of their environment.

Cunningham's approach (1972) applies Hull's concept of neurological "cell-assemblies" to Piaget's sensorimotor period, and begins with an organism endowed with primitive reflexes—e.g., sucking and grasping. Initially these reflexes run in parallel, and each involves a circular reactivity between sensations and motor responses (see fig. 8.2a). Thus, an infant might be seen grasping or sucking in a void, or might begin these actions as a response to tactile stimulation of the hand or mouth. Besides this concept of circularity, a key idea in this model is the relationship between successive reactions, or practices, and "attention span."

When a hungry infant is presented with a bottle, it will initially focus all of its attention on the sucking reflex. After consuming some of the bottle, the infant may then begin to engage in a form of primitive play: grasping, scanning, or playing with the nipple. The first reaction improves coordination within the reflex circuit, while this second, playful, reaction leads to a new cell-assembly: a crossing of reflex modalities (see fig. 8.2b). Thus, during a relaxed state, the infant may chance to grasp what he is sucking, and this initially haphazard event will become sharpened and differentiated via circular practice; as these secondary assemblies are practiced, then, they are subject, more and more, to "purposive" action.

Following this kind of assembly pattern, Cunningham's model simulates the development of a series of cell assemblies into a hierarchy of sensorimotor habits—what Piaget calls "schemes." Of particular interest is the sequence which the circular reaction represents: from an established habit-structure to new applications under relaxed conditions, which then may become higher-order habits. In this way, the first two years of life represent the movement from an active, but open, state to the beginning substructures of purpose and directed activities (see fig. 8.2c), supported by memory. In this sense, "attention span" refers to the number of underlying cell-assemblies with which an infant (or an older person) can engage his environment.

In their study of human problem-solving, Newell and Simon (1972) attempt to simulate a "sufficient" representation of this underlying structure and process. Of particular interest is their distinction between the subjective system and the objective environment, and the description of the processes involved in problem-solving. The subjective system, or "problem space," has two parts: a set of parameters which define the *natural* (short-term memory) limits on information processing, and a set of variables which describe the *acquired* strategies (cell-assemblies) which arise through experience, and which are stored in long-term memory. Taken together, these two aspects constitute the system's view of the problem and its potential for solving it.

The "task" environment is some objective problem whose structure is usually well-known to the experimenter, but which constitutes a form of "organized complexity" for the problem-solver. When we place an individual in a task environment, the process initially tends to be of a slow, serial, trial-and-error sort. The solver employs past experiences as "heuristics" for tentatively circumscribing the environment and for evaluating its progress. These heuristic "schemes" will vary in their degree of organization, depending upon past experiences, and they may or may not match, or be perceived to match, the environment.

As an overall image, then, this study suggests that the individual is a limited processor, who attempts to solve a problem by calling upon the organization ("chunks"; see Simon 1974) of prior experiences to constrain it. The environment itself is a "normative" construction—e.g., chess and crytarithmetic—scaled down to an individual level.[10] The linkage between system and environment is therefore contingent, and this, in the authors' terms (Newell and Simon 1972:55), provides two kinds of information. Successful problem-solving tells us a great deal about the task-environment by confirming or extending our knowledge of its structure. Departures from "rational" solutions, on the other hand, tell us a great deal about the natural limits—biological parameters— or acquired structures of the subject.

2. *Piaget's Concept of "Egocentrism"*. As implied above, knowledge is the outcome of a constructive process. This view suggests that the child begins its commerce with the environment through a profoundly deficient structure, gradually builds up a system of representations, and then, through this system, is able to solve problems, etc. The initial condition is referred to as "egocentrism"—the inability of the child to differentiate itself from the environment—and the course of development involves a gradual "decentering" from this initially absolute and unconscious perspective.[11] A full appreciation of this concept requires that we distinguish between performance and competence.

For instance, Piaget posed two questions for male children with male siblings: (1) "Do you have a brother?" (2) "Does your brother have a brother?" As early as two years, and because of recurrent experiences, the children responded appropriately to the first question; however, it was not until much later that they understood the *meaning* of the question. Not until the child can dissociate terms and objects, and organize these into a logic of classification, will it be able to handle the kind of problem which the second question posed: treating oneself as the object of a question. Structurally identical forms of "egocentrism" can be demonstrated in experiments on such problems as chance, conservation of matter and quantity, classification and seriation, or conceptions of time and space.

When we take up the question of moral development, this concept of egocentrism will be complemented by the concept of "heteronomy." Heteronomy means that social rules and duties— their source, meaning, and purposes—are initially external to the child's mind; thus, their observance requires a constructive, decentering process.

3. *Structures: The Three-Term Relationship.* As distinct from an empiricist approach, structuralism involves an interaction between a native, genotypic system, and its social and physical environment, which are linked by a circular and developmental process. Since this contrast produces some striking differences in the nature of the scientific enterprise, we shall briefly illustrate the nature of the argument and indicate some of its implications. While there are points of disagreement between them (Piaget 1970a), Piaget and Chomsky argue along similar lines. Chomsky (1972), for instance, asks "how are similarities of meanings, between individuals, possible?"[12] He then proceeds to reject the either/or arguments of innate or environmental determinism, as follows. There are two possible environmental explanations: ostensive learning or learning by definition. While the former would have to presuppose an implausibly homogeneous environment, the latter would require an initial stock of definitions for it to count. As an alternative Chomsky then proposes a biological "species of instincts" which provides a deep basis for similarities, without involving an excessive determinism:

Knowledge of language results from the interplay of initially given structures of mind, maturational processes and interaction with the environment. Thus there is no reason to expect that there will be invariant properties of the knowledge that is acquired. . . . Suppose, however, that we discover invariant properties [deep structure] of language. In such a case, it is always a plausible . . . hypothesis that these invariant properties reflect properties of the mind. (1972:23)

We shall see that this notion of invariant (syntactic) properties of mind, and the programs of research which aim at their discovery, carries several important implications. First, the hypotheses of variable knowledge, yet invariant properties (syntax) of mind, constitutes an approximation to the problems of similar judgments. Secondly, the notion of invariant properties makes the competent individual the primary source of "good" and "duty," so that observable social arrangements, rather than constituting the independent source of verification for social theories, take on a dependent status, subject to constructive principles and individual potentials and purposes.

4. *The Notion of "Stages": Continuity and Discontinuity.* The idea of a "circular reaction" indicates a continuous exchange between the individual and its significant environment. This exchange is represented by two concepts: "assimilation," where the child incorporates features of objects into existing structures of meaning, and "accommodation" where the existing structures are adapted to novel or obtrusive features of the environment. As these competent structures develop, there are abrupt discontinuities in the underlying organization which Piaget has been able to identify by employing logical representations, and which he marks by a four-stage sequence.

The four broad stages are outlined in table 8.2 along with the appropriate labels, the kinds of behaviors which each permits, and the age norms, which are not to be taken literally; it is the sequence, not the age norms, which are important. We shall illustrate their manifestations in more detail when we examine the stages of moral judgment.

5. *The Concept of "Conscious Realization".* Thus far, we have been stressing the view of "understanding" as the outcome of a process, and its correct application to a "task environment" as problematic and indirect. Since the process is gradual and essentially unconscious, thought has a "retrospective" quality (Weick 1969:30) to it: future projections reflect previous connections between acts, intentions, and consequences. Furthermore, formal thought does not arise until the fourth stage (adolescence), and since experiences are unconsciously stored in long-term memory, this concept of *conscious realization* (Piaget 1965:177) consists in an ideal and unusual process. It represents the ability for "decentering" from a particular locus of activity—motives, acts, and environmental structures—to engage in a process of reflection which entertains "all possible worlds" and subjects these to the necessity of logical implication. In effect, the process of decentering means that the individual *relativizes* any form of absolutes—belief, postulates, ego-perspective—and subjects these to reflective scrutiny.

Table 8.2. Piaget's Four Stages Covering the Period From Infancy to Early Adolescence

Stage	Age	Structural Assembly	Behaviors	Titles
I.	0–2	Sensory/Motor Schemas (Individual rites and habits.)	Play, ritualization—characterized by imitation and autism	Sensorimotor.
II.	2–7	Perceptual whole, without the property of "reversibility."	Object permanence, but not part/whole, or instance/class relationships.	Pre-operational.
III.	7–11	Classification and Seriation, and simple forms of "reversibility."	Capacity for physical experimentation, but dominated by actions and material results.	Concrete Operational.
IV.	11–15	Structured Whole, with complex composition of reversible operations.	Symbolic experiments, with actual results conceived as one of all possible results: hypothetical-deductive.	Formal Operational.

In their discussion of problem-solving, Newell and Simon refer to this process as "progressive deepening" (1972:752), meaning that once a solution is found, and can be repeated, the solver will be in a better position to know why he arrived, and by what path, at the solution.

Rawls' concept of "reflective equilibrium" (1972:20f.) is remarkably similar, and suggests a form of thinking which is nonlinear and reversible. For instance, as we shall see, he is able to specify the origin and nature of the social contract not by moving back into the real past, but by probing deeply into the nature or human judgment and its implications for social practices.

There are several reasons for alluding to this concept in these preliminary remarks. First, it suggests an image of the scientific enterprise which is rather unusual (Piaget 1970b).[13] Second, it helps to reinforce our focus of inquiry: the essential place which reasoning, and its underlying invariant properties, plays in the social construction process.

6. *Piaget's Notion of Two Moralities.* Throughout the morality volume, and especially in the fourth section, Piaget (1965) critically assesses sociocentric theories of duty and responsibility. He refers to these theories as the "morality of constraint and heteronomy" (rules and duties that are external and collective) and compares them with the "morality of cooperation." In his criticism, Piaget begins by agreeing with the main sociocentric thesis: morality starts within a context of existing rules and duties. However, since existing systems of rules are full of anachronisms, we need to distinguish between "actual" and "ideal" societies. Furthermore, since "duty" tends to be external, a sociocentric theory cannot fully account for the individual's commitment to, and observance of, rules; for these, we must appeal to some form of inner dynamics. But such an explanation introduces a further distinction: that between objective duty and the individual's own sense of "goodness." Finally, given these distinctions, any form of imposed authority, because the child is initially egocentric and rules are initially heteronomous, would lead to observance of rules which, at best, would tend to be haphazard and blind, and, at worst, would require the constant supervision of powerful invigilators.

At this point, Piaget begins to strike out in a different direction. Since rules have an a priori and social origin, he chose to study children's play groups: child-centered societies, relatively free of adult interference. By observing performances and consciousness in the games, Piaget is led to the conclusion that moral equilibrium requires nothing more than experiences in common, where practice and consciousness evolve under conditions of reciprocity.[14] As we shall see, this natural evolution of competent judgment occurs irrespective of the degree of arbitrariness or heteronomy of the environment; although, under conditions of unilateral authority, judgments tend not to become coordinated with behavioral repertoires. The principal effect of this is to suggest that the problem of morality requires a constructive solution where judgments and practices are brought into correspondence by a meaningful elimination of the authoritarian features of the social environment.

B. THE INQUIRY INTO MORAL JUDGMENT

As an application and test of his general theory, Piaget conducted three distinct inquiries; all of these are concerned with the evolution of individual judgment, but each varies the degree of heteronomy, and its bearing on moral practices. The first is a study of the integration of behavior and judgment in the context of children's games. The second study is primarily concerned with child-adult relationships, and the connection between adult constraint and the child's moral "realism" (egocentrism). The final study is addressed to the question of "justice"—where such concepts as duty, responsibility and sanctions are relevant—so that the interplay between individual competence and social institutions can be brought into full view. We shall begin by providing a summary of each of the studies, and conclude by discussing these results in the light of Piaget's theory; in turn, this discussion will serve as a foundation for the succeeding two sections.

1. Practice and Consciousness of Rules in Games. By choosing children's games for this inquiry, Piaget was able to examine the evolving relationship between behaviors and judgments. Games facilitate this kind of inquiry because they constitute relatively "closed" realities. They are also child-centered; adult intrusiveness is ordinarily minimal. Thus, while the rules of the game are initially external to the child's mind, and the child begins in an egocentric state, we are permitted to see the full play of development as it leads to a morality of autonomous cooperation: the gradual decentering from egocentric and heteronomous structures.

In analyzing his results, Piaget identified four stages of "practice," which correspond to the four general stages, and three stages of "consciousness." The difference in the number of stages and the time of their appearance denotes the time lag in the circular reaction between experiences and their representation. Figure 8.3 summarizes the two sets of stages and indicates the shifts in observables which mark each of these. To facilitate and sharpen our review, we shall overemphasize the abrupt shifts between stages.

In the earliest stage (P_i), children engage in a rudimentary form of play under the dictates of sensorimotor schemes—curiosity or assimilation, regulation or accommodation. A child might use the marbles as food for a doll, as cannonballs, or as objects to be stacked or rolled. Piaget interprets this early playing-without-rules as the substructure of later developments: "We believe that the individual rite (motor habit) and the individual symbol (motive) constitute the substructure for the development of rules and collective signs" (1965:32).

During the Egocentric stage (P_{ii}) the child's behavior begins to resemble that of the older children, but he is unable to get beneath the surface of imitation; he is unable to represent the connection between what others do, and what this means to them. At the same time, there is a moderate disjunction between the child's own behaviors and his intentions. With respect to consciousness (C_i), while the child may have a glimmer of the rules, and hold them in awe, he is consistent neither in their application nor expression.

By the time they reach the competitive period (P_{iii}) the children are able to coordinate a sufficient set of rules to constitute a game. Because understanding is minimal, however, the games themselves may dissolve into squabbles and other forms of "collective monologues." In the early part of this period children must make a great effort to keep their attention on the game, but this effort subsides with experience. Nevertheless, the correspondences between the players' practices is due more to a conjunction of habits then it is to true and mutual understanding; for instance, their

Figure 8.3. The Stages of Practice and Consciousness in Children's Games[a]

	Practice		Consciousness
P$_I$	Purely motoric—under the dictates of sensorimotor curiosity and regulation.		
P$_{II}$	Egocentric—a combination of behavioral imitation of older children and autism (playing alone even in presence of others).	C$_I$	Rules are interesting, but neither systematic nor coercive.
P$_{III}$	Incipient Cooperation—playing competitively to "win," with rigid adherence to rules	C$_{II}$	Rules are sacred and immutable—emanating from high authority.
P$_{IV}$	Cooperative—material aspects subordinated to symbolic aspects. Rules are interesting and give rise to "juridical" discussion.	C$_{III}$	Rules viewed as emanating from group. May be changed but only by mutual consent. Considerable freedom of speech.
			Perspectives given by social milieu.[b]

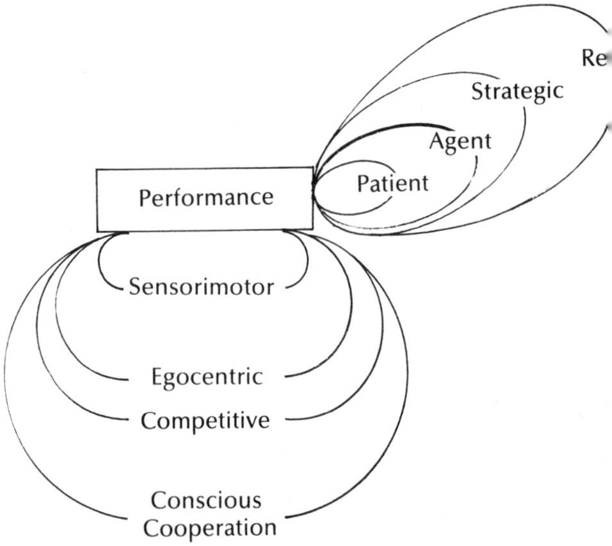

Competency or underlying structure of thought.

[a] Summarized from Piaget (1965).
[b] See Moore and Anderson (1971).

responses to questions (C_{ii}), regarding the rules and their origin, have an intuitive, absolute quality.[15]

Despite this adhesive quality between practice and consciousness, the competitive stage is a remarkable achievement. Over a series of encounters, the children learn to "win" and to "lose," and can accept these outcomes as fair, based upon the rules and their observance of them. Thus, once a minimal situation can be managed, the competitive aspect of the game serves as a substructure, over a long run of experiences, for the emergence of a form of symbolic reciprocity.

In the final stages (P_{iv} and C_{iii}) the game takes on the qualities of an aesthetic experience. Once the children have learned to coordinate a complex of meanings and activities, their mutual experiences lead them to a symbolic sense of play; they subordinate the material aspects of the game (cf. Mauss 1967). There are several concordant signs of this subordination effect. First, the children might accept as legitimate an "act of piracy" whereby a winner of all the marbles is required to redistribute them in order to keep the game alive. Second, they take great pleasure in "juridical" discussions which have the distinct quality of a true dialogue. Finally, they trace the origin of rules to traditions, not as eternal essences, but as working and mutable guidelines that can be altered by mutual consent.[16]

These results constitute the major outcropping from the first inquiry: by ages 11 or 12, children have assembled the mental basis for a miniature and ideal society, based on autonomous reason and mutual cooperation. This result arises from the possibility of coordinating competence and mutual experiences within a solidary peer group. Nevertheless, and precisely because of the solidarity, it is conceivable that the children could reach P_{iv} without completing C_{iii}; that is, without bringing consciousness to the level of formal operations. Such conditional social factors as "role distance," role-playing with younger children, etc., would appear to be essential for "conscious realization" to reach full bloom.[17] On the other hand, such insipid practices as adult-sponsored games— e.g., little leagues or hockey schools—would tend to prevent the children from reaching C_{iii} by usurping the "referee" perspective.[18] At the bottom of fig. 8.3 we have diagrammed the connecting loops between experiences and consciousness.

2. Adult Constraint and Moral Realism.   The second inquiry was addressed to the relationship between children's judgments and adult constraint. In the covering discussion (1965:ch. 3) Piaget is at great pains to describe how certain adult responses to childish activity—where parents and teachers, for instance, attend to the child's behavior and its consequences, rather then to the child's thought—are a powerful force which tends only to consolidate egocentrism.

The stimuli used for this phase of the study were paired stories, which varied the following factors: (a) the child's intent (e.g. helpful or mischievous); (b) his behavior (clumsy or culpable); (c) the consequences (some negative outcome). For instance, in one member of a stimulus pair a child might happen to break a number of cups *accidentally*, while in the other member he might break one cup while engaging in *mischief*. In his usual careful manner, Piaget elicited judgments from the children regarding the seriousness of the actions and the degree of responsibility. Table 8.3 contains a summary list of the more striking results which Piaget obtained, together with a set of remarkably similar results which Connell (1971) obtained in a study of political socialization.

All of these results suggest the underlying transformation of judgments between the egocentric and operational stages. Furthermore, since the stimuli were themselves arbitrary and described a heteronomous context, these judgmental transformations are more likely due to genetic then to social constructions. However, because of his unilateral respect for adults, the egocentric child is strongly inclined to adopt their perspectives and behaviors, as he perceives them, in response to such things as clumsiness, etc. Therefore, in moderate to extreme authoritarian relations, and due precisely to this combination of awe and respect, on the one hand, and the lack of free experimentation on the other, judgmental competency and moral conduct may fail to connect, subverting the growth of autonomy and conscious realization.

3. Cooperation and the Idea of Justice.   This third inquiry (1965:ch. 4) brings us to a thoroughly social application of the two moralities: does justice have its origin in objective, collective, and communicable forms of rules and sanctions, or is its origin to be found in the free expression of autonomous judgments. The test itself is quite demanding since, from the point of view of

Table 8.3. A Comparison of the Transformation in the Child's Judgments of Responsibility and Intention Between the Stages of Pre-operations and Operations, and Piaget's Results Compared to Connell's from a Study of Politics

Piaget's Study
(Note: Older children transformed these judgments.)

Younger children defined "lies" as "naughty" words—they tended to associate them with a global class of naughty words, an example of egocentric "syncretism."

Younger children viewed the seriousness of a lie in terms of its implausibility, whereas older children regarded plausible lies as the more serious—their plausibility made them more antisocial.

Younger children felt that it is worse to deceive an adult than it is to deceive a peer.

Among the younger children, the closer a punishment followed a violation, the naughtier the behavior, (egocentric "juxtaposition"). Similarly, the more severe a punishment, the more serious the deed must have been. (This result reflects the effects of heteronomy and the nature of retrospective thought.)

For younger children mistakes can count as lies, since they are unable to dissociate behavior and intention.

There were some exceptions to this overall pattern of differences between younger and older children. For instance, a young child might judge an act in terms of intention, rather than consequences, *if* it had had an experience similar to the one described by the stories.

Connell's Study (1971)
(Note: Even older children were "egocentric" because of the degree of heteronomy of subject matter.)

Children learn and cognitively respond to the idea of citizen's responsibility earlier than they learn about citizen sovereignty and populist rights.

Adversaries of government (the press and opposing parties) lack the charisma of leaders, and consequently are more open to suspicion and skepticism.

Children have a considerable fascination for military leaders and detectives. This fascination may reflect a series of factors: the conduct of such actors is more "visible," the children have a "threat schema" which is easily cultivated, and children are inclined to impute sacredness to authority.

* Political figures are frequently remembered within particular settings (TV News) so that people and geography become associated in a curiously distorted fashion. For instance, they might perceive a city mayor as directly responsible for services they hear about or actually experience.

children, not only are rules heteronomously arbitrary, but their connection with socially prescribed sanctions (e.g., punishments) is similarly arbitrary. Thus, by inquiring into the child's understanding of authority and responsibility and the child's sense of fairness in the application and distributions of sanctions, we are able to put Piaget's thesis to a decisive test.

In support of his conclusions, Piaget marshals several sets of data, and is quite thorough in his discussion of the results and their implications. We shall briefly summarize his discussion here. Authority and sanctions go through three stages, which roughly correspond to the three stages of consciousness from the first study:

Stage I.   Authority and Expiation. In this primitive stage, justice is based upon precepts controlled by adults. Adult authority combines with childish egocentrism, especially its tendency toward mystery and magic, to produce forms of justice which are remarkable for their severity and inconsistency.[19]

Stage II.   Egalitarianism and Retribution.[20] This second stage is marked by conflict between authority and affective solidarity with peers. Where actual conflicts arise (as in a classroom) the children prefer to accept collective punishment rather than break the bonds of solidarity. Among themselves, justice and punishment are still objective though reciprocal—an eye for an eye, or equal shares for all.

Stage III. Equity and Restitution. In this stage, authority is based upon cooperation and judicial discussion. Sanctions, whether in the form of shares of advantages or punishments, are to be "motivated." They are to take account of the intentions of both the individual and the group. In effect, the arbitrary nature of authority and sanctions has been transformed into a motivated system of procedures and interpretations.

Piaget concludes from these results that:

the sense of justice, though naturally capable of being reinforced by the precepts and practical example of the adult, is largely independent of these influences, and requires nothing more for its development than the mutual respect and solidarity which holds among children themselves. It is often at the expense of the adult, and not because of him, that the notions of just and unjust find their way into the youthful mind. In contrast to a given rule, which from the first has been imposed upon the child from outside and which for many years he has failed to understand, such as the rule of not telling lies, the rule of justice is a sort of immanent condition of social relations or a law governing their equilibrium. (1965:198)

C. SUMMARY AND CONCLUSIONS

For full appreciation of Piaget's conclusions in the above quote, it is necessary to recall that "genetic structuralism" is a synthesis of "genetic" and "social structural" components, as was outlined in the introduction. By the time a child reaches the age of 14 or 15, his mind will be structured by principles of formal operations—reversible judgments and thoughts. However, this competence (akin to the syntactic competency of speech) as a "sort of immanent condition" of justice, may or may not coordinate with conscious behaviors. The possibility of such coordination depends upon qualities of social experiences (see fig. 8.5). When rules are imposed as specific principles—when rules reflect relational patterns like "status consolidation"—we can expect egocentric performances. On the other hand, the greater the freedom of exploration, the more rules are seen as "agreements by mutual consent" ("multiform heterogeneity") and above all, the greater the cultivation of rules as "systems" of convention, the greater the degree of coordination of competent judgment with social practices.

Relatedly, one symptom of this maturing competency of performance is the tendency of the youthful mind to subordinate material (genetic) aspects of justice to symbolic (cultural), formal (logical) aspects. This transition from material to symbolic is the distinctive mark of the shift from "egalitarian" to "equity" principles of justice.

In sum, Piaget's studies of moral judgment indicate that the ordinary individual will evolve from an initial state of natural "selfishness" (egocentrism) to a state of symbolic equity. So the problem of "justice" becomes a problem of social morphology: "to what extent do the rules and relationships of social structure facilitate the adoption of the "referee" perspective?" (fig. 8.3). For instance, in Fig. 8.4 we employ the four perspectives as a means for focusing on the "researcher/subject" relationship. The table implies that when we assume a superior position, or structure our instruments, or guarantee anonymity with assurances that our in-

Figure 8.4. A Consideration of the "Blind Spots" in the Researcher/
Subject Relationship[a]

The Range of Perspectives Available
to the Researcher Who Controls the
Relationship:
Patient Agent Strategist Referee

The Range of
Perspectives   Patient
Available to   Agent
the Subject,   Strategist
Controlled by   Referee
Researcher:

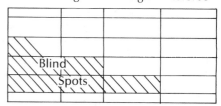

Note: social construction requires that
subjects, both as autonomous actors
and as members of society, adopt a
"referee" perspective.

[a] The four "perspectives" are drawn from Fig. 8.3. Since it is the researcher who
ordinarily initiates and controls the meaning of the relationship, and also publishes
the results of inquiry, the Figure addresses two issues: "how many of his four possible
perspectives can the subject enact?" and "what blind spots does the enacted relationship create, vis à vis social construction of reality?"

terest lies in aggregate trends, we "blind" ourselves to the individual inputs essential for social construction (fig. 8.4).

III. SOCIAL (AGGREGATE) WELFARE: "MARKET," "UTILITY" APPROACHES TO SOCIAL ORDER

In light of the above conclusions, the argument now shifts to
a consideration of social morphology and process: procedures for,
and the "substance" of, arriving at social decisions. The exposition
is based upon Arrow's (1963) axiomatic treatment of the mechanism for aggregating individual values into collective choice.[21]
After summarizing this market mechanism, we turn to consider
its logical aspects as well as its historical context. Finally, since the
results are negative, we summarize Arrow's reflections on how
the problem might be resolved. Arrow locates the key to the
problem within the individual; we suggest that it lies within the
procedures themselves. These considerations lead us to the final

section: Rawls' conception of a mechanism for constructing a just society.

A. SUMMARY OVERVIEW OF ARROW'S THESIS AND RESULTS

1. Problem Context. After reviewing alternative mechanisms for arriving at social welfare decisions, Arrow selects a "consensus" mechanism. Besides its inherent appeal to Western societies, this choice fixes individual reasoning as the basis for welfare decisions. He then joins this mechanism to a hybrid theory of values—one which combines the utilitarian notion of a common good with the pragmatic notion of self-interest—that has the effect of requiring a logical connection between the outcome of collective decisions and the inputs of reasonable, self-interested individuals.

2. Statement of the Problem. Is it possible to consistently transform, by aggregation, individual values into a collective choice which is sensitive and faithful to these values, in context of all possible worlds, and within the natural limits of the environment?

3. The Process of Social Choice. We are to imagine that each member of the society has reviewed, and decided his preferences between, all conceivable social states, yielding an ideal and true ordering of his values. Next, at a more realistic level, we are to imagine that the citizens are presented with, and express their preferences between, a particular set of alternative social states—candidates, commodity bundles, etc. It is these expressed preferences, reflecting the underlying true values, which enter as raw materials into the aggregation procedure.

4. Condition of Rationality. This condition requires that individual preferences, and the social choice derived from them, be "connected" and "transitive" to form a weak ordering. As the *test* of this condition we require an ordering of at least three alternatives by at least three persons.

5. Other Conditions. Individuals must be free to choose and express their preferences between alternative states, and each individual's vote must count. Two conditions require that the collective decisions be sensitive and faithful to individual preferences. The last two conditions prohibit social choices imposed by dictators or tradition.

6. Results of the Analysis. Under these requirements and con-

Table 8.4. Paradox of Voting

Individuals	Preference Orderings			Social Decision (Majority rule)
	1st	2nd	3rd	A over B by 2 to 1; B over C by 2 to 1; therefore A over C by rule
1	A	B	C	of transitivity. But actually C
2	B	C	A	over A by two to one. Thus the
3	C	A	B	result violates the condition of rationality—i.e., transitivity.[a]

[a] See Guilbaud (1966).

ditions, and within a context of all possible worlds, the analysis leads to the conclusion that no procedures will consistently produce admissible collective choices (the Impossibility Theorem). This result is exemplified by the Condorcet effect or the so-called "paradox of voting," illustrated in table 8.4.

In reviewing this result, Arrow works from both ends of the problem in an effort to pinpoint the nature of the paradox. On the one hand:

if no prior assumptions are made about the nature of individual orderings, there is no method of voting which will remove the paradox. . . . neither plurality voting nor any scheme of proportional representation, no matter how complicated. Similarly, the market mechanism does not create a rational social choice. (1963:59)

In short, the aggregation mechanism is flawed in its handling of free and independent choices.

On the other hand, were we to try to weight individual inputs in an attempt to make "interpersonal comparisons" of utility, sensitivity, needs, etc.—as social scientists do at the level of interval scales—then decisions reached must be either dictatorial or imposed by custom or tradition.

B. HISTORICAL AND FORMAL BACKGROUND OF THE WELFARE PROBLEM

As one positivist critic (Mishan 1969) puts it, welfare economics is torn between two mutually untenable masters: subjective ideals and objective arrangements. His "solution" is an "infusion of empiricism" (p. 80). Nevertheless, as he is well aware, this is not really a solution. Mishan asks us to imagine two families, each having experienced an increase in "real" income, but each envious of the other. If an economist treats the rise of income as an increase in welfare, this is sophistry given the envy. But, if envy becomes relevant, then his positive basis for analysis will dissolve. So, welfare as opposed to positive economics is hung upon a dilemma: the passages between subjective and objective states, and between individuals and their collective. The question naturally arises: "is this the best that can be done?"

In reviewing the historical background of the welfare issue, Arrow reviews two major streams of thought. On the one hand, his arguments indicate the sense in which "consensus" mechanisms are preferable to the alternatives of "tradition" (wise kings or elders) and "dictatorship," since, in effect, consensus is balanced between *stability* and *variety*.[22] The second stream is concerned with definitions of "goodness" or "utility." Idealism (e.g. Kant) presupposes "an objective social good defined independently of individual 'tastes'" (Arrow 1963:22). "Taste" suggests a corruption of true values. Pragmatism assumes that "each individual's good was identical with his desires" (p. 23). So, welfare is stranded between these two antithetical positions: seeking a "good" by aggregating individual preferences.

C. ARROW'S SUGGESTIONS FOR RESOLVING THE PARADOX

Arrow suggests two promising paths to a solution. The first is individualist and pragmatic. It substitutes tastes for values, so that expressed preferences are directly connected to personal consumption. But when personal consumption is not directly involved, an individual would be "indifferent"—he would vote for the status quo. When most persons are not indifferent, their interests are likely to be in conflict. Then, when a decision is reached it is imposed.

His second path is idealist: it presumes that individual values reflect each person's opinion of the common good—shared views of the same ultimate ends for the community. To bring these values to the surface, Arrow suggests a process of enlightenment: different opinions on social issues arise from lack of knowledge and can be removed by discovering the truth and letting it be widely known" (p. 88). As our discussion of Piagetian competency would indicate, this path appears quite promising. It has the effect of focusing our attention upon the social environment: knowledge, social relations, etc. This is the path the argument will follow in the next section.

D. SUMMARY AND CONCLUSION

Since Arrow's formal, interpretive analysis, and the dismal conclusion to which it leads, reflects our *actual* mechanisms for making political and economic choices, it ought to be quite jarring to the suppositions of empirical, oriented-to-actual, sociology. Market mechanisms address only two of our four perspectives: aggregating individuals (atoms) into wholes. Hence, they fail to take account of existing patterns of relationship, such as status consolidation, and the possible biases these introduce.

Moreover, like the child of Stage III., they provide no means for subordinating material objects ("good") to a fair and equitable symbolic discussion of the "rules" of welfare, justice, etc. To reach successive approximations to "enlightened" judgments, then, we need, like the amateur chess player aspiring to a level of master play, to construct better heuristics.

IV. RAWLS' THEORY OF JUSTICE: A "GENETIC STRUCTURALIST" APPROACH TO THE PROBLEM OF SOCIAL CHOICE[23]

As we have just seen, the problems of social welfare are of three kinds: (1) qualities of individuals as these affect the kinds of judgments rendered (for example, pragmatic self-interest vs. idealist opinions of the common good); (2) the related problem of defining "good" (the connection between material and symbolic aspects of our "objects" of choice); (3) finding a mechanism for transforming "parts" into a "whole" according to rules of consistency and a requisite balance between variety and stability. In a most ingenious manner, Rawls provides a constructive framework for solving these problems. In discussing his solution, we shall begin by showing how he handles the three problems. Next, we shall describe the basic principles his procedures produce. Finally, we shall illustrate how the theory can be applied to several key social issues.

A. THE THREE PROBLEMS

1. Individual Judgments. The problem here is whether individuals are *pragmatic* (selfish, self-interested) or *idealistic* (fundamentally similar in their judgments of common good). Rawls unravels this issue in a "genetic structuralist" manner. Like all other forms of human social behavior, "social judgments" are a compound of native and learned properties. As we have seen, in our discussion of Piaget's work, an individual begins his commerce with his world in a state of profound egocentrism, or "self-centeredness." But through experiences in common, with his peers or other facilitating environments, he gradually evolves mental structures marked by their logical consistency and reversibility. In a developmental-nativist sense, then, individuals are capable of meeting the "idealist" criterion. Furthermore, such competence is independent of what is actually learned.

Rawls is keenly aware of the arbitrary and systemic nature of "acquired" properties. Social values and norms are arbitrary in the linguistic sense: there is no materially necessary connection between symbols and the objects for which they stand. Consequently, the "meaning" of symbols is first and foremost contextual. Words and gestures have meaning within a system of other words and gestures.

By disentangling these native and arbitrary components, Rawls is able to make a considerable advance over Arrow's position. In a deep-structural sense, individuals are competent idealists, searching for the common good. Since the suprastructure is arbitrary and conventional, it is, unlike our biogram, subject to change in a Lamarckian sense. Hence, at one and the same time, the arbitrary system is the origin of social meaning and is subject to our purposeful manipulation. Our degree of freedom necessary to produce such changes is the competency of the individual. Following Piaget, Rawls reasons that "thought" is prior to, and a necessary condition for, language.

2. Defining the "good". In a thorough manner (1972, sections 5, 28–30), Rawls critiques the "utilitarian" approach to good. As we have just indicated, "goods" like "persons" are both material and symbolic. This symbolic-arbitrary aspect of good (the problem of drawing interpersonal comparisons) bedevils utilitarianism. It is also the origin of such social vices as "envy" and "spite." Finally, this symbolic-arbitrary aspect of good is apt to make us feel indifferent about decisions whenever our interests are not involved. So, Rawls differentiates the natural from the arbitrary (see his "thin theory of the good," section 60) sense of good. This has a twofold effect: (a) it residualizes our learned, self-interested sense of good, in order to make it the *object of choice*; (b) it brings formal reasoning into the fore as a means for constructing good. Hence, our sense of "good" is based upon our ability to reason formally, from whence we might construct our "contents" of good as a reflection of our social judgments.

3. *The Mechanism of Choice.* A great deal of heat has been generated by the principles (the substance) to which Rawls' procedures lead.[24] Hence, it is imperative to keep separate his "means" and the substance to which he thinks these would take us.

Since he properly regards social content as arbitrary, and thus an impediment to our reaching stable social decisions, Rawls proceeds to define a position from which we might choose the ground rules for constructing social relationships. We are, as it were, to become "referees" of the social construction process. In order to suspend the social contents, Rawls develops his concept of the "veil of ignorance." Behind this veil, we do not know any of the particular contents of social life (who or what we are) but only that social positions and relations exist. We are a group of strangers meeting to play touch football. We know there are rules, teams, goals, moves and positions, but we have not yet decided how to map persons onto positions. Before choosing the teams and playing the game, we need to decide how we want to play: for all-out for blood, money, and glory?—or for fun and enjoyment? This kind of decision context is called the "original position" where the basic terms of our game-contract are to be struck.

In short, in the "original position" and behind the "veil of ignorance," we are to choose the basic terms of our social contract. Once these terms are established, we lift the veil in stages (Rawls 1972:sect. 31), as we set rules, choose the teams, and flip the coin for kickoff. In other words, the "positive" or actual arrangements rest at the top of a four-stage sequence; formal-operational thought, where actual is subordinate to the possible and desirable, constitutes the foundation for such positive arrangements. So, Rawls' mechanism for choosing the principles by which we are to construct social arrangements achieves two important advances over the "market mechanism": it suspends the arbitrariness of actual social contents (say, particular and special interests), and it calls upon Piaget's "formal operations" as the rational vehicle for reaching basic social decisions. The effect of this is to produce a vertical hierarchy to our grounds of sociation. Since formal reasoning is a perfect self-regulator, we can expect "strict compliance" with the rules, based upon a general and shared "concept" of justice (pp. 454f.). When the veil of ignorance is lifted, at the level of positive arrangements, then "partial compliance" and different "conceptions" of justice come to the fore. Thus, where at the deepest level we find stability, at the surface we would find variety: competition, markets, discourse, etc. But the two extreme levels are linked by a process of circular reactions or "reflective equilibrium" (pp. 20f.).

B. THE BASIC PRINCIPLES

After going through a cautiously iterative process (see Rawls 1972:sects. 11, 13, and 46), Rawls arrives at his best guess as to the principles which reasonable and representative men would choose behind the veil of ignorance:

1. *First Principle ("equity"):* "Each person is to have an equal right to the most extensive total system of equal basic liberties compatible with a similar system of liberty for all" (p. 302).
2. *Second Principle ("equality"):* "Social and economic inequalities (if we choose to permit them) are to be arranged so that they are both:
   "(a) to the greatest benefit of the least advantaged, consistent with the 'just savings principle,' and,
   "(b) attached to offices and positions open to all under condition of 'fair' equality of opportunity" (p. 302).

Note that these two principles are Rawls' best guess, so could be subject to revision. Since procedure and substance can be separated, the theory is subject to test and falsifiability. In addition, since the principles are to be chosen behind a veil of ignorance, no one in the original position knows positively who he is. It would behoove the individual to choose principles he could live with no matter who he became: "just savings" means no one generation is allowed to waste resources or spoil the environment. Finally, the principle of liberty has priority (see sects. 8 and 39) over opportunity and distribution. This takes account of: (a) the fundamentally *social* (systemic) nature of the contract; (b) social construction as an agreement to tie up our fates in a stable, mutually agreeable way, yet permitting variance and differences to appear in our separate pursuits. Finally, the principles possess a reversible deep-to-surface-to-deep organization, which we shall now illustrate.

C. APPLICATIONS

"Civil disobedience" and "conscientious refusal" (Rawls 1972:sects. 53–59) arise as reflections of the theories' vertical structure. At the deepest level we have inviolable principles and strict compliance (logical necessity). But at the surface, where actions, intentions, and consequences are not always correlated, partial compliance comes into play. The two concepts are an inherent but circumscribed part of the theory because: (a) justice has its roots in the (formal) reason of men; (b) but reasonable men may differ on the justice of a positive law; (c) hence, disobedience is an appeal to others for "reflective equilibrium"—to heed and weigh his objections by descending to the "original position" to test the case.

Religious "toleration" (see note 6) is another illustrative example of how Rawls' theory works. It reflects the deep/surface organization of the theory (Rawls 1972:4). Rousseau had posed the apparent dilemma: members of the "faithful" must find it intolerable to live with those infidels believed damned, so must either seek to convert or eliminate them. However, the dilemma is merely a positive appearance. In the "original position": (a) no one would know to which faith he would belong; (b) each would choose basic principles with which he could live, regardless; so, (c) Rousseau's dilemma confuses *positive* and *deep structures*. Fanatical and absolute commitments, are, in other words, *arbitrary*, and as Blau's concept of "heterogeneity" suggests, they are subject to attenuation.

Finally, we come to the key question in the theory: "is man genetically "selfish" as the sociobiologists maintain; or does his nature require taming, as orthodox sociology would have it; or does ontogeny, as a free development, lead to social sentiments and a deep conception of justice?" Recall that Arrow, in seeking to resolve the paradox, raised such questions. The type of answer we find is crucial to Rawls' theory, since the possibility of a just and well-ordered society depends upon the moral nature of men—the kinds of decisions they would reach in the "original position."

By basing his procedures upon Piaget's sturdy research foundations (see esp. Rawls 1972:ch. 8), Rawls is able to move beyond speculative philosophy to entertain a precise answer: our nature leads from egocentricity to formal-operational cooperation. Hence, moral judgment is the foundation for constructing a *just* social structure. In fig. 8.5 we show how ontogeny is transformed from an initial state of egocentrism to its final state of formal operations, where material aspects become subordinate to the form of symbolic logic. From this perspective, the paradox of voting is no longer a problem. The paradox, as it were, is bracketed between deep and surface structures. While intransitive choices might appear at the surface of social life, where competitiveness and indifference exists, they do not arise at the deepest level, where social agreements are based upon discussion and decisions in common, since reasoning transcends any "actuals."

For the sake of simplicity, we view ontogeny from A's perspective. In the earliest stage, where play is seldom governed by rules, the child (fig. 8.5a) prefers to "win." Fate, however, conspires to let B (x = transform) or C (y = transform) win; at times, A comes in last ($x \cdot y$ = transforms). In this stage, the mind is unable to "identify" (symbolized by a single arrowhead in fig. 8.5) with these outcomes. Gradually, however, and with experience, A is able to represent, concretely, the different classes of outcomes (the double arrowheads), as in the Competitive Stage. Finally, as operations become fully reversible, material aspects are subject to the logic of transformations ($x \cdot y$ = z; $x \cdot z$ = y, etc.) as is characteristic of "Cooperation."

In fig. 8.5b we geometrically represent these transformations: beginning with $A>B>C$, rotation on the x axis produces $B>A>C$; rotation of the y axis produces $C>A>B$, and rotation of both axes

Figure 8.5. The Stages of Moral Judgment Anchor Rawls' Theory of Justice and the Decisions Reached in the "Original Position"

a. The three stages of judgment.

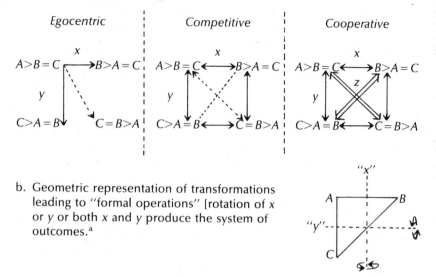

b. Geometric representation of transformations leading to "formal operations" [rotation of x or y or both x and y produce the system of outcomes.[a]

c. Comparison of competent and expressed (long and short-run) preferences

Stage	Competency (True Preference)	Expressed Preference	
		Short-Run	Long-Run
I	Habits or Rituals:	—	—
II	Imitation and Autism: children are egocentric and game is collective monologue	$A:a$ $B:b$ $C:c$	
III	Competition and Strategy $A:a>b=c$ $B:b>c=a$ $C:c>a=b$	(one admissible ordering leads to Condorcet effect) $A:a>b=c$ $B:b>c=a$ $C:c>a=b$	$A:a>b=c$ $B:b>c=a$ $C:c>a=b$
IV	Cooperative—Formal (all possible worlds) $A:a=b=c$ $B:b=c=a$ $C:c=a=b$	(desire to win) $A:a>b=c$ $B:b>c=a$ $C:c>a=b$	(fairness) $A:a=b=c$ $B:b=c=a$ $C:c=a=b$

[a] See Barbut (1970).

produces $C = B > A$. Finally, (fig. 8.5c) we show the four stages of competency broken down into "true" and "expressed" preferences for outcomes. Because of the long-run of experiences in common (where A = person; a = preferred outcome), each individual may play to win (surface structure = short run) subject to an agreement of fairness, equity, and role-playing ability (deep structure = long run). In short, experiences in common produce a correlation of competency and practices.

V. GENERAL SUMMARY AND CONCLUSIONS

We began the discussion by comparing and contrasting three approaches to social structure. Sociobiology is construed as an atomistic and mechanical theory of social behavior. While it pretends to scientific superiority, its claims are generally unjustified.[25] Next, we identified two sociologies. The dominant form is addressed to "actual" structure only, and as yet lacks an adequate theoretical orientation. In this sense, it is "structure without genesis." The alternative form views the origin of structure as residing in systems of ideas, not genes, and so seeks to identify the general principles of organization, utilizing logic as a means for locating the "actual" in a context of the "possible." Finally, "genetic structuralism" is a synthesis of biological and social structures. It seeks to represent how emergent properties of mind interact with the conventional idea-systems to produce a correlation between competent judgment and actual behaviors.

Since "competence" of the individual appears to evolve even in a minimal social environment, two conclusions may be drawn from the discussion. (1) The invariance of individual competence provides the framework within which to judge, adjust, and otherwise construct the rules of social relationships. (2) The main problematic of social construction is the system of rules which underlie actual patterns of relationships vis à vis matters of justice, and the distribution of resources and opportunities. Hence, in stark contrast to the elementary and mechanical determinism of sociobiology, the emphases within the sociological enterprise begin with the composition of rules, followed by the rearrangements and adjustments necessary to realize the rules. To emphasize the contrast between elementary determinism and composition analysis, we shall review each level of the argument.

1. While sociobiology is based upon modern genetics, this genetics is not compositional. To date, its models are addressed to simple, additive mappings of a few genes onto simple traits. Few efforts are addressed to the full ensemble of the 10,000+ genes in the human genome. (Curiously, it is the Marxist geneticists [Lewontin 1976] who are addressing these questions.) Hence, concepts of predispositions to native "selfishness," "conformity," etc. appear unwarranted. Nevertheless, sociobiology is of value on two counts: (a) it is an exceptional articulation of Western ideology (Sahlins 1976); (b) its zoology-ethology provides a rich lore for comparative sociology.

2. The human brain is an incredibly rich, interconnected ensemble. The cerebrum contains 10 billion neurons, each of which is connected to from 1,000 to 10,000 other neurons (Eccles 1977). This ensemble is extremely active: neurons atrophy from disuse or grow from use. In this context, the "robot" analogy is extremely impoverished. It is upon this richly endowed platform that sociocultural constructions are based. Curiously, the dominant hemisphere is the locus of language, arithmetic, and analytic skills. This, perhaps, explains the "reductionist" bias of sociobiology. The minor hemisphere contains the tools essential for compositional analysis: geometry, pattern-recognition, etc. Hence, the task of sociology implies a balance in the workings of the two hemispheres.

3. The neonate, while endowed with primitive reflexes, actively constructs its world, via a circular reaction, by building combinatorial structures of mind. It is this same imagery which distinguishes the performances of "amateur" from "accomplished" chess players. Their differences are, in the main, attributable to experience: the master learns systems of expected relationships within a context of legitimate rules and conventions.

4. Piaget, employing a "psychologic" as his model, identified four broad stages of mental development. The last, relatively invariant stage is marked by "formal operations"—mental structures which are fully reversible and therefore perfect self-regulators. "Morality" he defines as that stage of respect an individual acquires for rules and their applications. In turn, the stage of application reflects qualities of the social environment—say, *heteronomy* vs. *mutuality*. This notion takes account of the conjecture that "self" and "consciousness" are social constructions.

At this point, the argument shifted to consider the relationships between competent individuals and social structure.

5. Arrow's negative results cast doubt on the merits of the "market mechanism" and the doctrine of "utilitarianism." The first fails to take account of structure, since it is essentially an atomistic model. The latter fails to separate the material from the symbolic components of "goods." Once we take the "meaning" of material goods seriously, our attention is diverted from elementary objects to the fabric or tissue of the sociocultural system (from the *actual* to the *possible*).

To illustrate, Ekman (1973) has identified six "universal" facial expressions. He regards these as innately programmed; thus the universality. No learning is required for their production or recognition. Ekman is curiously adamant in his insistence that facial expression does *not* constitute a language (*cf.* Birdwhistell). Still, as any actor knows, the six basics can be combined: (a) simultaneously, yielding a rich vocabulary of subtle differentiations; (b) sequentially yielding a paralinguistic *text* in either an "honest" or "deceptive" manner. But the contrast to be drawn is between an innate, simple vocabulary and the rich, contextual elaborations.

6. Finally, Rawls' genetic structuralism takes account of the developmental and native competency of actors culminating in the Stage of "formal operations," and, the arbitrary and compositional quality of social rules and symbols, and the structures to which these give rise. When social structure is limited to the "actual," social construction is retarded. But when we suspend this concreteness, behind the veil of ignorance where formal reasoning is brought to the fore, then basic rules, and the relationships these imply, facilitate social construction.[26] But this procedural strategy does not imply that social structure is epiphenomenal; to the contrary, it is precisely due to the importance of the composition of social structure that Rawls designed his theory.

Hence, we have the possibility of choosing our rules of association: the construction of "multiform heterogeneity" or the entropy of "status consolidation"—tolerance or intolerance.

NOTES

1. Stability *and* variety constitute the poles of a fundamental dimension of opposition for biology, sociology, and constructionism. In biology, the gene is

more "stable" than chromosomes or organism, thus is contrued as the unit-of-selection; still, genetic variety is essential for adaptations to random shifts in the environment. Similarly, Blau's two concepts (below) represent stability and variety.

2. Wilson's insistence on locating ethics and motives in the hypothalmic-limbic regions of the mammalian brain may reflect the fact that this structure is conjectured to precede cerebral structures in natural evolution. However, from the point of view of "objective knowledge," it is the cerebrum, as the enabling structure for language, culture, "self," and consciousness, which precedes lower brain structures (see Popper and Eccles 1977; Jaynes 1976). Besides this "reversibility" issue, we would argue that brains must interact with symbols to produce "motives" or "ethics."

3. "Tolerance" is one of our general issues for two reasons: It applies to the rules of relationship between persons; it is not an object but a relationship. It is explicitly treated by Blau and Rawls (see below).

4. Dawkins suggests that there are 250,000 genes in the human biogram. The count may have no upper limit, as subatomic physics continues to search for, but not find, the basic building blocks of material life (see Capra 1975).

5. See Eccles (1977:221) for a description of the discrete functions of the dominant and minor hemispheres. (The fact that both language and analytic reasoning are dominant hemisphere functions may account for the excessive emphasis upon such analysis as sociobiology.) For an example of their coordination, see Bronowski's discussion of the Pythagorean proof (1973:158–59) and the Alhambran tiles (*ibid.*, pp. 172–73).

6. As table 8.1 indicates, the market mechanism has only two levels—a collection of independent units (atoms) and the collectivity or social whole. The lack of attention either to patterns of relationship or to the systemic-symbolic nature of rules, in both biology and sociology, may be traced to the reliance upon parametric statistics. That this may cause scientists to neglect much that is important can be seen in Schelling's (1978) recent work on micro-motives—critical mass—macrobehavior, which employs a model like Boyle's gas laws, (cf. Hardin 1968; Hirsch 1976).

7. Arrow's analysis requires that each individual's vote must count in any derived social decision. Obviously, as inequality spreads, the influence of the powerful becomes increasingly disproportionate. By focusing on the basic rules of sociation, Rawls is able to overcome or circumscribe such disequilibrating inequality.

8. The theory has a four-stage, deep to surface structure. At the deepest level, formal reasoning produces stability in the form of a general "concept" of justice and a form of stable ("strict") compliance. It is at the surface where we, if we so decided, would find "market mechanisms." So, from deep to surface levels we find, successively: rules, relations, autonomous actors, and the chance factors of the environment.

9. Rawls' concept of "reflective equilibrium" is modeled after this concept, which implies self-regulation as opposed to the linear, asymmetrical and additive models which characterize orthodox sociology and biology.

10. By "normative" two things are intended. First, it is opposed to "positive," so introduces the subjective into the behavioral; secondly, it takes account of the view that the origins of social structure are idea-systems, not gene (natural) systems.

11. Note the important conceptual affinity of "egocentrism" with Dawkins' "selfish gene"; both concepts refer to "self-centeredness." However, through the processes of successive decenterings which characterize ontogenetic stages, selfishness is gradually displaced by the self-other coordinations of formal reasoning.

12. The question of "similarities" has a deep significance. Arrow attempts to probe the issue as a means for resolving the dilemma of social–decision-making; Rawls articulates a procedure, based upon Piaget's research, for producing a convergence between different "conceptions" of justice to arrive at one, shared "concept" of justice.

13. Recall Blau's description of the "genetic difference" between an empirical-oriented-to-factual sociology, and the more formal approach which employs logical tools is a search for general principles of organization. This second, unorthodox approach seeks to interpret, not explain or predict, social organization.

14. For a model of how reciprocity leads to the application of formal reasoning to social relations, see fig. 8.5.

15. Wilson (1975:562–63) chastises Rawls for his "intuitionist," non-limbic ethical position. This seems unwarranted for two reasons: Rawls explicitly rejects intuition (1972:sect. 7); the limbic system is implicated in intuition. Moreover, Wilson's stance—his concrete behaviorism—is a step below that of Rawls' formal-operational reasoning. Wilson is at the level of concrete operations.

16. Recall Blau's description of "heterogeneity": "it attenuates ingroup relations, which confine people's perspectives, and intensifies intergroup relations, which foster tolerance and flexibility (variety)." So, mutual consent implies both formal reasoning and qualities of the social environment, as the two conditions for justice. Rawls' theory is modeled after this sort of conception (see section IV).

17. For an insightful study of role-playing phenomena, as these are reflected in language use and understanding, see Carol Chomsky (1969:41–102).

18. "Referees" are those who see "rules" as emanating from social life under the conditions of mutual consent. For an application of this concept to the relationships between researchers and their subjects see table 8.4.

19. Jaynes (1976) conjectures that "magic" is a function of the bicameral mind: the interaction of brain (minor hemisphere) and social environment (the need for social control as social structures began to elaborate). In bicameral times, self-consciousness did not exist, so the "me" and the "I" resided in separate spheres. The voices of the "gods" resided in the minor hemisphere, as guides to actions, explanations, etc.

20. Equalitarianism is the stage of "concrete" operations—where reason takes over from the "voices of the gods," but where thought is still subordinate to data. In the formal operational period, this relationship is reversed. For a variety of data to explicate these images, see Inhelder and Piaget (1958).

21. "Aggregation" calls to mind the simple, two-level relationship between individuals and society (e.g., Schelling's micromotives and macrobehavior). In contrast to aggregation, genetic structuralism is concerned with "composition"; it begins with the *rules* or *relationships*.

22. See note 1.

23. For a sociological discussion of Rawls' theory, see Coleman (1974), and the subsequent commentary on Coleman's interpretations (Condon 1976).

24. Heated discussions of Rawls' work appear in all manner of social science and humanities journals. One very common criticism is addressed to Rawls' "maximin" decision rule. Within the context of decision theory, the criticisms would make sense. But, in the context of Rawls' theory they do not. First, he merely chose maximin as a "heuristic" to illustrate how he thought men would decide behind a veil of ignorance. Second, and more importantly, the procedures for contructing a position of choice can and should be kept separate from the decision rule or the substance to which applications would lead. What appears to confound his critics is the lack of appreciation for the depth (levels) of the theory. Decision theory is "utilitarian" not "contractual."

25. The concept of "claim" may have two meanings: an "objective," "truthful" meaning, as in the domain of scientific materialism; or as a sociolinguistic expression. Within this latter tradition, the concept can be assimilated to the more general category of "accounts" (Scott and Lyman 1968). There, claims are honored, not so much as a matter of empirical validity, but, as a matter of the prestige of the speaker. The implication is that the emergent, cultural "whole" (symbols) is greater than the sum or product of its "parts" (genes).

26. For instance, if we derive "rules" from "origins" with respect to "selfishness" we have a number of possibilities: (a) man is innately selfish, so social relations must conform therewith; (b) the notion of "selfishness" is learned, so its function requires justification; (c) the study of ontogeny indicates initial selfishness which is attenuated by social experience. Obviously, choosing between these options ought to be based upon behavioral analysis; so a complication can be introduced: the possibility of "deception": (d) we learn that man is innately selfish, or, (e) we learn to conceal innate selfishness behind the appearances of altruism.

REFERENCES

Arrow, Kenneth J. 1963. *Social Choice and Individual Values*. 2 ed. New Haven: Yale University Press.

Ashby, W. Ross. 1956. *An Introduction to Cybernetics*. New York: Wiley.

Barbut, Marc. 1961. "Does the majority ever rule?" *Portfolio and Arts News Annual* 4:79–83, 161–168.

—— 1970. "On the meaning of the word 'structure' in mathematics." In Michael Lane, ed., *Introduction to Structuralism*. New York: Basic Books.

Blau, Peter. 1974. "Parameters of social structure." *American Sociological Review* (October)39:615–35.

Bronowski, Jacob. 1973. *The Ascent of Man*. Science Horizons, Inc., and the B.B.C.

Capra, Fritjof. 1975. *The Tao of Physics*. Boulder, Colorado: Shambhala.

Chomsky, Carol. 1969. *The Acquisition of Syntax in Children from 5 to 10*. Cambridge: MIT Press.

Chomsky, Noam. 1968. *Language and Mind*. New York: Harcourt, Brace and World.

—— 1972. *Problems of Knowledge and Freedom* (The Russell Lectures). London: Barrie and Jenkins.

Coleman, James A. 1974. "Review Essay: Inequality, sociology and moral philosophy" *American Journal of Sociology* (November)80:739–63.

Condon, Thomas F. 1976. Comment on Coleman [1974] *American Journal of Sociology*. (July)82:205–17.

Connell, R. W. 1971. *The Child's Construction of Politics*. Carlton, Victoria: Melbourne University Press.

Coombs, Clyde H. 1964. *A Theory of Data*. New York: John Wiley and Co.

Cunningham, Michael. 1972. *Intelligence: Its Organization and Development*. New York: Academic Press.

Dawkins, Richard. 1978. *The Selfish Gene*. London: Granada Publishing Co.

Eccles, John C. 1977. *The Understanding of the Brain*. New York: McGraw-Hill.

Ekman, Paul, ed. 1973. *Darwin and Facial Expression*. New York: Academic Press.

Ekman, P. and H. Oster. 1979. "Facial expressions of emotions" *Annual Review of Psychology*. Palo Alto, California: Annual Reviews, Inc.

Guilbaud, G. Th. 1966. "Theories of the general interest, and the logical problem of aggregation." In P. F. Lazarsfeld and N. W. Henry, eds. *Readings in Mathematical Social Science*. Cambridge: MIT Press.

Hardin, Garrett. 1968. "The tragedy of the commons." *Science* 166:1243–48.

Hirsch, Fred. 1976. *Social Limits to Growth*. Cambridge: Harvard University Press.

Inhelder, Barbel and Jean Piaget. 1958. *The Growth of Logical Thinking*. Anne Parsons and Stanley Milgram, trans. New York: Basic Books, Inc.

—— 1964. *The Early Growth of Logic in the Child*. E. A. Lunzer and D. Papert, trans. New York: Humanities Press.

Jaynes, Julian. 1976. *The Origin of Consciousness in the Breakdown of the Bicameral Mind*. Boston: Houghton-Mifflin.

Lévi-Strauss, Claude. 1963. *Structural Anthropology*. Trans. C. Jacobson and B. G. Schoepf. Garden City: Doubleday Anchor.

Lewontin, Richard. 1975. "The heritability hangup." *Science* 190:1163–68.
—— 1976. "The fallacy of biological determinism." The *Sciences* 16:6–10.
Mauss, Marcel. 1967. *The Gift: Forms and Functions of Exchange in Archaic Society.* New York: W. W. Norton.
Mishan, E. J. 1969. *Welfare Economics: Ten Introductory Essays.* New York: Random House.
Moore, O. K. and Alan R. Anderson. 1971. "Some principles for the design of clarifying educational environments." In J. Aldous, et al. eds. *Family Problem Solving.* Hinsdale, Ill.: The Dryden Press.
Newell, Allen and Herbert A. Simon. 1972. *Human Problem Solving.* Englewood Cliffs, N.J.: Prentice-Hall.
Piaget, Jean. 1965. *The Moral Judgment of the Child.* M. Gabain. trans. New York: The Free Press.
—— 1970a. *Structuralism.* C. Maschler trans. New York: Harper.
—— 1970b. "The place of the sciences of man in the system of sciences." *Main Trends of Research in the Social and Human Sciences.* Part I: Social Sciences. Mouton/UNESCO.
Popper, Karl R. and John C. Eccles. 1977. *The Self and Its Brain.* London: Springer International.
Rawls, John. 1972. *A Theory of Justice.* Cambridge: Harvard University Press.
Sagan, Carl. 1977. *The Dragons of Eden.* New York: Random House.
Sahlins, Marshall. 1976. *The Use and Abuse of Biology.* Ann Arbor: University of Michigan.
Schelling, Thomas C. 1978. *Micromotives and Macrobehavior.* Toronto: Geo. C. McLeod.
Scott, M. B. and S. M. Lyman. 1968. "Accounts." *American Sociological Review* 33:46–62.
Sen, Amartya K. 1970. *Collective Choice and Social Welfare.* San Francisco: Holden-Day.
Simon, Herbert. 1969. *The Sciences of the Artificial.* Cambridge: MIT Press.
—— 1974. "How big is a chunk?" *Science* 183:484–88.
Weick, Karl E. 1969. *The Social Psychology of Organizing.* Reading, Mass.: Addison-Wesley.
Wilson, Edward O. 1975. *Sociobiology: The New Synthesis.* Cambridge, Mass.: Belknap Press.
—— 1978. *On Human Nature.* Cambridge: Harvard University Press.
Wilson, Edward O. and William H. Bossert. 1971. *A Primer of Population Genetics.* Sunderland, Mass.: Sinauer Associates, Inc.

CHAPTER NINE

TOWARD A DEEP STRUCTURAL ANALYSIS OF MORAL ACTION

CHARLES W. LIDZ

Since Durkheim, it has become almost impossible to do a general sociological analysis of any institution or situation without a description of the moral, or as it is sometimes called "normative," aspects of a social phenomenon. A description of the normative order of a group is part of the sociological analysis of everything from skid row alcoholics to industrialization in the Third World. Terms like "norm," "value," "group ethic," "normative boundaries," "normative structure," "rules," and "law" are so pervasive in sociological writing that the point requires no elaboration. What Durkheim proposed was the centrality of the moral order to the social order (Durkheim 1947, 1951, 1958, 1961). Durkheim saw that every society had its own basic moral core or collective conscience and that its functioning provided the basic orientation to social life. Durkheim also saw that each institutionalized differentiated role relationship had its own, societally specified, moral order which provided more specialized regulation (Durkheim 1947). These findings are now central to modern sociology.

However, the importance of this topic to descriptive sociology, and its centrality to many general theoretical solutions to the problem of social order, does not mean that we have produced adequate theories of the structure of the moral order. My aim here is to raise some questions about the adequacy of current theories of the structure of moral action and to describe a possible

I owe special thanks to Eviatar Zerubavel, Rainer Baum, Thomas Farraro, Andrew Walker, Howard Schwartz, Talcott Parsons and my brother Victor Lidz for help with earlier drafts.

alternate line of approach using some notions of generative grammars borrowed from transformational-generative linquistics. I shall propose some tenative formulations of how such a grammar might function. However these are not intended to be empirically adequate theories but only illustrations of the general position. Although I shall be proposing rather basic changes in it, it is my goal to try to keep this analysis within the framework of the General Theory of Action as developed by Talcott Parsons and his many collaborators, students, and followers (Parsons 1937, 1951, 1961; Smelser 1963; Laubser et al. 1976).

Emile Durkheim introduced the concern with moral order and its effect on social action as a topic for modern sociology. The brilliance of his use of such concepts as "the collective conscience," "anomie," "the cult of the individual," and "non-contractual elements of contract"—all of them his ways of thinking about *la morale*—remains a delight to many sociologists. However Durkheim's concern was not primarily with the structure of morality. As a functionalist, his concern was mainly with the interrelationship between morality and social behavior and social institutions. Thus Durkheim wrote about the effects of patterns of moral structure on suicide, societal development, and crime rates, and looked at the ways in which other institutions—especially religion—affected the moral structure of society.

Durkheim was not concerned with the analysis of the functioning of the underlying structures of moral systems.[1] His first concern was demonstrating that moral systems do indeed have an order and that the patterns of those systems have an effect on social structure in general. His radical insistence that sociological analysis be kept separate from psychological analysis, and social systems from psychological systems, kept him from a concern with how individuals could continuously create and re-create moral structures and make them visible through their actions. Durkheim, and those that have followed his path, assumed that the only psychological processes necessary for an individual to properly employ societal moral schema were the elementary mechanisms of learning and a socialized commitment to the basic moral principles of the society (Durkheim 1961). This is the rough equivalent of the position which the Bloomfieldian linguists took toward the analysis of language. They argued that it was possible to understand the structure of language without any concern for psychology, including how the speaker could generate sentences (Leiber 1975). In their commitment to make linguistics a "positive science" they tried to abolish any concerns with the "mental element." Although Durkheim certainly did not try to do away with the mental element in sociology, his reiteration of the concept of society as a real entity rather than an analytic one hindered an adequate analysis of the interrelations between moral structures and their use in interaction by individuals. This prevented an adequate formal analysis of the structures of moral action and ultimately of the functions of morality in the social order.

THE CONCEPT OF MORALITY

Critics of Durkheim and his followers have often objected that Durkheim overestimated the pervasiveness and importance of moral structure. They have tended to emphasize the importance of self-interested actions in the development and maintenance of social structure.[2] At least part of this trouble evolves from Durkheim's tendency to equate morality with an unsituated concept of what is universally and nonselfishly good. Despite Durkheim's work on organic solidarities, the tendency has been to accentuate the collective, common, mechanical, or universal aspects of moral prescriptions. Durkheim himself tended to emphasize the disinterested and obligatory nature of morality (Durkheim 1961). It constrained the selfish desires of the individual. Thus, in his analysis of the marketplace, Durkheim tended to see morality as entering into the interactions only in the noncontractual elements of contract (Durkheim 1947). He failed to see that the rational pursuit of one's "self-interest" in the marketplace is also a morally prescribed and sanctioned expectation.[3] What I want to suggest here, among other things, is that universalistic, collectivity-oriented moral prescriptions are only one type of moral formulation.

The second difficulty with most current formal concepts of morality is that they focus almost exclusively on the evaluation of *acts*. As we shall see later, when we discuss the ways Talcott Parsons used the concept of normative control, this arises in part out of the specific theoretical use to which theorists have tried to put morality. However many aspects of action are evaluated in everyday life including the *persons* or *groups* involved, the *goals* of the action, the *means* employed, and the *settings* in which the action occurs. These various evaluations are, of course, intimately connected with one another. For example, the evaluations of persons are based in part on their acts. Conversely, we evaluate acts and goals on the basis of what we know about the people who do or propose them.[4] At any rate, we need a definition of morality which does not preclude such an analysis. Thus preliminarily we can define morality as the *aspect of action concerned with the evaluation of meaningful objects using the concepts of "good" and "bad" and other similar evaluative dualisms*.

The phrase "similar evaluative dualisms" cries out for some clarification even on a preliminary basis. Many adjectives and adverbs fit within this description to a greater or lesser degree. "Friendly" and "mean" are, in most situations of talk, almost subcategories of the concepts of "good" and "bad," although to call a defensive lineman in football "mean" is sometimes meant as a compliment. Adjectives like "strong" and "weak" are usually somewhat less morally involved, although again, probably not for defensive linemen. At the extreme, a list of house paints will describe some as "flat" and others as "high gloss" intending no evaluation whatsoever of the two types of paint. An actor might, however, use the terms in a moral manner ("And what was worse, they painted the walls with a high gloss paint!").

However the particular terms must not be treated as moral or not moral in and of themselves. Rather, any particular term must be seen simply as part of the verbal interaction which is meant to index, or refer to, the underlying meaning. I shall try below to make this clearer by the use of the concepts of "surface" and "deep" structure as they are used in linguistics. However, for present purposes it is enough to note that whether or not a word is a moral evaluative term is a situated and not an "objective" property. In the context of its use the particular term indexes the deep evaluation rather than being that evaluation itself. This is true even of the prototypical terms "good" and "bad" themselves. The greeting "Good morning" is not usually an evaluative statement about the particular temporal location of the actor. Equally interesting is the fact that these terms can be used to index their moral opposites, as when an actor describes another as "so good it's sickening." Or consider a colloquial use of the term "bad": "He's a really bad dude" is a laudatory description. We shall consider below these paradoxes of usage. For present purposes, it is important to note that the theoretical program proposed here operates within an explicit recognition of the indexicality of moral action. The phenomenon we are dealing with cannot be understood or even defined independent of the processes by which meaning is constituted.[5]

It might be objected that by defining morality in the broad way we have here, everything is included and the term means nothing—or at least it is not the same phenomenon that has traditionally been referred to as morality. That objection is, of course, partially valid. Any change in definition leads to a change in the boundaries of the subject. The definition of morality offered here focuses on the social world as moral action rather than defining some parts of social action as moral and others as not. It is continuous with traditional sociological analyses of morality in its concern with good and evil, its collective prescription, and its obligatory character. In the end, the justification for this refocusing of the concept of morality is its utility as an empirical and theoretical tool.

Before we leave the issue of definition, a word must be said about the various levels of the problem of morality in General Action Theory. An adequate theory of moral action must deal with its integration into the four levels of action systems. First, morality has a cultural aspect (Parsons 1961). It is part of the system of symbols, and an adequate theory of moral action must articulate well with what we know about the functioning of symbol systems in general and particularly with our knowledge of linguistic systems. After all, linguistic systems are the primary organizing foci of cultural dynamics. Thus it seems necessary that any theory of morality must in general be compatible with transformational-structuralist linguistics as it has evolved over the past two decades.

The second level of any analysis of action is the social level, which will be the primary focus of this analysis. Although I shall deal quite critically with the conventional sociological theories of morality, there can be no question, after Durkheim, that institutionalized moral schemas play a central role in the maintenance of the social order. Although we shall try to show that the normative structures described by Durkheim and his theoretical descendants cannot be thought of as the governing structures of moral action (the deep structures of morality), any theory of moral structure must be able to account for the production of such moral forms as laws, allegories, informal rules, and institutionalized values. Moreover, it must produce clear enough moral evaluations of acts and objects so as to generate some consensus for the purpose of collective sanctioning (Parsons 1951).

Finally we must deal with two differing levels of "psychological" structures and morality's relationship to them. First, most moral action is deeply involved with the actor's affective functioning. The Freudian superego is properly conceptualized as the aspect of personality which produces commitment to products generated by the deep moral structures. That is, the properly functioning superego produces guilt and self-righteousness which are internally generated sanctions for compliance with moral prescriptions (Parsons 1952).

At a different level, any theory of moral structure must be cognitively usable by the actor. The predominant theoretical description of cognition is, of course, contained in the work of Jean Piaget. Although Piaget's own formulations of moral development are too closely tied to the Durkheimian and Kantian formulations of morality to be adequate for our purposes (Piaget 1965), theories of moral structure must be generally compatible with Piaget's concept of cognitive structure.[6] Provisionally then, any description of the structure of moral action must be able to show how these could used by actors of all post-sensorimotor developmental levels. Any theory of morality which requires cognitive abilities of a very high level would have to account for how children are capable of moral functioning at the level they do without such cognitive abililities.

In this paper, however, the main attention will focus on the social and cultural level problem. In order to do this we must first review the state of the current theory of moral action. The best place to begin this effort is with the work of Talcott Parsons and his followers and coworkers. The reasons for this choice are rather obvious. Although Parsons' work no longer dominates the discussion in sociological theory the way it did two decades ago, his work remains the most comprehensive and systematic attempt to account for social order. Moreover, Parsons, following Durkheim, made morality a key focus of that account and his theory of moral action remains the leading effort in that field. There have been some substantial critiques of his theory, but we should nevertheless begin with Parsons.

TALCOTT PARSONS AND THE PROBLEM OF ORDER

The role of morality in social action was the central focus in Talcott Parsons' work from *The Structure of Social Action* until the time of his death. However, Parsons was never interested in morality per se. His works do not contain a serious attempt to describe the role of morality in empirical interaction, or any effort to get at the dynamics which generate moral actions in any situated occasion.[7] Moreover, the origin of Parsons' essential terms and concepts in his analysis of moral action (values and norms) demonstrates that his interest is not in morality for its own sake but in its relationship to the concept of social order. There is nothing inherently wrong with this but, as I shall try to show, it led Parsons to generate a theory which focused on certain aspects of moral action while ignoring others. In the end it also led to certain mistaken conclusions about the nature of the social order.

For Parsons, the moral (or normative) order is the central component in the maintenance of social order. Parsons developed this position in the analysis of the unit act in *The Structure of Social Action* (Parsons 1937:43–76) which involved three components of action, the *actor*, the *ends* or goal states, and the *means* to those goal states. Included in the analysis were the "conditions of action," which he saw as factors external to action. The means were seen as conditions of action transformed into elements of action through their intentional use by the actor to attain goals. Parsons was not concerned with which of these elements were morally evaluated but with what their role was in the production of the social order. He tried to show that no theory of action could possibly account for the nature of social order unless it had two moral components—one which involved the prescription of ends and another which regulated the means of action.

This analysis allowed Parsons to establish, beyond effective challenge, the predominance of Durkheimian and Weberian theory over earlier positivistic and utilitarian theories of action. The point here is neither to reiterate Parsons' arguments, nor least of all, to dispute his refutation of utilitarian and positivistic theories. What is important is that, in the process, Parsons developed the dominant theories of normative (moral) regulation of action based on the concept of the unit act. The moral regulation of ends eventually came to be referred to as "values" and the regulation of means came to be identified as "norms."

Although Parsons was to abandon the concept of the unit act after this work, the concepts of "norm" and "value" have come to be central to the analysis of the moral components of action both in Parsons' work and in the rest of sociology. What we must now consider is whether this model of the structure of morality can serve as a scientifically adequate account of moral action.

SOME PROBLEMS WITH THE PARSONIAN PARADIGM OF MORALITY

Because of the grounding of Parsons' concepts in the effort to deduce social order from the concept of morality, the Parsonian paradigm, and sociological theory in general, has not dealt with other moral structures in the general manner that it dealt with norms and values. Specifically, Parsons did not find it important for his argument to attend to the fact that both the actor and the conditions of action are also routinely subject to moral evaluation and the object of societally institutionalized moral prescription. Let us begin by considering the evaluation of actors. (In order to separate "actor" as the group or individual *source* of the act from "actor" as the *object* of evaluation, we shall refer to the actor, using Kenneth Burke's [1945] term, as the *agent* when it is the object of evaluation).

A close reading of Weber's thesis on the Protestant Ethic will show rather clearly that Calvinism and, to a lesser degree, other Christian dogmas, involve moral prescriptions of the nature of the agent. The elect soul was distinguished from the damned soul not by what it did but by its intrinsic nature. The core of the Calvinist doctrine of election through grace rather than through works was the insistence that the ultimate moral issues concerned the agent, not his or her acts. Indeed, Weber's analysis highlights the persistence of the importance of the moral evaluation of the agent in the secular economic sphere. A very different type of agent-based moral evaluative system is institutionalized in the practice of psychiatry. It specifies the appropriate types of agents rather than prescribing explicit norms or values to which actions should conform. Psychiatric diagnoses specify types of agents, not types of acts. It is a basic tenet of psychiatry that outward conformity does not provide evidence of health nor does deviant behavior necessarily reflect mental illness. Yet, as such critics as Thomas Szasz (1961) and Erving Goffman (1961) have pointed out, there are clearly substantial moral evaluative components to psychiatric practice. Indeed, given its central place in a variety of social control institutions in American society—from mental health clinics to probation and parole offices and "Dear Abby" columns—psychiatric ideology would seem to be a major moral structure in modern American society. It is possible to argue, of course (Szasz 1963), that the psychiatric medical model is simply a pseudo-scientific cover for the enforcement of conventional norms and values without the restrictions which "due process" places on the legal system. If this is true, it is hard to account for a psychiatrist's obsessive concern with such ordinarily moral trivial issues as an individual's response to an EEG, Rorschach, or MMPI test. A system which sanctioned only norm and value violation would probably not attend to such concerns, since neither would be morally important in such a system.

Likewise, it is clear that the evaluation of the "conditions of action" (or what we shall call, following Burke, the "scene") is also an important aspect of moral action. For example, whatever the scientific merits of the sociology of deviance in the first half of the century, much of it consisted of denunciation of certain types of scenes as "socially disorganized" and productive of various types of evils (Mills 1943). The morality that animates many social reform movements is much the same. They involve the judgment that certain scenes are in some way or another "bad." For example, urban renewal efforts seek to destroy "slums" and replace them with "better" housing in neighborhoods. Likewise, a discovery by a Soviet scientist is often treated as suspect in the U.S. simply because a Soviet scientist made it. These scenes are believed to be associated with various types of evils and affect our evaluation of their products.

Empirical evidence that moral evaluation is not limited to norms and values has piled up in the last two decades of work in the sociology of deviance. Following Edwin Lemert's (1951) suggestion that a proper understanding of the patterns of deviance would begin with the study of the mechanisms of social control, innumerable studies have shown the importance of scenic and agent-focused evaluation. For example, Aaron Cicourel's (1968) study of how juvenile probation officers and police decide which children should be treated as delinquent shows that such agent-based categories as ethnicity, intelligence, and personality structure, and such scenic features as the nature of the parents' marriage, the section of the city in which the juvenile lives, and the reputations of his friends, are routinely used in evaluating whether or not a child is delinquent.

Equally impressive is David Sudnow's (1965) study of the criminal court system which shows that such factors as the time of day in which the crime was committed, the age of the perpetrator, the location of the house in which the crime was committed, etc., are all used, or may be used, in deciding whether or not an arrest should be treated as a burglary or simply trespassing. Scenic and agent-based categories of evaluation are not simply incidental but routine and essential parts of the functioning of criminal court as a decision-making system.

It is, of course, no shocking discovery that many actual moral evaluations are agent- or scenic-focused. Durkheim (1947) recognized this as part of mechanical solidarity; they were part of Maine's (1894) notion of status based societies; Parsons (1951) treated such evaluations when considering ascriptive-particularistic norms and Marxists have treated them as part of the injustice inherent in the capitalist order. All this reflects the fact that our formal moral systems treat such evaluations as illegitimate. Indeed, much of the research describing such moral elements in practical decision-making has been of the muckraking sort. Such evaluations have been called "prejudicial" and "stereotypical," but the pervasiveness of the finding that "stereotypes" and "prejudice" enter into almost all evaluations should indicate a need for a broader analytic system.

An adequate theory of moral action must not treat only certain concrete structures of action as moral. Rather it must see morality as a continuously present, or at least potentially present, aspect of all action. Moral vs. nonmoral action is an analytic not a concrete distinction.

GOODE'S PROBLEM

Some two decades ago William Goode raised another objection to current theories of the moral order.

What in fact is "the" norm? You should not lie (only a loose conformity is demanded); or you may tell lies of the following types in these situations but not in others, and the wrongness of the lies is to be ranked in the following order. The first is a general norm, and of course there will be only rough compliance with it. . . . but no one has established such a matrix of obligations on empirical evidence . . . (as the second demands). (Goode 1960:254–55)

There seems to be considerable reason to believe that neither of these answers which Goode summarized would be an adequate account for the moral structure of action.

The idea of the moral regulation of behavior by detailed and situation specific norms is open to objection on several grounds. First, it would require the actor to know an enormous number of norms. The complexity of even the simplest routines of behavior is enormous (Garfinkel 1967:76–104). Furthermore, as Goode notes, the appropriateness of any behavior is not a context-free decision. The concept of the definition of the situation is the standard sociological way of handling this problem. Yet if every revision of the definition of the situation requires different specific appropriate norms and values, the amount of normative information that is necessary to perform even simple social activities would begin to approximate infinity. To illustrate: Suppose I meet Professor Jones for the first time; how am I to behave toward him? Is it relevant that Professor Jones is from the same university that I am? That I am new to the university? That we are from different disciplines? That he is older? That I know his published works? That we are on a camping trip together? That his wife is a dentist?, etc. All of these may influence what we say to and do with one another in the first few minutes of conversation. But it seems difficult to believe that I know a set of rules that should govern all my potential behavior with older male professors from different disciplines, in the same university, where I am a newcomer, whose published works I know and whose wife is a dentist, when I am on camping trip with him. The potentially relevant contingencies in any specific situation are so great that it is hard to believe that we have a list of rules stored in our heads that would be relevant for all or even most of them.

Furthermore, there is reason to believe that, to the degree that my behavior is normatively oriented in such situations, it is to very *general* rules and not to a long series of *specific* rules. If Professor Jones drops something from his knapsack, norms of politeness dictate that I try to pick it up. However, if it is right next to him, I may decide not to bother. It is difficult to imagine that there exists a rule which would specify how close to Professor Jones and how far away from me it would have to be for it to be appropriate for him to pick it up on an occasion like this one, rather than, for example, if Professor Jones was a woman in the same discipline and it was during working hours.

This seems to support what I believe to have been Durkheim's position: that the norms are general in nature rather than highly specific. Thus Durkheim emphasized the autonomous judgment of the individual and the importance of commitment to the normative code so that he or she faithfully tries to apply it properly (Durkheim 1961). However, this position raises as many problems as it solves because neither Durkheim nor anyone else has yet spelled out how the individual applies the norms and makes decisions on how to orient this behavior in this specific situation. The only solution in this theoretical stance seems to be to provide more rules of interpretation. These rules, however, seem to face the same problems the previous ones did. Ultimately, this position also generates more rules than it is possible for anybody to know.

Admittedly, this does not seem to have particularly bothered anybody working on Action Theory. Smelser (1963), in what is generally acknowledged to be one of the best theoretical statements of Action Theory, simply deals with all of the levels of rules that we have been discussing as one of his seven levels of norms, "specification of schedules and programs to regulate activity" (Smelser 1963:68). Apparently, as Smelser sees it, this is not a serious problem. In Smelser's work, and less explicitly in Parsons, the idea seems to be that there exists one or a series of very general norms which is increasingly specified down through several levels of generality to the particular situation. We are left with a model that looks like an inverted branching tree. At the top is one or a small number of very general norms, and at the bottom a multiplicity of specifications of the general norm(s) to specific situations. This general model is what can be called a surface structural model. The defining criterion of a surface structural model of morality is that there is one particular specific moral component for each specific situated behavior. There is no process for generating these except deduction and specification. At any given moment, the rules exist independent of the action of the individual applying them.

THE INFINITY PROBLEM

It is perhaps possible to make some of these problems clearer by reference to some of Harold Garfinkel's (1967) work on background expectancies in social interaction. What Garfinkel has described, in a variety of different quasi-experiments and studies, is the immense complexity of the background knowledge which is required for any interactive social order. As Garfinkel puts it:

Commonsense knowledge of the facts of social life to the members of society is institutionalized knowledge of the real world. Not only does commonsense knowledge portray a real society for its members, but in the manner of a self-fulfilling prophecy the features of the real society are produced by persons motived compliance with these background expectancies. (1967:53)

Moreover, Garfinkel insists repeatedly that the core of these background expectancies is essentially moral. In his study of "Agnes," a transsexual who "passes" for several years as a female, Garfinkel makes visible the tremendous complexity of the achievement of the rather simple ascribed category of female. This category, and its behavioral, contextual, and essential features is, for the ordinary population, a matter that is attended to only rarely. Few of us have ever heard a behaviorally adequate description of what it consists to be an ordinary male or female. Yet, the complexity of these roles which adults play with relative ease, is enormous.

For our purposes, the most interesting aspect of Garfinkel's findings about Agnes, and indeed in the rest of his studies of the moral structure of social life, is that Garfinkel found that the background knowledge necessary to properly fulfill a social role is not limited. There do not exist a limited set of moral prescriptions with which Agnes could properly act as a female. To use Garfinkel's term, a "game" analysis of Agnes' activities would be insufficient in a number of ways. The most important of these is that Agnes often found herself complying with rules that she did not know existed prior to the effort to comply with them. In Garfinkel's words:

Its "rules" are learned over the course of the actual interaction, as a function of actual participation, and by accepting the risks involved. . . .

Agnes was required to live up to the standards of conduct, appearance, skills, feelings, motives, and aspirations while simultaneously learning what these standards were. To learn them was, for her, a continous project of self-improvement. They had to be learned in situations in which as a matter of course. . . . they had to be learned by participating in situations where she was expected to know the very things that she was simultaneously being taught. (Garfinkel 1967:146–47).

In these situations Agnes had to continually use the talk and responses of others as a basis for constructing rules by which she could make a plausible appearance as a female. Conversely in many situations she had to find ways of "guessing" what would be an appropriate behavior, attitude, biographical particular, future ambition, or whatever for a female in her publicly known situation.

Our interest in this study is twofold. To begin with, the moral knowledge necessary to be what Agnes chose to be was infinite. This does not mean that it was a very large amount. Rather, there were, in the formal sense of the word, an infinite number of new and situationally unique moral performances necessary for her to demonstrate her "naturalness" as a female. Garfinkel has referred to the process necessary to manage such problems as "adhocing." In studying the way graduate students coded material in a social scientific study, he found that repeatedly and continuously they relied on cognitive procedures like "et cetera," "unless," "let it pass," and "factum valet" (in which an action prohibited by a rule is taken as correct once it is done). (Garfinkel 1967:20–22.)

Garfinkel's model of the practice of moral action thus requires a rule structure which involves judgments that cannot possibly be included in any surface structural model. For example, a series of rules which include the etcetera rule would have to be formulated as: "Situation A is covered by rules A, B, C, D, and other similar appropriate rules." Garfinkel's position is essentially that implicit in any set of moral rules is the idea that they will be applied by a "reasonable" person.

The second point that is critical for our purposes is the concept of "reasonableness." Although it is central to their inquiry, neither Garfinkel nor his students presented a systematic theory of how it would be possible for an actor to be able to be "reasonable." While Garfinkel has spoken of these as "artful occasioned accomplishments" he has suggested that a systematic theoretical account cannot be generated. Garfinkel is, of course, quite right that the creation of an adequate role performance is a cognitive achievement which depends on the "occasion," in the broadest sense of the word, for its accomplishment. What Garfinkel has left unanswered is the nature of the "reasonableness" of the accomplishment. Granted that it is an accomplishment, what is accomplished? The answer to this can only be satisfactorily gained by looking at the work of Noam Chomsky and other transformational generative linguists.

Chomsky (1957) and others have posed, and partially solved, a problem similar to the one we have discussed here: how is it possible for a finite set of linguistic rules to produce an infinite number of sentences? Chomsky (1959) has pointed out that it is inadequate to say that an individual is simply conditioned to know which sentences are grammatical and which are not by previous experience since we routinely produce sentences that we have never heard before. For example, William Faulkner once wrote a novel constructed entirely of one very long sentence. If Faulkner simply produced sentences which he had learned were correct, he could not have written this unique sentence. Furthermore, Chomsky pointed out that we can distinguish grammatically correct statements which we could not have heard from similar incorrect statements. Consider the following statements (Chomsky 1957):

a. Colorless green ideas sleep furiously.
b. Furiously sleep ideas green colorless.

Although both are meaningless, and it is fair to assume that neither had ever been stated before in the English language, the first is recognizable as syntactically correct and the second is not. Clearly the reader who recognizes (a) as grammatical and (b) as ungrammatical must have some sort of mechanism for generating grammatical sentences and for recognizing as grammatical sentences never seen before. This is, of course, exactly parallel to our problem with Professor Jones. It is a situation in which the actor must deal with an entirely new set of circumstances in which he or she is nonetheless expected to behave properly. Moreover "properly" is a criterion which is highly situationally specific. Likewise for Garfinkel's Agnes. She was constantly faced with situations in which she was required to create or generate the appropriate action or response to situations with which she had never before dealt.

How is this possible? Using highly formal models of what types of sentence-generating "devices" might account for the linguistic abilities of ordinary actors, Chomsky has been able to show that certain assumptions about the nature of linguistic competence are invalid and that others are necessary.

Chomsky's primary discovery is probably the concept of *deep structure* and its associated concept of *transformational devices*. The basic notion is that there exists a series of relatively simple linguistic "deep structures" which can yield an infinite variety of surface structures (ordinary sentences) through the use of what are known as transformational devices. Moreover these devices have made clear a series of properties of linguistic usage which could not be accounted for in previous grammars.

This is hardly the place to provide a description of even the elements of transformational generative grammars.[8] However, the fundamental idea is not too complex. What Chomsky has shown is that an infinite number of sentences exists in any language. Moreover, this infinity is not produced by the almost infinite number of word combinations but by such processes, built into the language, as rules which allow the insertion of a new clause or prepositional phrase into any sentence, including ones already containing such structures. Thus there exist not only an infinite number of sentences but also an infinite number of sentence structures. If the competent speaker is to know how to assess the grammaticality—i.e., the normative correctness of an infinite number of sentence structures—a "grammar of lists" simply won't do. *One cannot learn an infinite list.*

However, it is possible to construct rules which allow one to transform relatively simple basic sentences into all of the infinite variety of sentence structures. For example, an optional transformational rule (gapping) allows the transformation of four simple sentences:

I went home. Bill went to the store. Mary went to the movie. You went to New York.

into,

I went home, Bill to the store, Mary to the movie and you to New York.

Or consider a phrase structure rule such as the one which allows the addition of an infinite number of subordinate clauses and prepositional phrases on the end of this sentence:

The boy went to the house, on the block, near the school, behind the house, where I was born, when my father worked at the factory, in the valley, near the mountain. . . .

A DESCRIPTION OF MORAL STRUCTURE

What follows is an attempt to present a *preliminary* account of some aspects of a transformational structural grammar of morality. It is intended only to illustrate a direction in which work might proceed. The development of such a formal representation is a complex task and involves many more considerations than we can deal with here. The method of analyzing moral structure which follows is one that I have used for several years and has yet to encounter any insuperable barriers. However, I make no implication that this is ultimately an adequate procedure.

The core of the moral grammar are the five *basic terms* which Kenneth Burke (1945) explicated: Agent (Ag), Scene (Sc), Act (A), Agency—or what we will call the Means (M)—and Purpose (P). This may be thought of as the equivalent of the Subject, Verb, and Predicate of linguistic grammars. They form the basic elements of any general description of motives and constitute what we will refer to as a *motive set*.

The moral aspect of the description of motives is provided by what can be called a *moral modifier*. It consists of an evaluation of one of the basic terms. Such modifiers may be present or absent in any particular piece of social reality, and if present they may be either positive or negative. Symbolically these can be represented by p(positive), n(negative), or a(absent).

The most elementary moral act is the association of a moral modifier with basic term. Such a structure may be symbolized as, for example, A(p) (positively evaluated act) or M(n) (negatively evaluated means). If we use "good" and "bad" as our most pure examples of linguistic modifiers we get "the act is good," "the means are bad."

The other essential element of moral structure is the association of one morally modified object with another object, modified or not. This association can be used to define the moral character of this unknown.

A PRIMITIVE GRAMMAR

We are now in a position to describe a simple grammatical system with which moral evaluations could be made and one which will generate an infinite number of evaluations. Start with two terms A and B, which for present purposes can represent two agents, Sue and Mary. Suppose that we know that Sue is good and Mary is a friend of Sue's. The assumption of this system, and indeed of normal evaluating behavior, is that Mary is also good. This can be called the *consistency principle*, which says that when two grammatical terms are associated with each other, they will have like moral characters. Thus, the child who grows up in the slums is assumed to be more likely to become a criminal, the acts of God are sacred, and the purposes of the President are assumed to be high-minded.

Formally stated, if we have terms A, B, C, D and E and they are associated and if we know that A(p), then A(p) and B(?), C(?), D(?) and E(?) → A(p), B(p), C(p), D(p), E(p).

Such a grammar is generative in the sense that new terms (F, G, H, etc.) can always be added and immediately evaluated. This satisfies one of our criteria for an adequate grammar. Another important point is that the actor may employ his or her knowledge of institutionalized norms to generate evaluations since a general category (Doctor, suburb, driving a Corvette, etc.) may be used to categorize the term and thus provide a preliminary evaluation. Moreover, the generative quality allows the actor to be morally socialized, to understand new moral evaluations, without being explicitly told.

However, whatever advantages such a grammar has, it is inadequate for at least three reasons. The first problem with this grammar is quite simple. If one makes the reasonable assumption that there is a consistency to moral evaluations of terms across particular motive sets, the entire social universe would take on the same moral quality. For example, if one were to evaluate a colleague positively, it would follow that every activity he or she engaged in would be positively evaluated; since those activities took place within the same organization, the entire organization would be positively evaluated. At the extreme, since the colleague and the organization both existed in the Universe, the Universe and everything in it must be positively evaluated. The basic problem is that this first primitive grammar does not allow the maintenance of any moral boundaries.

The same weakness in the grammar leads to another practical problem. While the grammar accounts for how one can know the moral properties of unknowns within the same motive set, it does not allow two terms within the same motive set to have opposite moral qualities. The only resolution allowed in this grammar would be to change the evaluation of one term or another. This is not a theoretical impossibility, but if actors were faced with the problem of either giving up their adherence to a norm or value or giving up a friend everytime the friend acted badly or demonstrated adherence to a bad purpose, even the most elementary social order would disappear.

Finally, an empirical examination of even the most simple sorts of moral evaluations will show that the consistency principle cannot be upheld unqualifiedly. Two nations at war are not necessarily held to have the same moral quality; indeed it is most often assumed that they have opposite moral qualities. Furthermore, an agent's intentions may be good but his actions bad. Likewise, Horatio Alger's heroes were exemplary precisely because they transcended their poor backgrounds. For all of these reasons a system of relations between moral terms which goes beyond a simple consistency principle must be developed.

OPPOSITION AND A-MORAL ASSOCIATION

In moral evaluation "opposition" plays a critical part. Opposition places the conflicting parties on different sides and gives them differing moral evaluations. An agent and his or her enemy are seen as having basically different moral qualities. The social worker in the slum partakes neither of the negative evaluation of the slums in which he or she works, nor of the positive evaluation of its culture some of its residents might have. The social worker is trying to change the slum and is thus in opposition to it. Equally the person who organizes a revolution in a totalitarian country does not suffer from our evaluation of totalitarianism. Quite the opposite!

In brief, there exists a class of relationships whose core is opposition between one term and another. These relationships require that the two terms which are related in this way have opposite moral characteristics. If we symbolize this relationship by a minus sign, we can state the relationship using the symbols previously used to express the consistency principle. The following are grammatical relationships between two terms related through conflict:

$$A(p) - B(n) \text{ and } A(n) - B(p)$$

This can be illustrated nicely with a moral grammatical analysis of a version of the Horatio Alger story. Let A = the agent (call his Horatio), B = the predominant societal value of material success, C = crime and D = hard work.[9] If we know that $A(p)$ and $A + B$, $A - C$ and $C - D$, we can generate the classic structure of the Horatio Alger story:

1) $A(p) + B(p)$
   Horatio wants to succeed.
2) $A(p) + D(p)$
   Horatio works hard.
3) $B(p) + D(p)$
   Hard work yields success.
4) $A(p) - C(n)$
   Horatio rejects crime.
5) $C(n) - B(p)$
   Crime does not yield success.

6) $D(p) - C(n)$
   Crime and hard work do not go together.

Despite the addition of this new mode of association, the grammar remains generative. It is possible to know the relationship of any additional term to the entire structure if either its moral modifier or an association with one other term is known.

If the notion of opposition helps to set boundaries on the principle of consistency, it also raises serious problems which cannot be overlooked. Prior to the introduction of the concept of opposition, we assumed that any association between two terms was to reflect the principle of consistency. Now, however, we have two types of association which have opposite ramifications. How then is the actor to decide which type of association he should make between the two terms. Obviously if the association between two terms gives no moral directive then the grammar will not provide the actor with any evaluative information.

One solution to this problem is that actors learn to classify specific words and phrases as one type of association or another. The actor could learn, as part of his cultural heritage, that in the process of deciding who and what are good or bad, that terms such as "likes," "grew up in," "is friends with," "spends time with," indicate that the consistency principle should apply, whereas terms such as "hates," "is trying to change X," "is on the other side of," "is done against," indicate that the opposition principle applies. This is a familiar idea in linguistic theory where the actor is presumed to be capable of distinguishing between phrases used as verbs, nouns, adverbs, etc. This concept cannot be accepted unequivocally, however, since as we indicated above, terms are sometimes used to index their opposites. For the moment, however, let us use it as a temporary expedient.

The concept of opposition raises another problem however. When we admit that all types of association between terms are not consistency associations, the question arises whether there might not exist other types of association between terms which are neither inherently positive nor negative, which have no moral evaluative ramifications for the terms they connect. The answer is clearly that there are. Consider the connecting phrase "drove past" as in "Yesterday I drove past his house." Even if the "his" refers to Adolf Hitler, it is not likely that the auditor will assume a moral connection between "I" and "Hitler." Similarly the statement "I read the book" does not seem to imply much in terms of my evaluation of the book.

GRAMMATICAL AND UNGRAMMATICAL FORMS

The above relationships can now be stated in a series of formal statements of what types of relationships are "grammatical" and what types are not. If:

1. A and B symbolize any two basic terms,
2. (p), (n), (a) indicate respectively positive, negative, and no moral evaluations of A and B and,
3. +, −, and 0 indicate respectively the application of consistency, opposition, and no moral association types of association between terms,

then the following relationships seem to be grammatical.

1. $A(p) + B(p)$	6. $A(p) \ 0 \ B(a)$
2. $A(n) + B(n)$	7. $A(n) \ 0 \ B(n)$
3. $A(p) - B(n)$	8. $A(n) \ 0 \ B(a)$
4. $A(p) \ 0 \ B(p)$	9. $A(a) \ 0 \ B(a)$
5. $A(p) \ 0 \ B(n)$	

The following relationships are not grammatical; it would seem incongruous or peculiar to interpret moral statements in that manner.

1. $A(p) + B(p)$	6. $A(p) - B(a)$
2. $A(p) - B(p)$	7. $A(n) - B(a)$
3. $A(n) - B(n)$	8. $A(a) + B(a)$
4. $A(p) + B(a)$	9. $A(a) - B(a)$
5. $A(n) + B(a)$	

This list of forms has eliminated some redundancies by treating A and B reversibly. The moral relationship is unaffected by which term appears first in an account, at least for present purposes. Thus $A(p) - B(n)$ also stands for $A(n) - B(p)$.

I want to explicitly suggest that these rules are at least central components of the deep structural rules of moral action.[10] In order to consider the nature of moral transformational rules, it will now be useful to describe some empirical data.

AN EMPIRICAL PROBLEM

For the last several years my colleagues and I have been studying the interaction of patients and staff in an acute care psychiatric hospital and clinic.[11] Of special interest has been the initial few minutes of contact in the admission and referral service.

The most striking finding pertains to the way the interviews begin. With the exception of patients who the staff member suspects may not be capable of any reasonable dialogue or cases in which the admission is already determined by a private doctor, the opening questions always seem to be the same. While the words that the staff use vary, they seem to be conveying the same meaning and to be entirely interchangeable. Thus patients are asked such questions as "What is your problem?" "Why do you happen to be here?" "What is your trouble?" "What is the main reason you came here?" "What can we do for you?" "Why are you here today?" "How can we help you?" "Why did the doctor send you to see us?"

Perhaps even more striking evidence that these are analogues of one another is what happens when the patient does not give the proper response. Consider the following case:

Psychiatrist: "Why are you here?"
Patient: "I don't know. Why I am here?"
Psychiatrist: (after asking a few questions to ascertain whether or not she is oriented at all) "Why did you go to (other psychiatric hospital)?"
Patient: I didn't go, they took me there.
Psychiatrist: Why?
Patient: I didn't ask to go. I have no idea why they took me.
Psychiatrist: Why do you think they took you?
Patient: I really don't know. I didn't ask to go. There's nothing wrong with me.
Psychiatrist: Have you been drinking today? How much?
Patient: I've been drinking all day. . . .
Psychiatrist: How come?

In spite of the patient's refusal to accept the psychiatrist's moral structure for the situation, the psychiatrist persists in using it as the basis for his questions. The deep structure of these interchanges is fairly clear. It involves two agents—clinician and patient. The patient is composed of two parts, the patient and his or her problem. This can be diagramatically expressed.

$$\frac{\text{Clinician(p)} + \text{Patient(p)}}{\text{problem(n)}}$$

The other components of the standard motive set, the hospital (positively evaluated), medical technology (positively evaluated) and the purpose (a cure of the disease, also positively evaluated), are typically not developed in these initial interchanges.

The patient's response in the above case that there was nothing wrong with her only leads to the psychiatrist reformulating the question but insisting on the same model. When the patient persists in her denials that there is a problem, the psychiatrist tries another tactic and emphasizes that the patient was drunk and asks why she drank. This procedure eventually elicited a problem.

In the opening exchange, the psychiatrist or other clinician always seeks agreement from the patient that there is something wrong with him or her and that the patient should cooperate in correcting it. Some of the above questions, which clinicians use as openers, are more explicit than others. Questions like "Why do you happen to be here?" admit of many deep structural interpretations (as, of course, do many linguistic products). However, patients usually correctly interpret them and respond with a "problem" to be dealt with. When they do not, the staff rephrases the questions. Consider:

Clinician: Why are you here today?
Patient: Because they made an appointment for me for today.
Clinician: Well, what can we do for you?

However, a major problem remains unresolved. A close look at the clinician's opening questions, which are given above, and even the patient's responses, will show that they do not describe the entire deep structure. Indeed a similar close look at all 48 cases that we observed failed to show a single case in which all elements of the deep structure were made explicit in any one case. Rather *the surface structures invariably are elliptical presentations of the deep structures.* Yet the patient rarely fails to understand what is meant. Even when the patient disagrees with the appropriateness of the moral structure as grounds for conducting the relationship (as the first patient presented above did, "There's nothing wrong with me"), the disagreement did not come from misunderstanding.

The theoretical questions we face here are how can the patient read this deep structure out of the questions which the staff ask and how can the staff know the patient's acceptance of it from his or her responses. What is required are some transformational rules which allow one to infer the deep structure from the surface. Consider the question "Why are you here?" that the doctor used as an opening in the above case. Formally and verbally it indicates nothing of the moral structure. However, what it asks for is a purpose and allows the patient to indicate his knowledge and acceptance of the deep structure by presenting a "problem" in himself. The most frequent opening question is more explicit about this, "What is your problem?" The question is, what sort of rules would allow these interchanges to be interpreted in that way.

The critical transformational rule is what may be called the "modesty transformation." This leaves the speaker the option to delete a positive reference to himself or herself. It allows the auditor to assume, unless it is contradicted in other ways, the speaker's positive self-evaluation. The second critical piece of information is not contained in a transformation at all but is given simply in nonverbal interactions. The clinician goes out of his or her way to smile and try to show a friendly face. Sometimes this is made more explicit in the opening question, for example, "How can we help you?"

What the patient now knows from the opener of "Why are you here?" is:

$$\text{Staff}(p) \ + \ \text{Patient}(?)$$
$$? \qquad ?$$
$$\text{purpose}(?)$$

Furthermore, he or she can generate through the deep structural rules that the staff's model of the situation involves a positive evaluation of the patient. Thus when the patient presents a negatively evaluated problem he or she demonstrates a general acceptance of the staff's deep structure. A similar analysis is possible for all of the opening interchanges between staff and patients that we observed. Of course, when the opening line is "What is your problem?" the negative evaluation of the object toward which action is focused (the purpose) is clear. In this case the staff member presents the patient with the complete structure and expects acceptance in the form of cooperation.

What must be emphasized here is that the use of the generativity of the deep structure rules and the deletion power of the modesty transformation allows a relatively restricted verbal and nonverbal communication to become the basis for both participants to understand the basic moral assumptions of the situation.

CONCLUSION

I have sought to provide some basic elements of a transformational generative theory of the moral order. In addition, I have made an effort to build a structuralist account of the functioning of moral systems which will overcome the deficiencies inherent in conventional efforts to describe the substance of moral systems while ignoring the systematic structures which generate the morality.

The reliance on a Chomskian model for such a theory seems warranted given the enormous success such a model has had in providing accounts of linguistic phenomena. While I have proposed nothing that could be considered an adequate account of either deep structural or transformational rules, my analysis of the interactive data presented does provide some reason to hope that this type of model will provide us with a much more powerful analysis of the place of morality in social life.

NOTES

1. The structuralist elements in Durkheim's thought, particularly the essay on primitive classification (Durkheim and Mauss 1963) involves material more distant from the general essays on morality.

2. For example, Wrong (1962).

3. Although this frames the problem somewhat differently than he did, this is what I believe Weber (1958) was saying in the "spirit of capitalism."

4. Many of the findings of the interactionist school of deviance can be mustered to support this. As Suchar (1978:8) put it, "who you are has often been a more significant factor in bringing about societal disapproval than what you have done."

5. The concept of indexicality has been used in a generally similar way by

Garfinkel (1967) and his students. See Mehan and Wood (1975) for an inter-acting discussion.

6. See Flavell (1963) and Lidz and Lidz (1976).

7. The most significant exception to this is Parsons' study of the doctor and patient roles, in *The Social System* and elsewhere. Even there, however, Parsons seems more concerned with the institutional order than with how the morality is used in interaction for, in any detail, how it affects behavior. This is to say that, in Parsons' terms, this was primarily a social system analysis rather than an action system analysis.

8. A fine introduction is contained in Ruwet (1973).

9. In this example we leave the Act and the Scene out of the account for simplicity.

10. The similarity between these deep structural rules and the balance theory rules proposed by Fritz Heider (1958) became apparent to me only rather late in my work. I optimistically assume that this is grounds for hoping that the rules might have some validity.

11. This work has been partially supported by P.H.S. grant #MH27533.

REFERENCES

Burke, Kenneth. 1945. *A Grammar of Motives*. Berkeley: University of California Press.

Chomsky, Noam. 1957. *Syntactic Structures*. The Hague: Mouton.

—— 1959. "Review of *Verbal Behavior*, by B. F. Skinner [1957]." *Language* 35:26–58.

Cicourel, Aaron. 1968. *The Social Organization of Juvenile Justice*. New York, Wiley.

—— 1973. *Cognitive Sociology*. London: MacMillan.

Durkheim, Emile. 1947. *The Division of Labor in Society*. Glencoe, Ill.: Free Press.

—— 1951. *Suicide*. Glencoe, Ill.: Free Press.

—— 1958. *The Rules of Sociological Method*. Glencoe, Ill.: Free Press.

—— 1961. *Moral Education*. New York: Free Press.

Durkheim, Emile and Marcel Mauss. 1963. *Primitive Classification*. Chicago: University of Chicago Press.

Flavell, John H. 1963. *The Developmental Psychology of Jean Piaget*. Princeton: Van Nostrand.

Garfinkel, Harold. 1967. *Studies in Ethnomethodology*. Englewood Cliffs, New Jersey: Prentice-Hall.

Goffman, Erving. 1961. *Asylums*. New York: Anchor.

Goode, William J. 1960. "Norm commitment and conformity to role-status obligations." *American Journal of Sociology* 66:244–261.

Heider, Fritz. 1958. *The Psychology of Interpersonal Relations*. New York: Wiley.

Laubser, Jan, et al., eds. 1976. *Explorations in the General Theory of the Social Sciences: Essays in Honor of Talcott Parsons.* New York: Free Press.

Leiber, Justin. 1975. *Noam Chomsky.* New York: St. Martin's Press.

Lemert, Edwin. 1951. *Social Pathology.* New York: McGraw-Hill.

Lidz, Charles and Victor Lidz. 1976. "Piaget's psychology of intelligence and its place in the theory of action." In J. Laubser et al., eds. 1976.

Maine, Henry. 1894. *Ancient Law.* London: Murray.

Mehan, Hugh and Houston Wood. 1975. *The Reality of Ethnomethodology.* New York: Wiley-Interscience.

Mills, C. Wright. 1943. "The professional ideology of social pathologists." *American Journal of Sociology* 49:2.

Parsons, Talcott. 1937. *The Structure of Social Action.* New York: McGraw-Hill.

—— 1951. *The Social System.* Glencoe, Ill.: Free Press.

—— 1952. "The superego and the theory of social systems." *Psychiatry* 15:1.

—— 1961. *Theories of Society.* New York: Free Press.

Piaget, Jean. 1965. *The Moral Judgment of the Child.* New York: The Free Press.

Ruwet, Nicolas. 1973. *An Introduction to Transformational Grammars.* Amsterdam: North-Holland.

Skinner, B. F. 1957. *Verbal Behavior.* New York: Appleton.

Smelser, Neil J. 1963. *Theory of Collective Behavior.* New York: Free Press.

Suchar, Charles S. 1978. *Social Deviance.* New York: Holt, Reinhart and Winston.

Sudnow, David. 1965. "Normal crimes." *Social Problems* 12(3):255–70.

Szasz, Thomas. 1961. *The Myth of Mental Illness.* New York: Hoeber-Harper.

—— 1963. *Law, Liberty and Psychiatry.* New York: Collier.

Weber, Max. 1958. *The Protestant Ethic and the Spirit of Capitalism.* New York: Norton.

Wrong, Dennis. 1962. "The Oversocialized Concept of Man in Modern Sociology." *American Sociological Review* 26:183–93.

PART FOUR

THE STRUCTURAL MARXIST
PERSPECTIVE

CHAPTER TEN

THE PROBLEM OF THE "REPRODUCTION" OF SOCIOECONOMIC SYSTEMS

A NEW EPISTEMOLOGICAL CONTEXT

MAURICE GODELIER

A new epistemological situation has been arising during the last decade within the field of social sciences which permits a new form of cooperation between anthropology, history, economics, ecology, and even biology in the analysis of the history or evolution of socioeconomic systems.

This epistemological situation is characterized by two complementary aspects: on the one hand, a theoretical problem is increasingly commanding attention in the front line of research; on the other, this problem is being tackled in a new methodological context. The problem is that of the analysis of the conditions of "reproduction" (and of "nonreproduction") of social systems, taking into account the constraints imposed by their internal structures and their ecological environments.

The methodological context arose in the wake of recent attempts to find a way out of the succession of difficulties or even blind alleys encountered by traditional functionalism or structuralism when attempting to account for the appearance and disappearance of social structures within the specific and irreversible history of real societies.

Of these attempts I shall consider as important the school of "cultural ecology," which sees itself as being materialist, neofunctionalist, and neo-evolutionist and has developed chiefly in the United States; also important is that school which claims to be

Translated and edited by Ino and Irene Rossi.

based on a renewed Marxist approach and which has been pursued mainly in Europe.

These two lines of development have taken on this importance not only by virtue of their methodological innovation, but also because they both accorded particular attention to the roles of the economy in the logic governing the adaptation of societies to their environment and in the logic of evolution.

In order to be able to gauge the originality of these recent efforts, we must go back to the deadlock reached by nineteenth-century sociological evolutionism and the partial success obtained within the framework of the functionalist and structuralist approaches. The problem of the evolution of social systems is a fundamental one, but it is not new. In the nineteenth century it was one of the major themes of scientific thought and engrossed the minds of men like Spencer, Morgan, Maine, and Taylor. This was all the more readily discernible in that, in their time, every new science assumed the form of a "history," of races, of languages, of the family, of moral and religious ideas, etc. But the problem was gradually to be stripped of its value and cast into the shadow, by the functionalists first of all, and then by the structuralists, in the face of the contradictions and the pseudo-demonstrations accumulated by the very method employed by the evolutionists to reconstruct the "history" of human institutions and societies.

This method—which is still to a large extent that of the contemporary American neo-evolutionists such as White, Service, Sahlins (in the first phase of his thought), etc., and partially invalidates their findings—consisted in constructing a "logical" outline model of the evolution of societies on the basis of the conclusions drawn from the evolution of nature and particularly from the evolution of living beings. These conclusions were summed up in a few principles: there is a tendency for the internal complexity of organisms to increase and for specialized organs to become differentiated in order to integrate this complexity, etc. These principles were then transferred from the field of biology to that of anthropology, sociology, and history, within which disciplines they served to define in advance and in abstract terms the general trend, the direction, and the main stages of man's social evolution.

The task then consisted in singling out particular societies from among those covered by anthropological field studies, and without calling into question the significance of the data thus presented, with a view to illustrating as well as possible the sociological features of a stage through which mankind must logically have passed in order finally to organize itself into large civilized societies founded on the existence of a state, starting out from small segmentary and scarcely differentiated societies of palaeolithic hunters and food collectors.

It is to be noted that the very fact of placing these real institutions or societies in this or that pigeonhole automatically transformed such data into a "typical" representation of the organization of human society at this or that necessary stage of its development. By this method, "descriptive" data became falsely explanatory by becoming "illustrative." Thus, automatically, no trace remained of the real and specific evolution of the societies selected, or of their history, and at the same time, since these societies served to illustrate a stage which, historically, they had not themselves passed through, they consequently acquired an imaginary future at the very moment that their real past was eclipsed.

These negative results inevitably led to critical reactions and to the formulation of the functionalist, structuralist, and, to a certain extent, Marxist approaches. I shall briefly outline the theoretical positions of each of these schools concerning the method of analyzing social phenomena and the interpretation of the history of societies.

Functionalist empiricism starts not from individuals but from the relations between them. These relations are not taken one by one, but together, and this group of relations is regarded as an "integrated" whole to the extent that these different relations are functionally complementary. These functions determine the role and status of individuals in their social system, and this system constantly tends toward a state of equilibrium. Study of a society thus means study of a system, of a totality that is functionally integrated and that reproduces itself as such. Knowing the history of this system does not help one to know how it functions. History itself appears as "a succession of accidental events," which are left to the ethnologist or the historian, while theoretical analysis of the systems is reserved for the anthropologist or the sociologist. These views are well known, and it is unnecessary to do more than refer the reader to the classical writings of Radcliffe-Brown and Nadel, or, for sociology, to the work of Talcott Parsons (1949, ch. 10).

What structuralism and Marxism alike reject is not, of course, the principle that science must take as its subject of analysis the *relations* between men, or the principle that relations must be analyzed in their unity within a whole, or the principle that priority must be given to studying the logic of these relations and the whole before studying their origin and evolution. Malinowski and Radcliffe-Brown were right to turn away from that pseudo-history, the evolutionism of the nineteenth century which saw in a given society a collection of customs inherited from a past period that one reconstituted by means of assumptions that were unverified and often unverifiable, and instead to study the facts themselves as they presented themselves before their eyes.

I shall show farther on that Marx, turning his back on the "historicist" method, dealt with the origin of the capitalist mode of production only after studying its internal logic and establishing his theory of value and surplus-value. This methodological principle of priority for the analysis of a structure over that of its origin is the principle of modern linguistics and of Lévi-Strauss, even though the latter, unlike Marx, accepts the empiricist view that history is a "succession of accidental events."

What both structuralists and Marxists reject are the empiricist definitions of what constitutes a social structure. For Radcliffe-Brown and Nadel, a social structure is an aspect of *reality* itself; it is order, the ordering of the *visible* relations between men, an ordering that explains the logic of the complementariness of these visible relations (Radcliffe-Brown 1952).[1] For others—and, despite his criticisms of functionalism, Leach is the best example of these—the structure is an *ideal* order which the mind introduces into things by reducing the multiform flux of reality to simplified images that give one a hold upon reality and make possible social action, social practice (Leach 1964).[2]

For Marx, as for Lévi-Strauss, a structure is *not* a reality that is *directly* visible, and so directly observable, but a *level of reality* that exists *beyond* the visible relations between men, and the functioning of which constitutes the underlying logic of the system, the subjacent order by which the apparent order is to be explained.

Let me recall the insistence with which Lévi-Strauss returns to this essential point, combating the idealistic and formalistic interpretations to which his ideas are commonly subjected. In his reply to Maybury-Lewis, he emphasizes that:

> Of course the final word should rest with experience. However, the experiment suggested and guided by deductive reasoning will not be the same as the unsophisticated ones with which the whole process started. . . . The ultimate proof of the molecular structure of matter is provided by the electronic microscope, which enables us to see *actual* molecules. This achievement does not alter the fact that henceforth the molecule will not become any more visible to the naked eye. Similarly, it is hopeless to expect a structural analysis to change our way of perceiving concrete social relations. It will only *explain* them better.

Introducing to the public the first volume of *Mythologiques*, Lévi-Strauss again declared categorically:

> I have thus completed by demonstration of the fact that, whereas in the public mind there is frequently confusion between structuralism, idealism and formalism, structuralism has only to be confronted with true manifestations of idealism and formalism for its own *deterministic and realistic* inspiration to become clearly manifest. (Lévi-Strauss 1964:27; see also Godelier 1967)

The idealist and formalist interpretations of structuralism are based on the opening sentence of the well-known passage that Lévi-Strauss devoted to the concept of social structure:

> Passing now to the task of defining "social structure," that is a point which should be cleared up immediately. The term "social structure," has nothing to do with empirical reality but with models which are built up after it [d'apres celle-ci]. (Lévi-Strauss 1968;279)

This sentence, taken out of its context, conveys the illusion that the theoretical positions of Lévi-Strauss and of Leach are identical, or at least are fundamentally linked. But Lévi-Strauss' sentence cannot be interpreted correctly unless it is taken in relation to the sentence that follows:

> Social relations consist of the raw material out of which the models

making up the social structure are built [qui rendent manifeste la structure sociale elle-même]. (*Ibid*)

To make a structure *manifeste* does not mean creating it out of nothing or assuming that it exists only in the human mind, either in the form of models indigenous to social reality or in that of the abstract models of the sociologists.

To sum up this complex group of theoretical positions and oppositions as simply as possible, let me say that Lévi-Strauss affirms, like Radcliffe-Brown, the "reality" of social structures as existing outside the human mind, and so opposes Leach. But Lévi-Strauss at the same time opposes Radcliffe-Brown, since for him the reality of a social structure is not the "ordering" of the social relations that are directly observable by the informant or the anthropologist (Fortes 1949:56).[3] He is thus led to criticize functionalism for its inability to grasp the order underlying visible social relations and construct a solid basis for a comparative science of societies. Consequently he finds himself side by side with Leach, who also criticizes the truisms of functionalism, but moves in the opposite direction from Lévi-Strauss, toward a formalism that keeps intact the empiricist view of reality as a multiform, unstructured flux. It is understandable that such an interplay of agreement and disagreement at different levels should give rise to confusions and misconceptions in the social science field which make it necessary but difficult for researchers to undertake a critical analysis of the epistemological conditions and principles of their methods of cognition.[4] This is why a thorough analysis of the relations between structuralism and Marxism presents itself as a fundamental task, since it is possible for a radical difference and opposition to exist beneath and within a common acceptance of certain methodological principles and a common affirmation that science must be materialistic and deterministic.

Let us recall once again what these points of agreement are. There is first the methodological principle that social relations must be analyzed as forming "systems." Then there is the principle that the inner *logic* of these systems must be analyzed before their *origin* is analyzed. We see at once that, as regards these two principles, Marxism is not opposed either to structuralism or to functionalism.

These two principles are set forth in Marx's methodological Introduction to his *Contribution to the Critique of Political Economy*, where he defines the order in which it is necessary to study and expound the way the capitalist mode of production works: "Rent cannot be understood without capital, but capital *can* be understood without rent. Capital is the economic power that dominates everything in bourgeois society. It must form both the point of departure and the conclusion and it has to be expounded before landed property. After analyzing capital and landed property separately, their interconnection must be examined.

It would be inexpedient and wrong therefore to present the economic categories successively in the order in which they have played their dominant role in history. *On the contrary, their order of succession is determined by their mutual relation in modern bourgeois society and this is quite the reverse of what appears to be natural to them or in accordance with the sequence of historical development.* The point at issue is not the role that various economic relations have played in the succession of various social formations appearing in the course of history; even less is their sequence "as concepts" (Proudhon) (a nebulous notion of the historical process), but their *position* within modern bourgeois society. (Marx 1904)

Marx thus does not make the question of the origin or the history of social relations the key question for science, as did the evolutionists and diffusionists of the nineteenth century; his thinking on this point converges with that of Malinowski or of Lévi-Strauss (1967).[5] This accounts for the existence of a text such as *Pre-Capitalist Economic Formations* in which Marx, after having discovered the true, hidden nature of surplus-value, turns back to the history of Antiquity and the Middle Ages and analyzes the differences between various archaic or ancient modes of production and the capitalist mode.

This is the underlying reason for the internal structure of *Capital*, as well as for the existence of texts like *Pre-Capitalist Economic Formations* and also the drafts of Marx's letter to Vera Zasulich (March 8, 1881). In *Capital*, it is only *after* establishing that the content of the exchange-value of commodities is socially necessary labor time, and that capital is not a thing but a social relation between two classes, one of which appropriates the value created by the other (surplus-value), that Marx turns to the problem of the origins of capitalism, and deals with it under the title of "the primitive accumulation of capital." In *Pre-Capitalist Economic Formations* he had gone beyond the question of the origins of capitalism and outlined, writing as historian and anthropologist, a remarkable analysis of the original logics of the functioning of certain ancient and archaic modes of production, endeavoring to imagine some of the conditions of their internal transformations and their history. Marx's method in relation to history can be grasped very clearly in the passage he devoted to defining the nature of money as a commodity *specialized in the function* of expressing the value of other commodities, as "universal equivalent." When Marx says that he is going to show "the genesis of the money-form" of exchange-value, what he does is to determine at one and the same time the *specific function* of one particular category of commodities in relation to all the others, the *form* that a commodity has to assume in order to fulfill this specialized function as universal equivalent, and the practical *conditions* that make both necessary and possible the specialization of a certain category of commodities in this function. And Marx emphasizes that this theoretical procedure, which he calls the "ideal genesis" of money, is not at all a "history" of the different forms of money that are encountered in human societies. Such a "history" is possible, and can be scientific, only on the basis of results won by preliminary structural research, and the results of these historical researches will also contribute to the development of structural research. In this circular movement of cognition—the starting point of which is always analysis of functions and of the structures that realize them in defined conditions—a single science of man is constituted, which does not isolate, for example, ethnology and anthropology, history and theory, in closed fetishized compartments, or put them in opposition to each other.

A method like this, which aims at grasping simultaneously the basis, the *raisons d'être*, of the *functions*, *form*, and *conditions* of existence (and so of the rise and evolution of social relations, which thereby exist *only* as *structures* endowed with objective properties), lays down rigorous lines for a new and fruitful relation between scientific disciplines, both the different departments of history (economic, political, social, ideological, cognitive activities, etc.), and what are called the theoretical disciplines (anthropology, sociology, political economy, etc.). After that has been established the functionalists' view may cease to be true, or to seem true, according to which: "the historian can *only* provide us with the succession of *accidental* events which have *caused* a society to become what is is."[6]

But the functionalists' criticism of the historian's work, a criticism to which Marx subscribed in advance when he himself criticized the "historians" of capitalism or of Antiquity, goes further than a mere criticism of the present state of a theoretical method, a situation that one may still hope and endeavor to improve. Beyond the criticism of history as a craft (*Historie*, historiography) there is the empiricist view that history as reality (*Geschichte*) is only a succession of events, and of events that are themselves only accidents. On this fundamental point concerning not just the epistemological conditions of a *science* of history but the nature of the *actual process* of human history, Marx is opposed both to Radcliffe-Brown and to Leach or Lévi-Strauss.[7] I shall come back to this point. Before doing so, however, let me recall a third methodological principle which opposes Marxism and structuralism to functionalist empiricism, namely, that what is visible is a *reality* concealing *another*, deeper reality, which is hidden and the discovery of which is the very purpose of scientific cognition.

We are here at the very heart of Marx's method as displayed in *Capital*—at the point of origin of the theoretical revolution he effected in political economy and in the human sciences (Godelier 1970). What is this method? Marx shows the absurd, falsely obvious character of the conceptions that individuals *spontaneously* form regarding the nature of commodities and of economic relations in commodity societies: "A commodity appears at first sight a very trivial thing, and easily understood" (1938:41).

Marx shows that the reason why a commodity is a complex and obscure reality is that what makes a product of labor a commodity, namely, its value, is social labor that does not *appear* as such.

The existence of the things *qua* commodities, and the value relation between the products of labour which stamps them as commodities, have absolutely no connexion with their physical properties and with the material relations arising therefrom. There it is a definite social relation between men, that assumes, in their eyes, the fantastic form of a relation between things. In order, therefore, to find an analogy, we must have recourse to the mist-enveloped regions of the religious world. In that world the productions of the human brain appear as independent beings endowed with life, and entering into relation both with one another and the human race. (Marx 1938:43)

The fetishizing of commodities is not the effect of the alienation of consciousnesses but the effect *in* and *for* consciousnesses of the disguising of social relations *in* and *behind* their appearances. Now these appearances are the necessary point of departure of the representations of their economic relations that individuals spontaneously form for themselves. Such images thus constitute a more or less coherent body of illusory beliefs concerning the social reality within which these individuals live, and serve them as means of acting within and upon this social reality.

We see the full implication for the social sciences of Marx's demonstration of the existence of a process of fetishization of social relations, a demonstration carried out on the basis of the particular example provided by the fetishizing of commodity relations of production.[8] In showing that, by his labor, the worker creates *not only the equivalent* of the value represented by his wages but also *additional* value for which he is not paid, and which constitutes the origin and essence of surplus value, Marx shows at the same time that, in practice, the wage-relation "makes the actual relation invisible and, indeed, shows the direct opposite of that relation." Thus, at the level of visible social relations, everything happens, in the eyes of both the capitalists and the workers, as though wages paid for all the labor contributed by the worker and profit were not produced by labor but by capital. The economic categories of wages, profit, interest on capital, etc., therefore express quite well the visible relations of the capitalist system, and as such they have *pragmatic utility*, being of service in management and the making of decisions; but they possess no scientific value, for they do not reflect the true, underlying logic of the system. No econometrical refinements can alter this fact—which does not at all signify that the use of mathematics does not increase the pragmatic *utility* of the categories of vulgar economics; in fact, at the level of the day-to-day practice of business management of enterprises and competition, what is essential is not to have a scientific theory of the real functioning of the system in its totality, but to anticipate the functioning of variables—wages, investments, profits—which must and can be treated separately.

The final pattern of economic relations as *seen* on the surface in their real existence and consequently in the conceptions by which the bearers and agents of these relations seek to understand them, is very much different from, and indeed quite the *reverse*, of *their inner but concealed essential pattern and the conception corresponding to it.* (Marx 1938, 3:205)

It is therefore impossible for scientific cognition to be built up from the spontaneous representations formed by individuals for their social relations, and this radically refutes empiricism in all the fields where it operates. There is no fundamental difference between the spontaneous models of their society that individuals make for themselves, the "set of ideas" they have regarding their "social structure in practical situations" (Leach), and the learned models contructed by sociologists and economists who start from the same spontaneous representations and whose models "exist only as logical constructions in their own mind" (Leach). On this point Marx and Lévi-Strauss are in agreement, and the latter's analysis of the mechanisms by which mythical representations of reality are constructed is an essential scientific gain. However, Marx requires of science that it discover not merely the mechanisms of mythical thought but also the mechanisms which, existing *outside of* thought, impose upon the latter the illusory conceptions which it forms of reality—that is to say, both their content and their historical *necessity*.

It is, in reality, much easier to discover by analysis the earthly core of the misty creations of religion than, conversely, it is to develop from the actual relations of life the corresponding celestialized forms of those relations. The latter method is the only materialistic, and therefore the only scientific one. (Marx 1938, 1:367)

It is the actual significance of the structural analysis of myths and of all ideology that is called in question by this reflection of Marx's on the history of religion.

Before pursuing our analysis of the difference and opposition between Marxism and structuralism, let me mention an important consequence of the Marxist criticism of "bourgeois" political economy and of its empiricist premises. The most abstract categories of political economy, those which seem the most innocent of any ideological content, constitute only abstract cognition of the determinations that are common to all societies, and not real cognition of the specific structures of these societies.

The establishment of the individual as a mere *worker* is itself a product of historical development.

> Labour is quite a simple category. The idea of labour in that sense, as labour in general, is also very old. Yet 'labour' thus defined by political economy is as much a modern category as the conditions which have given rise to this simple abstraction. . . . This example of labour strikingly shows how even the most abstract categories, in spite of their applicability to all epochs—just because of their abstract character—are by the very definiteness of the abstraction a product of historical conditions as well, and are fully applicable only to and under those conditions. (Marx 1971:37, 39)

This analysis would not be repudiated by any anthropologist.[9] It shows well enough the extent to which abstract categories such as "economy," religion, politics, seen as so many subsystems of a social system (Talcott Parsons), rigidly contain the *apparent form* of the social relations of capitalist society. In the latter, the economy seems to function in a purely autonomous way, independently of political and religious relations which are seen as "exogenous" variables. Authentic Marxism, however, does not prejudge the form and content of real economic relations in the various societies known to history. Their modes of production are not objects available for direct cognition through experience, but realities which have to be "recognized" by discovering them where the vulgar and abstract conceptions of economy and society do not accompany them—that is, also in the functioning of political or religious or kinship relations. A mode of production is not reducible to the so called subsistence activities of a society, but is a complex reality that has to be "reproduced" by reconstructing its content by thought. We can now appreciate better the ridiculous and ideologically-marked nature of the advice given to English-speaking apprentice anthropologists in that little manual of instruction, *Notes and Queries on Anthropology*:

> If the investigator has been trained in ordinary economic theory but has no anthropological training, he should remember continually the im-

portance of the social setting of the economic institutions he is studying, otherwise he will not grasp the value system upon which the economic organization depends. If he has had no economic training he is recommended to study the fundamental principles expounded in one of the recognized economic textbooks. (Royal Anthropological Institute 1960)

Poorly concealed behind the look of innocent common sense are the contradictions of an empiricism that simultaneously declares and denies that it suffices to use "ordinary economic theory," that of the "recognized textbooks," in order to analyze original economic systems that *cannot be conceived* otherwise than in their *inner* relation with a definite "social setting." It is clear that for conceiving this inner relation, "ordinary economic theory," even the theory of "fundamental principles," does not offer an adequate instrument. Actually—and this is the radical originality of Marx's thought, which opposes it both to structuralism and to functionalism—Marxism assumes that this inner relation, which provides the underlying logic of the functioning of societies and of their history, is determined, in the last analysis, by the conditions of *production and reproduction* of their material basis, or, to use his terminology, their mode of production.

Marxism is not a philosophy of history, or a "model of history." History is not a concept that explains, but one that is explained. Marxism is above all a theory of society, a hypothesis regarding the articulation of its internal levels and the specific hierarchical causality of each of these levels. Marxism assumes both the relative autonomy of social structures and their reciprocal relation in a specific way of referring back to a system of *constraints*, which determine in the last analysis, but which are never directly visible, and which express the conditions of production and reproduction of the material basis of social existence. Developing the theory of these structures, their articulations, their causality, and the conditions necessary for them to appear and to disappear, signifies making history a science and developing it as such, as provisional synthesis and conclusion, as "reproduction of the concrete by means of thought."[10]

From the moment, however, when one accepts the assumption of the existence of necessary conditions for the appearance and disappearance of social structures, for their specific articulation and causality, history as reality can no longer be reduced to a succession of purely accidental events. Events have their own necessity, and accidents are seen to impose a necessity which ultimately does not depend on them since it expresses the objective properties of social relations, properties of compatibility and incompatibility, which underlie the limited system of their possible transformations. There is no point in counterposing the internal cause of the transformations of societies to the external ones, since in the end it is the same unintentional properties of the social structures that are expressing themselves. It is pointless to bring forward as an objection to Marxism the dominance of kinship relations in one case or politicoreligious relations in another case; for Marxism does not deny these facts and declines to reduce structures to one another as epiphenomena of material life; rather, Marxism *explains* the dominance of a given structure by *seeking* the reasons for it in specific determinations of different modes of production.[11] Faced with these facts of dominance, British anthropology has often proved incapable of doing anything more than repeat that the dominant structures serve to integrate the various parts of the social whole, while failing to explain why it is that in one case kinship and in another case politics or religion played the role of integrator.

The British social anthropologists were less concerned about total configurations of cultural knowledge than about the functional integration of institutions which supported and maintained society. . . . The key to the complex and beautiful unity of society was conceived to be its structure based on kin, marital and political relations. . . . Here were hidden elaborate networks and subtle symmetries to be discovered, whereas subsistence activities were considered simple, undifferentiated and boringly repetitive wherever one found them. (McNetting 1971:3–4)

And yet, on many occasions in their practical work, British anthropologists have contradicted this common doctrine of the older functionalism (as against the neofunctionalism of cultural ecology), without drawing radical conclusions from their having done so.[12] Thus, Leach, in his work *Political Systems of Highland Burma*, when he analyses the concepts of property and ownership, states:

The concepts which are discussed in the present section are of the utmost importance for my general argument for they provide the categories in terms of which social relations are linked with economic facts. In the last analysis the power relations in any society must be based upon the control of real goods and the primary sources of production, but this Marxist generalization does not carry us very far. (1964:141)

One cannot but wonder at the inconsequence of the conclusion, a pirouette by which the author shrugs off a hypothesis "of the utmost importance," and applicable to "any society," so as not to seem to be casting doubt on the non-Marxist theses of the functionalists.

Much more seriously, however, R. Firth says in the preface to the second edition of his *Primitive Polynesian Economy*:

After publishing an account of the social structure, in particular the kinship structure (*We, the Tikopia*, London, 1936), I analysed the economic structure of the society, because so many social relationships were made more manifest in their economic content. Indeed, the social structure, in particular the political structure, was clearly dependent on specific economic relationships arising out of the system of control of resources. With these relationships in turn were linked the religious activities and institutions of the society. (1939: chapter 11)[13]

Throughout his work Firth encouraged the development of economic anthropology, "for a deeper understanding of social conditions and structures in the communities the anthropologist studies" (1939:14).[14] But he never failed to show confidence in the general principles of non-Marxist political economy, as the theoretical framework needed in order to analyze the economic systems of primitive and peasant societies (1964).

However, is not functionalism engaged in ridding itself of its inconsistencies and its traditional theoretical hesitations, thanks to the efforts of the American school of "cultural ecology"? (Vayda and Rappaport 1968). This school declares itself to be resolutely materialist, and aims to reinterpret all human cultures on the basis of the material conditions of the adaptation of man to definite environments.[15] Every society is studied as a subsystem of a wider totality, the ecological system within which it lies, and the functioning and conditions of reproduction of this ecological system are analyzed by means of systems and communication theory (feedback mechanisms, entropy, etc.). The whole of functionalism seems to have been recast, in its orientation (materialistic), its method (modern systems theory) and its theoretical possibilities and aspirations (comparison of societies and construction of a multilinear schema of social evolution). Are we not here in the theoretical universe, if not of Marx himself, then at least of Marxism as it is generally understood and practiced?

I do not here propose to draw up a survey, even a provisional one, of the works of the anthropologists who adhere to the doctrine of cultural materialism. Robert Netting has recently done this, very firmly and perceptively, by compiling a list of the positive discoveries that were quickly made as soon as *detailed* study was undertaken of the ecological environment and conditions of production of the peoples who live by hunting and food-gathering (Richard Lee, De Vore, Steward), the Indians of the Northwest Coast (Suttles), the pastoral societies of East Africa (Gulliver, Deshler, Dyson-Hudson), and slash-and-burn cultivators (Geertz, Roy, Rappaport). Confronted by facts, the theses that had been repeated over and over again by cultural anthropology and which every anthropology student had accepted as gospel truth, gradually collapsed—the "hardship" of the life of the hunters and food-gatherers, the potlatch "excesses" of the Northwest Coast Indians, the "cattle complex" and "love for their cows" of the African herdsmen, and the "irrational practices" of slash-and-burn agriculture (see Vayda 1969). To the work of the anthropologists must be added that of archeologists such as Braidwood, Flannery, and McNeish, who have devoted themselves since the 1950s to reconstituting in minute detail the ecological conditions of existence of the pre-neolithic populations of Mesopotamia and Mesoamerica, and have transformed our knowledge of the processes of domestication of plants and animals and of the appearance of new economic and social systems based on agriculture and stockbreeding. Here too an old-established and respected idea, that of the "neolithic revolution" (Childe), had to be called in question and profoundly revised (see Ucko and Dimbleby 1969; Struever 1971).

It was inevitable that these positive results should be obtained as soon as a systematic effort was devoted to analyzing essential aspects of the functioning of primitive societies which had been dogmatically neglected or wrongly handled (brilliant exceptions were Malinowski, Firth, and Evans-Pritchard) on the pretext that they were "undifferentiated and boringly repetitive." Neverthe-

less, what is called the ecological approach comes to grief as soon
as it tries to become a general theory of social life and history. It
meets its downfall on such essential points as the causality of the
economy or the environment, the nature of the functional relations between social structures, and the driving-forces of the evolution of systems. It relies upon the dogmas of vulgar materialism,
which ultimately prove to be not merely helpless in face of the
idealism that is widespread in the social sciences but actually justify
this idealism and contribute to reproducing it.

Let me briefly review some of the weaknesses of this new form
of materialism. The economy, as a system of social relations between men engendered in and from the process of producing their
material conditions of existence, is reduced to technology and the
relation between men and nature. Instead of determination in the
last analysis by the economy, we have determination in the last
analysis by the ecological environment, to which man *adapts himself* by inventing the appropriate techniques. Social structures are
seen as so many means that are functionally necessary for this
ecological adaptation.[16] Their hidden, latent rationality lies in providing adaptive, selective advantages which are disguised under
forms that appear to be, say, irrational or noneconomic. Thus,
Marvin Harris, wishing, so to speak, to "desacralize" the sacred
cattle of India, writes:

I have written this paper because I believe the irrational, non-economic
and exotic aspects of the Indian cattle complex are greatly overemphas-
ized at the expense of the rational, economic and mundane interpeta-
tions. . . . Insofar as the beef-producing industries it is part of an ecological adjustment which maximizes rather than minimizes on the calorie
and protein output of the productive process. (1966)[17]

Of course I agree with the first sentence, but not with the second
in which one can recognize the empirical materialism, the "economism" that *reduces* all social structures to epiphenomena of the
economy which is itself reduced, through technique, to a function
of adaptation to the environment. With this view of the matter,
the problems presented by the dominance and the plurality of
functions of kinship relations or politicoreligious relations remain
inaccessible to materialist analysis; it is impossible to conceive the
specific articulation of structures; and reciprocal causality is re-

duced to probabilist correlation and history to a series of events of greater or less frequency.

Dependent as we are on the unfolding of the natural continuum of events our generalizations must be couched in probabilistic terms derived from the observation of the frequencies with which predicted or retrodicted events occur. (Harris 1968:614)

Actually, as Lévi-Strauss has noted, invoking the secret rationality of adaptive advantages in order to explain distinct forms of social organization leads one very quickly into either truisms or absurdities.[18] As soon as a society exists, it functions; and it is tautological to say that a variable is adaptive because it fulfills a necessary function in the total system.

Proof that a certain trait or cultural arrangement has positive economic value is not an adequate explanation of its existence or even of its presence. The *problematique* of adaptive advantage does not specify a uniquely correct answer. As a principle of causality in general and economic performance in particular, adaptive advantage is indeterminate: stipulating grossly what is impossible but rendering suitable anything that is possible. (Sahlins 1969, and 1972)

We see then that a materialism like this is unable to explain the fundamental necessity of what exists; it cannot explain the history of societies that are not always completely "integrated" totalities, but instead, totalities whose unity is the provisionally stable effect of a structural compatibility. Such a compatibility would enable different structures to reproduce themselves until they reach the point at which the internal (and external) dynamic of these systems prevents this totality from continuing to exist as such.

The "new materialism" seems analytically innocent of any concern for contradiction—although it sometimes figures itself a client of Marxism (minus the dialectical materialism). So it is unmindful of the barriers opposed to productive forces by established cultural organizations each concealed by its adaptive advantages in some state of fractional effectiveness. (Sahlins 1969)

Marshall Sahlins is right but in order to be fully convincing he should have given a scientific content to the notion of contradiction. All of us remember the dialectical "miracles" of Hegel and of so many Marxists (or so-called Marxists) and we know that most of the time scientific analysis was leaving the stage as soon as the "contradictions" were stepping into the middle of it. In some way, marvin Harris was expressing this common feeling when he wrote that:

Despite the Hegelian monkey on their back, Marx and Engels must be credited with an important breakthrough . . . (because) they proclaimed that it was in the economic base that the explanation for both parts of the superstructure—social organization and ideology were to be found. (1968:230–31)

Unfortunately for Marvin Harris, Marxism is not an aborted cultural materialism—an abortion due to an overdose of Hegelian logic—and to use Jonathan Friedman's words, cultural materialism is not good causal materialism, good Marxism minus the non-sense of dialectic (1971:7). And the reason is simply, as I have shown elsewhere, that Marx's dialectic is just not the hegelian dialectic (1967:22). Let us not forget that it is Marx himself who wrote that it just sufficed "to turn the dialectical (of Hegel) right side up again" to make it scientifically useful and to strip off all the mystifications with which Hegelian idealism has surrounded it.

It is Louis Althusser who has to be credited with having forced us to see the unlikely obscurity (even absurdity) of this hypothetical "inversion of Hegel." For him the specific difference of Marx's dialectic is to be found in the fact that the latter's contradictions are not "simple" like Hegelian ones but "overdetermined" in principle (Althusser 1965). This answer seems to miss two essential points, although it provides valuable positive elements at another level. These two points are: (1) There are two notions of contradiction in Marx: contradiction within a structure and contradiction between structures (or to use the vocabulary of systems theory, intrasystemic and intersystemic ones); (2) the basic principle of Marx's dialectic is not the theological, unscientific principle of identity of contraries but the principle of the conflicting unity of contraries. Without distinguishing these two kinds of contradiction, it is impossible to give sense to Marx's notion of "correspondence" between relations of production and the level of development of forces of production or between infrastructure and superstructures, and the "correspondence" is transformed immediately into a simplistic, mechanical cause-effect relationship.

Without this distinction it is impossible to grasp the logic of the development of a social system, to understand its possible evolutions. An example of the first kind of contradiction is that between capital and labor, between the capitalist class and the working class. One owns the capital, the other is excluded from ownership of it. One's profit is the unpaid labor of the other. What characterizes this first contradiction? It is inside capitalist "relations of production." It is thus an "internal contradiction of a structure" (Marx 1938, 3:244).

This contradiction is specific to the capitalist mode of production. It characterizes it as such, distinguishing it from other, slave-based or feudal modes of production. As it is specific, it characterizes the system from the beginning, and the functioning of the system continually reproduces it. It is therefore original, in the sense that it is present from the beginning and remains until the disappearance of a system. It develops with the development of the system, it is transformed by the evolution of capitalism from free competition to monopoly and by the evolution of the trade union and political organization of the working class. This contradiction is antagonistic: the function of one class is to exploit the other. It reveals itself in the class struggle.

Is this basic antagonism, which would seem to occupy the forefront of the historical stage, in fact the basic contradiction of capitalism? No. For Marx, the latter is the contradiction between the development and the socialization of the productive forces and the private ownership of the means of production.

The contradiction, to put it in a very general way, consists in that the capitalist mode of production involves a tendency towards absolute development of the productive forces, regardless of the value and surplus-value it contains, and regardless of the social conditions under which capitalist production takes place; while, on the other hand, its aim is to preserve the value of the existing capital and promote its self-expansion to the highest limit (i.e., to promote an ever more rapid growth of this value). (Marx 1938:237)

What are the characteristics of this contradiction? It is not a contradiction within a structure, but one between two structures. It is thus not directly a contradiction between individuals or groups, but between the structure of the productive forces (their ever

greater socialization) and the structure of the relations of production (the private ownership of the productive forces).

Now the paradox is that this contradiction, which is basic because it explains the evolution of capitalism and its inevitable
disappearance, appears at "a certain stage" of evolution, at a "certain stage of maturity" (Marx 1938:861) of the system.[19] And this
stage is the stage of large-scale industry—i.e., a certain state of
development of the productive forces. Marx clarifies this in an
1868 letter to Kungelmann: "He would have seen that I represent
large-scale industry not only as the mother of the antagonism, but
also as the creator of the material and spiritual conditions necessary
for the solution of this antagonism."

In the beginning, however, far from contradicting the development of the productive forces, capitalist relations of production
gave it impetus in its progress from the organization of manufacture to the appearance of mechanization and heavy industry.
Mechanized industry, completing the separation of agriculture and
domestic rural industry (which is annihilated), "for the first time,
conquers for industrial capital the entire homemarket" and gives
it "that extension and consistence which the capitalist mode of
production requires." The latter had become "combined and scientific (Marx 1938, 1:748–749) with the progress of the division
of labour. Before machinery, manufacturing production could not
achieve this "radical transformation."

Thus, initially, far from there being a contradiction between
capitalism and the development of the productive forces, there
was a correspondence, a functional compatibility which was the
basis for the dynamism of technical progress and the capitalist
class. But this very structural correspondence between capitalism
and the forces of production means a noncorrespondence of these
forces of production with feudal relations of production. And for
Marx this noncorrespondence is the foundation of the objective
contradiction between feudal and capitalist relations, between the
seignorial class and the capitalist class. For as we have seen, if
there are to be capitalists, there must also be laborers facing them,
free in their person, forced to put their labor power up for sale—
i.e., excluded from ownership of the meaning of production (Marx
1938, 1:168).

Thus the basic contradiction of the capitalist mode of production emerges with the development of this mode of production, without anyone wishing to make it appear. This contradiction is therefore unintentional. It is a result of the action of all the agents of the system and of the development of the system itself, and is never the project of any consciousness, and is never anyone's goal. Marx is therefore drawing attention to aspects of reality which cannot be referred to any consciousness nor explained by consciousness. It is the mode of production itself, the valuation of capital, which produces this result "unconsciously" (Marx 1938, 1:254).

But this basic, unintentional, contradiction is not the opaque involuntary residue of intersubjective action. It is unintentional and without teleology, but transparent to science because it is "significant." It signifies the limits within which it is possible that capitalist relations of production, based on private property, may correspond to the development of the productive forces to which they have given birth.

These limits are "immanent" to capitalist relations of production, and cannot be "overcome" (Marx 1938, 3:245), since the evaluation of capital depends on the exploitation of the great mass of producers: they are thus limits expressing objective properties of the capitalist mode of production, (not of capitalists or workers as individuals or economic agents): "The entire capitalist mode of production is only a relative one, whose barriers are not absolute. They are absolute only for this mode, i.e., on its basis" (Marx 1938, 3:252). These are the limits within which the relations of production can remain constant, allowing for gigantic variations in the productive forces. These limits are thus objective properties of the system and these properties establish the necessity for its evolution and disappearance. They can act on the system itself and are the causality of the structure on itself. "The real barrier of capitalist production is capital itself" (Marx 1938, 3:245). As we can see, contradictions within a structure and contradictions between structures are not of the same order. The former is a property of a structure itself and, in Jonathan Friedman's words, exists "between systematically self-contradictory aspects of a social relation." The second is the limit of functional compatibility between structures within a system or, more precisely, between the internal properties of structures and their mutual constraints. The relative autonomy of structures means, first of all, the autonomy of their internal and objective properties.

I think that this theory of contradiction is implicit in Marx and radically opposes Marx's dialectic to Hegel's one. Clearly, the basic principle of Marx's dialectic cannot be the principle of identity of contradictories, which is a metaphysical principle only necessary to provide a proof of absolute idealism and to establish Hegelianism as the absolute knowledge of the Absolute Spirit. This absolute spirit is a totality which contradicts itself in the exteriority of nature and the interiority of the Logos and maintains its identity through all its contradictions; by being the Real is also the Rational.

But for Marx the capitalist is not the worker, production is not consumption, and the internal contradiction between capitalists and workers cannot be solved without the development of the productive forces. The solution of an internal contradiction is not created solely by the internal development of that contradiction, but depends largely on the development of contradictions between structures, which are linked to the first one but are not identical to it.

It is now easy to understand why Marx declared from the *Contribution* on: "Hence, it is the simplest matter with a Hegelian to treat production and consumption as identical," and added: "The result we arrive at is not that production distribution, exchange and consumption are identical, but that they are all members of one totality, differences within one unity" (Marx 1904:282).[20]

And in *Anti-Duhring*, Engels defended Marx's dialectical method by showing that it could not be reduced to "these dialectical . . . mazes . . . this mixed and misconceived idea (according to which) it all amounts to the same thing in the end" (Marx 1904:291), where the negation of the negation serves "as the midwife to deliver the future from the womb of the past," declaring that a rose is a rose and that it is not a rose" (Engels 1943:169).

As I understand it, Marx's analysis of the basic notion of contradiction between structures tallies with the most recent scientific practice (Engels 1943:195). The notion makes explicit certain objective properties of structures, that is, objective limits to the possibilities of their reproduction, to their remaining essentially constant, given the variations of their internal and external conditions of functioning, and more profoundly, to their reproduction of their relation and connection with other structures. The appearance of a contradiction is, in fact, the appearance of a limit to the conditions of invariance of a structure. Beyond this limit a change in structure becomes necessary. In this perspective the notion of contradiction I am putting forward would perhaps be of interest to cybernetics. This science explores the limits and the possibilities of internal regulations that allow any system (whether physiological, economic or whatever) to maintain itself despite a determined range of variation of its internal and external conditions of functioning. This analysis brings together the sciences of nature and the sciences of man. Now we see better why Marxism is not cultural materialism and why a cultural materialist, even if he uses cybernetics and systems theory, will not become a Marxist, since he lacks the basic notions of contradictions and structural causality needed to perform what he wants to ultimately accomplish: explain the multilinear evolution of mankind. But maybe history is not evolution nor even multinear evolution—because a multilinear evolution is still linear and so it conceals the fact that history proceeds with the creation of new points of departure for evolution, and there are departures which are not entirely contained in embryo in their own past.

Lévi-Strauss from the outset, rejects empiricism and evolutionism in all their forms and deals with structures, their internal and transformational properties and their mutual compatibilities and claims to be a materialist; is he, like Marx, trying to build up a science of History? From some of his texts the answer would seem positive.

For Claude Lévi-Strauss, "It is tedious, as well as useless . . . to amass arguments to prove that all societies are in history and change; that this is so is patent. History is not merely a cold history in which societies which create the minimum of that disorder which the physicists call enthropy . . . tend to remain indefinitely in their iditial state" (1961:38). It is also made up of these "non-recurrent chains of events whose affects accumulate to produce economic and social upheavals" (1962:311).

In order to explain these fundamental historical transformations, Lévi-Strauss accepts "the undoubted primacy of infrastructures" (1962:173).

I do not at all mean to suggest that ideological transformation gives rise to social ones. Only the reverse is in fact true. Men's conception of the relations between nature and culture is a function of modifications of their own social relations. . . . We are however merely studying the shadows on the wall of the cave. (1962:117)

Lévi-Strauss himself states: "It is to this theory of superstructures, scarcely touched upon by Marx, that I hope to make a contribution: (1962:173).

One cannot but note that this theory of society, of the "law of order" of the relation between economy and of society, has vanished: Lévi-Strauss, in the conclusions to *Du Miel aux Cendres* sees a fundamental historical upheaval at the end of which, "at the frontiers of Greek thought, mythology gave way to a philosophy that emerges as the preliminary condition for scientific reflection, . . . an historical occurrence whose whole significance lies in having happened in that place at that time" (1966:407). History, even though endowed with a "law of order," is thus deprived of any necessity, and the births of Western philosophy and science are seen as more accidental events. "Neither here nor there was the transition necessary, and if history retains its position in the front rank, this position is the one that rightfully belongs to irreducible contingency" (1966:408).

We see before us a theoretical method which, underneath the apparently harmonious character of the author's work, is based upon the opposed systems of theoretical principles—one of which affirms the necessity of historical transformations while the other affirms their irreducibly contingent nature. (Incidentally, Marx did not contrast necessity and contingency as two irreducible realities). The question arises whether Lévi-Strauss' theoretical method leads necessarily from the first conclusion to the second.

Why, then, does Lévi-Strauss' structural analysis, although it neither denies or tears itself away from history, still never "meet" history in its concrete diversity and reality?

Structural analysis does not meet history because, from the outset, Lévi-Strauss has separated analysis of the form of kinship relations from the analysis of their functions. It is not that these functions are denied, but they are never explored as such.[21] As a result, the problem of the real articulation of kinship relations and the other social structures that characterize concrete, historically determined societies (concrete realities within which Lévi-Strauss limits himself to distinguishing the "formal system" of kinship relations to be studied in itself and compared with other forms of kinship, similar or contrasting) is never analyzed either. Of course Lévi-Strauss is not unaware of these problems, but he has not tackled them.[22] And yet these are fundamental problems, the solution of which will enable us to understand both the form and the content of social relations, the conditions for their appearance and for their disappearance, and hence the history of mankind through their history. Thus, in connection with "the correlation established by Murdock between patrilineal institutions and the highest levels of culture" (1937; see also Driver and Schuessler 1967), Lévi-Strauss says: "It is true that in societies where political power *takes precedence* over other forms of organization the duality which would result from the masculinity of political authority and the matrilineal character of descent could not subsist. Consequently, societies attaining this level of political organization tend to generalize the paternal right" (1967:36).

A structural morphology without analysis of functions, with "physiology," is incomplete, and only joint development of these two fields of investigation can enable us to pose correctly the problems of the transformation and evolution of systems—the problems of history.

A functional system, e.g., a kinship system, can never be interpreted in an integral fashion by diffusionist hypotheses. The system is bound up with the total structure of the society employing it, and consequently its nature depends more on the intrinsic characteristics of such a society than on cultural contacts and migrations. (Lévi-Strauss 1967:144)

It is therefore necessary to take up the task where it has been abandoned, and go beyond structural analysis of the forms of kinship or the reconstruction of a formal grammar of the myths of the American Indians. To go further than a structural morphology means, therefore, trying to account for the forms, functions, mode of articulation, and conditions of transformation of the social structures within the concrete societies studied by the historian and the anthropologist. It is precisely in order to accomplish this complex task, which presupposes a combination of several theoretical methods, that Marx's hypothesis of the determination, in the last analysis, of the forms and the evolution of societies by the conditions of production and reproduction of their material life is needed as the central hypothesis. It is to this central hypothesis that we are inevitably brought by a rigorous functionalism and structuralism when these try to penetrate more deeply into the logic of the facts and societies they analyze.[23]

But here is a last trap to avoid. Observing that in the society they study, kinship, politics, or religion plays a dominant role, most empiricist historians or anthropologists conclude that the economy has but a secondary role in the functioning and evolution of these societies. That was the position of Karl Polanyi, but it is also the position of Louis Dumont, Fuhrer-Haimendorf, and many other anthropologists. So the main problem for a Marxist is to explain the dominance of, say, kinship or politics from the structure of economic relationships. That seems to be quite a challenge. Among the Marxists there are two ways of solving this apparent contradiction. The first one is developed by Althusser and his disciples, Terray, Rey, and Meillassoux. They state, without demonstration, that if kinship or religion is playing the dominant role within one society, it is because of the economic conditions existing in this society. They interpret the causality of economy as a mechanism of selection among various sets of social relationships, one of which will be put in the dominant position. It is not difficult to see why they never succeeded in demonstrating their position. In fact, just like the empiricists they are fighting against, they are still viewing the causality of economy as the relationship of an institution to other ones.

There is another way to understand the causality of economy. It is in proving that kinship or religion or politics dominates if and only if these social relations function as "relations of production." When I say that "they function as relations of production" I mean that they assume the triple function of determining access to and control of the means of production, of allocating the social labor force between different sectors of production, and of determining access to and control of the social output, for the groups and the individuals which make up a given type of society. The main problem for both historians and anthropologists is to discover the reasons why and the conditions in which kinship relationships or any other social relationships function as relations of production. To study the causality of economy is not to develop economic anthropology but to discover the reasons why economy does not occupy the same locus and hence does not assume the same forms and has not the same mode of development in different societies and at different epochs.

From this standpoint it will no longer be possible to go on counterposing anthropology to history or to sociology as three fetishized separate domains, nor to present economic anthropology or economic history as more specialized lines of research belatedly added to other specialized domains that are more advanced. What is involved in the study of societies, on the basis of their mode of production and reproduction, is the complete and radical reworking of all the theoretical methods that have been developed in the process of man's cognition in his social life and his historical evolution. What is involved is the crisis, latent or overt, which prevails today in the human sciences—the problem of their unity and their progress. Beyond the problems of knowledge, there are the problems of the transformation of our society and of radical change.

NOTES

1. The elements of the social structure are human beings, "what is meant by social structure" being "any arrangement of persons in institutionalized relationships."

2. I hold that social structure in practical situations (as contrasted with the sociologist's abstract model) consists of a set of ideas about the distribution of power between persons and groups of persons." Then, referring to the models constructed by sociologists and anthropologists, Leach adds this definition of an orthodox functionalism: "Social structure . . . the principles of organization that unite the component parts of the system," and concludes with a subjectivist pirouette: "The structures which the anthropologist describes are models which exist only as logical constructions in his own mind."

3. This is a criticism that Meyer Fortes directed at Radcliffe-Brown when he wrote in 1949 in the Radcliffe-Brown Festschrift: "Structure is not immediately visible in the "concrete reality." . . . we are, as it were, in the realm of grammar and syntax, not of the spoken word" (1949:56).

4. This is why Edmund Leach appears in the eyes of his Anglo-American colleagues as the isolated but turbulent representative of structuralism, and he

himself declares his "sympathy with his [Lévi-Strauss'] general point of view" and his "obvious debt" to him (Leach 1961:vi).

5. "A functional system, e.g., a kinship system, can never be interpreted in an integral fashion by diffusionist hypotheses. The system is bound up with the total structure of the society employing it, and consequently its nature depends more on the intrinsic characteristics of such a society than on cultural contacts and migrations" (Lévi-Strauss 1967:449; Engl. trans. p. 390). And again, on p. 165 (English translation, p. 142): 'We have been careful to eliminate all historical speculation, all research into origins, and all attempts to reconstruct a hypothetical order in which institutions succeeded one another." And Evans-Pritchard, similarly: "A history of the legal institutions of the England of today will only show us how they have come to be what they are and not how they function in our social life" (1951:48).

6. This is how Evans-Pritchard sums up the attitude of the functionalists toward history, without, however, endorsing it himself. See the next note.

7. Let me recall that on this crucial point there is disagreement among the functionalists. Evans-Pritchard stresses, for instance, that: "History is not merely a succession of changes but . . . a growth. . . . Furthermore . . . history alone provides a satisfactory experimental situation in which the hypotheses of functional anthropology can be tested" (1951:60).

8. I have tried to analyze other forms of fetishism connected with noncommodity modes of production (Godelier 1970; 1971).

9. Marshall Sahlins states: "A man works, produces in his capacity as a social person, as a husband and father, brother and lineage mate, member of a clan, a village. Labor is not implemented apart from these existences as if it were a different existence. 'Worker' is not a status in itself nor 'labour' a true category of tribal economics" (1968:80).

10. Marx states: "The concrete concept is concrete because it is a synthesis of many determinations, thus representing the unity of diverse aspects. It appears therefore in reasoning as a summing-up, a result, and not as the starting-point, although it is the real point of origin, and thus also the point of origin of perception and imagination" (1904:206).

11. "In the estimation of [a critic of Marx], my view that each special mode of production and the social relations corresponding to it, in short, that the economic structure of society, is the real basis on which the juridical and political superstructure is raised, and to which definite social forms of thought corresponds; that the mode of production determines the character of the social, political and intellectual life generally, all this is very true for our own times, in which material interests preponderate, but not for the Middle Ages when Catholicism had dominated, nor for Athens and Rome, when politics reigned supreme. In the first place it strikes one as an odd thing for anyone to suppose that these well-worn phrases about the Middle Ages and the Ancient World are unknown to anyone else. This much, however, is clear, that the Middle Ages could not live on Catholicism, nor the Ancient World on politics. On the contrary, it is the mode in which they gained a livelihood that explains why here politics and there Catholicism played the chief part. . . . On the other hand, Don

Quixote long ago paid the penalty for wrongly imagining that knight errantry was compatible with all economical forms of society" (Marx 1938, 1:54). Marx gave only fragments of explanations of these different dominances, but his thought is very clear, and does not justify the criticisms made by Louis Dumont of his alleged utilitarian and Victorian conception of man: "Marx shut himself within the confines of the modern view of man as an individual. Marx fully shared the outlook of the scholars of the Victorian age" (1964:39).

12. R. Firth writes: "W. L. Warner argued that the Murngin did not create a separate economic structure . . . but were dependent on their other institutions, primarily their kinship system, to regulate indirectly their technology and control their distribution and consumption of goods and services (Warner 1937:138). But the lack of what may be classed as specifically economic *institutions* does not mean the lack of economic *process*" (Firth, 1939:7; emphasis his).

13. Among other valuable works by Anglo-American anthropologists on primitive economic systems should be mentioned Nadel's excellent book *Black Byzantium*, devoted to the Nupe of Nigeria, and *The Nuer*, by Evans-Pritchard.

14. His evaluation of Herskovits (1952) which was for a long time one of the few textbooks available to anthropologists on the subject, should be called to mind: "Herskovits examines material from a wide range of sources dealing with 'non-literate' economic systems. His treatment tends to be eclectic rather than rigorously theoretical and it is difficult to discern what is the general framework of his analysis" (Firth 1959:32).

15. "The tendency in social anthropology has been to study societies as if they were isolated, self-sufficient systems, subsisting on thin air, with no visible roots in the soil. The guiding principle, derived in large part from Durkheim and more explicitly from Radcliffe-Brown, has been that social facts require sociological explanations" (Gray and Gulliver 1964:6).

16. I refer the reader to the cuttingly-written, debunking paper by Jonathan Friedman (1971).

17. See also Harris 1968:614.

18. Lévi-Strauss: "To say that a society functions is a truism, but to say that everything in a society functions is an absurdity" (1968:13).

19. From the beginning the private ownership of the productive forces was opposed to the "social character of these productive forces. But during the first stages of development of the capitalist relations of production, this opposition— far from hampering the development of the productive forces—created and sustained this development. I do not depart from what I wrote in my (1967). It would be more precise to say that the relations of production and productive forces "become more and more in contradiction" with the development of the capitalist mode of production.

20. When Lenin declares that the dialectic is "the theory of the identity of opposites" or "the study of the contradiction in the very essence of things," I suggest that he is proposing a false equivalence between two definitions.

In the same way, Mao Tse-tung constantly confuses the unity of opposites with their identity: "How . . . can we speak of identity or unity (of opposites)? The fact is that a contradictory aspect cannot exist all by itself. If there is not the opposite aspect, each aspect loses the conditions of its existence. . . . Without landlords, there would be no tenant-peasants; without tenant-peasants, there would be no landlords. Without the bourgeoisie there would be no proletariat; without the proletariat there would also be no bourgeoisie. . . . All opposite elements are like this: Under certain conditions they are on the one hand composed to each other and on the other hand interconnected, interpenetrated, interpermeated and interdependent; that is what we mean by identity" (Mao Tse-tung 1960:47; see also 1954).

21. Why are they not explored? The reason is to be found not in the method itself, the analysis of structures, but in Lévi-Strauss' own personal and social background. Lévi-Strauss mentioned this kind of research when in *Anthropologie Structurale* he spoke of an "order of the orders" which accounts for societies as entities, but he never again dealt with the problem.

22. Lévi-Strauss writes: "Actually there is nothing in the exchange of women faintly resembling a reasoned solution to an economic problem (although it can acquire this function in societies which have already learnt in some other way what purchase and sale are)" (1967:162). I do not think that kinship relations acquire economic functions only when an economy of buying and selling (a market economy) has been established.

23. Cf. Marx in the famous "sixth chapter" of *Capital*, long unpublished, which has recently appeared in French in the 'Collection 10/18,' Plon, Paris, 1971, as *Un chapitre inédit du 'Capital'* (the original, with a Russian translation, was published in 1933 in *Arkhiv Marksa i Engelsa*, vol. 2 [VII], under the title: *Erstes Buch. Der Produktionsprozess des Kapitals. Resultate des unmittelbaren Produktionsprozess*): "My conception differs fundamentally from that of the bourgeois economists who, prisoners of capitalist conceptions, see indeed how production takes place within capitalist relations, but now not how these relations are themselves produced, at the same time creating the material conditions for their own dissolution—abolishing with the same stroke their historical justification, as a necessary form of economic development and production of social wealth" (translation from the original, p. 176).

REFERENCES

Althusser, L. 1965. "Contradiction et surdetermination" and "Sur la dialectique materialiste," reedited in *Pour Marx*. Paris: Maspero.

Driver, H. and K. Schuessler. 1967. "Correlational analysis of Murdock's 1957 ethnographic sample." *American Anthropologist* 69(3):332–52.

Dumont, Louis. 1964. "La civilisation Indiènne et nous." *Cahiers des Annales*, Paris: Armand Colin.

Engels, F. 1943. *Anti-Duhring*. London: Lawrence and Wishart.

Evans-Pritchard. 1951. *Social Anthropology*. Oxford: Oxford University Press.

Firth, R. 1939. *Primitive Polynesian Economy*. London: Routledge.

—— 1959. *Economics of New Zealand Maori*. Wellington: Owen.

—— 1964. "A viewpoint from economic anthropology." In R. Firth and B. S. Yamey, eds. *Capital, Saving and Credit in Peasant Studies*. London: Allen.

Fortes, M., ed., 1949. *Social Structure: Studies Presented to A. R. Radcliffe-Brown* Oxford: Oxford University Press.

Friedman, J. 1971. "Marxism, structuralism and vulgar materialism." *American Anthropological Association* annual meeting.

Godelier, M. 1967. "Système, structure et contradiction dans le capital." *Les Temps Modernes*, 828–64.

—— 1970. "Fétichisme, religion et théorie générale de l'ideologie chez Marx." In *Annali*, Feltrinelli, pp. 22-40.

—— 1971. "Mythe et histoire, reflexions sur les fondements de la pensée sauvage." *Annales*, May-August, pp. 541–58.

Gray, R. F. and Gulliver, P. H., eds. 1964. *The Family Estate in Africa*. New York: New York University Press.

Harris, M. 1966. "The cultural ecology of India's sacred cattle." In *Current* Anthropology 7 (1).

—— 1968. *The Rise of Anthropological Theory*. New York: Crowell.

Herskovits, Melville J. 1952. *Economic Anthropology*. New York: Knopf.

Leach, E. 1961. *Rethinking Anthropology*. London: London School of Economics.

—— 1964. *Political Systems of Highland Burma*. London: Bell and Sons (orig. 1954).

Lévi-Strauss, C. 1957. *Anthropologie Structurale*. Paris: Plon.

—— 1960. "On manipulated sociological models." In *Bijdragen tot de taal-, land- en volkenkunde*. The Hague.

—— 1964. *Le Cru et le Cuit*. Paris: Plon.

—— 1961. *Entretiens avec Georges Charbonnier*. Paris: Plon.

—— 1962. *Le Pensée Sauvage*. Paris: Plon.

—— 1966. *Du Miel aux Cendres*. Paris: Plon.

—— 1967. *Les Structures Eléméntaires de la parenté*. Paris: Mouton.

—— 1968. *Anthropologie Structurale*. Paris: Plon.

McNetting, R. 1971. "The ecological approach in cultural study." A McCaleb Module in *Anthropology*. New York: McCaleb Publishing Co.

Mao Tse-tung. 1954. *Selected Works, I*. N.Y.: International Publisher.

—— 1960. *On Contradiction*. Peking.

Marx, K. 1904. *Contribution to the Critique of Political Economy*. London: Lawrence and Wishart.

—— 1938. *Capital*. London: Allen and Unwin.

—— 1971. *Grundrisse*. London: David McLellan.

Murdock, G. P. 1937. "Correlation of matrilineal and patrilineal institutions." In *Studies in the Science of Society*. New Haven: A. G. Keller.

Nadel, F. 1957. *The Theory of Social Structure*. London: Cohen and West.

Parsons, T. 1949. *Essays in Sociological Theory, Pure and Applied*. New York: Free Press.

Radcliffe-Brown, A. R. 1952. *Structure and Function in Primitive Society*. London: Cohen and West.

Royal Anthropological Institute. 1960. *Notes and Queries in Anthropology*. London: Routledge.

Sahlins, M. 1968. *Tribesmen*. Englewood Cliffs, N.J.: Prentice-Hall.

—— 1972. *Essays in Stone Age Economics*. Chicago: Aldine.

—— 1969. "Economic anthropology and anthropological economics." In *Social Sciences Information* 8(5):29–30.

Struever, S. 1971. *Prehistoric Agriculture*. New York: Natural History press.

Ucko, P. J. and Dimbleby, C. W. 1969. *The Domestication and Exploitation of Plants and Animals*. Chicago: Aldine.

Vayda, A. P., ed. 1969. *Environment and Cultural Behavior*. New York: The Natural History Press.

Vayda, A. P. and R. A. Rappaport. 1968. "Ecology, cultural and noncultural." In J. A. Clifton, ed. *Introduction to Cultural Anthropology*. Boston: Houghton Mifflin.

Warner, W. L. 1937. *A Black Civilization*. New York.

CHAPTER ELEVEN

THE OPPRESSION OF WOMEN

A STRUCTURALIST MARXIST VIEW

MARTHA E. GIMÉNEZ

Modern feminism has led to the emergence of an ever-growing body of literature seeking to ascertain, using social science and Marxist theories, the origin of the oppression of women, the reasons for its perpetuation throughout history, its functions in contemporary society, and the conditions that would lead to its demise. The heterogeneous class and ethnic composition of the women's movement as well as the differences in the academic training of individual writers are reflected in the political splits within the movement and in the theoretical and methodological heterogeneity of these writings. More importantly, as intellectual productions rooted in a historically specific political and ideological conjucture, these writings have been affected by the hegemony of idealist and empiricist assumptions underlying current common sense views of the world, social science paradigms, and dominant interpretations of Marxism. Indeed, idealist (i.e., Hegelian, phenomenological, humanistic, existentialist, psychological, voluntaristic) versions of Marxism seem to be more acceptable and respectable within feminist, Marxist, and non-Marxist academic and nonacademic circles in the U.S. On the other hand, theoretical developments that claim to maintain the dialectical materialist outlook of classical Marxism and stress the nonsubjective dimension of social processes are generally ignored or criticized and dismissed on the grounds of their alleged determinism, economism, or functionalism.

This is a revised version of a previously published article: "Structuralist Marxism on 'The Woman Question,'" *Science & Society* (Fall 1978) 42(3):301–23. I want to thank Sandra Bartky and Francine Rainone for their support and critical readings of an earlier draft. I am particularly indebted to Suzanne and Michael Neuschatz for their insightful criticisms, helpful suggestions, and generosity with their time.

An interesting case in point that highlights the nature of the parameters governing intellectual production in the U.S. today is the absence of Structuralist Marxism from American feminist theory. Neither non-Marxist social scientists seeking new ideas for theory construction nor feminists sympathetic to Marxism seem to have found Structuralist Marxism compelling enough to warrant some consideration.

An investigation of the complex historical determinants of this theoretical conjuncture is beyond the scope of this essay which is intended, primarily, as a exploration of the potential relevance of Structuralist Marxism for the development of a Marxist theory of women's oppression under capital. The noted feminist Juliet Mitchell once made a suggestion which has been taken with approval by most other feminists attempting to develop a Marxist analysis of the oppression of women: "We should ask feminist questions, but try to come up with some Marxist answers" (Mitchell 1971:99). In my view, the only way to come up with Marxist answers is to begin by asking Marxist questions. For that purpose, Structuralist Marxism offers important conceptual tools conducive to the formulation of Marxist questions and the elaboration of Marxist analyses of concrete issues: analyses that go beyond the use of Marxist categories in isolation from the logic of Marxist theory and methodology.

In the first section of this essay I shall offer a summary version of important Structuralist Marxist theoretical and methodological contributions; in the second section, I shall critically examine some sociological and feminist theoretical statements, and in the third section, I shall present theoretical and methodological insights obtained by approaching the question of the oppression of women in the light of Structuralist Marxism. While Structuralist Marxism is not exempt from problems, it is my contention that a judicious incorporation of its major insights into the analysis of the oppression of women cannot but further our understanding of its structural supports and the conditions necessary to overcome them.

STRUCTURALIST MARXISM: THEORETICAL AND METHODOLOGICAL ISSUES

Structuralist Marxism is not a fully developed theory; it is a descriptive label which, although rejected by those to whom it is applied, is currently used to indicate the heterogeneous production of Marxists who have introduced structuralist terminology in their writings and have acknowledged some degree of overlap between structuralist and Marxist principles. The most important representatives are Louis Althusser and Maurice Godelier and it is with their work that this essay will be primarily concerned.

The reason why Structuralist Marxism has had a deep impact in the development of Marxist scholarship is because it articulates fundamental methodological principles and theoretical constructs which were largely tacit in classical Marxist works. Godelier convincingly argues that the two main principles of structuralism were discovered by Marx who can thus be considered as "a forerunner of the modern structuralist movement" (Godelier 1970:343).

The first principle is that *"a structure is part of social reality but not of visible relationships"* (Godelier 1970:347). This principle has the following implications:

A. *There are two levels of social reality*: The level of visible social relationships and the level of invisible structures whose laws of functioning and transformation account for changes at the observable level.

B. *The aim of scientific study is to discover those hidden structures*. Marx's scientific project was precisely that of the discovery of the structure and laws of motion of the capitalist mode of production concealed by the visible reality created by its functioning.

C. *The systematic study of appearances cannot provide a scientific knowledge of social reality*.

D. *This failure to attain knowledge taking appearances as starting point is not a cognitive failure*. The concealment of the structure by appearance is inherent in the nature of the structure itself. Structures are made up of social relations which cannot be directly apprehended, for they vanish behind forms of physical or social objectification. For example, capital appears as machines, money, etc.

E. *To each structure corresponds a form of appearance*. And scientific study must take into account both, explaining the appearance in terms of the structure.

F. *To each structure corresponds a form of consciousness or spontaneous representations held by individuals whose activities reproduce the structure*. The systematic study of those representations, far from disclosing the underlying logic of the structure, can only reproduce, at the level of theory, the mystifications created by the very functioning of the structure.

The second principle of structuralism is that "*the study of the internal functioning of a structure must precede and will throw light on the study of its coming to being and subsequent evolution*" (Godelier 1970:347). The historical analysis of the emergence of the constituent elements of a structure and their interrelations presupposes a prior knowledge of the structure and its processes. Thus Marx presents his brief historical discussion of the genesis of primitive accumulation *after* the basic structure, processes, and contradictions of capitalism have been identified (Godelier 1970:348–50). After the structural level of social reality has been discovered, the next step is that of establishing the articulation between that structure and its observable manifestations which can now be defined according to their "real function in the system and their internal compatibility with the essential structures already studied." This process amounts to the description of "the ideal birth of the various elements of a system on the basis of its internal laws of composition" (Godelier 1970:352). This "ideal birth" or "ideal genesis" of categories cannot be confused with their historical or real genesis. Godelier argues that Marx's stress on the priority of structural over historical analysis "is total and anticipates by more than half a century the radical rethinking in linguistics and sociology which led de Saussure and Lowie to reject the evolutionist approach of the 19th century" (Godelier 1970:353). Marx is very specific in this respect:

> It would be impractical and wrong to arrange the economic categories in the order in which they were the determining factors in the course of history. Their order of sequence is rather determined by the relation which they bear to one another in modern bourgeois society, and which is the exact opposite of what seems to be their natural order or the order of their historical development. . . . we are interested in their organic connections within modern bourgeois society. (Marx 1972:41–42)

This is an important principle which establishes the difference between Marxist historical analysis and history as chronology or as the study of arbitrary periodizations based, for example, on the dominance of specific ideas or of "great men." It indicates the methodological priority of the theoretical investigation of the mode of production as a whole over the historical investigation of the real (i.e., chronological) origin of its isolated elements.

The two main methodological principles of Structuralist Marxism have been presented. It is now necessary to examine the Structuralist Marxist contribution to the analysis of historical phenomena: the concepts of mode of production and social formation. Mode of production is a theoretical construct that denotes the historically specific combination of the elements of the production process (laborers, nonlaborers, and means of production) in the context of structurally compatible political, legal, and ideological structures. These elements are combined in two kinds of relations: relations of "real or material appropriation" or technical relations of production (e.g., cooperation, manufacturing, modern industry, automation); and "property connections" or social relations of production which are the relationships between laborers and nonlaborers mediated through their property relations to the means of production. In the capitalist mode of production, these are the relations between capitalists and wage workers (Althusser and Balibar 1970:215). The forces of production, which cannot be considered as things or techniques taken in themselves, are all the factors of production in their historically specific combination within the process of production, considered from the standpoint of their actual and potential productivity (Althusser and Balibar 1970:233–41). Modes of production differ qualitatively from one another in the way in which unpaid surplus labor is extracted from the direct producers. The mode of surplus extraction corresponds to the level of development of the productive forces and the nature of the relations of production and constitutes the unifying principle of the mode of production as a whole (Marx 1968:791–92).

The concept mode of production is an abstract one that captures the fundamental features that constitute the organizing principle of the economic, legal, political, and ideological structures that characterize different historical epochs. Empirically, in a given social formation, modes of production are always found in varied combinations with other modes of production. In the structuralist reading of Marx, the alternative to the abstract notion of society is the concept of social formation, a "complex structured whole where the mode of production is determinant 'in the last instance' and the superstructure (legal, political, and ideological structures) is relatively autonomous" (Althusser 1970:111). In all social formations it is possible to identify the following: a complex economic base formed by the historically specific articulation of several modes of production one of which is always dominant; and a complex superstructure whose elements have forms and functions the origins of which can be traced to the different modes of production that make up the economic base (Godelier 1978:63). Scientific analysis must be aimed at establishing first the nature of the hierarchical articulation of modes of production (i.e., the specific ways in which the dominant mode of production subjects the others to its own requirements and transforms them into conditions of its own reproduction) and, second, the nature of the hierarchical articulation among the elements of the superstructure which is also constituted as a set of conditions for the reproduction of the dominant mode of production (Godelier 1978:63). The structure of the superstructure reflects the articulation of the economic base; it overdetermines the base as it reproduces it in historically specific ways—ways peculiar to the characteristics of the social formation being considered. On the other hand, the economic base determines the superstructure "in the last instance," through a system of internal constraints which has its origins in the material conditions of production and expresses the conditions of reproduction for the dominant mode of production. The structural compatibility between the form and content of the elements of the superstructure and the system of constraints is itself a structural effect of the system of constraints which ensures the reproduction of the mode of production. It is, consequently, through the structural effects of the system of constraints, which simultaneously affect all the elements of the social formation, that the mode of production determines, in the last instance, the overall structure of the social formation as well as the form and function of its instances (Godelier 1978:52–53). The category of determination "in the last instance" has a twofold theoretical importance: it reaffirms the materialist philosophical standpoint of Marxism (it is the base that determines the superstructure, not vice versa) and, at the same time, it stresses the dialectical nature of the Marxist concept of determination by making explicit the relative autonomy and causal efficacy of the other instances of the social formation which, in turn, "overdetermine" the base (Althusser 1976:177; see also Althusser 1970:89–128).

Modes of production based on the private ownership of the means of production are inherently contradictory and subject to qualitative changes brought about by the operation of those contradictions. Given that the mode of production is the locus of the two main contradictions of capitalism (the contradiction between capital and labor and the contradiction between the forces and the relations of production), the fact that the mode of production is "overdetermined by the superstructure means that those contradictions are never found 'active in the pure state but, on the contrary,' overdetermined . . . always specified by the historically concrete forms and circumstances in which it is exercised" (Althusser 1970:106). This process of specification operates from the different elements of the social formation and includes the national and international circumstances affecting the social formation at a given time. Whatever the nature of those processes, "in the last instance" it is in the internal and contradictory properties of the mode of production that the crucial source of change is to be found. Godelier makes this point as follows:

whether the causes . . . [of change] are external or internal they only have an effect because they bring into play (and are made to act as final causes) the structural properties of systems . . . these properties are always, in the final count, immanent in this system, explaining the unintentional role of its functioning. (Godelier 1978:37)

Althusser makes a similar point:

For Marxism the explanation of any phenomenon is in the last instance *internal:* it is the *internal* "contradiction" which is the "motor." The external circumstances are active: but "through" the internal contradiction which they overdetermine. (Althusser 1976:80; emphasis in the text)

Within class-based modes of production, structures are thus both complementary and contradictory; the relationship of complementarity through which the mode of production is reproduced throughout time is, at the same time, unstable and operates within limits beyond which contradictions assert themselves. Within capitalism, the contradiction between the forces and the relations of production emerges as the unintentional product of the objective property of various structures and their interrelationship, including the class struggle; it is not a consciously willed result. Quoting Marx's concise statement of this key point, "the real barrier of capitalist accumulation is capital itself" (Godelier 1970:353). Godelier stresses the nonteleological nature of the processes leading to the demise of capitalism and the creation of the material conditions for the rise of socialism. It is not "the revolt of the 'true essence' of man against the 'dehumanized existence' imposed on the workers by the bourgeoisie" (Godelier 1970:355), but the social processes generated by the objective properties of the forces and the relations of production that necessitates the emergence of socialism.

Through his emphasis upon the analysis of structures, their hierarchical articulation, objective properties, and conditions of emergence, reproduction, and change, Godelier makes a methodological point similar to that expressed by Althusser's dictum: "History is a process without a Subject or Goals" (Althusser 1976:94). While individuals act *in* history within the parameters set by modes of production, they are not, Althusser argues, the *subjects of* history in a philosophical sense. It is Althusser's aim to establish a clear-cut difference between idealistic interpretations of history based upon the identification of a Subject (Man, God, the Human Race, the transcendental ego, etc.) as the Origin, Cause, and Goal of History, and the Marxist historical and dialectical materialist view of history as the history of modes of production unfolding in terms of the class struggle: while history lacks a Subject, it does have a *motor:* the class struggle (Althusser 1976:94–99; emphasis and capitalized words in the text).

Althusser's theoretical anti-humanism is thus akin to Godelier's anti-teleological standpoint. Both are rooted in their appraisal of the scientific importance of the theoretical and methodological discoveries of the mature Marx. In their view, Marx's analysis of the processes whereby capitalist development creates the material conditions for its own end and for the rise of a new mode of production does not rest upon a philosophical anthropology or upon a theory of the human essence; it rests, on the contrary, on the scientific investigation of the material conditions surrounding the emergence, development, and disappearance of historically specific modes of production. Both are concerned with delimiting the boundaries between Marxism as a science, and Marxism as an idealistic, humanistic ideology; they do so by stressing the anti-humanistic, anti-historicist, anti-psychologistic nature of the Marxist method. It is precisely this methodological standpoint which makes it possible to formulate specifically Marxist questions and come up with Marxist answers.

I have outlined and discussed some of Althusser's and Godelier's most significant insights. Given the specific objective of this essay, I have neither explored the full range of their contributions to Marxist theory nor the extent of their political and theoretical differences. The question of the relative importance of structuralism in their reading of Marx is, however, pertinent to this work and I shall examine it briefly.

Althusser argues that the rationalistic, mechanistic, and formalistic tendencies of structuralism are antithetical to Marxism; he pleads guilty to "a very ambiguous flirtation with structuralist terminology" (Althusser 1976:128) and emphatically denies any commitment to structuralism. On the other hand, Althusser identifies an area of overlap between Marxism and structuralism: both reject historicist, psychologistic explanations of social phenomena. It was precisely in the effort to formulate his Marxist thesis of theoretical antihumanism that Althusser found it necessary to borrow structuralist terminology without, at the same time, adopting structuralism in its entirety (Althusser 1976:128). Althusser, for whom the class struggle is the motor of history, cannot be appropriately described as a structuralist. Godelier, on the contrary, finds a greater convergence between Marxism and structuralism. He considers Marx as a forerunner of modern structuralism and, more importantly, he seems to have incorporated, in his analysis of social change, the mechanistic tendencies of structuralism. To my knowledge, the class struggle is absent from Godelier's work, where modes of production succeed one another purely through the mechanistic operation of the objective properties of their structures. While Althusser might agree with Godelier's rejection of purely idealistic, humanistic justifications of the necessity of socialism, he would most certainly disagree with Godelier's assumption about the automatic nature of the process. This theoretical and political difference does not, in my view, invalidate Godelier's methodological contributions. After all, a crucial feature of Marxist "theoretical practice" (and the works of Marx, Engels, and Lenin are an object lesson about this point) is the critical dialogue with one's theoretical opponents. In the sections that follow I hope to show, through my own "theoretical practice" the significance of Althusser's and Godelier's insights for the analysis of the oppression of women.[1]

A CRITICAL LOOK AT CURRENT PERSPECTIVES
ON SEXUAL INEQUALITY

Empirically, at the level of "visible relationships." and personal, immediate experience, women's disadvantages appear and are experienced as men's advantages. Social scientists have produced abundant historical and cross-cultural evidence documenting the different rewards, power, and prestige allocated to men and women by past and present societies. This has shaped the questions that have been raised about the origins of the oppression of women and the conditions that reproduce it through time. Questions about the oppression of *women* unavoidably become questions about the power of *men*, and about the differences between the sexes that may account for the ubiquitousness of sexual inequality. This "men vs. women" problematic has been reinforced by the dominant empiricist approach to the question of socialism and its impact on the status of women. Socialism is a transitional stage between two modes of production, capitalism and communism; it is characterized by a contradictory combination of features pertaining to both modes and, consequently, by heightened class struggles. Like the transition from feudalism to capitalism, the socialist transition is a complex and protracted process whose impact upon people's lives should be assessed taking into consideration the lessons from the past as well as the unique characteristics of each socialist social formation and its place in the international political conjuncture. The dominant view, however, suggests that socialism has already happened and it has not fulfilled its promises, particularly with respect to women. Accepting this view means judging the socialist experience ahistorically, from the standpoint of an ideal model of what socialism should be. Taken thus outside its historical context, the persistence of sexual inequality in the socialist countries is unwarrantedly perceived as "proof" that changes in the mode of production will not liberate women. This, together with the obvious fact that sexism predates capitalism, has lent support to the conceptualization of sexism independently from modes of production and to the search for its origins (in the chronological sense) and mechanisms of support elsewhere. Given this formulation of the problem, what kinds of theoretical insights have been produced?

Sociologically, an early and influential explanation for sexual inequality was found in the interaction between sex differentiation and sex stratification. Sex differentiation refers to the division of labor by sex within and outside the family. In contemporary society, occupational roles are the core of the male role cluster while family roles are the core of the female role cluster. Sex stratification refers to the different power and prestige attached to the male and female roles. Differential power and prestige stem from individuals' differential access to socially valued scarce resources. Sex differentiation, in confining women to household tasks, childbearing, and childrearing, has impaired their opportunity to secure wealth and power in comparison to men. Functional sex differentiation or sexual division of labor would appear as the source of sex stratification as well as the condition for its maintenance: "sex stratification, like other functional differentiations, entail a 'rank ordering' of the position of men and women. It is noted that this tendency towards rank differentiation has a feedback effect that contributes to the support of the underlying functional differentiation" (Holter 1973:53; emphasis added).

Current patterns of sex differentiation or sexual division of labor which assigns public roles to men while relegating women primarily to domesticity became the core of feminist theorizing about the determinants of women's oppression. Collapsing the two levels of analysis, differentiation or division of labor and stratification or differences in status and power, the notion of hierarchical sexual division of labor was developed to denote the power differences between the sexes linked to the sexual division of labor reflected in the public/private split. Projected into the past, the hierarchical sexual division of labor served as the basis for a theory of patriarchy, a social system in which men oppress women, as the earliest form of social organization.

Firestone (1970) argues that sex class (male dominance) stems from men's and women's unequal biological roles in procreation. The fact that women bear children and care for them during the lengthy period of dependency required by human infants to develop has placed them, from the beginning, in a situation in which their physical survival as well as the survival of their children was dependent on their relationship to men. Inequality, in her view, is thus inherent in the biological family, structurally and psychologically. The type of psychosexual development determined by biological inequality generates a need for power as a crucial dimension of male personality, which eventually results in the development of class societies. Class differences have their root, therefore, in sex class which, in turn, arises from the biological inequality between the sexes linked to procreation.

Firestone's biological determinism has found few supporters. More recent theories about the origins of male dominance give, like Firestone, a determinant role to the family, to sexual and reproductive relations, and to the type of psychosexual development generated within the family. Representative of the major trends in American Feminist theory today are the works of Rubin (1975), Chodorow (1978) and Eisenstein (1979) whose contributions I shall briefly outline.

Rubin's two major contributions to feminist theory are the following:

1. The notion of sex gender system, a societal universal that denotes the existence, in all societies, of "a set of social arrangements by which the biological raw material of human sex and procreation is shaped by human intervention" (Rubin 1975:165).

2. A theory of the oppression of women based on Lévi-Strauss' theory of kinship, and on the psychoanalytic theory of gender formation. The origin of human society, for Lévi-Strauss, is the incest taboo which ensures the exchange of women between kinship groups. Marriage is not a relationship between individuals but an exchange relation between kinship groups that reinforces a sexual division of labor that makes the interdependence between the sexes essential for their survival. Rubin carries Lévi-Strauss' analysis further by arguing that because men exchange women (whereas women can neither exchange women nor exchange themselves), the sexual division of labor thus created is inherently oppressive. The exchange of women generates enforced hetero-

sexuality, the social repression of female sexuality, and the creation of gender identity in ways that repress the natural similarities between the sexes. The stages of psychosexual development articulated by Freud are, on the other hand, the processes through which male dominance and female oppression are perpetuated. In Rubin's view, there is a "striking fit" between Lévi-Strauss and Freud which implies that the sex-gender system today "is still organized by the principles outlined by Lévi-Strauss" (Rubin 1975:198).

For Rubin, the value of Lévi-Strauss' and Freud's works lies not only in the importance of the questions they raise but in the fact that their theories are conducive to the development of an analysis of sex and gender in isolation from the mode of production (Rubin 1975:203). She does point out, on the other hand, that as sex, politics, and economics are mutually interrelated, a complete analysis of women should take "everything" into account.

At the highest level of abstraction the concept sex-gender system denotes a social science truism; i.e., the fact that the personality structure associated with gender, sex roles, sex stratification, and kinship relations is socially determined. To say that every society has a sex-gender system is as enlightening as to acknowledge that every society has an economic system; both are "sensible abstractions" that follow from the fact that at all times, "the subject, mankind, and the object, nature, are the same" (Marx 1970a:190). However, as Marx points out, "even the most abstract categories, despite of their validity in all epochs . . . are equally a product of historical conditions even in the specific form of abstractions, and they retain their full validity only for and within the framework of these conditions" (Marx 1970a:210). From the standpoint of Marxist theory, a major problem with the use of ahistorical categories like sex-gender system is that questions about the historical conditions determining their full validity— i.e., questions about their historically specific origins and underlying conditions of reproduction—are displayed by questions about their historical and cross-cultural variations. Such categories are mere empty vessels to be "filled" with empirical "content"; theory is replaced with description and taxonomy and the discovery of empirical correlations pre-empts the task of theoretical investigation as a prerequisite for significant empirical research. Studies about the historical and cross-cultural variations of the sex-gender system could provide useful descriptions and predictions about, for example, the kinds of institutional factors likely to be correlated with a given kind of sex-gender system; those findings, however, would not provide an explanation, because questions about the underlying, hidden, historically specific structures, processes, and contradictions that produce those empirically observable phenomena remain outside the purview of such approaches to the study of social reality. But there are other considerations that limit the usefulness of this concept. It can be used descriptively, as a shorthand way to refer to several levels of analysis: gender identity, sexual and reproductive behavior, sex differentiation, sex stratification; or it can be synonymous with kinship system. Theoretically, on the other hand, the concept offers no clue as to the nature of the system to which it presumably refers; it does not specify the nature of the interrelationship between its elements except, of course, at the metatheoretical level established on the basis of Lévi-Strauss' and Freud's works. Given its ahistorical origins and conditions of reproduction (the exchange of women, the Oedipal struggle), questions about the historically specific determinants of each level, about the historically specific way they might be interrelated and about their "mutual interdependence" with "politics" and "economics" are ultimately irrelevant. Sexual inequality, given that the social organization of sex and gender rests upon gender identity as constructed through the Oedipal struggle, will only be abolished through qualitative changes in psychosexual development leading to the emergence of an androgynous, "genderless" world (Rubin 1975:204). The call for the abolition of differences as a sufficient condition for the abolition of inequality cannot but follow from an analysis that postulates the identity between the two. This is also Chodorow's standpoint: historically and cross-culturally, it is impossible to separate the sexual division of labor from sexual inequality (Chodorow 1978:214).

Chodorow's (1978) theory of the origins of male dominance and the conditions that reproduce it combine feminist theoretical insights with those of Parsons' sociology, psychoanalytic object-

relation theory, and the Frankfurt School's—particularly Horkheimer's—analysis of changes in the personality structure brought
about by the impact of capitalism upon the family. For Chodorow,
the root of male dominance is the universal fact that women
mother; mothering and the reproduction of mothering have psychological and social consequences which create and perpetuate
sexual inequality. Mothering is the unintentional effect—at the
level of the personality structure—of the asymmetrical organization of parenting. Women are the primary parent for both sexes,
and that creates crucial differences in children's relational experiences, which determine qualitative differences in masculine and
feminine personality. Women's sense of gender identity develops
through a process of identification with their mothers in a context
of primary relationships between them. The female role-learning
process is thus characterized by diffuseness, affectivity, and par-
ticularism; and these features shape women's personality and
women's roles inside and outside the family. Men, on the other
hand, develop their gender identity and relational capacities
through the denial of their first identification with their mothers
and the development of secondary relations with their father in
a context of affective neutrality. The male role learning process
is characterized by specificity, affective neutrality, and universal-
ism and—because it rests upon the rejection of the mother and
the devaluation of the feminine—it results in the development
of a psychology and ideology of male dominance. Furthermore,
the sex roles and occupational roles men and women find outside
the family partake of similar characteristics: women's roles are
essentially "particularistic" and centered around the family and
"primary" interpersonal relations, while male roles are "universalistic" and centered around the requirements of the organization
of production.

This is indeed an astonishing account. The "fit" between Parsons
sociology and the discoveries resulting from the use of psychoanalytic object relations theory is as striking as the previously mentioned "fit" between Lévi-Strauss and Freud. The private/public
split mirrors the traditional/modern society dichotomy and Ort-
ner's (1974) question, "Is Female to Male as Nature is to Culture?"
could now be restated as Is Female to Male as Traditional Society

is to Modern Society? without increasing our comprehension of these issues. It is, undoubtedly, important to investigate the structural effects of the asymmetrical organization of parenting to determine the extent to which the "message" (if it is the case that there is one) that is metacommunicated by the structure has its sources in the structure itself or in the historical context of which the structure is a part. Chodorow's analysis, in my view, only succeeds in legitimating Parsons' categories of analysis by endowing them with a veneer of universality and atemporality grounded in the ahistorical fact of mothering.

Looking at the reproduction of mothering under capitalism, Chodorow points out that women's mothering in the isolated nuclear family "reproduces both the ideology and the psychodynamic of male superiority and the submission to the requirements of production" (Chodorow 1978:181). Women's mothering during the transition to capitalism produced capitalists endowed with "inner direction, rational planning and organization," and workers endowed with "a willingness to come to work at certain hours and work steadily, whether or not they needed money that day" (Chodorow 1978:186). Today women's mothering produces a malleable "other directed" personality characterized by a "generalized achievement orientation" among the middle and upper middle classes (Parsons' argument, which emphasizes the intense mother-child relationship that emerges in isolated nuclear families where fathers are relatively absent), and an "authoritarian personality" among the working classes (the Frankfurt School argument that stresses the decline in the "real" authority of the father brought about by the growth of wage labor and the concomitant vulnerability of workers to the market). Given the primacy given to mothering in determining sexual inequality and sex roles, it is not clear why it should produce such different effects. It would seem, rather, that inner direction and other direction as personality types have their origins outside the family and that mothers simply convey socially determined personality structures, sex roles, etc. Chodorow's efforts to introduce history in her analysis are not very successful because history remains external to the core of her theory: the universal fact of mothering. Her answers to critics who point out the basically ahistorical nature of her account (see, for example, Chodorow 1978:215–16) do not clarify the nature of the relationship between mothering, modes of production, personality structure, sexual differentiation, and sexual stratification.

Eisenstein (1979) develops her theory through a critique of Marx, Marxism in general, and radical feminism. Marx and Marxist theorists are guilty of "breaking the real connections of everyday life" and of oversimplification of political reality," because they posit class exploitation as the primary contradiction (Eisenstein 1979:21). Radical feminists are guilty of similar sins because they posit sexual oppression based on biological inequality as primary (Eisenstein 1979:18). Marxists have an "economic theory of power" while radical feminists have a "sexual theory of power." The alternative Eisenstein proposes is socialist feminism, an approach that seeks to integrate Marxism and radical feminism in a theory of capitalist patriarchy according to which capitalism and patriarchy are mutually interdependent (Eisenstein 1979:22).

Patriarchy is defined as male power through sexual roles or relations of reproduction based on male control over reproduction. The basis for patriarchy is the "sexual division of labor and society" which has "material form (sex roles themselves) and ideological reality (the stereotypes, myths and ideas that define those roles)" (Eisenstein 1979:24–25). The sexual division of labor and society has its origins in "ideological and political interpretations of biological difference. . . . men have chosen to interpret and politically use the fact that women are the reproducers of humanity" (Eisenstein 1979:25). Patriarchy seems to be synonymous not only with sex roles and relations of reproduction but also with the family. Patriarchy and capitalism (i.e., family and economy) cannot be treated as separate systems because they are interrelated by the sexual division of labor and society which cuts across them and is "at the base of them; because it divides men and women into their respective hierarchical sex roles and structures their related duties in the family domain and within the economy" (Eisenstein 1979:27). Both systems are analytically irreducible to each other; they are functionally interdependent and responsive to each other's needs for self-perpetuation although their relationship is becoming increasingly "uneasy" because the growth in women's participation in the labor force tends to undermine some aspects of patriarchal control (Eisenstein 1979:28–29). Because of her reliance on Ollman's (1971) interpretation of Marx's philosophy as a philosophy of internal relations, Eisenstein cannot avoid the pitfalls of multiple causality. This is reflected in the stress given to the mutual interdependence between capitalism and patriarchy throughout her work, which, however, does not yield very useful conclusions: capitalism uses patriarchy and patriarchy uses capitalism and both "operate within the division of labor and society" (Eisenstein 1979:27), a rather confusing concept that seems to denote a reality that dates both capitalism and patriarchy.

Underlying these otherwise different perspectives is a theoretical analysis of sexism in isolation from modes of production, a standpoint that has serious theoretical and methodological drawbacks because it unerringly leads to the search for the chronological origins of the oppression of women while neglecting the historically specific context that surrounds concrete instances of sexual inequality (for a trenchant non-Marxist critique of this perspective see Rosaldo 1980:389–417). This is tantamount to separating men and women from their historical conditions of existence; instead, they are thrown into the limbo of the genesis of human society where, isolated from concrete relations of production, they mate in a context that seems to unavoidably generate sexual inequality either because of biological "inequality" in procreation (Firestone); because men exchange women (Rubin); because men "choose" to control reproduction in order to oppress women (Eisenstein); because women mother (Chodorow); or because of functional, adaptive sex role differentiation based on women's role in procreation and childcare (Sociology). These are universal, ahistorical explanations that lead to the elaboration of universal, formal categories of analysis (e.g., sex class, sex-gender system, patriarchy, mothering, sexual division of labor and society, sexual differentiation, sexual stratification) themselves produced and perpetuated by unchanging and universal sexual, reproductive, and family relations. The content of those categories may vary through time because of their "interrelationship" for "mutal interdependence" with social institutions. Nevertheless, they persist in spite of qualitative changes in modes of social organization because their origins as well as the conditions for their continuity and change have been postulated independently from modes of production, as if the forces of historical change were impotent to substantially change the nature of sexual, procreative, and parental relations and their impact on individuals' psychosexual development.

THE STRUCTURALIST MARXIST ALTERNATIVE

From the standpoint of Structural Marxism, the key to developing an adequate explanation of sexual inequality is to be found not in individual biology or psychology, in the organization of parenting, in ahistorical accounts about the origins of human society, or in abstract processes of functional adaptation and structural differentiation. Instead, regardless of its ubiquitousness, sexual inequality should be investigated, in each instance, as a historically specific phenomenon with historically specific roots located in the invisible levels of social reality; namely, in structures concealed by those visible processes which are, in fact, the effects through which the existence of those structures manifests itself. This concept of structure corresponds to social relations which evolve in the process through which people produce their material and social existence and which are independent from individuals' will (Marx 1970a:20). Production has a twofold nature: "on the one side, the production of the means of existence. . . . on the other side, the production of human beings themselves" (Engels 1972:71). The variety of visible, institutionalized ways that "men oppress women" are effects, at the levels of "society" and "market relations," of the articulation between the two aspects of the mode of production which determine relations between men and women that are independent of their will: i.e., relations determined not by what individuals think, believe, want or need—consciously or unconsciously—or by whatever social constraints the "market" or "society" imposes upon them; instead, they are relations mediated by the historically specific relation of men and women to the material conditions of production and of physical and social reproduction (Althusser 1976:200–7). The general methodological principle is that the material basis of sexual inequality is to be sought in the articulation between class relations or relations of production and the relations of physical and social reproduction valid within a historically specific mode of production. I shall limit my analysis of the capitalist mode of production in an effort to delineate, following the second structuralist methodological principle, the capitalist basis of sexual inequality.

By mode of physical and social reproduction it is meant the historically specific combination of labor and means of reproduction (the material basis for the performance of reproductive tasks: the tools, goods, utensils, raw materials, foodstuffs, etc.) with relations between men and women. Such a combination reproduces the present and future members of social groups by procreation, physical care (cleaning, food preparation, etc.) and nurturant and supportive services (sexual relations, socialization of children, cooperation, etc.). Such groups have different locations in the productive process. (For a detailed discussion of these concepts see, for example, Giménez 1978; Secombe 1974.) The dominant visible forms taken by modes of physical and social reproduction throughout history have been family and kinship structures as well as kinship structured groups (groups in which adults and children are not related by blood). In capitalist social formations, the nuclear family emerges as the dominant but not exclusive context in which social classes are reproduced; empirical variations documenting not only the existence of other forms (e.g., single-parent households) but also the conditions under which nuclear families remain to a greater or lesser extent embedded in broader kinship networks must be understood in terms of underlying relations of physical and social reproduction which are determined, for each class, by the capitalist organization of production, distribution, and consumption.

Capitalist families live off profits from capital and are surrounded by extensive kinship networks which are also economic networks through which wealth is preserved, increased, and circulated. Men and women own the means of production and are free from the necessity of selling their labor to survive; they are the "bearers" or "supports" of the capitalist class (cf. Althusser 1976:206) and reproduce it under legal and ideological conditions that ensure the preservation of property and its transmission to legitimate heirs, the future bearers of the class. Given the different biological role of men and women in procreation, these superstructural conditions involve control over women's sexuality and reproductive capacity; the pre-capitalist relationship between private ownership of the means of production and class control over women as producers of the future members of the class is preserved and reproduced under capitalism through superstructural conditions (legal, ethical, religious, ideological, etc.) that universalize it for all classes, obscuring the qualitative differences between classes in the process of defining everyone as a legal, political, ethical subject (Althusser 1971:162–86). These superstructural conditions (the legal apparatus surrounding marriage, divorce, and inheritance; bourgeois morality; ideologies about abortion, contraception, etc.) contribute to create the circumstances in which the control exerted by the capitalist class over the conditions for the reproduction of all classes, including itself, appears, at the level of visible relations, as control exerted by men over women. Class control over the means of production and over the conditions for its own reproduction as a class places capitalist men and women into social relations independent of their will. They are unequal relations in which, at the level of "society," men appear in control of capital, female sexuality, and reproductive capacity. On the other hand, within capitalist households, labor and means of reproduction are brought together through a division of labor or technical relations of reproduction that ensure women's complete freedom from the routine and menial dimensions of reproduction as well as partial freedom from social reproduction. Paid domestic workers (most of whom are likely to be women) do housework, childcare, and some aspects of child socialization under the direct or indirect supervision of capitalist women who often delegate the managing tasks to workers hired for that purpose. The existence of a primarily female strata of domestic servants is, therefore, the basic underpinning of the almost exclusive dedication of capitalist women to social reproduction on a daily and generational basis (child socialization, social activities that enhance and complement their husbands' public roles, etc.), and of the unique characteristics of domestic relations between men and women in the capitalist household; a context in which contemporary discussions about the desirability of childcare by persons other than the biological parents, or about the need to change the division of labor between men and women to increase men's domestic activities in order to liberate women for greater social involvement and self-fulfillment, have no meaning.[2]

Working class families live off the sale of the labor power of their adult members and rely on the domestic labor of women for the daily and generational reproduction of labor power. The dominant pattern is one in which men are the only or most important wage earners and wives are the primary domestic workers, whether or not they are also employed. The mutually reinforcing relationship between women's domestic responsibilities and their social and economic oppression has been discussed and documented in great lengths and need not be reexamined here. Also, I am not going to dwell on the debate about the nature of domestic labor: whether it is paid or unpaid labor and whether or not it produces surplus value (see for example, Secombe 1974; Coulson et al. 1975; Gardiner 1975). What is relevant here is that domestic labor is a form of socially necessary labor that expands the goods and services available to the working class beyond what it would be possible to purchase with wages. Domestic labor is thus an important component of the standard of living of the working class and a source of use values which enter in the process through which labor power is produced and reproduced on a daily and generational basis. On the other hand, domestic labor benefits the capitalist class because its presence lowers the overall level of wages, thus increasing the amount of surplus that can be extorted from the direct producers. But neither the division of labor within the home and its impact on the status of women, nor the relationship between domestic labor and the level of wages, can explain in themselves the existence of sexual inequality within the working class. To find the specifically capitalist material basis of sexual inequality it is necessary to examine the material conditions leading to family formation within the working class.

Capitalism, as a historically specific mode of production, rests upon a class structure based on the private ownership of the means of production and the concomitant expropriation of the direct producers who, as free laborers owning nothing but their labor power, must sell it to the owners of capital to get access to the means of subsistence necessary for themselves and their children. Hence, there is inherent in capitalism a tendency toward the universalization of commodity production generated by the separation of the direct producers from the conditions of production and reproduction which affects not only capital goods and consumer goods but also an ever growing variety of services. An important exception to this trend is labor power, a crucial commodity which is not produced on a capitalist basis although its daily and generational reproduction requires a constant flow of market goods and services and is, consequently, shaped by the requirements of capitalist production. Within the working class household, goods and services purchased with the means of exchange obtained through the sale of labor power are combined with domestic labor in the context of relations of reproduction that presuppose the employment, as a wage laborer, of at least one member of the household. Domestic labor produces use values for the consumption of *all* the members of the family (Benston 1969); this is "consumptive production" because persons produce their own body, and I may add their own physical and intellectual capacities, through the consumption of goods and services (Marx 1970:195). The consumption of the use values produced at home is thus, simultaneously, the production and reproduction of the present and future members of the working class. The capitalist mode of producing material goods *produces* consumption, i.e., consumptive production "by providing the material of consumption. . . . by creating in the consumer a need for the objects which it first presents as products and *by determining the mode of consumption* (Marx 1970a:197; my emphasis). Crucial for the understanding of sexual inequality in the working class is the determination exerted by the mode of production upon the mode of consumption or, which is the same, the mode of consumptive production or physical and social reproduction.

Under capitalist conditions, the production of surplus and its extraction from the direct producers is concealed by the appearances of the market and social relations; this is the sphere of Freedom, Equality, Property, and Bentham (Marx 1970b:196). At this level, individuals meet and engage in equitable exchanges that result in the distribution of the product: rent, profits, interest, and wages are allocated to different individuals on the basis of their function in the production process. This level is an intermediate phase between production and distribution (Marx 1970a:204). It is both a structural effect of the underlying relation of production and a crucial condition for the reproduction—over time—of the capitalist mode of production as a whole. It mystifies the nature of the production process by hiding class rule and its effects under the guise of unmanageable laws (e.g., supply and demand, the Malthusian population principle) and other "social facts."

The relations of structural compatibility between these phases or moments of the mode of production as a whole—i.e., production, exchange, and distribution—set structural limitations to the possible forms in which labor power can be reproduced. The mode of consumption or consumptive production cannot itself be isomorphic with the mode of production: the reproduction of labor power on a capitalist basis would destroy the material basis for the production of free individuals, autonomous and responsible for their own success or failure, which constitute the cornerstone of capitalist social and market relations. On the other hand, the lack of isomorphism between the mode of production and the mode of reproduction of labor power is not the product of design but the complex structural effect of the relations of production, exchange, and distribution, overdetermined by the superstructure and mediated by the biological level and by the class struggle.

At the level of production, the creation of a propertyless class, bound to capital for its survival in a context of chronic unemployment and periodic economic crises, has created an objective situation of job scarcity and fierce competition among the members of the working class. This situation is exacerbated by the tendency toward the universalization of commodity production and the concomitant transformation of all social relations into market relations.

At the level of exchange, this objectively competitive situation is ideologically understood and experienced in terms of visible and "obvious" cleavages based on sex, age, racial, or ethnic differences or differences in national origins, religion, and so forth. It is in the interest of capital to have a divided labor force, and sexual antagonism is one among the many divisions that capital uses and reinforces to its advantage. While segregated labor markets may reduce the amount of competition, they never obliterate its objective existence, which tends to reassert itself in times of economic crises, shifts in the organic composition of capital, and drastic reorganization of the labor force.

These objective conditions place men and women in antagonistic and competitive relations. At the biological level, on the other hand, men and women are placed in complementary sexual and procreative roles; this is the material basis for the fact that, at the levels of distribution, exchange, and visible social relations, they also confront each other as potential sexual partners and potential parents—i.e., as potential agents of reproduction. While other cleavages within the working class can be overcome through unionization and other forms of collective organization, the family—the major locus of the reproduction of labor power—emerges as the most important institution bringing the sexes and generations together. At this level of analysis, men and women freely meet and enter into apparently free relationships; this is the sphere not only of Freedom, Equality, Property, and Bentham but also of Love, Motherhood, ideologies about femininity and masculinity, and other forms of legitimation. These "freely" entered family relations create bonds of interdependence between men and women and between families; kinship relations become an important source of economic support for unemployed workers as well as for those unable to work because of age, illness, or other circumstances (see, for example, Humphries 1977).

But the interdependence between families and between men and women rests upon underlying relations of personal economic dependence. The relations of production, exchange, and distribution place those who earn wages in a position to gain access to the material conditions of reproduction and, consequently, in a position of power over those with little or no access to those conditions. Kinship relations legitimate the claims of the latter upon the former while the absence of such bonds place people in an objective situation of dependence leading to the emergence of forms of political control (e.g., welfare) and personal dependence. Sexual inequality is one among the many forms of inequality thus generated by the mode of production within the working class. The overall effect of the capitalist relations of production, exchange, and distribution is to recruit men and women for the positions of agents of reproduction within the mode of physical and social reproduction in a context that places those agents of reproduction who are also wage earners in a position of power over those who are only domestic workers and that turns the position of domestic worker into a structural alternative to that of wage worker. These conditions are outside the control of individuals whatever their sex may be and express the rule of the capitalist class—mediated by the anarchy of the market and the relations of dependence thereby generated at the level of distribution. Under such conditions, domestic labor becomes an unavoidable economic "option" for women which places them in a dependent position with respect to men which is independent of their will.

It may be argued that this account does not explain why women, rather than men, are expected to become domestic workers and that an answer to that question would have to rely on arguments such as those discussed in the previous section which seek the origins of sexual inequality outside the mode of production (on biological or psychological differences between men and women or on pre-capitalist "patriarchal" ideologies, division of labor, power relations, etc.). My answer to those arguments is that pre-existing structural and superstructural instances do indeed overdetermine the relations between the sexes within and outside the family. Pre-existing ideologies and practices set the parameters for the way men and women—at the level of visible relations—have perceived their options and the nature of their relationships from the very beginning of capitalism. But one must "distinguish between the material transformation of the conditions of production . . . and the legal, political, philosophical . . . ideological forms in which men become conscious of this conflict and fight it out" (Marx 1970:21). It is the transformation of the conditions of production and reproduction (the mode of producing and distributing goods and its impact upon the reproduction of life) which places working class men and women in different locations which imply unequal access to the conditions of reproduction. This unequal access, which is the basis for their asymmetrical relations at the level of visible relations, stems from their relationship to the conditions of production, as propertyless workers, and to the conditions of procreation and reproduction, as agents involved in the daily and generational reproduction of labor power. Pre-capitalist sexist patterns can persist, new ones can develop, and all of them can overdetermine the relationship between the sexes because the material conditions that place men and women in an unequal relationship determine, in the last instance, the efficacy of those patterns. These material conditions are the outcome of the combined effects of the relations of production, exchange, and distribution *mediated* by the biological level of sexuality and procreation and by the class struggle and *overdetermined* by precapitalist and capitalist superstructures.

Mediation is a mode of determination according to which a given social process or a given set of material conditions shape the consequences of other processes (Wright 1976:25). To acknowledge biology as an important mediating condition is neither "vulgar materialism" nor biological determinism; it simply means to take into account the effect of the biological level *in itself*, which cannot be reduced to its social construction or production nor to a moment in the subject–nature dialectic (Timpanaro 1975:34). Biology shapes the consequences of capitalist relations of production, exchange, and distribution which place all individual workers in competition for scarce jobs by establishing the material conditions for the development of relations of cooperation between male and female workers based on sexuality and procreation. The class struggle, in turn, modifies the impact of the capitalist organization of production by reinforcing the working class family as a locus of resistance. Humphries (1977) has convincingly argued that the persistence of the working class family as well as its changing fortunes cannot be purely explained in terms of the sexism of male workers or the needs of capital accumulation, as an institution passively reflecting such needs while fulfilling ideological functions supporting the hegemony of the capitalist class. An adequate explanation should also take into account the state of the class struggle and its relative success in securing a family wage and other benefits.

The mode of production sets structural limitations to the possible modes of reproducing labor power that could be structurally compatible with capitalism and to the possible survival strategies that working class people could develop to overcome their fragmentation and vulnerability to the vagaries of the labor market and to changing forms of surplus extraction. The class struggle, on the other hand, modifies and challenges those limitations in manifold ways. Through the combined mediation of the biological level and the class struggle, the working class family emerges as the dominant survival strategy open to male and female workers. It should then be clear that it is not the power of working class men (or women's reproductive roles) that keeps women as the primary agents of reproduction within working class households nor is it the power of men that creates segregated labor markets and other barriers to equality between the sexes. It is the power of capital which establishes structural limitations to the possible ways in which the propertyless class can have access to the conditions necessary for its daily and generational reproduction and it is the relative powerlessness of working class men and women as *individuals* struggling for survival that forces them into these relations of reproduction which are both relations of cooperation and unequal relations of personal economic dependence. The contradiction between capital and labor, between production and reproduction, and the protracted class struggle thereby generated are the determinants of the contradictory nature of the relations between working class men and women. The mode of reproducing labor power can thus be accurately understood as a unity of opposites, where bonds of cooperation and solidarity are also bonds of dependency grounded in the set of structural possibilities open to male and female members of the working class under capitalist conditions.

CONCLUSION

Capitalist and working class relations of physical and social reproduction are subject to similar structural constraints in all capitalist social formations. On the other hand, their empirically observable manifestations will reflect the unique characteristics of each social formation such as, for example, the specific form in which capitalist and precapitalist modes of production are articulated; the characteristics of the superstructure which reflect the complexity of the base and overdetermine it; and the internal characteristics of the social formation itself as well as its location in the international structure.

The essence of my argument is that, in capitalist social formations, the observable forms of sexual inequality are determined, in the last instance, by the historically specific way in which the mode of production (conceived as a complex structured whole in which the capitalist mode of production is dominant) affects the access of the laboring and nonlaboring members of the subordinate classes (wage and salaried workers, peasants, agricultural workers, the unemployed, etc.) to the material conditions necessary for their daily and generational reproduction. While the actual effects of the mode of production upon the mode of physical and social reproduction among those classes is always modified or overdetermined by the class struggle and other mediations, the maintenance of capitalist relations of production sets structural limits to such modifications, and may even reverse them on occasion, depending on the nature of the crises affecting the social formation at a given time. Moreover, in any social formation the level of social stratification reflects the complexity of the base; consequently the empirical study of sexual inequality must rest upon the previous theoretical work of developing propositions about the underlying relations of production and reproduction determining the observable relations between men and women within classes, fractions of classes, and "contradictory class locations" (see Wright 1976 for a definition of that concept).

It should be clear, then, that from the standpoint of Structuralist Marxism, the issue of whether "class" or "sex" is primary or what forms their "mutal interdependence" may take are oversimplifications of very complex matters that cannot be resolved by a priori political commitments or by automatically reacting against the ghost of the "economism" of "orthodox Marxism," which seems to haunt the American intellectual scene. A straightforward analysis of the capitalist mode of production in all its moments (production, exchange, distribution, and consumption) clearly shows that the mode of production determines the mode of consumptive production or physical and social reproduction. The control exerted by the capitalist class over its own conditions of reproduction and over the conditions necessary for the reproduction of the laboring classes determines, in the last instance, the nature of the relations between the sexes and the relative significance of the family within social classes. The major theoretical task becomes, therefore, that of unraveling the specific parameters within which the reproduction of different classes and fractions of classes takes place under capitalism and, in so doing, mapping out the historically possible relations between the sexes that those parameters regulate. From this standpoint, all explanations of the observable forms of sexual inequality within capitalist social formations based on various analyses of the biological, psychological, or social differences between the sexes, or an analysis of the mode of reproduction in isolation from but "interacting" with the mode of production, are overlooking the historically specific determinants of the phenomena they attempt to explain. On the other hand, sociological analyses of sex differentiation and sex stratification and feminist analyses of sexuality, reproductive oppression, psychological oppression, etc. could be *critically*—not eclectically—integrated with the Structuralist Marxist analysis of their specifically capitalist structural and superstructural determinants. The main theoretical assumption underlying such critical integration is the following: the capitalist relations of production and the relations of physical and social reproduction (which are relations into which men and women enter independently of their will) impose historically specific structural limits to the range of empirical variations in sexual inequality in capitalist social formations which feminist scholarship has abundantly documented. Theoretical and empirical investigation of the specific articulation between the visible forms of sexual inequality and their underlying structural determinants would presuppose the investigation of the most important mediating and overdetermining instances. This would not only heighten the scientific understanding of sexual inequality but would also give feminists a sound basis for the evaluation of short and long run political and economic objectives.

The analysis of sexual inequality developed in this essay is a preliminary contribution to the work of others similarly engaged in the task of elaborating a Marxist theory of the oppression of women, asking Marxist questions, and developing Marxist answers (see for example, Vogel 1979; Chinchilla 1980; Dixon 1979). Structuralist Marxism is not indispensable for this project, but greatly facilitates it; Structuralist Marxism formulates important methodological considerations and key analytical distinctions which are not clearly and systematically stated in the works of the classics. Given the nature of the present historical conjuncture, Structuralist Marxism is not likely to have noticeable impact in the development of American feminist theory. But what is at stake is more than an academic debate about the explanatory power of different theories. Theories inform policies and political struggles and the success of the struggle against sexual inequality depends on the extent to which the factors that produce it and reproduce it through time are correctly identified. From the standpoint of Structuralist Marxism, the development of theories that acknowledge the determinant role of the mode of production are more likely to succeed in identifying those determinants and in generating effective political strategies.

NOTES

1. In the Althusserian framework, the notion of practice refers to "any process of *transformation* of a determinate given raw material into a determinate *product*, a transformation effected by a determinant human labor, using determinate means" (of "production") (Althusser 1970:106; his emphasis). Theory is a "specific form of practice" in which intellectual labor transforms existing concepts (raw materials)—themselves the products of previous practices—into knowledges (products) through the use of theoretical tools. Theoretical practice must be understood in a materialist way (i.e., in the historical conjuncture that makes it possible) to avoid falling into a theoreticist error. (For further elaboration of this point see Althusser 1976:119–125.)

2. The use of domestic servants is not restricted to the capitalist class; at certain levels of income, "middle class" and "upper middle class" women do purchase domestic labor. The qualitative differences between the capitalist use of servants and the practice of hiring household "help" with varying degrees of regularity is a matter that cannot be fully explored at this time. It is important to point out, however, that the existence of differences in class and socioeconomic status that allow some women to purchase their full or partial freedom from the "drudgery of housework" contributes to the maintenance of class relations and of sexual inequality within the working class.

REFERENCES

Althusser, Louis. 1970. *For Marx.* New York: Vintage Books.
—— 1971. *Lenin and Philosophy.* New York: Monthly Review Press.
—— 1976. *Essays in Self Criticism.* Atlantic Highlands, N.J.: Humanities Press.
Althusser, Louis and E. Balibar. 1970. *Reading Capital.* New York: Pantheon Books.
Benston, Margaret. 1969. "The political economy of women's liberation." *Monthly Review* (September) 21:13–25.
Chinchilla, Norma. 1980. "Ideologies of feminism: Liberal, radical, marxist." Social Sciences Research Reports 61 (February). School of Social Sciences, University of California, Irvine.

Chodorow, Nancy. 1978. *The Reproduction of Mothering.* Berkeley: University of California Press.
Coulson, Margaret et. al. 1975. "The housewife and her labor under capitalism: A critique." *New Left Review* (January–February) 89:59–71.
Dixon, Marlene. 1979. *Women in Class Struggle.* San Francisco: Synthesis Publications.
Einsenstein, Zillah R., ed. 1979. *Capitalist Patriarchy and the Case for Socialist Feminism.* New York: Monthly Review Press.
Engels, Friedrich. 1972. *The Origin of the Family: Private Property and the State.* New York: International Publishers.
Firestone, Shulamith. 1971. *The Dialectic of Sex.* New York: Bantam Books.
Gardiner, Jean. 1975. "Women's domestic labor." *New Left Review* (January–February) 89:47–58.
Giménez, Martha E. 1978. "Structuralist marxism on 'The woman question.'" *Science and Society* (Fall) 42:301–23.
Godelier, Maurice. 1970. "System, structure and contradiction in *Das Kapital.*" In Michael Lane, ed. *Introduction to Structuralism,* pp. 340–58. New York: Basic Books.
—— 1978. *Perspectives in Marxist Anthropolgy.* New York: Cambridge University Press.
Holter, Harriet. 1973. *Sex Roles and Social Structure.* Oslo: Universitetsforlaget.
Humphries, Jane. 1977. "Class struggle and the persistence of the working class family." *Cambridge Journal of Economics* 1:241–58.
Marx, Karl. 1968. *Capital,* vol. 3. New York: International Publishers.
—— 1970a. *A Contribution to the Critique of Political Economy.* New York: International Publishers.
—— 1970b. *Capital,* vol. 1. New York: International Publishers.
—— 1972. *The Grundrisse.* David McLellan, ed. New York: Harper & Row.
Mitchell, Juliet. 1971. *Woman's Estate.* New York: Pantheon Books.
Ollman, Bertell. 1971. *Alienation: Marx's Conception of Man in Capitalist Society.* New York: Cambridge University Press.
Rosaldo, M. Z. 1980. "The use and abuse of anthropology: Reflections on feminism and cross-cultural Understanding." *Signs* (Spring) 5:389–417.
Rubin, Gayle. 1975. "The traffic on women: Notes on the 'political economy' of sex." in R. R. Reiter, ed. *Toward an Anthropology of Women,* pp. 157–210. New York: Monthly Review Press.
Secombe, Wally. 1974. "The housewife and her Labor under capitalism." *New Left Review* (January–February) 83:3–24.

Timpanaro, Sebastiano. 1975. *On Materialism.* Atlantic Highlands, N.J.: Humanities Press.

Vogel, Lise. 1979. "Questions on the woman question." *Monthly Review* (June): 31:39–59.

Wright, E. O. 1976. "Class boundaries in advanced capitalist societies." *New Left Review* (July–August) 98:3–41.

POST-STRUCTURAL SEMIOTICS

CHAPTER TWELVE

STRUCTURES, INSTRUMENTS, AND READING IN SOCIOLOGY

THE CASE OF NURSES' COMPLIANCE WITH MEDICAL DOCTORS

CHARLES C. LEMERT and WILLARD A. NIELSEN, JR.

There is no structuralist sociology. Nor should there be if the intention is merely to borrow principles and techniques from an essentially alien intellectual source. Sociologists interested in European structuralism (and its heirs) should take caution from the witness of colleagues who have borrowed from afar. The best recent example is phenomenological sociology. There is none. Twenty years after Schutz was first available in English there is at best a sensitivity to issues provoked by phenomenology. Only in ethnomethodology, among those who have taken phenomenology seriously, has any truly empirical research been done, and then only by emasculating its phenomenologicity. There are other examples. Existential and systems theory sociologies were stillborn. Pragmatist sociology (symbolic interactionism) had a beautiful childhood and promising adolescence, but now seems to have burned itself out.

Our caution in the use of structuralism is not pure skepticism. We suspect that Lévi-Strauss et al. may well translate better than did Schulz, Husserl, James, Dewey, Mead, Sartre, Bertalanffy. But, equally, we believe that translations, anymore than borrowings, are *not* the issue. The failure of these other experiments might well lie in the fact that they expected too much of the alien source, sought to remake sociology *tout de nouveau*, and ignored the specificity of sociology itself.

Therefore, we have no interest in constructing a structuralist sociology, only in benefiting, as sociologists, from structuralism and its aftermath in Europe. We begin, therefore, with two elementary questions: (1) What is, at the moment, sociology's most specific problem? (2) What is the problematic of structuralism and how does it help solve sociology's problem?[1]

The first question is easily answered if one understands the specificity of a scientific field in concrete terms, that is, with reference to the epistemological and political struggles taking place at a historic moment.[2] It seems clear that, at this moment in North American sociology, one problem is debated more widely and seriously than any other: How are measurements, hence explanations, possible given the frailty of our instruments? Since the mid-60s—taking ethnomethodology (Cicourel 1964) and path analysis (Duncan 1966) as points of departure—no question has been more fundamental. Ethnomethodology pushed us beyond the naïveté of humanist idealism, which believed that positivism's absolutism could be corrected merely by the conceptual and humane sensitivity of the field researcher. At the other extreme, path analysis (and the subsequent theory, constructionist movement, which drew its faith therefrom) was taken as a technical advance overcoming the naïveté of operationalism. We saw, coming from all quarters, proposals for more "mature" measurement procedures: Breaching experiments (Garfinkel 1967), triangulated field observations (Denzin 1972), stochastic disturbance term measures (Siegel and Hodge 1968), indirect measures (Blalock 1970), and so forth. The weakness of these proposals was not, as Lewis Coser (1975) has claimed, the want of a topic, but the very inadequacy of these techniques themselves. Ethnomethodology, having relativized both formal and informal measures (see Cicourel 1964; cf. Lemert 1979c), was left with measures of measures, talk about talk—that is, a sociology of the sociology of conversations. Path analysis, when it ceased computing long enough to reflect on its formalism, led quickly to half-solutions such as auxiliary theory (Blalock 1970) or the reduction of measurement to the diagnosis of error terms (Namboodiri et al. 1975), which it could be said is only a more complex and abstract version of ethnomethodology's dilemma. Measurement was problematized in the mid-1960s, and remains our central problem still, if only because the ratio of promises kept to promises made is so intolerably low. We have more techniques, but proportionately fewer explanations.

Second, the problematic of structuralism can be stated in straightforward terms: Metaphysics is dead. Language and discourse have entered. Knowledge is only at the juncture of language as it is practiced and language as it is structured by social (hence, historic) convention.[3] We hold, therefore, that the distinctive contribution of structuralism is not that of a specialized program for the formal analysis of social totalities. The formalizing phase of structuralism did not survive the 1960s. Barthes' *Système de la mode* gave way to *Plaisir du texte*; formalism gave way to the eroticism of discursive practices. We argue (without having the space to justify) that what is new for sociology in "structuralism" is to be found more in Derrida, Foucault, Kristeva, the "later" Barthes, and Eco than in Lévi-Strauss, Piaget, or Hjelmslev. We agree with Bourdieu (1968) that structuralism is specific for sociology only when read with reference to Durkheim and Marx, and, we would add, Saussure.[4] In other words, we believe that the distinctive and specific features of structuralism truly emerge only in the later movement, post-structuralism, which made explicit the critiques of historicism, subject-reductionism, metaphysics, and—generally—homocentric humanism.[5] Post-structuralism's *loci classici* are Foucault's *Archaeologie de savior* or Derrida's *De la grammatologie*, while structuralism's point of reference is Lévi-Strauss' *Les structures élémentaires de la parenté*. In both lines, discourse (mythic, poetic, vocal, etc.) is the primary surface of investigation, but it is only in the former cases that the embeddedness of language and discursive practices in concrete social formations is taken as essential. In Foucault, for example, discursive analysis reveals not the universal structures of mind, but the specificity of social relations in a given historic *epistème* (Foucault, 1973).

READING

In more general terms, the problematic of the sociologically interesting structuralism is: How does one read in discursive practices the social relations which engender and limit social actions? To this we juxtapose our understanding of the problem of American sociology: How does one measure the social in order to explain it? Therefore, the argument we shall develop is: When measurement is understood as the reading of discourses, sociology explains practices with reference to structures.

We are serious in saying that sociological measurements' basic question ought to be: How do we read? Reading involves a literature. Sociologists refer constantly to their literature, but always in a haphazard way. Reviews of the literature are seldom more than weak contexts for an author's own position. Virtually everyone bemoans the fact that there has been little cumulation of knowledge "in the literature." We think that this is due to poor reading: the general absence of an explicit-for-sociology theory of reading which would permit us to read our literature (the source of ideas, concepts, variables, etc.) with positive reference to our measures. This involves the assumption that measuring is the reading of a more natural literature—letters, documents, reports to census takers, answers to survey questions, self-assessments, behaviors written into economic trend reports, market indicators, SES profiles (etc.), ritual dances, and so forth. Hence, the reader of a secondary literature (what other sociologists have said) is bound to our reading of our primary literature (what actors say and do). The relationship between the two is one in which the secondary literature is the basis upon which an "*instrument*" is constructed, while the primary literature is the field into which "*data*" are built.[6] We are not speaking metaphorically when we say that reading is the fundamental work of sociology.

In order to make our case concretely, we have selected a secondary literature which puts our proposal to a test. We shall discuss the literature "on" the presumption of compliance as the normal type for the nurse (RN)–medical doctor (MD) relationship in hospital settings.[7] These literary materials are well-bounded and extensive (as the citations we provide show). However, from the beginning, they seem to render our proposal of a structural reading theory impotent. This literature debates the idea that the RN–MD relationship in hospitals is typically and appropriately the compliance of RN behaviors to MD's orders. This proposition is aggravating to a structural reading because it implies that the fundamental issue is sociopsychological: that the explanation for RN behavior is an attitude (compliance or noncompliance). Where more than diadic social structural features are considered (structure of medical vs. surgical wards [Coser 1958], structure of hospital administration [Bates and White 1961; Sills 1976], etc.) structural factors are often relegated to the background. Even when given the role of independent variables (e.g., Flood and Scott 1978), their independence is purchased at the price of a formalism which destroys the positivity of the crucial relationship between "observed" behaviors of RNs and MDs and the structural factors of ward or hospital organization.[8] Thus, this literature, by ignoring or formalizing structural effects, challenges the structuralist problematic by virtue of being an essentially (if not avowedly) sociopsychological literature. The challenge to a structural theory of measurement and explanation is most acute in the face of this sort of literature, as opposed to literatures limiting themselves, however important their problems, to questions of state–class relations, class conflict, or social mobility. We add (perversely, but not facetiously) that the literature of RN behavior serves us well because it is garden variety. This literature is manifestly dull, sometimes laughable. In short, it is the stuff most sociologists read and with which they are obliged to work.

MEASURES AND INSTRUMENTS

Sociologists use "instruments" to "measure" "observables" in order to *produce* "data" for "explanations"—a reasonable statement rendered powerless by recent sociology. Sociologists know—now more than ever—that "instruments" cannot be operations linking observables to facts (Willer and Webster 1970; Blalock 1968). The weakness of our instruments is not a question of observer–subject effects, the inexactness of error term descriptions, or the imprecision of data taking; it lies in the language of instrumentation (Cicourel 1964; Blalock 1969; Galtung 1969; Lemert 1979b). Instruments are theories (Blalock 1969) or products of researcher's formal discourse. With the demise in the 1960s of overt and crypto operationalism, the ideal of a positive relationship between a measured datum and an observed real world (RW) stimulus–response unit was itself destroyed. There exists no positive relationship between words and things. The RW is at best a Presumably Real Social World (PRSW); and measurement reads this illusion.

The most stunning demonstration of this fact is found in recent advances in measurement error theory (Siegel and Hodge 1968; Sonequist 1970; Blalock 1968). It is assumed that the stochastic disturbance term "measures" the deviation between the languages of theory and research. If, for example, our variable is 'X,' then, normally:

$$X_{\text{measured}} = T_{\text{true value}} \text{ of } X + e_{\text{disturbance term}} \qquad (12.1)$$

Even though (12.1) states explicitly, through the stochastic term e, that all relevant features of X are unknown, it creates the illusion that the variable is measured completely and accurately. However, "any measure is subject to both errors incurred through definition of a less than completely valid measure of a theoretical construct and error incurred through an operational measure which is not perfectly reliable" (Siegel and Hodge 1968:55). Therefore, (12.1) must be rewritten as:

$$X = (C + v) + e \qquad (12.2)$$

where, "C equals the value assumed by the theoretical construct we are measuring, and v represents departures of the true values of the measured variable from the values of the theoretical variable we are attempting to operationalize" (Siegel and Hodge 1968:55). Through the arbitrary *theoretical* decision to accept the stochastic disturbance term of (12.1) as incorporating both errors to which Siegel and Hodge refer, there exists no sound *methodological* device for the determination of v in (12.2). Measures of illusions are themselves illusory.

Criticisms of empiricism (Willer, n.d.; Sonequist 1970), while salutory, are often merely a displacement of the problem. Recognizing that words and things do not necessarily have anything to do with each other, they turn to words—but without a serious theory of words and texts. Galtung (1969) is an excellent example. He is ready to abandon the notion that measures can detect actor's "real" intentions, and turns to actor's words as such, hence transforming "the problem from the problem of correspondence between thoughts and words to the problem of how representative the interview situation is as social intercourse" (Galtung 1969:124). This is a sophisticated formal version of the ethnomethodological principle of the validity-destroying effect of the context embeddedness of social discourse. Neither seems to fully admit that the gulf between PRSW things and measures (hence, data) is unbridgeable even by the partial reformist strategies of humanistic or technical "sensitivity." This is evident when Galtung's implicit theory of measurement is restated with reference to the RN–MD literature (see figure 12.1).

A measured datum available for use in a compliance theory of RN–MD relations is the measurer's coded sign for a real world impression, or text (the written entry by RNs of their behavior: administration of a specific drug to a patient). The impression (RN's chart entry) is a product of a behavioral response (RN drug administration) which in turn is created by the action of a stimulus (MD's order) on a responding object (RN as addresses of MD's orders). Though few today would admit it (for an exception see Salancik 1977:1–2), this amounts to the same thing as an earlier naïveté: that a datum is a one-to-one emblem for a stimulus. In more general terms, this is the position that observables produce measured data. This can be seen more clearly when the concept "*data*" is clarified. A datum is a measured unit. If—as everyone seems to agree—a datum is unable to stand for a real world thing, then *how* does it mean?

A datum is an expression vehicle for a content. When an RN enters the "fact" that she administered a drug of a certain dosage to a certain patient at a certain time subsequent to and directed by an MD order, a sociologist is warranted—let us assume—to enter a purely sociological mark in his records (perhaps on a standardized observer's check sheet, or simply in a field notebook). This mark becomes an encoded *sign* only in the context of a theory; that is, the formal discourse which led the sociologist to believe certain things which became his proto-"instrument"; for our example, sociologist presumably believes: (1) that there is something interesting about RN–MD relations, a problem of some kind; (2) that whatever is interesting is contained in RN-response-to-MD sequences; (3) that certain behaviors—administration of drug, entry making—are a way of observing the RN to MD response; (4) that the specific behaviors could legitimately be recorded in a sociologist's preliminary text, perhaps by means of a simple x in the "RN makes chart entry" column of the sociologist's log book. This x or check-mark is a proto-datum which

			PRSW		Measurement
Galtung:	Stimulus →	Object →	Response →	Impression	→ Datum
Example:	MD's Order →	RN as addressee →	RN behavior^1: Administration of Drug →	RN behavior^2: Chart Entry	→ Compliance datum
			.	.	→ .
			.	.	→ .
			.	.	→ .
			N	N	→ N

Figure 12.1. Traditional Measurement Theory

becomes a true datum only in the context of "data"—that is, a larger number of x's in the same column which at some subsequent point have been certified by sociologist's technology as valid, reliable, and significant. This certification, of course, is possible if the aggregated x's, rewritten as numbers, are supplied proper contents. This content is of course generated from the same theory which generated the instruments by which the datum and its fellow significant data were collected. In our example, a given x in the proper column becomes an expression unit for the meaningful content: //compliance// (e.g., Rank and Jacobson 1977). In other words, the x-marks in the "RN makes entry" column are—both prospectively and retrospectively—expression units for the content //compliance//. They are thereby sign functions existing exclusively in sociologists' texts.

A measurement theory such as Galtung's relies on an unjustified procedure. It must arbitrarily and without explanation exclude certain entirely possible meanings from the x-marks. The very drawing of an "RN makes entry" column (an element in an instrument) is, we know very well, designed to "infer" the content x-marks can have, //compliance//. Since the placing of the x in some other column ("no chart entry," "sequence incomplete," "other," etc.) is the equivalent of the content "noncompliance," instruments so designed can only collect positive entries. They solve the problem of the datum's unrepresentiveness of a real-world thing by the use of contents from the instrument (its columns, and the theory according to which they were written).[9] Although a sensible beginning, the strategy soon collapses because it ignores a crucial possible content: the RN's intentions, which could of course be marked, for example, by such entries as "patient in bed 12 resting comfortably at 12:30 A.M.," which, in the context of an inappropriate MD medication order for 12:30 A.M. could supply to a datum the content, //noncompliance//. But in a scheme like Galtung's such data contents cannot be generated because the logic of the instrument requires a correspondence between data logged by a sociologist and the observed, preestablished behaviors. In other words, possible contents are arbitrarily excluded at the point of measurement by the instrument's assumption that a behavior is equivalent to a datum whose content can only be //compliance// or //noncompliance//. These unexplained exclusions are the monologicity of positivist measures. All the talk of indirect measurement, auxiliary theory, disturbance term, and the like do nothing to change the situation. The exclusion of possible contents is the necessary consequence of the refusal to recognize the extent to which empiricism and its avatars (like operationalism) remain the driving force behind any theory of measurement which holds that data values correspond to and are generated by (however obliquely) real world events. If words have nothing to do with things, they have nothing to do with things. Words (even sociologist's words) have only to do with words. The solution is not in the refinement of measures, but in a proper theory of words and their relationship to each other—that is, of the intertextual relationship between sociologists' and actors' words. This, we believe, is managed only by a theory of reading which explains sociologists' readings of PRSW texts.

TEXTS AND LITERATURES [10]

Texts are, to use Eco's (1978) words, "multi-level discourses." Texts are not composed of straightforward syntagmatic links between words, or simple denotative contents necessarily associated with terms. Texts are not read automatically (as in positivist measurement), but on the basis of a reader's competence, that is, his learned ability to properly associate possible contents with expressions addressed to him.[11] Thus, when an MD writes a medication order such as: "Valium 5mg. p.o. Q.i.D. × 1 mo.," the nurse must know that this means //give a certain tablet at a certain dosage four times a day for one month//. A competent RN-reading of this text involves the RN's training, including knowledge of the effect of the dosage on the patient. In effect, this is knowledge of the chemical and physiological implications of the behavioral response to the MD's medication order text (e.g., an improperly administered medication may lead to a coma, mental stress, etc.). Likewise, the RN knows, also on the basis of training, that the administration of a drug requires an appropriate chart entry, which includes knowledge (however conscious or preconscious) that the social structure of the medical ward would collapse if RNs fail to make such entries. Were all RNs to refuse to chart drug administrations, this would require the presence at all times of MDs or some other more reliable representative thereof. Thus, all MD orders are read with reference to competent knowledge of drug order codes, physiological effects of drugs, social effects of chart entries, and hospital organizational rules, among other pertinent knowledges.

With respect to measurement, the problem for the sociologist is to read these RN readings. Sociologists at this point are in exactly the same situation as the RN. They must read with reference to their competent knowledges: namely, the literature on hospital structures, formal organizations, medical systems, compliance relationships, status attributions, and so on. Sociologists' literatures are multiple—including, of course, at least: (1) materials published in sociological journals or books published in the name of sociology (e.g., the RN-to-MD compliance literature); (2) general documentation provided by private and public agencies (such as government statistics on health care system structures, costs, training needs, etc.); (3) oral texts provided in conversation by nurses, medical doctors, patients; (4) newspaper accounts of events in hospital settings, and so forth. Though the first (to which we restrict ourselves) is primary, the others are equally—or in certain instances more—important. These literatures are the *only* resources available for those who desire to create instruments to measure "events" in the PRSW. Sociological instruments of whatever kind (survey instruments, field notebooks, experiment protocols, interview schedules) are exclusively and necessarily constructed on the basis of a reading of literatures. It is, therefore, surprising that there has never been an explicit theory for the reading of these texts. It is assumed, apparently, that sociologists possess a native skill by which they read out instruments from literatures—an assumption which naïvely entails the corollary: literatures are neutral resources which do not complicate the measurement process. These assumptions explain why all the attempts to control for measurement error concentrate on the observer or his instrumentation, as if the reliability and validity of instruments were only problems and as if instruments were created without difficulty. Since this is patently absurd, we must turn to a theory of reading able to suggest the way an instrument can be read from literatures (remembering that, for the sake of our example, we refer only to formal sociological literatures).

The first and fundamental principle of reading is that the reader and the text are bound to each other by a common set of historically relative conventions. Texts in an unknown foreign language cannot be read. A reader's basic competence is the ability to recognize at least something familiar in the texts: its language, its contents, its grammars, its connotations, and so forth. This mastery is never complete precisely because the reading, the text, and their social formation are historic conventions. We know this from the fact that certain literary forms (the novel, for example) once did not exist, may not exist in the future, and during their tenure have changed considerably. One cannot read Flaubert and Balzac as one reads Butor or Updike. The contents of reading competencies change. This leads to a second principle: readers, texts, and readings are socially produced. Neither the author nor the reader are able to write or read in mutual or respective isolation from their social circumstances. Reading is the product of the relations of literary production. Though the situation is even more complex than this, we shall work with these elementary principles, drawn quite clearly from post-structuralist reading theory (Culler 1974).

To simplify a bit: a literature is encoded by the same social and productive relations which determine readers' reading. Reading competence is the ability to recognize enough of these codes in order to make some sense of the text. Readings are never perfect because, (a) there is no reason to decode a text perfectly and (b) the code is constantly changing even as it is read (Eco 1976:2.13).

All this is particularly true of a sociological literature which aims, presumably, to describe the very social conditions in which it is itself produced. Thus, a literature must be read with reference to what we know of the society in, by, and for which it was produced. In brief, we know that all sociological literatures written since the 1950s in advanced capitalist societies were produced under the following social conditions: increasing structuration and centralization of social functions in state and corporate organizations; decreasing autonomy of individuals as workers, producers, inventors of social norms; decreasing significance of nation–state distinctions as a result in increasing internationalization of capital; increasing fiscal crisis in the late capitalist world; increasing formalization, routinization, and control in individual's work and personal lives. Consequently, no sociological reading of a literature can produce competent instruments if it fails to permit a reading of at least the following "levels": individual intentions and behaviors, organizational constraints thereupon, socioeconomic constraints on both actions and organizations. Simply put, readings must consist of social structural (organizational and socioeconomic constraints) and actor-related (intentions and behaviors) factors.

Turning to the RN–MD literature, we see that texts exist which are pertinent to all these levels, even though any given text tends to be a selective reading. Some limit their reading to the RN–MD diadic relations (Rank and Jacobson 1977; Stein 1967; Hofling et al. 1966). Others (Reich and Geller 1976) read only the personality traits of RNs; still others (Alutto and Belasco 1977) read only RN decision-making abilities. At another level, there are studies, such as Coser's (1958) which pass beyond social psychology to the social structure of medical and surgical wards. Coser's claim is that the RN's interaction with the MD is a function of the differing structures of surgical and medical settings (high in the former, low in the latter). At a still "higher" level, Flood and Scott (1978) read encroachment behaviors as a consequence of the social structure of the hospital as a formal organization in which hospital administration and physician components are the only independent variables of significance, leaving the nursing administration component in a necessarily insignificant position. Then, at the level of the socioeconomic setting, there is an abundant literature (e.g., Navarro 1976; Waitzkin and Waterman 1974; Sills 1976) which might read any particular topic (RN–MD relations) in the context of social and economic structures determining hierarchical control mechanisms (thus, presumably, obliging RN compliance).

INSTRUMENTS

Of course, the literatures just cited are intended as "readings" of the PRSW. By listing them in this manner, we show that they were in fact selective readings and provide a literature with which to begin anew, in hopes of showing how to avoid their errors. We know now why the existing RN–MD literature is so selective. These readers did not begin by constructing instruments with reference to the social codes organizing their literature. For example, Coser (1958) limits herself to the relationship between role behavior and medical-surgical wards without the least explanation, as if nothing else mattered. Thus, the literature she cites refers predictably to the social order of the ward and little else. This selectivity was due to an uncritical employment of the traditional theory of measures. Believing that RW "stimuli" are the sources of "data," she simply selected an unexplained "interesting" problem.

To avoid this trap, we must deal with the problem of an instrument's selectivity—the problem of parsimony. Having claimed that all the pertinent structural levels must be read, we are open to the charge that everything must be read—clearly an impossible task.

This requires us to be more precise in describing the nature of the instrument as a reading of a literature intended for a reading of a PRSW. The inadequacy of the traditional theory of measures (exemplified by Galtung's model) is that too few contents are available for expression units. Having derived the possible contents from a selective reading of the literature (e.g., deciding that compliance–noncompliance are the contents to be "discovered" behind RNs' behaviors), traditional measures cannot collect contents which do not fit the instrument, even though in the literature these other contents are available. This inadequacy can be solved by a description of the form of an instrument.

What, after all, is an instrument but a collection of *types* derived from a literature? The //complying nurse// is a type, as is its opposite. But we know that other types exist. Two can be given as examples: One is the //influencing nurse// (Rushing 1962; Stein 1967; Hoekelman 1975) who is neither purely compliant or noncompliant. This is the nurse who, by subtle games (Stein 1967), influences MDs to change or even discover the proper order to be given. The other is the //competing nurse// (Rank and Jacobson 1977; Rushing 1962) who disregards the compliance game altogether and operates, in some circumstances, more or less independently; in effect, ignoring MD orders. The problem for measurement is that these types are not observable in the PRSW. It is possible to observe entries in a chart and *suspect* that the entry is: (1) a true entry reflecting strict compliance (complying type RN), (2) a true entry of a drug administration, but as a result of an MD order the RN influenced (influencing type RN), and (3) a modified or falsified entry reflecting a situation in which, for example, the nurse withheld the drug because she knew that the patient, on this evening, had no need of a sedative (competing type RN). It is totally irrelevant that one of these might be more probable than the others. The mere existence of any one, including the "extreme" third case, in any literature whatsoever is enough to make it a possible type behavior obligating an instrument to anticipate it.

But how? We must ask what an instrument actually observes. Not contents. And not types. Both are generated by a literature. What is observed is simply an expression token. The observation of an RN chart entry is, from the point of view of an instrument, only an expression vehicle for a content and a token of a type.[12] It is neither the content (//compliance//) nor a possible type (//professional// nurse). Only an expression token that is a concrete instance of a behavior is observed. The token behavior could be exactly the same in all three cases, but the type and content could vary (fig. 12.2). //Compliant//, //influencing//, and //competing// nurses could enter the same words in a chart, but as a result of different motives.

The problem is that those motives cannot be observed in any strict fashion (RNs will not tell us, they do not know themselves, they know and tell us lies to protect themselves, etc.). Galtung wisely urges us to read only the expression (his "impression") text; but, he is totally wrong to assume that we can infer from a behavior expression a meaningful content to the behavior. He is wrong because we know from a "reading" of the literature that other contents are available for the same token expressions.

Since we have only the literature from which to collect these contents, we must begin there. But let us recall that a literature is a coded product of a social formation and a set of productive relations; and let us recall further that the literature used is only partially sociological texts: it could include documents, letters, nurse's autobiographies, and so forth. Thus, the literature's code is, taken as a whole, an ensemble of behavioral types, any one of which could be enacted and expressed by a concrete token on a given observed hospital ward. We also know therefrom that any and all of the three types in figure 12.2 are themselves products of social and economic relations: formal organization relations

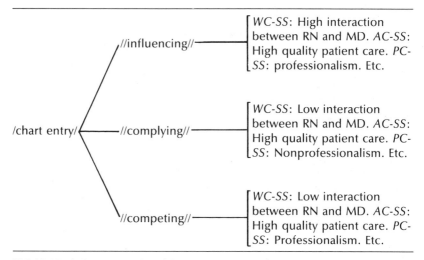

WC-SS: Work Component Social Structure. AC-SS: Administration Component Social Structure. PC-SS: Professional Component Social Structure. Etc.: Other social structures which are not considered above. Other components of the social structure which are not considered above.

Figure 12.2. Token, Types, and Ambiguity

between RNs and MDs (not to mention hospital administrators); informal professional relations defining proper RN comportment; economic relations establishing status differentials between RNs and MDs; economic conditions determining amount of available staffing or number of technical supports in a given hospital which constrain or free the RN and MD (e.g., paging systems providing the RN access to MDs at home or off the ward). These social structural relations are the source of types, available for inclusion in instrumentation. One example is the professional component social structure of the RN. RNs learn a code of professional ethics, which is itself a product of other social relations. They are taught, traditionally, to comply with MDs' orders on the basis of certain social conventions: the assumption that the MD's greater technical skill makes "him" primary in providing health care, the assumption of the MD's superior status, the assumption that medical wards *must* be arranged hierarchically, and so forth. Thus, being a subprofessional is, in medical literature, a simple connotation so well established that the two concepts (nurse and subprofessional) are virtually synonymous. However, in the sociological literature we know that this type-to-type relation is constantly infringed upon. Nurses who see themselves as "professionals" sometimes disobey MD's orders because: (1) the patient made a quick and unexpected recovery, (2) in the context of other orders by the same physician the order is contraindicated, or (3) the medication order is incorrect (e.g., in excess of the maximum dose; see Hofling et al. 1966; Linn 1971; and Rank and Jacobson 1977). In other words, the RN's professionalism is not necessarily associated with compliance. Competing nurses who understand their behavior as a means for providing "quality health care" (perhaps in the face of incompetent MD's, such as interns, nonspecialists), may be defining themselves as entirely professional in their noncompliance. In the process such an RN contends not merely with an MD but with prevailing structures of intrahospital relations: hierarchies, statuses, pay scales, vacation schedules, and so forth.

However, for our purposes, the important thing is that no sociological instrument could ever measure a behavioral token as belonging to an //RN–competing-professional// type unless this type is contained from the beginning in the instrument. What we are arguing is that a token can never be "measured" directly in the PRSW; nor, without a theory of reading, can it be taken from the literatures. And types can only be read from the literature if that literature is understood as texts encoded by the same social relations which also produce RN behaviors. In other words, and quite seriously, our only access to the PRSW is through the literature. Our observables (token expressions) make sense only when read with respect to a reading of the social structures which generate the possible types available for RN expression in concrete behaviors. We could call this a theory of "indirect measurement" were it not for the fact that we assume that all literatures have equal standing with respect to "reality." However near or far they are from whatever is "real," they are our only resources. This is true for actors and sociologists alike.

DISCOVERY

How can we have a discovery principle? How is it possible to know that we are reading what is actually "there" and not what we would like to read? This entails two additional concepts: *ratio difficilis* and *disambiguation*.

RATIO DIFFICILIS

A *ratio facilis* is a well-established conventional relationship between an observed token and its type.[13] This is exactly what we have in all the traditional literature which assumes (see figure 12.1) that an /RN chart entry/ is a proper token of the //RN–complying-professional// type. However, if we allow only instruments based on a *ratio facilis* we shall be no better off than traditional measurement theory. We shall measure only what the conventions of our literature tells us ought to be there (in other words, by allowing only *ratio facilis* we run the risk of perpetuating the status quo and discovering nothing new). A *ratio difficilis* is, on the other hand, a relationship between an established type and an unexpected, hence unique, content. Instruments must be able, in principle, to produce surprising results (discoveries); otherwise they are not measuring, only mapping. A complying RN token is scientifically meaningful only if we have some reason to believe that it is not a /competing/ or /influencing/ RN token. Since RNs cannot or will not tell us which token they are enacting, we can only explain the RN behavior by means of an instrument able to collect (i.e., produce) a *ratio difficilis*. This amounts to an instrument which so incorporates all social structural dimensions and their combinations as to yield, at least: an //RN–competing-professional// type, and an //RN–influencing-professional// type, alongside the expected //RN–complying-professional// type (see figure 12.2).

Since it is always possible that the literature does not contain a possible type available for a *ratio difficilis*, and since the PRSW cannot itself tell us of this relationship, the possibility of discovery in social science rests entirely on a structural reading of the literature. Discovery is possible only when one reads from structures to behaviors and not vice versa (as in traditional measurement). Though the structures in the literature (knowledge of economic and social relations, organizational forms, etc.) may not tell us in so many words what we ought to produce—in a specific case study, a certain *ratio difficilis*—those structures can tell us that such a relation might be discoverable. For example, knowledge of the changing status of nurses may be found in Johnson and Martin 1958; Minehan 1977; new forms of professional behavior for nurses involving increasing autonomy in Davis 1974; Mass et al 1975; changes in sex composition of the nursing field with the inclusion of males in various statistical abstracts, effects of feminist ideology on female RN in Ashley 1975; Bakdish 1978; Moniz 1978; increasing caution of MDs in the face of malpractice suits in newspapers; increasing medical and hospital costs in our bank accounts, and increasing size of administrative components in hospitals and welfare organizations in Blau 1970. All these structural effects must be included in the instrument (the means of primary observation). Without them there are no surprises (hence nothing is measured). With them at least the possibility of discovery, upon which science is founded, exists.

DISAMBIGUATION

We are still faced with the problem of parsimony. The above suggests that virtually everything must be incorporated in instrumentation. This, to be sure, is impossible. How then is one to perform a parsimonious reading out of instruments? One must read with reference to points of ambiguity in the literature. If RN–MD relationships are read from the point of view of traditional expectations about ward and hospital organization, there is little possibility of ambiguity. We expect (hence we find) compliance. Ambiguity becomes possible only when one can recognize that //RN–professional-quality medical care// could just as well be marked by //RN-competing// (or //RN-influencing//) as by //RN-complying//. And again, we can only anticipate this relationship if we have read the literatures to discover a possible structural explanation for an //RN-competing// with MD type. If we know that RNs increasingly define themselves as coequal professionals—that MDs, for fear of malpractice suits, might desire to diffuse and share legal responsibility; that hospital costs require a transfer of certain functions from high paid MDs to lower paid RNs, etc.—then we can discover an ambiguity in the traditional reading.

An ambiguity is not an explanation. It merely requires us to structure our instrumentation in a way that it can produce "*ex-*

planatory" "data." What after all, is explanation but the disambiguation of an intelligible ambiguity? But how is an ambiguity discovered? Only by knowledge of alternative explanations for a given observed behavior. This knowledge cannot be given by the RN (by the RW). It is found only in the literature which permits us to reconstruct the possible and probable social structures determining behaviors (see Eco 1978). Social structures, as opposed to behaviors, exist only in literatures; they can never be observed. Thus, in the literature, read structurally, one finds the point at which measures must be made and instruments created; that is, the point at which rival social structural *"explanations"* tell us that things might not be as they appear. In our example, we shall of necessity limit ourselves to a small portion of the structural effects necessary to discover an ambiguity in need of disambiguation: the structural effects having to do with RNs' definition of their professionalism, and RN and MDs' participation in a system which, in principle, serves to provide quality patient care.

Ambiguity can arise only when it is recognized that the behavior to which the //professional RN// type corresponds can also be explained by apparently "nonprofessional" types. Both can be marked by other contents and types existing in the literature, such as: //therapeutic harmony// and //providing quality patient care// (see Johnson and Martin 1958). Our thesis is that in order to talk of professionalism among nurses the analysis must be expanded. We must go beyond the traditional equivalencies established (in one part of the literature) among //professional RN//, //complying RN//, //therapeutic harmony//, and //quality patient care//. This involves discovering in the literature possible substitutions for any one of these type contents when substitution would allow us to account for otherwise confusing facts—such as the fact that //competing// nurses do not always lose their jobs and sometimes are respected by MDs. In other words, we must reread all the literature which assumes that //complying RN// and //professional RN// are synonymous (Froebe and Bain, 1976; Bates, 1978; Pearlin and Rosenberg, 1962; Hoekelman, 1975).

In fig. 12.2, we have diagramed and summarized a sample of the social structural (SS) effects which correspond to three types (//influencing RN//, //complying RN//, //competing RN//) each of which are taken as probable contents for an observed expression behavior /RN chart entry/. Fig. 12.2, in effect, creates an ambiguity:—Which SS path provides the type best able to explain the /RN chart entry/ token? Fig. 12.3 illustrates a possible disambiguation.[14]

Let us suppose, on the basis of reading of the literature, that an axis is formed by two content types—U_1: //complying RN// and U_2: //competing RN// which are mutually exclusive types of professionalism. Whatever else //complying// and //competing// nurses are, they are not the same. But we know that neither type of nurse intends to be nonprofessional (especially in a world of increasing professionalization). We know that a prevailing, socially structured, definition of the two types as professional does exist. However, we also know that some conventions change. There is permeability between the two types and the marker //professional//. This constantly shifting, unstable set of relationships is susceptible to metaphorical substitution or metonymical assimilation (see Eco, 1976; 3.8.4 and passim). A metaphoric relationship exists when one *type* (//professional//) can be substituted for another (//complying RN// or //competing RN//); and a metonymic relationship exists when the latter two types can be assimilated to each other. These possible relationships of substitution and assimilation are, obviously, only evident from a knowledge of *all* possible social structures which could determine a behavior. A selective reading of the literature could lead (and has led) to the assumption that RNs are merely subprofessionals, hence, not capable of autonomous decision-making because their training is "inferior." This entails the further assumption that only the MD can provide //quality patient care//, the RN being a mere auxiliary. Read in this way, the literature yields the "explanation" that //conforming RN// and //professional RN// are synonomous and that no substitutions can be made. In this formulation, they must be directly, and without ambiguity, assimilated to //quality patient care// ($U_1(mtn\alpha_1) \equiv \lambda_1$). However, it is now well known (by our reading of accounts of poor MD patient care, films such as *Hospital*, notices of MDs losing malpractice suits, and other more formal literatures) that MDs, if left to their own devices, do not automatically provide //quality patient care//. This entails, further, the possibility that //quality patient care// *might* be provided equally by continuous and competent nursing. This, in turn, raises

A. The Potential Ambiguity

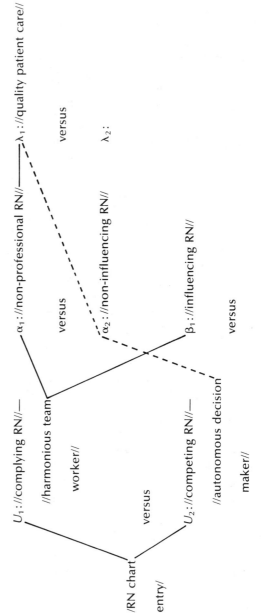

/RN chart entry/

U_1://complying RN//— //harmonious team worker//

versus

U_2://competing RN//— //autonomous decision maker//

α_1://non-professional RN//— λ_1://quality patient care//

versus

α_2://non-influencing RN// λ_2:

versus

β_1://influencing RN//

versus

β_2://non-influencing RN//

B. Because:

$$[(U_1(\text{mtn}\alpha_1) \equiv \lambda_1] \cdot [\lambda_1(\text{mtn}\alpha_2) \equiv U_2)] \rightarrow [U_1(\text{mtf}\lambda_1) \equiv U_2]$$

C. The Result:

//influencing RN//

Figure 12.3. Disambiguation of a Rhetorical Code Change

the prospect that a nonconforming RN, for example //competing//, could both provide //quality nursing care// and be //professional// (see Fagin 1975; Churchill 1977; Bandman and Bandman 1978). In this case, //quality patient care// can be assimilated metonymically to //competing RN// ($\lambda_1(mtn\alpha_2) \equiv U_2$). But this assimilation depends on the possibility of a metaphoric substitution of //competing RN// for //complying RN//. The result is attained by the addition of another marker to our reading of RN behaviors, namely: //autonomous decision maker// which is assimilated to //professional RN// after it is substituted for //harmonious team worker//. Ultimately, (see fig. 12.3), //autonomous decision maker// becomes a weak metaphoric substitution for //influencing RN// (see Rushing 1962; Stein 1967; Hoekelman 1975).

This is a structural effect. There is evidence (Johnson and Martin 1958:376; Cates 1965; Froebe and Bain 1976; Lewin and Damrell, 1978:39) that nurses actually produce new RN //professional// behaviors, such as modeling their //professional// behavior after that of MDs by performing nurses' ward rounds as a replication of doctors' rounds (Froebe and Bain 1976).

It is apparent that the explanation for new behaviors of this sort is contained in the shifting structural relationships between RNs' understanding of their professionalism, the changing structure of hospital wards, modification of the MD role in patient care, and so forth. We could never "*explain*" (or even "*measure*") these behaviors, which all of us can observe without the benefit of either sociology or "structuralism" and without a coherent reconstruction of the structural field of the RN–MD relationship. Furthermore, what is explained is that //autonomous decision maker// is not and need not be automatically assimilated to //competing//; and, accordingly, that //harmonious team worker// holds no necessary relationship to //professional RN//. Indeed when read in this way, one can see that the latter relationship is not only not "natural" but may even be an instance of another content //domination//, the explanation of which would involve still wider investigations of the RN–MD structural field (the structures of hospital administration, capitalist health care systems, etc.). This shows that one ambiguity leads to another and, as a result, the reading of structural effects is continuous (as it should be in any true science). But the continuous revision of sociological reconstructions of this structural field are not arbitrary. They move in a positive fashion, from ambiguity to ambiguity. Of course, ambiguities are only the beginning points of analysis by which parsimonious measurement becomes possible. Though instruments and, thereby, readings are constantly revised, the result is a nonpositivist, positive reading of the structural field upon which explanation depends.

NOTES

1. We use the term "structuralism" because "post-structuralism" is not very precise. We are not "structuralists," but we are not going to waste space and time with a history of the theoretical materials we use. We indicate our sources below.

2. See Pierre Bourdieu (1975) on the specificity of science. We are not interested in what sociology ideally "ought" to be (its most abstract theoretical problematic) but in what it actually is at the moment.

3. As explained below, this is the problematic of post-structuralism. Michel Foucault (1972, 1973) is the most important discussion of this position. There is an ample secondary literature of the topic. For examples, see Culler (1974) and Said (1975).

4. The affinities amongst Marx, Durkheim, and Saussure are discussed at greater length in Baudrillard (1972) and Culler (1976).

5. See Lemert (1979a) for an application of this view originally presented in Foucault (1972).

6. Instrumentation, like measurement, is a process of encodement. This discussion involves a theory of codes (not presented here). We rely heavily on Eco (1976). Throughout this article we use quotation marks, slashes, and italics technically. "Xxxx" refers to a concept or term used in common sense or sociological discourse which requires further analysis we cannot give here. We mark it in this way to note that we use it more or less in its "normal" sense, but recognize the problems associated with it. The marking *xxxx* refers to a term or concept we encode in this text, giving it our meaning. "*Xxxx*" means that our usage corresponds, roughly, with normal usage. Thus, "*data*" here marks the fact that we use a sociologically normal term, in our way: our usage adds to but does not change the normal sense. Also, below, single slashes /xxxx/ refer to an expression unit; double slashes //xxxx// refer to a content.

7. Within this text, the terms "*nurse*" (RN) and "*medical doctor*" (MD) are shorthand notations for persons who perform certain medical tasks. The holding of an RN or MD is not paramount for our discussion.

8. This involves an analysis of the problems of structural analysis which cannot be presented here (see Lemert 1979b).

9. We refer here to the distinction between words and things and the assumption that real worlds do not exist for sociology.

10. In the following, our reliance on Eco (1976; cf. 1978) is especially great.

11. We use the generic masculine in knowledge of the sexism involved, but in ignorance of an adequate substitute.

12. The following discussion depends on the distinction between a token, found in a PRSW, which is read by a type, a theoretical instrument. This usage (drawn from Eco 1976) serves here to make the point that stimuli from a "world" do not generate data; it is only the instrument which reads tokens of an empirical field which is itself established by a reading of the same literature that generates the types. One has tokens only on the basis of types.

13. We are, of necessity, omitting much that could be included here: especially, the theory of signs and sign functions, connotation, and denotation. Also, we are abbreviating by collapsing somewhat the relationship between expression types and expression tokens. Again, see Eco (1976).

14. This is only one methodological possibility. Figure 12.3 is based on Eco (1976:3.8.4). The following symbols appear: U_1, U_2, α_1, α_2, β_1, β_2, λ_1, λ_2; and are explained by the terms following the symbols. However, λ_2 is not explained. It can signify anything as long as it opposes directly the signification of λ_1. Hence, λ_1 and λ_2 form an oppositional axis as do $\alpha_1-\alpha_2$, $\beta_1-\beta_2$, and U_1-U_2. This indicates that "things" in themselves signify nothing. Therefore, the signified is defined only in relation to what it is not (e.g., a //complying RN// is not a //competing RN//). Part A indicates the potential ambiguity: How can a //complying RN// and a //competing RN// signify //quality patient care//? Part B offers one explanation for this ambiguity. The abbreviations *mtn* and *mtf* refer to metonymical assimilation and metaphorical substitution, respectively. Hence, the first part of B (to the left of the arrow) reads: the //complying RN// (U_1) via metonymical assimilation of the content of //nonprofessional RN// ($mtn\alpha_1$) is then rhetorically equivalent ($\equiv$) to //quality patient care// (λ_1). The remainder of the equation is translated in the same manner. Part C shows the result of Part B. The content of //influencing RN// collapses the opposition of α_1 to α_2 and therefore obliterates the opposition of U_1 to U_2.

REFERENCES

Alutto, J. A. and J. A. Belasco. 1977. "Determinants of attitudinal militancy among nurses and teachers." *Industrial and Labor Relations Review* (January) 27:216–27.

Ashley, Jo Ann. 1975. "Nurses in American history: Nursing and early feminism." *American Journal of Nursing* (September) 75:1465–67.

Bakdish, Diane P. 1978. "Becoming an assertive nurse." *American Journal of Nursing* (October) 78:1710–1712.

Bandman, B. and E. Bandman. 1978. "Do nurses have rights? No and yes" *American Journal of Nursing* (January) 78:84–86.

Bates, Barbara. 1978. "Doctor and nurse: changing roles and relations." In H. D. Schwartz and C. S. Kart, eds. *Dominant Issues in Medical Sociology*, pp. 221–27. Reading, Mass.: Addison-Wesley.

Bates, F. L. and R. F. White. 1961. "Differential perceptions of authority in hospitals." *Journal of Health and Human Behavior* 2:262–67.

Baudrillard, Jean. 1972. *Pour une critique de l'economic politique du signe.* Paris: Gallimard.

Blalock, Hubert M., Jr. 1968. "The measurement problem: A gap between the language of theory and research." In H. M. Blalock, Jr. and A. Blalock, eds. *Methodology in Social Research*, pp. 5–27. New York: McGraw-Hill.

—— 1969. *Theory Construction: From Verbal to Mathematical Formulations.* Englewood Cliffs, N.J.: Prentice–Hall.

—— 1970. "The formalization of sociological theory." In J. C. McKinney and E. Tiryakian, eds. *Theoretical Sociology: Perspectives and Developments*, pp. 271–300. New York: Appleton–Century–Crofts.

Blau, Peter. 1970. "A formal theory of organizations." *American Sociological Review* 35(2):201–19.

Bourdieu, Pierre. 1968. "Structuralism and theory of sociological knowledge." *Social Research* (Winter) 35:681–706.

—— 1975. "The specificity of the scientific field and social conditions of the progress of reason." *Social Science Information* 14(5):19–47.

Cates, Judith N. 1965. "Images of the health professionals." *The Sociological Quarterly* (Autumn) 6:391–97.

Churchill, Larry. 1977. "Ethical issues of a profession in transition." *American Journal of Nursing* (May) 77:873–75.

Cicourel, Aaron V. 1964. *Method and Measurement.* New York: Free Press.

Coser, Lewis A. 1975. "Two methods in search of a substance." *The American Sociological Review* 40(6):691–700.

Coser, Rose L. 1958. "Authority and decision-making in a hospital: A comparative analysis." *American Sociological Review* (February) 23:56–63.

Culler, Jonathan D. 1974. *Structuralist Poetics.* Ithaca, N.Y.: Cornell University Press.

—— 1976. *Saussure.* Glasgow: Fontana/Collins.

Davis, Margaret K. 1974. "Intrarole conflict and job satisfaction on psychiatric units." *Nursing Research* (November–December) 23:482–88.

Denzin, Norman. 1972. "The logic of naturalistic inquiry." *Social Forces* (December) 50:162–66.

Duncan, O. Dudley. 1966. "Path analysis: Sociological examples." *American Journal of Sociology* (July) 72:1–16.

Eco, Umberto 1976. *A Theory of Semiotics.* Bloomington: Indiana University Press.

—— 1978. "Possible worlds and text pragmatics: 'Un drame bien parisien.'" *Versus: Quaderni di studi semiotici* (July–August) 19–20:5–72.

Fagin, Claire M. 1975. "Nurse's rights." *American Journal of Nursing* (January) 75:82–85.

Flood, A. B. and W. R. Scott. 1978. "Professional power and professional effectiveness: The power of the surgical staff and the quality of surgical care in hospitals." *Journal of Health and Social Behavior* (September) 19:240–54.

Foucault, Michel 1972. *The Archaeology of Knowledge*. New York: Random House.

—— 1973. *The Order of Things*. New York: Vintage Books.

Froebe, D. and R. J. Bain. 1976. *Quality Assurance Programs and Controls in Nursing*. St. Louis: C. V. Mosby.

Galtung, Johan. 1969. *Theory and Methods of Social Research*. New York: Columbia University Press.

Garfinkel, Harold. 1967. *Studies in Ethnomethodology*. Englewood Cliffs, N.J.: Prentice–Hall.

Hoekelman, Robert A. 1975. "Nurse–physician relationships." *American Journal of Nursing* (July) 75:1150–52.

Hofling, C. K., E. Brotzman, S. Dalrymple, N. Graves, and C. M. Pierce, 1966. "An experimental study in nurse–physician relationships." *Journal of Nervous and Mental Disease* 143:171–80.

Johnson, M. M. and H. W. Martin. 1958. "A sociological analysis of the nurse role." *American Journal of Nursing* 58:373–77.

Lemert, Charles C. 1979a. *Sociology and the Twilight of Man: Homocentrism and Discourse in Sociological Theory*. Carbondale: Southern Illinois University Press.

—— 1979b. "Language, structure, and measurement: Structuralist semiotics and sociology." *American Journal of Sociology* 84(4):929–957.

—— 1979c. "De–centered analysis: ethnomethodology and structuralism." *Theory and Society* 7:289–306.

Lewin, E. and J. Damrell. 1978. "Female identify and career pathways: Post–baccalaureate nurses ten years after." *Sociology of Work and Occupations* (February) 5:31–54.

Linn, Lawarence S. 1971. "Physician characteristics and attitudes toward legitimate use of psychotherapeutic drugs." *Journal of Health and Social Behavior* 12:132–40.

Maas, M., J. Specht, and A. Jacob. 1975. "Nurse autonomy: Reality not rhetoric." *American Journal of Nursing* (December) 75:2201–08.

Minehan, Paula L. 1977. "Nurse role conception." *Nursing Research* (September–October) 26:374–79.

Moniz, Donna. 1978. "Putting assertiveness techniques into practice." *American Journal of Nursing* (October) 78:1713.

Namboodiri, N. K., L. F. Carter, and H. M. Blalock, Jr. 1975. *Applied*

Multivariate Analysis and Experimental Designs. New York: McGraw–Hill.

Navarro, Vicente. 1976. *Medicine Under Capitalism.* New York: Prodist.

Pearlin, L. I. and M. Rosenberg. 1962. "Nurse–patient social distance and the structural context of a mental hospital." *American Sociological Review* (February) 27:56–65.

Rank, S. G. and C. K. Jacobson. 1977. "Hospital nurses' compliance with medication overdose orders: A failure to replicate." *Journal of Health and Social Behavior* (June) 18:183–93.

Reich, S. and A. Geller. 1976. "Self–images of nurses." *Psychological Report* (October) 39:401–2.

Rushing, William A. 1962. "Social influence and the social–psychological function of deference: a study in psychiatric nursing." *Social Forces* 41:142–48.

Said, Edward. 1975. *Beginnings: Intention and Method.* New York: Basic Books.

Salancik, Gerald R. 1977. "Commitment and the control of organizational behavior and belief." In B. W. Staw and G. R. Salancik, eds. *New Directions in Organizational Behavior*, pp. 1–54. Chicago: St. Clair Press.

Siegel, P. M. and R. W. Hodge. 1968. "A causal approach to the study of measurement error." In H. M. Blalock, Jr. and A. Blalock, eds. *Methodology in Social Research,* pp. 28–59. New York: McGraw-Hill.

Sills, Grayce M. 1976. "Nursing, medicine, and hospital administration." *American Journal of Nursing* (September) 76:1432–34.

Sonquist, John 1970. *Multivariate Model Building: The Validation of a Search Strategy.* Ann Arbor, Mich.: Institute for Social Research.

Stein, Leonard I. 1967. "The doctor-–nurse game." *Archives of General Psychiatry* (June) 16:699–703.

Waitzkin, H. B. and B. Waterman 1974. *The Exploitation of Illness in Capitalist Society.* Indianapolis: Bobbs–Merrill.

Willer, David. n.d. "What is Exact Theory." Mimeographed. University of Kansas.

Willer, D. and M. Webster, Jr. 1970. "Theoretical concepts and observables." *American Sociological Review* 35:748–57.

INDEX

NOTES ON THE CONTRIBUTORS

Priscilla P. Clark, Professor of French at the University of Illinois (Chicago), holds a Ph.D. from Columbia University. Author of *The Battle of the Bourgeois* and several articles on the sociology of literature, she is currently completing a study of French literary institutions.

Terry Nichols Clark is Associate Professor of Sociology, University of Chicago and has taught at Columbia, Harvard, Yale, and the Sorbonne. Among his numerous publications are included *Prophets and Patrons: The French University and the Emergence of the Social Sciences*, Harvard University Press (1973) and *Gabriel Tarde on Communication and Social Influence*, University of Chicago Press (1969).

Thomas F. Condon is Associate Professor of Sociology at the University of Guelph. He holds an MA (1964) from the University of Notre Dame, and a Ph.D. (1971) from the University of Minnesota. He was a contributing editor of *Family Problem Solving* (1971). He has co-authored with Prof. Wieting, *The Context and Practice of Sociological Research* (1976). His current research includes a structural analysis of commercial television, including the popular M*A*S*H series.

S. N. Eisenstadt received his Ph.D. from the Hebrew University, Jerusalem, where he is Professor of Sociology. He has been a frequent visiting professor of sociology at Harvard University. His many books include *The Political System of Empires* (1963), *Revolutions and the Transformation of Societies* (1978) and, with M. Curelaru, *The Form of Sociology: Paradigms and Crises* (1976).

Peter P. Ekeh is currently professor in the faculty of political sciences in the University of Ibadan, Nigeria. He has earned an M.A. in Sociology at Stanford University (1967) and a Ph.D. at the University of Berkeley (1970). He has published *Social Exchange Theory: The Two Traditions* (1974) and is working on a new publication, *Colonialism and Social Structure*.

Martha E. Giménez, Associate Professor of Sociology at the University of Colorado, Boulder, received a Ph.D. from the University of California, Los Angeles (1973). She is the author of numerous articles in the fields of Population Theory and Marxist Theory.

Maurice Godelier is affiliated with the "Ecole des Hautes Etudes en Sciences Sociales" of Paris and is a leading exponent of Marxist-Structural Anthropology. Some of his numerous publications have been translated into English: *Rationality and Irrationality in Economics* (1972), *Perspectives in Marxist Anthropology* (1976).

Fred E. Katz, Visiting Fellow, Department of History, Johns Hopkins University. Formerly, Professor of Sociology, State University of New York at Buffalo and Tel Aviv University. He has a Ph.D. from North Carolina (1961). His books include: *Structuralism in Sociology: An Approach to Knowledge* (1976), *Autonomy and Organization* (1968), *Contemporary Sociological Theory* (ed., 1971). His current work is on Holocaust research.

Charles C. Lemert is Professor of Sociology at Wesleyan University. He is author of *Michael Foucault: Social Theory and Transgression* (with Garth Gillan) (Forthcoming), *Sociology and the Twilight of Man* (1979) and editor of *French Sociology* (1981). Lemert taught previously at Southern Illinois University at Carbondale, and is a Senior Editor of *Theory and Society*.

Charles W. Lidz is Associate Professor of Psychiatry and Sociology at the University of Pittsburgh. He received his Ph.D. from Harvard University. His major work is *Heroin, Deviance and Morality* (1980), with Andrew Walker. He is currently preparing a book on an ethnographic study of informed consent in psychiatry.

Willard A Nielsen, Jr. is Visiting Lecturer of Sociology at Southern Illinois University where he is currently studying for his Ph.D. He received his B.A. (1975) and M.A. (1977) from Trinity University.

Talcott Parsons studied at the London School of Economics and earned a Ph.D. at the University of Heidelberg. He taught at Harvard University from 1927 to 1979, the year of his death. Among his numerous books, whose influence has shaped much of American sociology, are *The Structure of Social Action* (1937), *The Social System* (1951), *Action Theory and the Human Condition* (1978).

Ino Rossi is Professor of Sociology and Anthropology at St. John's University. He holds an M.A. in sociology from the University of Chicago and a Ph.D. in sociology and anthropology from the New School for Social Research. Among his books are: *The Unconscious in Culture*, ed. (1974), *People in Culture*, ed. (1980), *The Logic of Culture*, ed. (forthcoming). He is now completing a volume on the interface between modern French structuralism and traditional sociological paradigms.

Arthur L. Stinchcombe is Professor of Sociology at the University of Arizona at Tucson. He is author of *Theoretical Methods in Social History* (1978) and *Rebellion in a High School* (1964).

Stephen G. Wieting, who received a B.A. from Whitworth College and a Ph.D. from the University of Minnesota, is an Associate Professor of Sociology at the University of Iowa. He has written articles on structuralism and ethnomethodology and is currently working on the relationship between fictional literature and painting, and on sociological theory.